A
History of China

A
History of China

Wolfram Eberhard
Professor of Sociology, University of California, Berkeley

ROUTLEDGE & KEGAN PAUL
London and Henley

'Chinas Geschichte' first published in Switzerland 1948
Translated by E. W. Dickes

English edition first published 1950
by Routledge & Kegan Paul Ltd
Reprinted 1952, 1955 and 1958

Second edition (revised by the author
and reset) 1960
Reprinted 1964 and 1967

Third edition (revised and enlarged)
published in America 1969
Reprinted 1971

This fourth edition (revised by the author
and reset) first published in Great Britain 1977
by Routledge & Kegan Paul Ltd
39 Store Street
London WC1E 7DD and
Broadway House, Newtown Road
Henley-on-Thames
Oxon., RG9 1EN
Printed in Great Britain by
Western Printing Services Ltd, Bristol
Copyright © Wolfram Eberhard 1977

ISBN 0 7100 8357 2 (c)
ISBN 0 7100 8358 0 (p)

To My Wife

CONTENTS

Chapter V: MILITARY RULE (250–200 B.C.)

Chapter VI: THE EARLY GENTRY SOCIETY (200 B.C.–A.D. 250)

Chapter VII: THE EPOCH OF THE FIRST DIVISION OF CHINA (A.D. 220–580)

(A) THE THREE KINGDOMS (A.D. 220–265)

(B) THE WESTERN CHIN DYNASTY (A.D. 265–317)

(C) THE ALIEN EMPIRES IN NORTH CHINA, DOWN TO THE TOBA (A.D. 317–385)

(D) THE TOBA EMPIRE IN NORTH CHINA (A.D. 385–550)

(E) SUCCESSION STATES OF THE TOBA (A.D. 550–580): NORTHERN CH'I DYNASTY, NORTHERN CHOU DYNASTY

(F) THE SOUTHERN EMPIRES

Chapter VIII: CLIMAX AND DOWNFALL OF THE IMPERIAL GENTRY (A.D. 580–950) 169

(A) THE SUI DYNASTY (A.D. 580–618)

(B) THE T'ANG DYNASTY (A.D. 618–906)

(C) THE SECOND DIVISION OF CHINA: THE FIVE DYNASTIES (A.D. 906–960)

Chapter IX: MODERN TIMES   205

(A) GENERAL CHARACTERISTICS

(B) PERIOD OF MODERATE ABSOLUTISM

(1) The Northern Sung dynasty

(2) The Liao (Kitan) dynasty in the north (937–1125)

(3) The Hsi-Hsia state in the north (1038–1227)

(4) The empire of the Southern Sung dynasty (1127–1279)

Chapter XI: THE REPUBLIC   315
(1912–1948)

Chapter XII: PRESENT-DAY CHINA   333

(A) THE GROWTH OF COMMUNISM

(B) NATIONALIST CHINA IN TAIWAN

(C) PEOPLE'S REPUBLIC OF CHINA (1949–   )

ILLUSTRATIONS

MAPS

INTRODUCTION

Histories of China have to be rewritten from time to time, and so I have attempted to rewrite some parts of my own History of China. There are several reasons for this. First, our knowledge of China's history has changed. Many new excavations have been made and many new studies have been produced which have corrected our former views. Perhaps we should admit that it is a bad moment to bring out a History of China, because many of the new excavations have not yet been described and analysed fully; many new texts have been found, but we do not have them yet in our hands and the necessary philological work on them is not yet done; many other documents will undoubtedly be found in the next years. Thus, in a couple of years, yet another 'revision' will be necessary.

Second, we have changed. Changes in our own society have raised new questions and made us aware of new problems. A scholar, even a historian who studies Chinese history, is necessarily influenced by these new trends; he looks at his Chinese data in a way which differs from the way he studied the data formerly. To give a simple example only: when the position of women in our society is discussed daily and often passionately, the writer is naturally stimulated to look into the question: what was and what is the position of women in Chinese society? Or, when we discuss the problems of ecology in our society, we are stimulated to find out what attitudes Chinese had towards their environment.

Finally, the greater the role becomes which China plays in the world, the greater their pride in their achievements tends to become; the deeper roots Marxist-Maoist thinking develops, the more will publications from the People's Republic be permeated by nationalist and Maoist thoughts. And the more will our own public be influenced by publications which consciously or unconsciously incorporate such traits. I admit, nobody is completely without bias, but it may be important to attempt to show an interpretation of Chinese history which tries to avoid the 'official' bias. Of course, both sides agree that the basic sources of Chinese history contain biases. It has been realized that the sources on which reliance has always been placed were not objective, but deliberately and emphatically represented a particular philosophy. The reports on the emperors and ministers of the earliest period are not historical at all, but served as examples of ideas of social policy or as glorifications of particular noble families. Myths such as we find to this day among China's neighbours were made into history; gods were made men and linked together by long family trees. We have been able to touch on all these things only briefly, and have had to dispense with any account of the complicated processes that have taken place here.

The official dynastic histories apply to the course of Chinese history the criterion of Confucian ethics; for them history is a text-book of ethics, designed to show by means of examples how the man of high character should behave or not behave. Practically all our written sources were produced by men of the upper class and represent the social and political values these men had. These historians and chroniclers were not much interested in and often not well informed about the great majority of the people. We have, thus, to try to go deeper and to extract the historic truth from these records. This is a tremendous task in which scholars from all countries are engaged, but, to this day, we are far from having really worked through every period of Chinese history; there are long periods on which scarcely any work has yet been done. Thus the picture we are able to give today has no finality about it and will need many modifications.

The present work is intended for the general reader and not for the specialist. It attempts to pay more attention to social and cultural developments than to purely political history; to try to find out how the 'common man' lived and not only how the leaders lived. I have also been concerned not to leave out of account China's relations with her neighbours. Now that we have a better knowledge of China's neighbours, the Turks, Mongols, Tibetans, Tunguses, Thai, not confined to the narratives of Chinese, who always speak only of 'barbarians', we are better able to realize how closely China has been associated with her neighbours from the first day of her history to the present time; how greatly she is indebted to them, and how much she has given them. We no longer see China as a great civilization surrounded by barbarians, but we study the Chinese coming to terms with their neighbours, who had civilizations of quite different types but nevertheless developed ones.

These special stresses make, I think, this book different from others, and try to make the reader see the Chinese people in a different light. I have to admit that even in such a limited field as Chinese social-cultural history, almost innumerable studies have appeared in recent

years in all languages of the world that it is impossible to be fully
'up-to-date'. Perhaps a group of scholars, each specializing in a
limited period of history, might have been able to overcome this
weakness, but in all collective works on China that I know, unity of
thought and method is missing.

It is usual to split up Chinese history under the various dynasties
that have ruled China or parts thereof. The beginning or end of a
dynasty does not always indicate the beginning or the end of a
definite period of China's social or cultural development. We have
tried to break China's history down into the three large periods—
'Antiquity', 'The Middle Ages', and 'Modern Times'. This does not
mean that we compare these periods with periods of the same name
in Western history although, naturally, we find some similarities with
the development of society and culture in the West. Every attempt
towards periodization is to some degree arbitrary: the beginning and
end of the Middle Ages, for instance, cannot be fixed to a year,
because development is a continuous process. To some degree any
periodization is a matter of convenience, and it should be accepted
as such.

Chinese words are transcribed according to the Wade-Giles system
with the exception of names for which already a popular way of
transcription exists (such as Peking). Place names are written without
hyphen, if they remain readable.

W.E.

CHAPTER ONE

Prehistory

1 *Sources for the earliest history*

Until recently we were dependent for the beginnings of Chinese history on the written Chinese tradition. According to these sources China's history began either about 4000 B.C. or about 2700 B.C. with a succession of wise emperors who 'invented' the elements of a civilization, such as clothing, the preparation of food, marriage, and a state system; they instructed their people in these things, and so brought China, as early as in the third millennium B.C., to an astonishingly high cultural level. However, all we know of the origin of civilizations makes this of itself entirely improbable; no other civilization in the world originated in any such way. As time went on, Chinese historians found more and more to say about primeval times. All these narratives were collected in the great imperial history that appeared at the beginning of the Manchu epoch. The older historical sources make no mention of any rulers before 2200 B.C., no mention even of their names. The names of earlier rulers first appear in documents of about 400 B.C.; the deeds attributed to them and the dates assigned to them often do not appear until much later.

Modern research has not only demonstrated that all these accounts are inventions of a much later period, but has also shown *why* such narratives were composed. We will discuss this later at the appropriate moment, but briefly mention that on the one hand these accounts can be seen as an attempt of Chinese philosophers to explain the development of culture and society and to use them to legitimize the system of government that existed in their time. On the other hand, the accounts served to legitimize the aspirations and actions of particular persons or groups of persons.

Furthermore, we can now state with certainty that all historical data which were given in written documents for times down to about 1000 B.C. are false. They are the result of astronomical-astrological calculations, made by specialists of later times who pursued their own special political aims by doing these calculations. To this day,

1

we do not have written sources which are earlier than c. 1300 B.C., but we have reason to say that persons and activities mentioned in sources written after that time and said to have lived before it, really did live and seem to have done certain actions, perhaps up to the time shortly before 2000 B.C. There is, however, no reason to accept anything that is said in later sources about periods before 2000 B.C. as 'historical'. Strictly speaking, then, a history of China should not begin before the time for which written documentation exists. During the last 50 years, numerous excavations have been made on the territory of the People's Republic of China, but to call the cultures which have been found, 'Chinese' is just about as logical as to call the people of Mohenjo Dharo 'Pakistani'. We now know definitely, though not all the evidence has been published, that on the territory of China people of different cultures and even of different races lived. We also know that in present-day China people of different cultures live as minorities, though 'racially' most of them are not different from 'Chinese', and we know that the people who now call themselves 'Chinese' do not all have all the same racial origins—in whichever way we may define this controversial term 'race'. The matter is not a matter of race or language and not a matter of territory. We should speak of 'Chinese' from the moment that we can find a group of people under an organized government, a form of 'state' that regards itself as a group with a common culture and as different from other groups. From at least 1000 B.C. on, we find a clear term which the Chinese used for themselves and which excluded others. As the state of that time was a clear continuation of an earlier state, we can speak of 'Chinese' probably from about 1500 B.C. on. What is before this time should be called 'pre-Chinese' and we can study this period only by means of archaeology and comparative ethnology. However, both methods tend to give different results.

2 *The earliest periods*

For the earliest period, we have nothing but a few excavations. Actually, we cannot expect very many traces of the first man, as there were probably only a few small hordes in some places of the Far East. The main settlement which we know consists of caves in Chou-k'ou-tien, south of Peking. Here lived the so-called 'Peking Man'. He is vastly different from the men of today, and forms a special branch of the human race, closely allied to the Pithecanthropus of Java. The formation of later races of mankind from these types has not yet been traced, if it occurred at all.

The Peking Man lived in caves; no doubt he was a hunter, already in possession of very simple stone implements and also of the art of making fire. As none of the skeletons so far found is complete, it is assumed that he buried certain bones of the dead in different places from the rest. This burial custom, which is found among primitive peoples in other parts of the world, suggests the conclusion that the Peking Man already had religious notions. We have no knowledge yet of the length of time the Peking Man may have inhabited the Far East. His first traces are attributed to a million years ago, and he may have flourished in 500,000 B.C.

The first remnants of the Peking Man were already found in the 1920s. Only in recent years, remnants of this race were found also in other parts of northern China.

In a later phase of the Pleistocene remnants of a different human race, perhaps related to the Neanderthal race of Europe and Western Asia, have recently been discovered, and the more developed stone scrapers and other implements show some relation to Aurignacian and Moustérian tools of the West. However, it is still much too early to state whether such similarities are the result of transmission or of pure chance.

Finally, in the last part of the Pleistocene, a modern race of Homo sapiens is found in China, first in the upper levels of the Chou-k'ou-tien caves, then in other parts of China; with him appear still further refined and specialized stone tools. Archaeologists are of the opinion that this Far Eastern race may be the ancestor of the Mongoloid races of the northern Far East, but at the same time also the ancestor of a Negroid Oceanic race. Such dark-skinned races are found in parts of the Malay peninsula and the Philippines, as well as in New Guinea. And there are literary allusions in Chinese texts suggesting that a dark-skinned race may once have lived in historical periods in some parts of south China.

Possibly, this new race, which certainly is the ancestor of still existing races, may have developed in the Far East from an earlier Neanderthal race, which again could have developed from the Peking Man race. In any case, none of these earlier human beings has survived anywhere. With the beginning of the 'recent period' of geological time, the separation of the Mongoloid and the Negroid race seems to have taken place. Yet the skeletal remains found in An-yang and dating somewhat before the year 1000 B.C. seem to indicate that, at least at that time, still other races may have lived in the area of China.

At the beginning of this 'recent period' we find in the Ordos area and north of it a microlithic culture, i.e. a culture in which stone implements of very small size, but well made, were used; similar cultures have also been discovered in the West. At probably the same time, a distinct mesolithic culture appears in the area of the south of China, roughly the area around Canton and west of it. It seems that these people were largely fishers living along the rivers and the coast. It is here that the earliest remnants of a simple, cord-marked pottery have been found. The use of cord indicates that fibres were used, and it is likely that these fishermen already made a kind of bark-cloth by beating fibres from trees into a vegetable felt. This is perhaps one of the most important human inventions, as it may have led to the invention of felt among animal breeders and to the invention of paper and printing many, many centuries later. And it may be that in this southern culture, the first experiments with the cultivation of plants were made. Rice, the staple food of the Chinese, seems to have been cultivated somewhere in South-East Asia; some archaeologists believe in Thailand, others seem to prefer south China. As far as we know, the population of both areas was closely related. Similarly, the cultivation of taro and yam must have begun in the same area.

It is different, however, with those plants which are still typical for the north. It is more generally assumed that wheat and millet came to the Far East from the West, the 'Fertile crescent' or even the eastern parts of Africa. Together with these plants came cattle and sheep.

3 *The eight basic cultures*

The principal drawback of archaeology is that what can be excavated is only a small, select section of the total culture of a society. Occasionally, we can draw conclusions from the findings on the religion and the social organization of the people. Thus, even in areas in which archaeologists have done very much work, it often remains impossible and usually questionable to assign to a specific layer that the archaeologists have established, a specific culture which is known from historical accounts to have lived in that same area. Because of the selectivity of archaeological findings, cultures seem to be very much alike over large areas in which numerous different types of societies may have existed. If later archaeologists were to excavate sites of our present time, and if they did not find written documents, they might easily conclude that there was a unified culture all over the world, because they would find the same automobiles, airplanes, radios and televisions everywhere. Here, historical ethnology may come to help. By carefully mapping the distribution of elements of material and non-material culture, by using legends and other traditions, and by tracing the distribution of still existing 'local cultures' as far back as possible, it seems possible to establish that in the area which is now China, a considerable number of different, local cultures existed, each developing along its own lines, but finally all contributing in different degrees to the formation of what we then begin to

4

call 'Chinese culture'. We will mention only the most important local cultures.

(a) The north-east culture, centred in the present provinces of Hopei (in which Peking lies), Shantung, and southern Manchuria. The people of this culture were ancestors of the Tunguses, probably mixed with an element that is contained in the present-day Paleo-Siberian tribes. These men were mainly hunters, but probably soon developed a little primitive agriculture and made coarse, thick pottery with certain basic forms which were long preserved in subsequent Chinese pottery (for instance, a type of the so-called tripods). Later, pig-breeding became typical of this culture.

(b) The northern culture existed to the west of that culture, in the region of the present Chinese province of Shansi and in the province of Jehol in Inner Mongolia. These people had been hunters, but then became pastoral nomads, depending mainly on cattle. The people of this culture were the tribes later known as Mongols, the so-called proto-Mongols. Anthropologically they belonged, like the Tunguses, to the Mongol race.

(c) The people of the culture farther west, the north-west culture, were not Mongols. They, too, were originally hunters, and later became a pastoral people, with a not inconsiderable agriculture (especially growing wheat and millet). The typical animal of this group soon became the horse. The horse seems to be the last of the great animals to be domesticated, and the date of its first occurrence in domesticated form in the Far East is not yet determined, but we can assume that by 2500 B.C. this group was already in possession of horses. The horse has always been a 'luxury', a valuable animal which needed special care. For their economic needs, these tribes depended on other animals, probably sheep, goats, and cattle. The centres of this culture, so far as can be ascertained from Chinese sources, were the present provinces of Shensi and Kansu, but mainly only the plains. The people of this culture were most probably ancestors of the later Turkish peoples. It is not suggested, of course, that the original home of the Turks lay in the region of the Chinese provinces of Shensi and Kansu; one gains the impression, however, that this was a border region of the Turkish expansion; the Chinese documents concerning that period do not suffice to establish the centre of the Turkish territory. Recent linguistic research has made it likely that Turkic, Mongolic, and Tungusic languages are to some degree related and may have developed from one single type of language; it seems also that the Korean language is related to these languages, while Japanese may have more complex origins, though still be related to Korean and through it to the Altaic languages.

(d) In the west, in the present provinces of Szechwan and in all the mountain regions of the provinces of Kansu and Shensi, lived the ancestors of the Tibetan peoples as another separate culture. They were shepherds, generally wandering with their flocks of sheep and goats on the mountain heights.

(e) In the south we meet with four further cultures. One is very primitive, the Liao culture, the peoples of which are the Austro-asiatics already mentioned. These are peoples who never developed beyond the stage of primitive hunters, some of whom were not even acquainted with the bow and arrow. Farther east is the Yao culture, an early Austronesian culture, the people of which also lived in the mountains, some as collectors and hunters, some going over to a simple type of agriculture (denshiring). They mingled later with the last great culture of the south, the Thai culture, distinguished by agriculture. The people lived in the valleys and mainly cultivated rice. The centre of this Thai culture may have been in the present provinces of Kuangtung and Kuangsi. Today, their descendants form the principal components of the Thai in Thailand, the Shan in Burma and the Lao in Laos. Their immigration into the areas of the Shan States of Burma and into Thailand took place only in quite recent historical periods, probably not much earlier than A.D. 1000.

Finally there arose from the mixture of the Yao with the Thai culture, at a rather later time, the Yüeh culture, another early Austro-nesian culture, which then spread over wide regions of Indonesia, and of which the axe of rectangular section became typical. Lin-guistically, the languages of the Tibetans (to which minorities in China proper, like the Lolo, belong) are related to the Chinese language. The Thai languages are even closer relatives of the Chinese, while the languages of the Yao and Yüeh seem to have been related to the languages of Indonesia and the South Pacific. The Liao may have relatives in Mon and Kmer cultures of South-East Asia.

Thus, to sum up, we may say that, quite roughly, in the middle of the third millennium we meet in the north and west of present-day China with a number of herdsmen cultures. In the south there were a number of agrarian cultures, of which the Thai was the most powerful, becoming of most importance to the later China. We must assume that these cultures were as yet undifferentiated in their social composition, that is to say that as yet there was no distinct social stratification, but at most beginnings of class-formation, especially among the nomad herdsmen. This picture of prehistoric cultures, each of which is a contributor in its own way to the later 'Chinese' culture, is much more detailed than the picture gained from archaeo-logy alone, but is, in my opinion, not in contradiction to the results of archaeology. Doubtless further research will clarify and correct this reconstruction of the last period of Chinese prehistory.

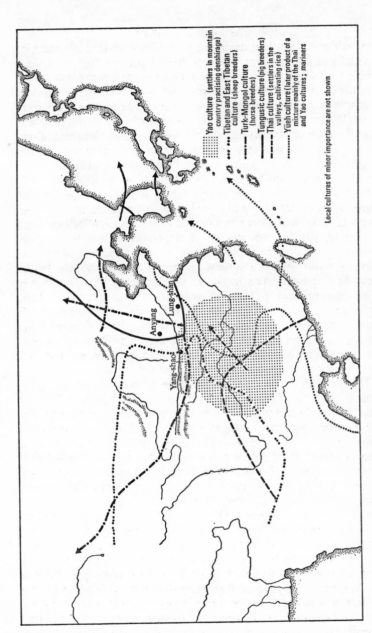

MAP 1 *Regions of the principal local cultures in prehistoric times*

Yao culture (settlers in mountain country practising denshirage)

●●● Tibetan and East Tibetan culture (sheep breeders)

—·—· Turk-Mongol culture (horse breeders)

——— Tungusic culture (pig breeders)

—··— Thai culture (settlers in the valleys, cultivating rice)

········ Yüeh culture (later product of a mixture mainly of the Thai and Yao cultures ; mariners)

Local cultures of minor importance are not shown

Anyang

Lung-shan

Yang-shao

4 *The Yang-shao culture*

The various cultures here described gradually penetrated one another, especially at points where they met. Such a process does not yield a simple total of the cultural elements involved; any new combination produces entirely different conditions with corresponding new results which, in turn, represent the characteristics of the culture that supervenes. We can no longer follow this process of penetration in detail; it need not by any means have been always warlike. Conquest of one group by another was only one way of mutual cultural penetration. In other cases, a group which occupied the higher altitudes and practised hunting or slash-and-burn agriculture came into closer contacts with another group in the valleys which practised some form of higher agriculture; frequently, such contacts resulted in particular forms of division of labour in a unified and often stratified new form of society. Recent and present developments in South-East Asia present a number of examples for such changes. Increase of population is certainly one of the most important elements which lead to these developments. The result, as a rule, was a stratified society being made up of at least one privileged and one ruled stratum. Thus there came into existence around 2000 B.C. some new cultures, which are well known archaeologically. The most important of these are the Yang-shao culture in the west and the Lung-shan culture in the east. Our knowledge of both these cultures is of quite recent date and there are many enigmas still to be cleared up.

The Yang-shao culture takes its name from a prehistoric settlement in the west of the present province of Honan, where Swedish investigators discovered it. Typical of this culture is its wonderfully fine pottery, apparently used as gifts to the dead. It is painted in three colours, white, red, and black. The patterns are all stylized, designs copied from nature being rare. This pottery is still handmade; the potter's wheel is a later invention. Together with this fine pottery, a common grey pottery was still used, and some scholars think that the painted pottery may be a development from earlier cord- or mat-marked pottery. Others have pointed out that the designs on the painted pottery have close parallels with pottery found in Iran (Anau) and other sites in western Asia. Doubtless some ethnocentrism has entered the debate here: Western scholars seem to have a tendency to derive Chinese culture from the West, while many Chinese scholars have tried to show that Yang-shao culture developed in the nuclear area of old China and spread later to the West. They claim that the earliest Yang-shao remains come from south Shansi, west Honan, east and central Shensi, and that the findings in west Shensi and Kansu are of a later period. This may be correct, but does not exclude the possibility that Yang-shao has at some time also received stimuli from western Asia. The more we know, the more we can see that Near and Far East were never as independent from one another as we formerly have thought. Certain it is, however, that the Yang-shao people lived only on the western highlands of China, along river terraces and along small basins. They did not live in the eastern great plains of China. The distribution of this culture is similar to that of the reconstructed Tibetan culture, though we certainly cannot regard Yang-shao as a 'proto-Tibetan' culture. Though they kept sheep and goats, and some cattle, their main animals were the pig and the dog. Much of their food still came from hunting and fishing, but they were already farmers who cultivated millet and wheat—and both, as we have noted, come from the West. Earlier scholars believed that they also cultivated rice, but this seems still to be doubtful. They seem to have used hemp for clothing, but there is an indication that they already produced some kind of silk from the cocoons of one variety of the silkworm. Until late in history, silk has been the typical invention of the Chinese which made them famous already in the times of the Roman Empire.

The tools of the Yang-shao people were already highly specialized; we can distinguish agricultural tools such as hoe, spade, digging stick, sickle and grain grinders, from tools used for carpentry and from weapons. Their stone tools were polished.

They lived in compact villages—a settlement type which remained typical until the present. However, it seems that the villages often shifted, perhaps in connection with their slash-and-burn agriculture which made periodic migrations necessary. The villages seem to exhibit some planning. Often, the cemetery was in the north of the village, and their pottery kilns were also outside the settlement. Houses were made of stamped clay (adobe), often semi-subterranean and mainly rectangular or square; however, round buildings were found as well as fully subterranean storage buildings. In a later period, Chinese archaeologists have claimed to have found 'long houses', in which more than one family lived, each in a compartment with its fire-place. As in Marxist theory 'communal settlement' plays an important role, such interpretations have to be taken with some scepticism. Such long houses still exist in parts of South-East Asia and Indonesia.

5 *The Lung-shan culture*

The Lung-shan culture, characterized by a black, fine pottery, often already made on the wheel, was discovered shortly before the Second World War. It is a culture of the east and of the plains. The discussion of its relation to Yang-shao and to the later historical cultures is again not free from elements of ideological speculation. As the eastern plains have always been regarded by Chinese historians as a part of the nuclear area of Chinese culture—it is the area in which China's greatest thinkers were born—a 'two culture' theory was hypothesized: Yang-shao and Lung-shan were both contemporary, each one independent of the other. The more recent consensus seems to be that Lung-shan is slightly later than Yang-shao. Some Western scholars, agreeing with this, tried to derive the Lung-shan culture again from a later period of West Asian cultures. In fact, there is a black pottery of quite similar type widely spread over Turkey and Iran. Chinese scholars, on the other hand, have tried to derive the Lung-shan culture from the Yang-shao culture. In favour of the first hypothesis speaks the fact that many Yang-shao vessels have forms which we know from the West, while Lung-shan vessels are clearly prototypes of vessels which later became typical of 'Chinese' pottery.

Lung-shan is certainly more highly developed than Yang-shao. Their villages were more permanent and were surrounded by mud walls; they seem to have had a higher agriculture with permanent use of the same fields. They had scapulimancy, i.e. used animal bones for the purpose of fortune-telling. Such and other characteristics have induced some scholars to assume that the people of the Lung-shan culture had already a social organization with some stratification, a beginning of the formation of social classes.

Most important for the Lung-shan culture is that it seems to have quickly spread over wide parts of the Far East, from Manchuria in the north to Canton and Taiwan. It is today possible to isolate several 'local cultures' of the Lung-shan type, and it may well be possible in the future to identify some of these local cultures with those hypothesized by the ethno-historic method. There is as yet no unanimity among scholars as to the age of Yang-shao and Lung-shan. It may perhaps be adequate to say that Lung-shan existed, perhaps even in different local forms, around 2000 B.C. Then, Yang-shao must have existed before 2400 B.C., but perhaps even a good deal earlier.

6 The first petty states in Shansi

At the time in which, according to archaeological research, the painted pottery flourished in west China, Chinese historical tradition has it that the model rulers Yao, Shun, and Yü ruled the empire. What we know about them comes from sources which were written not much before 400 B.C., and the traditional dates (Yao 2333–2234; Shun 2233–2184; Yü 2183–2177 B.C.) are found in much later sources still and are clearly the result of astrological calculations. These men became the models of good kings: it is said that Yao ceded the throne when he was old to a simple man, Shun, and not to his son; Shun supposedly did the same, while Yü tried to act the same way but 'people' wanted him to establish his son as successor, and from then on hereditary rule became established. All three are credited with acts which benefited mankind, especially Yü, who controlled a large flood by designing channels for the waters. It has been possible to show that these 'actions' in part are euhemerized myths, in part constructions of philosophers who wanted to explain the origins of society and culture. Much more creditable is another, equally late and questionable source which states that Shun made war against Yao and killed him, and that Yü acted similarly. The only conclusion which we may perhaps draw from all these texts is that sometime around 2000 B.C. small statelets may have existed in the area of the southern part of today's province of Shansi, similar to many such statelets of Chinese and of non-Chinese that still existed down to the middle of the first millennium B.C.

Perhaps the creation of statelets coincides with the next great cultural progress: bronze seems to appear in traces within the later Yang-shao culture about 1800 B.C. By about 1400 B.C. it had become very widespread and technically very well developed. As the forms of the oldest weapons and their ornamentation show similarities with weapons from north Central Asia and as also mythology seems to indicate that the bronze came from the north into China, some scholars assume that bronze was brought to the Far East either through the agency of peoples living north of China, perhaps people related to the later Turkish tribes, or by individual clans or families which migrated from customer to customer, as we meet them later in Turkish and Central Asian tradition. These tribes or clans, in turn, could have learned the technique from some Near Eastern society, as bronze was used there much earlier than in central and east Asia. Other scholars believe that bronze was independently discovered in the area of north China and spread from there to the areas north of China. The bronze vessels which made their appearance about 1450 B.C. seem to be a direct development from earlier pottery, while their ornamentation seems to be largely derived from earlier wood-carving of southern style. This is not astonishing as there were few deposits of tin and copper in north China, while in the south, an area at that time inhabited mainly by Thai tribes, both metals were plentiful, so that a trade from the south to the north must soon have set in.

It is at this time that Chinese tradition has its first 'dynasty', the Hsia, which is said to have been founded by Yü. The traditional date for the Hsia dynasty (2176–1725 B.C.) is certainly false. What the late sources say about this period cannot be accepted as historical, though there seems to be an indication that some kind of dynasty may have existed. Archaeology has to this time not yet been able to find incontestable traces of the Hsia, in spite of numerous excavation attempts in the supposed centres of this dynasty.

CHAPTER TWO

The Emergence of Feudalism
(c. 1600–1028 B.C.)

1 *Period, origin, material culture*

With the Shang dynasty, we come at last into the realm of history, though we still do not have reliable data for its duration. It can now be proved that the traditional date for the end of the dynasty (1112 B.C.) is wrong and the result of calculations. Therefore, the traditional year for its beginning (1751 B.C.) must also be wrong. We have lists of the Shang kings and excavated documents have proved that these lists are by and large correct. But in spite of these documents we still cannot say how long individual kings ruled and from when to when. While the written texts do not say much about Shang culture, numerous excavations show that the Shang civilization was a complex one with elements that clearly come from the Lung-shan culture, and others which seem to come from Yang-shao. The inscriptions on bone which have been found show that the Shang had quite a number of towns, some of which have tentatively been identified with excavation sites. These excavations seem to prove one point in the later documents, namely that the Shang changed their capital several times in the course of the dynasty. While it is still disputed that the place where the overwhelming number of inscriptions were found, a place near the present city of An-yang in Hopei province, really was the capital of the Shang shortly before the end of the dynasty, the important fact for us is that settlements enclosed by walls which first were found in the Lung-shan period now became the norm. Down to modern times, the walled city the symbol of Chinese rule and the seat of local or central government. The walls of one of the earliest cities seem to have had an average height of 10 metres and an average width of 20 metres, so that the wall of over 7,000 metres required the moving of almost 3 million cubic metres of soil. It has been calculated that such a structure would need 10,000 workers who worked for 18 years continuously. These calculations are rough ones, but indicate that only a society with stratification and a centralized government could have produced them.

Before the Second World War, only one site of Shang culture was excavated, the city of Yin, near An-yang. With new excavations made after 1950, we know much more and can now say that the earliest site with a clearly 'Shang culture' is near Yen-shih, between Lo-yang and Cheng-chou in Honan province. Tradition has it that the first Shang ruler lived in Po, and Po has, by some scholars, been identified with the area of Yen-shih. Here several different sites have been found, but not all of them have been excavated. Important is, that excavations found below the Shang level a Lung-shan level and below that a Yang-shao level. We should also keep in mind that Yen-shih is geographically at the beginning of the plains, where Lung-shan people touched Yang-shao people. The Yen-shih people did not yet have a script, though some of their incisions on pots may be symbols of some early script. They used stone, shells and bone for their implements, and had some bronze implements. This seems to be the earliest occurrence of metal in the Far East, much later than in the Near East.

The next important Shang settlement is very close to the present Cheng-chou. It may have been the city of Ao, reported in Shang texts. It seems that inside the city walls, only the upper class lived and was buried, so that the city can be regarded as an administrative centre. The commoners seem to have lived outside the walls. Later Chinese cities often have two walls: one enclosing the administrative centre or the imperial palaces, the larger one enclosing the area in which the ordinary people lived. Ao was already surrounded by a rectangular wall, the 'ideal' form of the Chinese city to the recent past. Inside the walls remnants of large buildings were found, perhaps remnants of a palace. Even the earlier Yen-shih may have had a palace-like building, it is assumed. In both places there are indications that some of the corpses found may have been victims of human sacrifice.

The city of Yin near An-yang, is by far the greatest Shang settlement and belongs to a later period. Here, the first written documents were found. Yin seems to have had a wall, too, although it is largely destroyed. Inside the walls was a complex which is regarded as a palace area, surrounded by houses which seem to have been houses of palace artisans, while the houses of others were more on the outside. The rectangular houses were built in a style still found in Chinese houses, except that their front did not always face south as is now the general rule. The Shang buried their kings in large, subterranean, cross-shaped tombs outside the city, and many implements, animals and human sacrifices were buried together with them. The custom of large burial mounds, which later became typical of the Chou dynasty, did not yet exist.

The Shang had sculptures in stone, an art which later more or less completely disappeared and which was resuscitated only in post-Christian times under the influence of Indian Buddhism. Yet Shang culture cannot well be called a 'megalithic' culture. Bronze implements and especially bronze vessels were now developed to a degree that has rarely been reached again in China or any other early civilization of the world. The implements were made by specialists whose 'trade marks' we often can see on the vessels. The bronze weapons have some similarity to weapons from central north Asia and are often ornamented in the so-called 'animal style' which was used among all the nomad peoples between the Ordos region and Siberia to Iran in the West until the beginning of the Christian era. But whether this 'animal style' was first developed by the Shang and from there spread towards the West or whether the process went the other way, is still unclear. Thus far, we cannot prove that the Chinese learned metallurgy and the earliest style of decoration of weapons from the West. Certainly, the famous bronze vessels show a decoration which is more closely related to the south than to the West.

There can be no doubt that the bronze vessels were used for religious service and not for everyday life. For everyday use there were earthenware vessels. Even in the middle of the first millennium B.C., bronze was exceedingly dear, as we know from the records of prices. China has always suffered from scarcity of metal. For that reason metal was accumulated as capital, entailing a further rise in prices; when prices had reached a sufficient height, the stocks were thrown on the market and prices fell again. Later, when there was a metal coinage, this cycle of inflation and deflation became still clearer. The metal coinage was of its full nominal value, so that it was possible to coin money by melting down bronze implements. As the money in circulation was increased in this way, the value of the currency fell. Then it paid to turn coin into metal implements. This once more reduced the money in circulation and increased the value of the remaining coinage. Thus through the whole course of Chinese history the scarcity of metal and insufficiency of production of metal continually produced extensive fluctuations of the stocks and the value of metal, amounting virtually to an economic law in China. Consequently metal implements were never universally in use, and vessels were usually of earthenware, with the further result of the early invention of porcelain. Porcelain vessels have many of the qualities of metal ones, but are cheaper.

The earthenware vessels used in this period are in many cases already very near to porcelain: there was a pottery of a brilliant white, lacking only the glaze which would have made it into porcelain. Patterns were stamped on the surface, often resembling the patterns on bronze articles. This ware was used only for formal, ceremonial purposes. For daily use there was also a perfectly simple grey pottery.

The houses and palaces which have been excavated were made of adobe, but in contrast to earlier periods, the houses were built on stamped-earth foundations, a technique that has remained typically Chinese. Of course, we should assume that in addition to these more solid houses, much of the population lived in simple huts of which no remnants remained. Similar to the ancient cities of India, like Harappa, the palace area seems to have had a system of water ditches, probably for drainage.

The area under more or less organized Shang control comprised towards the end of the dynasty the present provinces of Honan, western Shantung, southern Hopei, central and south Shansi, east Shensi, parts of Kiangsu and Anhui. We can only roughly estimate the size of the population of the Shang state. Late texts say that at the time of the annihilation of the dynasty, some 3·1 million free men and 1·1 million serfs were captured by the conquerors; this would indicate a population of at least some 4–5 millions. This seems a possible number, if we consider that an inscription of the tenth century B.C. which reports about an ordinary war against a small and unimportant western neighbour, speaks of 13,081 free men and 4,812 serfs taken as prisoners.

Inscriptions mention many neighbours of the Shang with whom they were in a more or less continuous state of war. Many of these neighbours can now be identified. We know that Shansi at that time was inhabited by Ch'iang tribes, belonging to the Tibetan culture, as well as by Ti tribes, belonging to the northern culture, and by Hsien-yün and other tribes, belonging to the north-western culture; the centre of the Ch'iang tribes was more in the south-west of Shansi and in Shensi. Some of these tribes definitely once formed a part of the earlier Hsia state. The identification of the eastern neighbours of the Shang presents more difficulties. We might regard them as representatives of the Tungus cultures, Thai tribes, or descendants of early states of the Lung-shan cultures. We should not think that all these neighbours were primitives. On the contrary, we should assume that they, too, had societies which could be regarded as states, similar to those early pre-Chinese statelets which we discussed above.

As in earlier time, the Shang Chinese used fibres of plants, and their nobility even silk, woven in intricate designs, for their clothing. They kept cattle, pigs, dogs, chickens, but in the later Shang period, horse-breeding becomes more and more evident. Some authors believe that the art of riding was already known in late Shang times, although it was certainly not yet so highly developed that cavalry units could be used in war. With horse-breeding the two-wheeled light war-chariot makes its appearance. The wheel was already known in earlier times in the form of the potter's wheel. Recent excavations have brought to light burials in which up to eighteen chariots with two or four horses were found together with the owners of the chariots. The cart is not a Chinese invention but came from the north, possibly from Turkish peoples. It has been contended that it was connected with the war-chariot of the Near East: shortly before the Shang period there had been vast upheavals in western Asia, mainly in connection with the expansion of peoples who spoke Indo-European languages (Hittites, etc.) and who became successful through the use of quick, light, two-wheeled war-chariots. It is possible, but cannot be proved, that the war-chariot spread through Central Asia in connection with the spread of such Indo-European-speaking groups or by the intermediary of Turkish tribes. We have some reasons to believe that the first Indo-European-speaking groups arrived in the Far East in the middle of the second millennium B.C. Some authors even connect the Hsia with these groups. In any case, the maximal distribution of these people seems to have been to the western borders of the Shang state. As in western Asia, a Shang-time chariot was manned by three men: the warrior who was a nobleman, his driver, and his servant who handed him arrows or other weapons when needed. There developed a quite close relationship between the nobleman and his chariot-driver. The chariot was a valuable object, manufactured by specialists; horses were always expensive and rare in China, and in many periods of Chinese history horses were directly imported from nomadic tribes in the north or west. One of the main sports of the noblemen in this period, in addition to warfare, was hunting. The Shang had their special hunting grounds south of the mountains which surround Shansi province, along the slopes of the T'ai-hang mountain range, and south to the shores of the Yellow river. Here, there were still forests and swamps in Shang time, and boars, deer, buffaloes and other animals, as well as occasional rhinoceros and elephants, were hunted. None of these wild animals were used as a sacrifice; all sacrificial animals, such as cattle, pigs, etc., were domesticated animals.

2 *Writing and religion*

Not only the material but also the intellectual level attained in the Shang period was very high. We meet for the first time with writing—much later than in the Middle East and in India. Chinese scholars have succeeded in deciphering some of the documents discovered, so that we are able to learn a great deal from them. The writing is a rudimentary form of the present-day Chinese script, and like it is a pictorial writing, but also makes use, as today, of phonetic signs. There were, however, a good many characters that no longer exist, and many now used are absent. There were already more than 3,000 characters in use of which some 1,000 can now be read. (Today newspapers use some 3,000 characters; scholars have command of up to 8,000; the whole of Chinese literature, ancient and modern, comprises some 50,000 characters.) With these 3,000 characters the Chinese of the Shang period were able to express themselves well.

The still existing fragments of writing of this period are found almost exclusively on tortoiseshells or on other bony surfaces, and they represent oracles. Thus, we have to keep in mind, that these texts cannot give us a full picture of their literature, not even of their vocabulary and grammar. Shang bronzes have usually only a very few characters, and often these are still illegible. As the old Chinese script is not based on the sounds of the words, we do not know how it was pronounced. To the present time, Chinese characters can be pronounced in different ways, according to dialects, even according to languages, i.e. Korean, Vietnamese, and Japanese formerly were written down with Chinese characters, though pronounced according to the Korean, Vietnamese, or Japanese languages. Thus, we cannot definitely say that the language of the Shang was the same as that of their successors, although most scholars assume that it was.

In spite of the limited scope of the oracle texts and the fact that almost all of them were found near An-yang and belong to the late Shang period, most of what we know about Shang society comes from these texts. But as the oracles were taken for the ruler, our knowledge of the culture of the common people remains limited.

Characteristic of Shang religion is the ancestral cult which is the forerunner of the ancestral worship typical of the Chinese to recent days. Deceased rulers and even ministers were given sacrifices at fixed dates and, apparently, they were regarded as intermediaries between their descendants and the highest deity, Shang Ti. Even the deceased mothers of the rulers received sacrifices. In addition to the worship of the royal ancestors, the Shang knew many nature deities, especially deities of fertility. There was no systematized pantheon, different deities being revered in each locality, often under the most varied names. These various deities were, however, similar in character, and later it often occurred that many of them were combined by the priests into a single god. The composite deities thus formed were officially worshipped. Their primeval forms lived on, however, especially in the villages, many centuries longer than the Shang dynasty. The sacrifices associated with them became popular festivals, and so these gods or their successors were saved from oblivion.

The Shang, as well as later Chinese, seem not to have had much interest in speculating about the origins of the world and mankind. It seems that Shang Ti was conceived as a male, living above and guiding all growth and birth, while the earth, also worshipped, was a kind of mother goddess who bore the plants and animals procreated by Shang Ti. It is likely that some myths which later sources report already existed in some parts of the Shang realm. Thus, we hear in a local myth that the two main deities were conceived as a married couple who later were parted by one of their children. The husband went to heaven, and the rain is the male seed that creates life on earth. In other regions it was supposed that in the beginning of the world there was a world-egg, out of which a primeval god came, whose body was represented by the earth: his hair formed the plants, and his limbs the mountains, and valleys. Every considerable mountain was also itself a god and, similarly, the river god, the thunder god, cloud, lightning, and wind gods, and many others were worshipped.

In order to promote the fertility of the earth, it was believed that sacrifices must be offered to the gods. Consequently, in the Shang realm and the regions surrounding it there were many sorts of human sacrifices; often the victims were prisoners of war. One gains the impression that many wars were conducted not as wars of conquest but only for the purpose of capturing prisoners, although the area under Shang control gradually increased towards the west and the south-east, a fact demonstrating the interest in conquest. In some regions men lurked in the spring for people from other villages; they slew them, sacrificed them to the earth, and distributed portions of the flesh of the sacrifice to the various owners of fields, who buried them. At a later time all human sacrifices were prohibited, but we have reports down to the eleventh century A.D., and even later, that such sacrifices were offered secretly in certain regions of central China. In other regions a great boat festival was held in the spring, to which many crews came crowded in long narrow boats. At least one of the boats had to capsize; the people who were thus drowned were a sacrifice to the deities of fertility. This festival has maintained its fundamental character to this day, in spite of various changes. The same is true of other festivals, customs, and conceptions, vestiges of which are contained at least in folklore.

The main problem in understanding Shang religion and even the religion of much later periods of Chinese history is that we find on their sacrificial bronzes numerous figures which are doubtless supernatural beings but which cannot be identified with deities mentioned in texts. It seems that texts mention, with few exceptions, only deities which were officially recognized and worshipped, while representations on bronzes and later on walls of buildings depict some of the popular deities.

There are some indications that the Shang had some star-worship. Certainly, they observed celestial phenomena and developed some elements of later astrology and geomancy. Their calendar was basically oriented according to the moon, but as they also had intercalatory months, they must have known that twelve moon cycles do not amount to one full cycle of the year. Thus, their calendar was already a luni-solar one, a calendar which tried to achieve a synchronism between the two luminaries. However, attempts to establish the exact form of their calendar and to interpret the dates given in Shang oracle texts in terms of our chronology have not yet been successful. As the tombs of Shang noblemen show some orientation (the heads are turned to the north), they also must have had some beliefs which we later find systematized in Chinese geomancy and astrology.

3 Early feudalism

At the head of the Shang state was a king, posthumously called a 'Ti', the same word as in the name of the supreme god. We have found on bones the names of all the rulers of this dynasty and even some of their pre-dynastic ancestors. These names can be brought into agreement with lists of rulers found in the ancient Chinese literature. The ruler seems to have been a high priest, too; and around him were many other priests. We know some of them now so well from the inscriptions that their biographies could be written. The priests as a special class, disappear later in Chinese society and are replaced by scribes.

Perhaps the best way to describe Chinese society at this time is to say that with the exception of the ruler, there were no free men: nobody was free, but the higher a person was in the social scheme, the more freedom he had. Around the king, in the capital, there were 'ch'en', officials who served the ruler personally, as well as scribes and military officials. We hear of different and often quite specialized ranks and have to assume that there was some bureaucracy, though we do not know whether there was already a true bureaucratic system with promotions and demotions according to merit and/or seniority. It seems clear, however, that important posts were in the hands of members of a nobility, lesser ones were manned by commoners. Characteristic of the nobility was the use of vehicles. Commoners did not have war-chariots; we do not know whether they were even allowed to own horses. The war-chariot was the decisive weapon and remained so until late Chou time.

The basic army organization was in units of one hundred men which were combined as 'right', 'left' and 'central' units into an army of 300 men. But it seems that the central power did not extend very far. In the more distant parts of the realm were more or less independent lords, who recognized the ruler only as their supreme lord and religious leader. The main obligations of these lords were to send tributes of grain, to participate with their soldiers in the wars, to send tortoiseshells to the capital to be used there for oracles, and to send occasionally cattle and horses. There were some thirty such dependent states. Although we do not know much about the general population, we know that in most parts of the Shang state, the society was patriarchal, patrilinear, and patrilocal. The Shang kings seem to have had a complicated system of succession as well as of marriage. After the death of the ruler his brothers followed him on the throne, the older brothers first. After the death of all brothers, the sons of the older or younger brothers became rulers. We do not know, however, whether a difference was made between sons of main and of secondary wives. Nor does it seem that the sons of the oldest brother were preferred to the sons of younger brothers. The main wives were, according to one recent study, selected according to a kind of moiety system, somewhat similar to marriage regulations among Australian aborigines. We do not know whether such a system was limited to the royal clan, to the whole upper class, or to the whole population. Until very recent times, different Chinese groups had different systems regulating the selection of the partner, coexisting at the same time. It has been said that Shang society had traces of an earlier matrilinear system. Certainly, the nobility had no matrilinear marriage rules, but it seems possible that matrilinear and matrilocal societies existed in some parts of the Shang state. Below the nobility, we find large numbers of dependent people. Modern Chinese scholars frequently call them 'slaves' and like to speak of a 'slave society'. If this means that the economy was based on the labour of a slave class, it is certainly not true. However, there certainly were slaves, i.e. people who had no social rights and were regarded as pieces of property. But we cannot prove that their labour was the basis of Shang economy. The majority of people were certainly farmers, and they were not 'free'; it seems that the Shang rulers claimed the right over the land these farmers used, and they imposed certain obligations, mainly forced labour, upon these farmers. Thus, we might call them 'serfs'. Some serfs were in hereditary group dependence upon some noble families and working on land which the noble families regarded as theirs. Families of artisans and craftsmen also were hereditary servants of noble families—a type of social organization which has its parallels in ancient Japan and in later India and

21

other parts of the world. The independent states around the Shang state also had serfs. When the Shang captured neighbouring states, they resettled the captured foreign aristocracy by attaching them as a group to their own noblemen. The captured serfs remained under their masters and shared their fate. The same system was later practised by the Chou after their conquest of the Shang state.

The conquests of late Shang added more territory to the realm than could be coped with by the primitive communications of the time. When the last ruler of Shang made his big war which lasted 260 days against the tribes in the south-east, rebellions broke out which led to the end of the dynasty, about 1028 B.C. according to the new chronology (1122 B.C. old chronology).

CHAPTER THREE

Mature Feudalism (c. 1028–500 B.C.)

1 *Cultural origin of the Chou and end of the Shang dynasty*

Many of the countries against which the Shang fought should probably be regarded as statelets, and some of them may already have ruled in cities. Among these, apparently, were the ancestors of the Chou who at first lived in central Shensi, an area which even in much later times was the home of many non-Chinese tribes. According to their tradition, they were forced to leave their homes due to the pressure of tribes, which may have belonged to the Turkish ethnic groups, though it is also possible that the movement of the Chou was connected with pressures from Indo-European tribes. There are some indications that the ruling house of Chou may have been related to the Turkish ethnic group, while their population consisted mainly of Tibetan tribes. Whether the Chou language contained elements of these languages is not yet clear. Certainly the language of the Chou is the ancestor of what we now call the Chinese language.

The culture of the Chou before their conquest is still little known, but it seems to be closely related to that of the earlier Yang-shao. They certainly had bronze weapons which differed in shape from those of the Shang; they had the war-chariot, and the horse seems to have played a much greater role among them than among the Shang. Their eastward migration, however, brought them within the zone of the Shang culture, by which they were strongly influenced, so that the Chou culture lost more and more of its original character and increasingly resembled the Shang culture. The Chou were also brought into the political sphere of the Shang, as shown by the fact that marriages took place between the ruling houses of Shang and Chou, until the Chou state became nominally dependent on the Shang state in the form of a dependency with special prerogatives. Meanwhile the power of the Chou state steadily grew, while that of the Shang state diminished more and more through the disloyalty of its feudatories and through wars in the east. Finally, about 1028

B.C., the Chou ruler, named Wu Wang ('the martial king'), crossed his eastern frontier and pushed into central Honan. His army was formed by an alliance between various tribes, in the same way as happened again and again in the building up of the armies of the rulers of the steppes. Wu Wang forced a passage across the Yellow river and annihilated the Shang army. He pursued its vestiges as far as the capital, captured the last emperor of the Shang, and killed him. Thus was the Chou dynasty founded, and with it we begin the actual history of China. The Chou brought to the Shang culture elements of Turkish and also Tibetan culture, which were needed for the release of such forces as could create a new empire and maintain it through thousands of years as a cultural and, generally, also a political unit.

2   Chou feudalism

In contrast to Marxist scholars, who tend to call feudal any society in which a class of landowners who at the same time also exercised political power, controlled a class of farmers and often also a class of slaves, we define feudalism as a system of government of agrarian societies in which we find a hereditary upper class which in itself is stratified, and in which some sovereign rights are given to lower members of the upper class, the nobility, in exchange for services to the highest members of that class. These services are mainly military services, but also can be others. The relation between the 'vassals' and the 'lord' are contractual and renewable each time at the time of the death of either partner. Below this class of aristocrats, we have one or several classes, constituting the majority of the population, and consisting always of farmers, often also of artisan classes and of slaves. There are different ways by which such a feudal society can be formed; the case of the Chou is a very common one: a case of 'super-stratification', in which a conquering federation puts itself over an already stratified society. The Chou conquering power consisted of members of the clan to which the future rulers belonged, clans which were related to them by marriage, and clans which had joined them or had been forced to join them already before the time of the war of conquest. The conquerors were regarded as an alien minority, so that they had to march out and spread over the whole country. Moreover, the allied tribal chieftains expected to be rewarded. The territory to be governed was enormous, but the communications in northern China at that time were similar to those still existing not long ago in southern China—narrow foot-paths from one settlement to another. It is very difficult to build roads in the loess of northern China; and the war-chariots that required roads had only just been introduced. Under such conditions, the simplest way of administering the empire was to establish garrisons of the invading tribes in the various parts of the country under the command of their chieftains. Thus separate regions of the country were distributed as fiefs. If a former subject of the Shang surrendered betimes with the territory under his rule, or if there was one who could not be overcome by force, the Chou recognized him as a feudal lord.

We find in the early Chou time the typical signs of true feudalism: fiefs were given in a ceremony in which symbolically a piece of earth was handed over to the new fiefholder, and his instalment, his rights and obligations were inscribed in a 'charter'. Most of the fiefholders were members of the Chou ruling family or members of the clan to which this family belonged; other fiefs were given to heads of the allied tribes. The fiefholder (feudal lord) regarded the land of his fief, as far as he and his clan actually used it, as 'clan' land; parts of this land he gave to members of his own branch-clan for their use without transferring rights of property, thus creating new sub-fiefs and sub-lords. In much later times the concept of landed property of a family developed, and the whole concept of 'clan' disappeared. By 500 B.C., most feudal lords had retained only a dim memory that they originally belonged to the Chi clan of the Chou or to one of the few other original clans, and their so-called sub-lords felt themselves as members of independent noble families. Slowly, then, the family names of later China began to develop, but it took many centuries until, at the time of the Han Dynasty, all citizens (slaves excluded) had accepted family names. Then, conversely, families grew again into new clans.

Thus we have this picture of the early Chou state: the imperial central power established in Shensi, near the present Sian; supposedly over a thousand feudal states, great and small, often consisting only of a small garrison, or sometimes a more considerable one, with the former chieftain as feudal lord over it. Around these garrisons the old population lived on, in the north the Shang population, farther east and south various other peoples and cultures. The conquerors' garrisons were like islands in a sea. Most of them formed new towns, walled, with a rectangular plan and central crossroads, similar to the European towns subsequently formed out of Roman encampments. This town plan has been preserved to the present day.

This upper class in the garrisons formed the nobility; it was sharply divided from the indigenous population around the towns. The conquerors called the population 'the black-haired people', and themselves 'the hundred families'. The rest of the town populations consisted often of urban Shang people: Shang noble families together with their bondsmen and serfs had been given to Chou fiefholders. Such forced resettlements of whole populations have remained

25

typical even for much later periods. By this method new cities were provided with urban, refined people and, most important, with skilled craftsmen and businessmen who assisted in building the cities and in keeping them alive. Some scholars believe that many resettled Shang urbanites either were or became businessmen; incidentally, the same word 'Shang' means 'merchant', up to the present time. The people of the Shang capital lived on and even attempted a revolt in collaboration with some Chou people. The Chou rulers suppressed this revolt, and then transferred a large part of this population to Loyang. They were settled there in a separate community, and vestiges of the Shang population were still to be found there in the fifth century A.D.: they were entirely impoverished potters, still making vessels in the old style.

3 Fusion of Chou and Shang

The conquerors brought with them, for their own purposes to begin with, their rigid patriarchate in the family system and their cult of Heaven (t'ien), in which the worship of sun and stars took the principal place; a religion most closely related to that of the Turkish peoples. Some of the Shang popular deities, however, were admitted into the official Heaven-worship. Popular deities became 'feudal lords' under the Heaven-god. Earlier conceptions of the soul were also admitted into the Chou religion: the human body housed two souls, the personality-soul and the life-soul. Death meant the separation of the souls from the body, the life-soul also slowly dying. The personality-soul, however, could move about freely and lived as long as there were people who remembered it and kept it from hunger by means of sacrifices. The Chou systematized this idea and made it into the ancestor-worship that has endured down to the present time.

The Chou officially abolished human sacrifices, especially since, as former pastoralists, they knew of better means of employing prisoners of war than did the more agrarian Shang. The Chou used Shang and other slaves as domestic servants for their numerous nobility, and Shang serfs as farm labourers on their estates. They seem to have regarded the land under their control as 'state land' and all farmers as 'serfs'. Thus, the following, still rather hypothetical, picture of the land system of the early Chou time emerges: around the walled towns of the feudal lords and sub-lords, always in the plains, was 'state land' which produced millet and more and more wheat. Cultivation was still largely 'shifting', so that the serfs in groups cultivated more or less standardized plots for a year or more and then shifted to other plots. During the growing season they lived in huts on the fields; during the winter in the towns in adobe houses.

In this manner the yearly life cycle was divided into two different periods. The produce of the serfs supplied the lords, their dependants and the farmers themselves. Whenever the lord found it necessary, the serfs had to perform also other services for the lord, most of all, military services in case of war, where they accompanied the war-chariots of the lords. Farther away from the towns were the villages of the 'natives', nominally also subjects of the lord. In most parts of eastern China, these, too, were agriculturists. They acknowledged their dependence by sending 'gifts' to the lord in the town. Later these gifts became institutionalized and turned into a form of tax. The lord's serfs, on the other hand, tended to settle near the fields in villages of their own because, with growing urban population, the distances from the town to many of the fields became too great. It was also at this time of new settlements that a more intensive cultivation with a fallow system began. At latest from the sixth century B.C. on, the distinctions between both land systems became unclear; and the pure serf-cultivation, called by the old texts the 'well-field system' because eight cultivating families used one common well, disappeared in practice.

The actual structure of early Chou administration is difficult to ascertain. The 'Duke of Chou', brother of the first ruler, Wu Wang, later regent during the minority of Wu Wang's son, and certainly one of the most influential persons of this time, was the alleged creator of the book 'Chou-li' which contains a detailed table of the bureaucracy of the country. The 'Chou-li' is certainly written down more than 800 years after the beginning of the Chou and gives an ideal picture of a bureaucratic state. But the study of Chou bronze texts has shown that the Chou had indeed a bureaucracy which was highly developed and complex. Some offices were fully feudal, i.e. officers were granted sovereign rights over certain pieces of land and the population living on it; others were given special offices near the capital or at the court and had income from these offices. Other officers around the ruler were comparable to personal servants, and still others had to have professional knowledge and training, such as the court scribes. We must assume that the majority of them came from the ranks of the nobility; upward social mobility seems to have developed only in a later period.

The Chou capital, at Sian, was a twin city. In one part lived the master-race of the Chou with the imperial court, in the other the subjugated population. At the same time, as previously mentioned, the Chou built a second capital, Loyang, in the present province of Honan. Loyang was just in the middle of the new state, and for the purposes of Heaven-worship it was regarded as the centre of the universe, where it was essential that the emperor should reside.

Loyang was another twin city: in one part were the rulers' administrative buildings, in the other the transferred population of the Shang capital, probably artisans for the most part. The valuable artisans seem all to have been taken over from the Shang, for the bronze vessels of the early Chou age are virtually identical with those of the Shang age. The shapes of the houses also remained unaltered, and probably also the clothing, though the Chou brought with them the novelties of felt and woollen fabrics, old possessions of their earlier period. The only fundamental material change was in the form of the graves: in the Shang age house-like tombs were built underground; now great tumuli were constructed in the fashion preferred by all steppe peoples.

One professional class was severely hit by the changed circumstances—the Shang priesthood. The Chou had no priests. As with the peoples of the steppes, the head of the family himself performed the religious rites. Beyond this there were only shamans for certain purposes of magic. And very soon Heaven-worship was combined with the family system, the ruler being declared to be the Son of Heaven; the mutual relations within the family were thus extended to the religious relations with the deity. If, however, the god of Heaven is the father of the ruler, the ruler as his son himself offers sacrifice, and so the priest becomes superfluous. Thus the priests became 'unemployed'. Some of them changed their profession. They were the only people who could read and write, and as an administrative system was necessary they obtained employment as scribes. Others withdrew to their villages and became village priests. They organized the religious festivals in the village, carried out the ceremonies connected with family events, and even conducted the exorcism of evil spirits with shamanistic dances; they took charge, in short, of everything connected with customary observances and morality. The Chou lords were great respecters of propriety. The Shang culture had, indeed, been a high one with an ancient and highly developed moral system, and the Chou as rough conquerors must have been impressed by the ancient forms and tried to imitate them. In addition, they had in their religion of Heaven a conception of the existence of mutual relations between Heaven and Earth: all that went on in the skies had an influence on earth, and vice versa. Thus, if any ceremony was 'wrongly' performed, it had an evil effect on Heaven—there would be no rain, or the cold weather would arrive too soon, or some such misfortune would come. It was therefore of great importance that everything should be done 'correctly'. Hence the Chou rulers were glad to call in the old priests as performers of ceremonies and teachers of morality similar to the ancient Indian rulers who needed the Brahmans for the correct performance of all rites. There thus came into existence in the early Chou empire a new social group, later called 'scholars', men who were not regarded as belonging to the lower class represented by the subjugated population but were not included in the nobility; men who were not productively employed but belonged to a sort of independent profession. They became of very great importance in later centuries.

In the first centuries of the Chou dynasty the ruling house steadily lost power. Some of the emperors proved weak, or were killed at war; above all, the empire was too big and its administration too slow-moving. The feudal lords and nobles were occupied with their own problems in securing the submission of the surrounding villages to their garrisons and in governing them; they soon paid little attention to the distant central authority. In addition to this, the situation at the centre of the empire was more difficult than that of its feudal states farther east. The settlements around the garrisons in the east were inhabited by agrarian tribes, but the subjugated population around the centre at Sian was made up of nomadic tribes of Turks and Mongols together with semi-nomadic Tibetans. Sian lies in the valley of the river Wei; the riverside country certainly had belonged, though perhaps only insecurely, to the Shang empire and was specially well adapted to agriculture; but its periphery—mountains in the south, steppes in the north—was inhabited (until a late period, to some extent to the present day) by nomads, who had also been subjugated by the Chou. The Chou themselves were by no means strong, as they had been only a small tribe and their strength had depended on auxiliary tribes, which had now spread over the country as the new nobility and lived far from the Chou. The Chou emperors had thus to hold in check the subjugated but warlike tribes of Turks and Mongols who lived quite close to their capital. In the first centuries of the dynasty they were more or less successful, for the feudal lords still sent auxiliary forces. In time, however, these became fewer and fewer, because the feudal lords pursued their own policy; and the Chou were compelled to fight their own battles against tribes that continually rose against them, raiding and pillaging their towns. Campaigns abroad also fell mainly on the shoulders of the Chou, as their capital lay near the frontier.

It must not be simply assumed, as is often done by the Chinese and some of the European historians, that the Turkish and Mongolian tribes were so savage or so pugnacious that they continually waged war just for the love of it. The problem is much deeper, and to fail to recognize this is to fail to understand Chinese history down to the Middle Ages. The conquering Chou established their garrisons everywhere, and these garrisons were surrounded by the quarters of artisans and by the villages of peasants, a process that ate into the pasturage of the Turkish and Mongolian nomads. Some of the nomadic tribes living between garrisons withdrew, to escape from the growing pressure, mainly into the province of Shansi, where the influence of the Chou was weak and they were not numerous; some of the nomad chiefs lost their lives in battle, and some learned from the Chou lords and turned themselves into petty rulers. We will have to discuss these processes again later. Within the area in which the Chou ruled over people who had been farmers for a long time, a kind of symbiosis developed in these first centuries of Chou rule between the urban aristocrats and the country-people. The rulers of the towns took over from the general population almost the whole vocabulary of the language which from now on we may call 'Chinese'. They naturally took over elements of the material civilization. The subjugated population had, meanwhile, to adjust itself to its lords. In the organism that thus developed, with its unified economic system, the conquerors became an aristocratic ruling class, and the subjugated population became a lower class, with varied elements but mainly a peasantry. From now on we may call this society 'Chinese'; it has endured to the middle of the twentieth century. Most later essential societal changes are the result of internal development and not of aggression from without.

4 Limitation of the imperial power

In 771 B.C. an alliance of northern feudal states had attacked the ruler in his western capital; in a battle close to the city they had overcome and killed him. This campaign appears to have set in motion considerable groups from various tribes, so that almost the whole province of Shensi was lost. With the aid of some feudal lords who had remained loyal, a Chou prince was rescued and conducted eastward to the second capital, Loyang, which until then had never been the ruler's actual place of residence. In this rescue a lesser feudal prince, ruler of the feudal state of Ch'in, specially distinguished himself. Soon afterwards this prince, whose domain had lain close to that of the ruler, reconquered a great part of the lost territory, and thereafter regarded it as his own fief. The Ch'in family resided in the same capital in which the Chou had lived in the past, and five hundred years later we shall meet with them again as the dynasty that succeeded the Chou. The period that now begins, is called 'Eastern Chou', and its first part, to 481 B.C., is the 'Spring and Autumn' period, called after an annalistic history on which Confucius worked.

The new ruler, resident now in Loyang, was foredoomed to impotence. He was now in the centre of the country, and less exposed to large-scale enemy attacks; but his actual rule extended little beyond the town itself and its immediate environment. Moreover, attacks did not entirely cease; several times parts of the indigenous population living between the Chou towns rose against the towns, even in the centre of the country.

Now that the emperor had no territory that could be the basis of a strong rule and, moreover, because he owed his position to the feudal lords and was thus under an obligation to them, he ruled no longer as the chief of the feudal lords but as a sort of sanctified overlord; and this was the position of all his successors. A situation was formed that may be compared with that of Japan down to the middle of the nineteenth century. The ruler was a symbol rather than an exerciser of power. There had to be a supreme ruler because, in the worship of Heaven which was recognized by all the feudal lords, the supreme sacrifices could only be offered by the Son of Heaven in person. There could not be a number of sons of heaven because there were not a number of heavens. The imperial sacrifices secured that all should be in order in the country, and that the necessary equilibrium between Heaven and Earth should be maintained. For in the religion of Heaven there was a close parallelism between Heaven and Earth, and every omission of a sacrifice, or failure to offer it in due form, brought down a reaction from Heaven. For these religious reasons a central ruler was a necessity for the feudal lords. They needed him also for practical reasons. In the course of centuries the personal relationship between the various feudal lords had ceased. Their original kinship and united struggles had long been forgotten. When the various feudal lords proceeded to subjugate the territories at a distance from their towns, in order to turn their city states into genuine territorial states, they came into conflict with each other. In the course of these struggles for power many of the small fiefs were simply destroyed. It may fairly be said that not until the eighth and seventh centuries B.C. did the old garrison towns become real states. In these circumstances the struggles between the feudal states called urgently for an arbiter, to settle simple cases, and in more difficult cases either to try to induce other feudal lords to intervene or to give sanction to the new situation. These were the only governing functions of the ruler from the time of the transfer to the second capital.

5 Changes in the relative strength of the feudal states
In these disturbed times China also made changes in her outer frontiers. When we speak of frontiers in this connection, we must take little account of the European conception of a frontier. No frontier in that sense existed in China until her conflict with the European powers. In the dogma of the Chinese religion of Heaven, all the countries of the world were subject to the Chinese emperor,

the Son of Heaven. Thus there could be no such thing as other independent states. In practice the dependence of various regions on the ruler naturally varied: near the centre, that is to say near the ruler's place of residence, it was most pronounced; then it gradually diminished in the direction of the periphery. The feudal lords of the inner territories were already rather less subordinated than at the centre, and those at a greater distance scarcely at all; at a still greater distance were territories whose chieftains regarded themselves as independent, subject only in certain respects to Chinese overlordship. In such a system it is difficult to speak of frontiers. In practice there was, of course, a sort of frontier, where the influence of the outer feudal lords ceased to exist. The development of the original feudal towns into feudal states with factual sovereignty over their territories proceeded, of course, not only in the interior of China but also on its borders, where the feudal territories had the advantage of more unrestricted opportunities of expansion; thus they became more and more powerful.

Along the northern borders, the difference between 'Chinese' lords and 'non-Chinese' rulers also became blurred. Statelets which in the early years of the Chou certainly were ruled by non-Chinese and inhabited largely by non-Chinese, slowly became more and more 'Chinese' by adopting institutions of their neighbours, the feudal lords, and probably also by immigration of Chinese into their area.

In the south (that is to say, in the south of the Chou empire, in the present central China) the garrisons that founded feudal states were relatively small and widely separated; consequently their cultural system was largely absorbed into that of the aboriginal population, so that they developed into feudal states with a character of their own. Three of these attained special importance—(1) Ch'u, in the neighbourhood and north of the present Hankow; (2) Wu, near the present Nanking; and (3) Yüeh, near the present Hangchow. In 704 B.C. the feudal prince of Wu proclaimed himself 'Wang'. 'Wang', however, was the title of the ruler of the Chou dynasty. This meant that Wu broke away from the old Chou religion of Heaven, according to which there could be only one ruler (*wang*) in the world. Though Chinese sources always regard these southerners as 'barbarians', i.e. as people with no civilization, archaeology has shown us that this was not at all the case. The south-eastern part of China developed cultures of its own, probably derived from the Lung-shan culture. A geometrical style of pottery becomes typical of the lower Yangtze area. But soon we find here the use of bronze and iron, and according to some scholars, the first iron cultures of China originated here. At our middle Chou period, archaeology confirms well what we can learn from Chou texts: mixed and side by side with these native

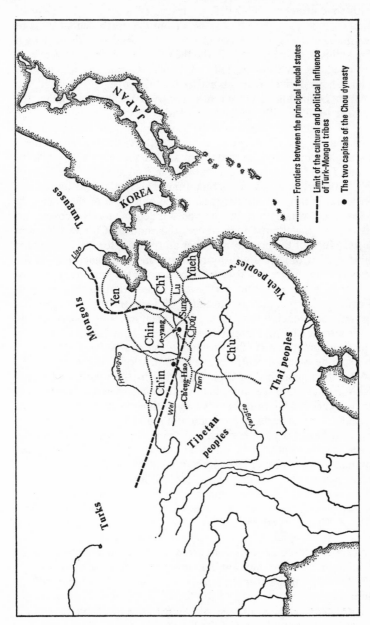

MAP 2   *The principal feudal states in the feudal epoch (roughly 770–481 B.C.)*

·········· Frontiers between the principal feudal states

– – – Limit of the cultural and political influence
         of Turk-Mongol tribes

● The two capitals of the Chou dynasty

southern cultures we find definite traces of Shang and mainly of Chou culture, indicating that settlers from the north, feudal lords of the Chou, had begun to settle in the south together with their own men, amidst local people. Similarly, the western province of Szechwan developed, as archaeology tells us, two local cultures which seem to have been derived from an earlier neolithic one.

At the beginning of the seventh century it became customary for the ruler to unite with the feudal lord who was most powerful at the time. This feudal lord became a dictator, and had the military power in his hands, like the shoguns in nineteenth-century Japan. If there was a disturbance of the peace, he settled the matter by military means. The first of these dictators was the feudal lord of the state of Ch'i, in the present province of Shantung. This feudal state had grown considerably through the conquest of the outer end of the peninsula of Shantung, which until then had been independent. Moreover, and this was of the utmost importance, the state of Ch'i was a trade centre. Much of the bronze, and later all the iron, for use in northern China came from the south by road and in ships that went up the rivers to Ch'i, where it was distributed among the various regions of the north, north-east, and north-west. In addition to this, through its command of portions of the coast, Ch'i had the means of producing salt, with which it met the needs of great areas of eastern China. It was also in Ch'i that money was first used. Thus Ch'i soon became a place of great luxury, far surpassing the court of the Chou, and Ch'i also became the centre of the most developed civilization.

After the feudal lord of Ch'i, supported by the wealth and power of his feudal state, became dictator, he had to struggle not only against other feudal lords, but also many times against risings among the most various parts of the population, and especially against the nomad tribes in the southern part of the present province of Shansi. In the seventh century not only Ch'i but the other feudal states had expanded. The regions in which the nomad tribes were able to move had grown steadily smaller, and the feudal lords now set to work to bring the nomads of their country under their direct rule. The greatest conflict of this period was the attack in 660 B.C. against the feudal state of Wei, in northern Honan. The nomad tribes seem this time to have been proto-Mongols; they made a direct attack on the garrison town and actually conquered it. The remnant of the urban population, no more than 730 in number, had to flee southward. It is clear from this incident that nomads were still living in the middle of China, within the territory of the feudal states, and that they were still decidedly strong, though no longer in a position to get rid entirely of the feudal lords of the Chou.

The period of the dictators came to an end after about a century, because it was found that none of the feudal states was any longer strong enough to exercise control over all the others. These others formed alliances against which the dictator was powerless. Thus this period passed into the next, which the Chinese call the period of the Contending States (403–221 B.C.).

6 Confucius and the Chinese basic values

After this outline of the political history we must consider the intellectual development of this period. The centuries between 500 and 280 B.C. are certainly the period in which we find the greatest variety of ideas, many of which remained decisive down to almost the present day. It is symbolic that Mao Tse-tung has recently called for the fight against Confucius and the praise of Shih Huang-ti, though both men have been dead for more than two thousand years.

We saw how the priests of the earlier dynasty of the Shang developed into the group of so-called 'scholars'. When the Chou ruler, after the move to the second capital, had lost virtually all but his religious authority, these 'scholars' gained increased influence. They were the specialists in traditional morals, in sacrifices, and in the organization of festivals. The continually increasing ritualism at the court of the Chou called for more and more of these men. The various feudal lords also attracted these scholars to their side, employed them as tutors for their children, and entrusted them with the conduct of sacrifices and festivals.

China's best-known philosopher, Confucius (Chinese: K'ung Tzŭ), was one of these scholars. He was born in 551 B.C. in the feudal state Lu in the present province of Shantung. In Lu and its neighbouring state Sung, institutions of the Shang had remained strong and traces of Shang culture can be seen in Confucius's political and ethical ideas. He acquired the knowledge which a scholar had to possess, and then taught in the families of nobles, also helping in the administration of their properties. He made several attempts to obtain advancement, either in vain or with only a short term of employment ending in dismissal. Thus his career was a continuing pilgrimage from one noble to another, from one feudal lord to another, accompanied by a few young men, sons of scholars, who were partly his pupils and partly his servants. Many of these disciples seem to have been 'illegitimate' sons of noblemen, i.e. sons of concubines, and Confucius's own family seems to have been of the same origin. In the strongly patriarchal and patrilinear system of the Chou and the developing primogeniture, children of secondary wives had a lower social status. Ultimately Confucius gave up his wanderings, settled in his home town of Lu, and there taught his disciples until his death in 479 B.C.

Such was briefly the life of Confucius. His enemies claim that he was a political intriguer, inciting the feudal lords against each other in the course of his wanderings from one state to another, with the intention of somewhere coming into power himself. There may, indeed, be some truth in that.

Confucius's importance lies in the fact that he systematized a body of ideas, not of his own creation, and communicated it to a circle of disciples. His teachings were later set down in writing and formed, right down to the twentieth century, the moral code of the upper classes of China. Confucius was fully conscious of his membership in a social class whose existence was tied to that of the feudal lords. With their disappearance, his type of scholar would become superfluous. The common people, the lower class, was in his view in an entirely subordinate position. Thus his moral teaching is a code for the ruling class. Accordingly it retains almost unaltered the elements of the old cult of Heaven, following the old tradition inherited from the northern peoples. For him Heaven is not an arbitrarily governing divine tyrant, but the embodiment of a system of legality. Heaven does not act independently, but follows a universal law, the so-called 'Tao'. Just as sun, moon, and stars move in the heavens in accordance with law, so man should conduct himself on earth in accord with the universal law, not against it. The ruler should not actively intervene in day-to-day policy, but should only act by setting an example, like Heaven; he should observe the established ceremonies, and offer all sacrifices in accordance with the rites, and then all else will go well in the world. The individual, too, should be guided exactly in his life by the prescriptions of the rites, so that harmony with the law of the universe may be established.

Today, we see this stress on harmony as one of the basic values of Chinese civilization. Harmony is seen as the principle of the cosmic order, therefore also as the principle of human social organization. It presupposes the subordination of the individual under the community; the will to give up freedom, the highest value of Western, European cultures, in favour of the security which the community has to offer when harmony is established. More and more we see that there is a contradiction between freedom and security; man cannot have both at the same time. Chinese society and its philosophers by stressing harmony instead of conflict, elected security.

A second idea of the Confucian system came also from the old conceptions of the Chou conquerors, and thus originally from the northern peoples. This is the patriarchal idea, according to which the family is the cell of society, and at the head of the family stands the eldest male adult as a sort of patriarch. The state is simply an extension of the family, 'state', of course, meaning simply the class of the feudal lords (the 'chün-tzǔ'). And the organization of the family is also that of the world of the gods. Within the family there are a number of ties, all of them, however, one-sided: that of father to son (the son having to obey the father); that of husband to wife (the wife had fewer rights); that of elder to younger brother. An extension of these is the association of friend with friend, which is conceived as an association between an elder and a younger brother. The final link, and the only one extending beyond the family and uniting it with the state, is the association of the ruler with the subject, a replica of that between father and son. The ruler in turn is in the position of son to Heaven. Thus in Confucianism the cult of Heaven, the family system, and the state are welded into unity.

The 'five relations', enumerated above, exhibit a second basic value of Chinese society: no two persons are equal. Inequality is expressed by three criteria. The person who is older has more rights than the younger one; the male person has more rights than the female; the person in higher rank has more rights. This basic inequality of people is, of course, the opposite to the idea of the 'brother' in Christianity and to the principle of democracy and equality in the West. But, as China's history shows, a well-functioning society can be built on this principle. There is almost no possibility that two persons who meet have any doubt as to how they have to deal with the other person and how this other person expects to be treated. A great number of conflicts and stresses in our society have their origin in the fact that it is very difficult for us to find out how the person with whom we interact expects to be treated—just think of the problems American fathers have with their children, or the heads of bureaucracies with their employees. By determining the status of each person within the state, frictions could be reduced. Existing vagueness was prevented by precise rules of etiquette. Every step, every action was prescribed (to some degree as in our books of etiquette, though these were never 'official'), and whoever followed these rules experienced no frictions and could expect to live in harmony. We might want to explain these first two basic values as a consequence of the compact way of settlement of the Chinese. With very few exceptions, Chinese never lived in open settlements, always in compact villages. They were compact, because Chinese settled along valleys, avoiding as far as possible the hills. Their fields were in these valleys, and the more space a settlement took, the less land for production was available, because fields could not be too far from the settlement, otherwise they would be exposed to attacks and thefts and their cultivation would cost too much time and labour. In a compact settlement, with the lightly built Chinese houses which, in early times, had no windows, later windows of paper, and which have no solid inner walls, every and any sound can be heard by everybody who is in the house, and also by everybody who passes by or lives in the next houses. With no 'rules of behaviour' incessant friction would occur. The individual had to restrain himself and be quiet. Down to the present time, one of the basic rules is that one should not talk 'empty talk', not talk about what is not one's own business.

So far as we have described it above, the teaching of Confucius was a further development of the old cult of Heaven. Through bitter experience, however, Confucius had come to realize that nothing could be done with the ruling house as it existed in his day. So shadowy a figure as the Chou ruler of that time could not fulfil what Confucius required of the 'Son of Heaven'. But the opinions of students of Confucius's actual ideas differ. Some say that in the only book in which he personally had a hand, the so-called 'Annals of Spring and Autumn', he intended to set out his conception of the character of a true emperor; others say that in that book he showed how he would himself have acted as emperor, and that he was only awaiting an opportunity to make himself emperor. He was called indeed, at a later time, the 'uncrowned ruler'. In any case, the 'Annals of Spring and Autumn' seem to be simply a dry work of annals, giving the history of his native state of Lu on the basis of the older documents available to him. In his text, however, Confucius made small changes by means of which he expressed criticism or recognition; in this way he indirectly made known how in his view a ruler should act or should not act. He did not shrink from falsifying history, as can today be demonstrated. Thus on one occasion a ruler had to flee from a feudal prince, which in Confucius's view was impossible behaviour for the ruler; accordingly he wrote instead that the ruler went on a hunting expedition. Elsewhere he tells of an eclipse of the sun on a certain day, on which in fact there was no eclipse. By writing of an eclipse he meant to criticize the way a ruler had acted, for the sun symbolized the ruler, and the eclipse meant that the ruler had not been guided by divine illumination.

Rendered alert by this experience, we are able to see and to show that most of the other later official works of history follow the example of the 'Annals of Spring and Autumn' in containing things that have been deliberately falsified. This is especially so in the work called 'T'ung-chien kang-mu', which was the source of the history of the Chinese empire translated into French by de Mailla. History, for Confucius, and down to the present time, is not an objective science, but an educational tool: history can tell us how to behave in a specific situation, by studying how others, before us, have acted in similar situations. Good history should make clear the values of society, and, if necessary, criticize the unworthy in clear terms. To the present time, the newspapers of the People's Republic call the leaders of the Republic of China 'bandits' and vice versa: they know very well, that these men are not real bandits, but they want to express that they violate moral standards which they (each of them differently) have set up and want to defend.

Apart from Confucius's criticism of the inadequate capacity of the emperor of his day, there is discernible, though only in the form of cryptic hints, a fundamentally important progressive idea. It is that a nobleman (chün-tzǔ) should not be a member of the ruling élite by right of birth alone, but should be a man of superior moral qualities. From Confucius on, 'chün-tzǔ' came to mean 'a gentleman'. Consequently, a country should not be ruled by a dynasty based on inheritance through birth, but by members of the nobility who show outstanding moral qualification for rulership. That is to say, the rule should pass from the worthiest to the worthiest, the successor first passing through a period of probation as a minister of state. In an unscrupulous falsification of the tradition, Confucius declared that this principle was followed in early times. It is probably safe to assume that Confucius had in view here an eventual justification of claims to rulership of his own.

Thus Confucius undoubtedly had ideas of reform, but he did not interfere with the foundations of feudalism. For the rest, his system consists only of a social order and a moral teaching. Metaphysics, logic, epistemology, i.e. branches of philosophy which played so great a part in the West, are of no interest to him. Nor can he be described as the founder of a religion; for the cult of Heaven of which he speaks and which he takes over existed in the same form before his day. He is merely the man who first systematized those notions. He had no successes in his lifetime and gained no recognition; nor did his disciples or their disciples gain any general recognition; his work did not become of importance until some three hundred years after his death, when in the second century B.C. his teaching was adjusted to the new social conditions: out of a moral system for the decaying feudal society of the past centuries developed the ethic of the rising social order of the gentry. The gentry (in much the same way as the European bourgeoisie) continually claimed that there should be access for every civilized citizen to the highest places in the social pyramid, and the rules of Confucianism became binding on every member of society if he were to be considered a gentleman. Only then did Confucianism begin to develop into the imposing system that dominated China almost down to the present day. Confucianism did not become a religion. The Jesuit missionaries in the sixteenth and seventeenth centuries came to that conviction and stated that the cult of the ancestors which is commonly associated with Confucianism as one of its important rituals, is not a cult to deified beings. To some degree, we could call Confucianism a 'community religion' if we compare it with such customs of ours, as to stand up when the national anthem is played, to erect war memorials and decorate them with flowers, to give precedence to older people or people of high rank in the government, and many other things by which we show our sense of belonging. A similar but much more conscious and much more powerful part was played by Confucianism in the life of the average Chinese, though he was not necessarily knowledgeable in the field of philosophical ideas. We may feel that the rules to which he was subjected were pedantic; but there was no limit to their effectiveness: they reduced to a minimum the friction that always occurs when great masses of people live close together; they gave Chinese society the strength through which it has endured; they gave security to its individuals. China's first real social crisis after the collapse of feudalism, that is to say, after the fourth or third century B.C., began only in the present century with the collapse of the social order of the gentry and the breakdown of the family system.

Confucius as a personality remains obscure to us, in spite of all studies. It is remarkable that the man who paid so much attention to the family, came from a family that was unusual, to say the least; apparently had little contact with his wife, and had only one son who hardly was as he would have expected. But these bits of information do not suffice to reconstruct Confucius as a man.

7 Lao Tzŭ

In eighteenth-century Europe Confucius was the only Chinese philosopher held in regard; in the last hundred years, the years of Europe's internal crisis, the philosopher Lao Tzŭ steadily advanced in repute, so that his book was translated almost a hundred times into various European languages. According to the general view among the Chinese, Lao Tzŭ was an older contemporary of Confucius; recent Chinese and Western research (A. Waley; H. H. Dubs) has contested this view and places Lao Tzŭ in the latter part of the fourth century B.C., or even later. Virtually nothing at all is known about his life; the oldest biography of Lao Tzŭ, written about 100 B.C., says that he lived as an official at the ruler's court, and one day, became tired of the life of an official and withdrew from the capital to his estate, where he died in old age. This, too, may be legendary, but it fits well into the picture given to us by Lao Tzŭ's teaching and by the life of his later followers. From the second century A.D., that is to say at least four hundred years after his death, there are legends of his migrating to the far west. Still later narratives tell of his going to Turkestan (where a temple was actually built in his honour in the

Medieval period); according to other sources he travelled as far as India or Sogdiana (Samarkand and Bokhara), where according to some accounts he was the teacher or forerunner of Buddha, and according to others of Mani, the founder of Manichaeism. For all this there is not a vestige of documentary evidence.

Lao Tzŭ's ideas are contained in a small book, the 'Tao Tê Ching', the 'Book of the World Law and its Power'. The book is written in quite simple language, at times in rhyme, but the sense vague and ambiguous. We now believe that it is an abstract of a full book, parts of which have recently been discovered. With its help, we may arrive at a better understanding of Lao Tzŭ's teachings.

Lao Tzŭ's teaching is essentially an effort to bring man's life on earth into harmony with the life and law of the universe (Tao). This was also Confucius's purpose. But while Confucius set out to attain that purpose in a somewhat rationalistic way, by laying down a number of rules of human conduct, Lao Tzŭ tries to attain his ideal by an intuitive, emotional method. Lao Tzŭ is always described as a mystic, but perhaps this is not entirely appropriate; it must be borne in mind that in his time the Chinese language, spoken and written, still had great difficulties in the expression of ideas. In reading Lao Tzŭ's book we feel that he is trying to express something for which the language of his day was inadequate; and what he wanted to express belonged to the emotional, not the intellectual, side of the human character, so that any perfectly clear expression of it in words was entirely impossible. It must be borne in mind that the Chinese language lacks definite word categories like substantive, adjective, adverb, or verb; any word can be used now in one category and now in another, with a few exceptions; thus the understanding of a combination like 'white horse' formed a difficult logical problem for the thinker of the fourth century B.C.: did it mean 'white' plus 'horse'? Or was 'white horse' no longer a horse at all but something quite different?

Confucius's way of bringing human life into harmony with the life of the universe was to be a process of assimilating Man as a social being, Man in his social environment, to Nature, and of so maintaining his activity within the bounds of the community. Lao Tzŭ pursues another path, the path for those who feel disappointed with life in the community. A Taoist, as a follower of Lao Tzŭ is called, withdraws from social life, and carries out none of the rites and ceremonies which a man of the upper class should observe throughout the day. He lives in self-imposed seclusion, in an elaborate primitivity which is often described in moving terms that are almost convincing of actual 'primitivity'. Far from the city, surrounded by Nature, the Taoist lives his own life, together with a few friends and

41

his servants, entirely according to his nature. His own nature, like everything else, represents for him a part of the Tao, and the task of the individual consists in the most complete adherence to the Tao that is conceivable, as far as possible performing no act that runs counter to the Tao. This is the main element of Lao Tzŭ's doctrine, the doctrine of *wu-wei*, 'passive achievement'.

Lao Tzŭ seems to have thought that this doctrine could be applied to the life of the state. He assumed that an ideal life in society was possible if everyone followed his own nature entirely and no artificial restrictions were imposed. Thus he writes:

> The more the people are forbidden to do this and that, the poorer will they be. The more sharp weapons the people possess, the more will darkness and bewilderment spread through the land. The more craft and cunning men have, the more useless and pernicious contraptions will they invent. The more laws and edicts are imposed, the more thieves and bandits there will be. 'If I work through Non-action,' says the Sage, 'the people will transform themselves.'

('The Way of Acceptance', a new version of Lao Tzŭ's 'Tao Tê Ching', by Hermon Ould (Dakers, 1946), Ch. 57.) Thus according to Lao Tzŭ, who takes the existence of a monarchy for granted, the ruler must treat his subjects as follows:

> By emptying their hearts of desire and their minds of envy, and by filling their stomachs with what they need; by reducing their ambitions and by strengthening their bones and sinews; by striving to keep them without the knowledge of what is evil and without cravings. Thus are the crafty ones given no scope for tempting interference. For it is by Non-action that the Sage governs, and nothing is really left uncontrolled. ('The Way of Acceptance', Ch. 3.)

Lao Tzŭ did not live to learn that such rule of good government would be followed by only one sort of rulers—dictators; and as a matter of fact the 'Legalist theory' which provided the philosophic basis for dictatorship in the third century B.C. was attributable to Lao Tzŭ. He was not thinking, however, of dictatorship; he was an individualistic anarchist, believing that if there were no active government all men would be happy. Then everyone could attain unity with Nature for himself. Thus we find in Lao Tzŭ, and later in all other Taoists, a scornful repudiation of all social and official obligations. An answer that became famous was given by the Taoist Chuang Tzŭ (see below) when it was proposed to confer high office

in the state on him (the story may or may not be true, but it is typical
of Taoist thought): 'I have heard,' he replied, 'that in Ch'u there is a
tortoise sacred to the gods. It has now been dead for 3,000 years, and
the king keeps it in a shrine with silken cloths, and gives it shelter in
the halls of a temple. Which do you think that tortoise would prefer—
to be dead and have its vestigial bones so honoured, or to be still
alive and dragging its tail after it in the mud?' The officials replied:
'No doubt it would prefer to be alive and dragging its tail after it in
the mud.' Then spoke Chuang Tzǔ: 'Begone! I, too, would rather
drag my tail after me in the mud!' (Chuang Tzǔ 17, 10.)

The true Taoist withdraws also from his family. Typical of this
is another story, surely apocryphal, from Chuang Tzǔ (Ch. 3, 3).
At the death of Lao Tzǔ a disciple went to the family and expressed
his sympathy quite briefly and formally. The other disciples were
astonished, and asked his reason. He said: 'Yes, at first I thought
that he was our man, but he is not. When I went to grieve, the old
men were bewailing him as though they were bewailing a son, and
the young wept as though they were mourning a mother. To bind
them so closely to himself, he must have spoken words which he
should not have spoken, and wept tears which he should not have
wept. That, however, is a falling away from the heavenly nature.'

Lao Tzǔ's teaching, like that of Confucius, cannot be described
as religion; like Confucius's, it is a sort of social philosophy, but of
irrationalistic character. Thus it was quite possible, and later it
became the rule, for one and the same person to be both Confucian
and Taoist. As an official and as the head of his family, a man would
think and act as a Confucian; as a private individual, when he had
retired far from the city to live in his country mansion (often modestly
described as a cave or a thatched hut), or when he had been dismissed
from his post or suffered some other trouble, he would feel and think
as a Taoist. In order to live as a Taoist it was necessary, of course,
to possess such an estate, to which a man could retire with his
servants, and where he could live without himself doing manual
work. This difference between the Confucian and the Taoist found
a place in the works of many Chinese poets. I take the following
quotation from an essay by the statesman and poet Ts'ao Chih, of
the end of the second century A.D.:

Master Mysticus lived in deep seclusion on a mountain in the
wilderness; he had withdrawn as in flight from the world,
desiring to purify his spirit and give rest to his heart. He
despised official activity, and no longer maintained any relations
with the world; he sought quiet and freedom from care, in
order in this way to attain everlasting life. He did nothing but

send his thoughts wandering between sky and clouds, and consequently there was nothing worldly that could attract and tempt him.

When Mr Rationalist heard of this man, he desired to visit him, in order to persuade him to alter his views. He harnessed four horses, who could quickly traverse the plain, and entered his light fast carriage. He drove through the plain, leaving behind him the ruins of abandoned settlements; he entered the boundless wilderness, and finally reached the dwelling of Master Mysticus. Here there was a waterfall on one side, and on the other were high crags; at the back a stream flowed deep down in its bed, and in front was an odorous wood. The master wore a white doeskin cap and a striped fox-pelt. He came forward from a cave buried in the mountain, leaned against the tall crag, and enjoyed the prospect of wild nature. His ideas floated on the breezes, and he looked as if the wide spaces of the heavens and the countries of the earth were too narrow for him; as if he was going to fly but had not yet left the ground; as if he had already spread his wings but wanted to wait a moment. Mr. Rationalist climbed up with the aid of vine shoots, reached the top of the crag, and stepped up to him, saying very respectfully:

'I have heard that a man of nobility does not flee from society, but seeks to gain fame; a man of wisdom does not swim against the current, but seeks to earn repute. You, however, despise the achievements of civilization and culture; you have no regard for the splendour of philanthropy and justice; you squander your powers here in the wilderness and neglect ordered relations between man. . . .'

Frequently Master Mysticus and Mr. Rationalist were united in a single person. Thus, Shih Ch'ung wrote in an essay on himself:

In my youth I had great ambition and wanted to stand out above the multitude. Thus it happened that at a little over twenty years of age I was already a court official; I remained in the service for twenty-five years. When I was fifty I had to give up my post because of an unfortunate occurrence. . . . The older I became, the more I appreciated the freedom I had acquired; and as I loved forest and plain, I retired to my villa. When I built this villa, a long embankment formed the boundary behind it; in front the prospect extended over a clear canal; all around grew countless cypresses, and flowing water meandered round the house. There were pools there, and outlook towers; I bred birds and fishes. In my harem there were always good

1 Painted pottery from Kansu: Neolithic.
(In the collection of the Museum für Völkerkunde, Berlin.)

2 Ancient bronze tripod found at An-yang.
(From G. Ecke, 'Frühe chinesische Bronzen aus der
Sammlung Oskar Trautmann', Peking, 1939, plate 3.)

musicians who played dance tunes. When I went out I enjoyed nature or hunted birds and fished. When I came home, I enjoyed playing the lute or reading; I also liked to concoct an elixir of life and to take breathing exercises [both Taoist practices], because I did not want to die, but wanted one day to lift myself to the skies, like an immortal genius. Suddenly I was drawn back into the official career, and became once more one of the dignitaries of the Emperor.

Thus Lao Tzŭ's individualist and anarchist doctrine was not suited to form the basis of a general Chinese social order, and its employment in support of dictatorship was certainly not in the spirit of Lao Tzŭ. Throughout history, however, Taoism of the type that the 'Tao Tê Ching' seems to propose remained the philosophic attitude of individuals of the highest circle of society; its real doctrine never became popularly accepted; for the strong feeling for nature that distinguishes the Chinese, and their reluctance to interfere in the sanctified order of nature by technical and other deliberate acts, was not actually a result of Lao Tzŭ's teaching, but one of the fundamentals from which his ideas started. But there appeared a religious system which claims to derive from Lao Tzŭ and which still exists today. We call it sometimes 'Vulgar Taoism' or 'Folk religion'. It is not clear whether it existed at the time of Lao Tzŭ or originated later. We believe that it contains many elements of an old folk religion of which hardly any traces were preserved in our sources. We will come back to this 'Taoism'. Here, it suffices that in the writings of their thinkers, Lao Tzŭ's book is interpreted as a religious text, given a different meaning and purpose. In this system, some thinkers were true mystics; others, more practical, tried to prolong their life by sexual techniques and by control of the breath and the diet; still others tried to develop an elixir of life and became alchemists. In all these schools, the 'Tao Tê Ching' was the basic book; all interpreted it in their way.

If the date assigned to Lao Tzŭ by present-day research (the fourth instead of the sixth century B.C.) is correct, he was more or less contemporary with Chuang Tzŭ, who was probably the most gifted poet among the Chinese philosophers. At the time of his writing, there was not yet a single 'real' book, except more or less annalistic books of history. So his book consists of short essays which exhibit a wealth of fresh metaphors and similes which nobody before him had thought of, and a wealth also of thoughts of a different kind, some even reminding us strongly of Indian thought, and, as we will see, it is not impossible that elements of Indian thought reached China around or before 400 B.C.

From Lao Tzǔ and Chuang Tzǔ a thin thread extends as far as the fourth century A.D.: Huai-nan Tzǔ, Chung-ch'ang T'ung, Yüan Chi (210–263), Liu Ling (221–300), and T'ao Ch'ien (365–427), are some of the most eminent names of Taoist philosophers. After that the stream of original thought dried up, and we rarely find a new idea among the late Taoists. These gentlemen living on their estates had acquired a new means of expressing their inmost feelings: they wrote poetry and, above all, painted. Their poems and paintings contain in a different form what Lao Tzǔ had tried to express with the inadequate means of the language of his day. Thus Lao Tzǔ's teaching has had the strongest influence to this day in this field, and has inspired creative work which is among the finest achievements of mankind.

CHAPTER FOUR

The Dissolution
of the Feudal System
(c. 500–250 B.C.)

1 Social and military changes

The period following that of the Chou dictatorships is known as that of the Contending States (480–222 B.C.). Out of over a thousand states, fourteen remained, of which, in the period that now followed, one after another disappeared, until only one remained. This period is the fullest, or one of the fullest, of strife in all Chinese history. The various feudal states had lost all sense of allegiance to the ruler, and acted in entire independence. It is a pure fiction to speak of a Chinese state in this period; the emperor had no more power than the ruler of the Holy Roman Empire in the late medieval period of Europe, and the so-called 'feudal states' of China can be directly compared with the developing national states of Europe. A comparison of this period with late medieval Europe is, indeed, of highest interest. If we adopt a political system of periodization, we might say that around 400 B.C. the unified feudal state of the first period of Antiquity had ceased to exist and that 'national states' had emerged which took a development in the direction of the national states of medieval Europe, although formally, the feudal system continued and the national states still retained many feudal traits.

As none of these states was strong enough to control and subjugate the rest, alliances were formed. The most favoured union was the north-south axis; it struggled against an east-west league. The alliances were not stable but broke up again and again through bribery or intrigue, which produced new combinations. We must confine ourselves to mentioning the most important of the events that took place behind this military façade.

Through the continual struggles more and more feudal lords lost their lands; and not only they, but the families of the nobles dependent on them, who had received so-called sub-fiefs. Some of the

47

landless nobles perished; some offered their services to the remaining feudal lords as soldiers or advisers. Thus in this period we meet with a large number of migratory politicians who became competitors of the wandering scholars. Both these groups recommended to their lord ways and means of gaining victory over the other feudal lords, so as to become sole ruler. In order to carry out their plans the advisers claimed the rank of a Minister or Chancellor.

The main literary source for this period is the 'Plans of the Contending States' ('Chan Kuo Ts'ê'), a book which is not so much a book of history as a kind of early novel which reports the clever tricks and schemes of these advisers. Thus, though certainly many events did not take place exactly as the book says, the spirit behind these events seems to be caught very well.

Realistic though these advisers and their lords were in their thinking, they did not dare to trample openly on the old tradition. The emperor was indeed a completely powerless figurehead, but he belonged nevertheless, according to tradition, to a family of divine origin, which had obtained its office not merely by the exercise of force but through a 'divine mandate'. Whether or not the lords believed in this 'mandate', rulers and pretenders always in history have tried to establish their 'legitimacy'. Accordingly, if one of the feudal lords thought of putting forward a claim to the imperial throne, he felt compelled to demonstrate that his family was just as much of divine origin as the emperor's, and perhaps of remoter origin. In this matter the travelling 'scholars' rendered valuable service as manufacturers of genealogical trees. Each of the old noble families already had its family tree, as an indispensable requisite for the sacrifices to ancestors. But in some cases this tree began as a branch of that of the imperial family: this was the case of the feudal lords who were of imperial descent and whose ancestors had been granted fiefs after the conquest of the country. Others, however, had for their first ancestor a local deity long worshipped in the family's home country, such as the ancient agrarian god Huang Ti, or the bovine god Shen Nung. Here the 'scholars' stepped in, turning the local deities into human beings and 'emperors'. This suddenly gave the noble family concerned an imperial origin. Finally, order was brought into this collection of ancient emperors. They were arranged and connected with each other in 'dynasties' or in some other 'historical' form. Thus at a stroke Huang Ti, who about 450 B.C. had been a local god in the region of southern Shansi, became the forefather of almost all the noble families, including that of the imperial house of the Chou. Needless to say, there would be discrepancies between the family trees constructed by the various scholars for their lords, and later, when this problem had lost its political importance, the commentators laboured for centuries on the elaboration of an impeccable system of 'ancient emperors'—and to this day there are sinologists who continue to present these humanized gods as historical personalities.

In the earlier wars fought between the nobles they were themselves the actual combatants, accompanied only by their retinue. As the struggles for power grew in severity, each noble hired such mercenaries as he could, for instance the landless nobles just mentioned. Very soon it became the custom to arm peasants and send them to the wars. This substantially increased the armies. The numbers of soldiers who were killed in particular battles may have been greatly exaggerated (in a single battle in 260 B.C., for instance, the number who lost their lives was put at 450,000, a quite impossible figure); but there must have been armies of several thousand men, perhaps as many as 10,000. The population had grown considerably by that time.

The armies of the earlier period consisted mainly of the nobles in their war-chariots; each chariot surrounded by the retinue of the nobleman. Now came large troops of commoners as infantry as well, drawn from the peasant population. To these, cavalry were first added in the fifth century B.C., by the northern state of Chao (in the present Shansi), following the example of its Turkish and Mongol neighbours. The general theory among ethnologists is that the horse was first harnessed to a chariot, and that riding came much later; but it is my opinion that effective horse-breeding was impossible without mastering the art of riding on a horse. However, it seems that cavalry could be used in war only after the domestication of horses had progressed and the riders had been trained in disciplined, co-ordinated action on horseback while being able to shoot accurately with the bow from the back of a galloping horse, especially shooting to the rear. In any case, its cavalry gave the feudal state of Chao a military advantage for a short time. Soon the other northern states copied it one after another—especially Ch'in, in north-west China. The introduction of cavalry brought a change in clothing all over China, for the former long skirt-like garb could not be worn on horseback. Trousers and the riding-cap were introduced from the north.

The new technique of war made it important for every state to possess as many soldiers as possible, and where it could to reduce the enemy's numbers. One result of this was that wars became much more sanguinary; another was that men in other countries were induced to immigrate and settle as peasants, so that the taxes they paid should provide the means for further recruitment of soldiers. In the state of Ch'in, especially, the practice soon started of using the whole of the peasantry simultaneously as a rough soldiery. Hence that state was particularly anxious to attract peasants in large numbers.

2 *Economic changes*

In the course of the wars much land of former noblemen had become free. Often the former serfs had then silently become landowners. Others had started to cultivate land in the area inhabited by the indigenous population and regarded this land, which they themselves had made fertile, as their private family property.

The natives probably in most parts of what was China at that time, still used digging sticks and other light tools. Chinese used a plough, drawn by an animal, and even before the cultivation of rice and irrigation had become widely accepted, fields had to be relatively level and rectangular. Thus, each new development of land needed much investment in labour. There was, in spite of the growth of the population, still much cultivable land available. Victorious feudal lords induced farmers to come to their territory and to cultivate the wasteland. This is a period of great migrations, internal and external. It seems that from this period on not only merchants but also farmers began to migrate southwards into the area of the present provinces of Kwangtung and Kwangsi and as far as Tonking.

As long as the idea that all land belonged to the great clans of the Chou prevailed, sale of land was inconceivable; but when individual family heads acquired land or cultivated new land, they regarded it as their natural right to dispose of the land as they wished. From now on until the end of the medieval period, the family head as representative of the family could sell or buy land. However, the land belonged to the family and not to him as a person. This development was favoured by the spread of money. In time land in general became an asset with a market value and could be bought and sold.

Another important change can be seen from this time on. Under the feudal system of the Chou strict primogeniture among the nobility existed: the fief went to the oldest son by the main wife. The younger sons were given independent pieces of land with its inhabitants as new, secondary fiefs. With the increase in population there was no more such land that could be set up as a new fief. From now on, primogeniture was retained in the field of ritual and religion down to the present time: only the oldest son of the main wife represents the family in the ancestor worship ceremonies; only the oldest son of the emperor could become his successor. But the landed property from now on was equally divided among all sons. Occasionally the oldest son was given some extra land to enable him to pay the expenses for the family ancestral worship. Mobile property, on the other side, was not so strictly regulated and often the oldest son was given preferential treatment in the inheritance. Daughters did not inherit land. Until recently, daughters were regarded as a kind of trust: their parents raised them for their husbands, and the husband had to repay to the parents the cost which was involved in raising the girl from birth to the moment of her marriage. Thus, the family of the groom had to pay a 'bridal gift', and the bride's family did not have to let her inherit parts of the family property.

The technique of cultivation underwent some significant changes. There seems to have been a plough, made of wood, which in use was drawn by one or two persons, together with a 'pull-spade'. From this time on, the animal-drawn plough seems to have become more common and it was often strengthened by an iron plough-share. Iron sickles, too, became common. A fallow system was introduced so that cultivation became more intensive. Manuring of fields was already known in Shang time. It seems that the consumption of meat decreased from this period on: less mutton and beef were eaten. Pig and dog became the main sources of meat, and higher consumption of beans made up for the loss of proteins. All this indicates a strong population increase. We have no statistics for this period, but by 400 B.C. it is conceivable that the population under the control of the various individual states comprised something around 25 million. The eastern plains emerge more and more as centres of production.

Iron, which now became quite common, was produced apparently in south China and also in Shansi. The blacksmiths of this time were able to produce cast as well as wrought iron which indicates that they must have had well-constructed furnaces and bellows in order to reach the necessary temperatures. Firing material was obviously at this period still charcoal; the use of coal seems to have come up somewhat later, and it is quite likely that the Chinese already at a relatively early time were able to transform coal into coke with a technique similar to that by which they produced charcoal. In any case, it seems to be clear that Chinese could handle iron and soon steel at a time much earlier than Western countries.

The raw materials for bronze came mainly from the south. We know now that Chinese made bronze mirrors already in the Shang time, but from our period on, mirrors become pieces of art, decorated with numerous symbolic figures. Swords of bronze appear already before our period, but belt hooks are new and indicate some change in clothing. The bronze vessels of the period of the Warring States replace the highly stylized animals and mythical beings by vivid scenes of battle, by wrestling matches, or other representations from daily life. This indicates that their use was no longer limited to ritual ceremonies, though bronze still was too expensive to be used in ordinary households.

The increased use of metal and the invention of metal coins greatly stimulated trade. Money normally was of copper and remained so until modern times; the value of the coin always was supposed to correspond to the metal value of the coin. Thus, a considerable capital in the form of copper coin took up a good deal of room and was not easy to conceal. If anyone had much money, everyone in his village knew it. No one dared to hoard to any extent for fear of attracting bandits and creating lasting insecurity. On the other hand the merchants wanted to attain the standard of living which the nobles, the landowners, used to have. Thus they began to invest their money in land. This was all the easier for them since it often happened that one of the lesser nobles or a peasant fell deeply into debt to a merchant and found himself compelled to give up his land in payment of the debt.

Soon the merchants took over another function. So long as there had been many small feudal states, and the feudal lords had created lesser lords with small fiefs, it had been a simple matter for the taxes to be collected, in the form of grain, from the peasants through the agents of the lesser lords. Now that there were only a few great states in existence, the old system was no longer effectual. This gave the merchants their opportunity. The rulers of the various states entrusted the merchants with the collection of taxes, and this had great advantages for the ruler: he could obtain part of the taxes at once, as the merchant usually had grain in stock, or was himself a landowner and could make advances at any time. Through having to pay the taxes to the merchant, the village population became dependent on him. Thus the merchants developed into the first administrative officials in the provinces.

In connection with the growth of business, the cities kept on growing. It is estimated that at the beginning of the third century, the city of Lin-chin, near the present Chi-nan in Shantung, had a population of 210,000 persons. Each of its walls had a length of 4,000 metres; thus, it was even somewhat larger than the famous city of Lo-yang, capital of China during the Later Han dynasty, in the second century A.D. Several other cities of this period have been recently excavated and must have had populations far above 10,000 persons. There were two types of cities: the rectangular, planned city of the Chou conquerors, a seat of administration; and the irregularly shaped city which grew out of a market place and became only later an administrative centre. We do not know much about the organization and administration of these cities, but they seem to have had considerable independence because some of them issued their own city coins.

From this period on, one can study the expansion of Chinese

settlement into areas of indigenous, non-Chinese societies by the spread of cities. A settlement became a 'city' (*ch'eng*) when it became the seat of an administration, and its outer symbol was its city wall. Normally, farmers did not live in cities. It was the aristocracy, its dependants, and a part of the craftsmen who had to work for the aristocracy that were the urbanites. We know, however, from neolithic times on that certain industries were usually outside the cities, mainly brick-making and metal founding. This has given rise to the theory that originally the cities were primarily cult centres to which the upper class which conducted the cult, became attached. The surrounding villages, specialized in farming or crafts, came to the city as their religious centre and their market; only at a subsequent period did the villages coalesce with the cult centre into a city. In general, this does not seem to be the best explanation for the Chinese type of urban development. We should regard the specialized rural settlements as outposts of the cities, where craftsmen were socially like Indian craft castes tied to the city aristocracy and had to work for their masters. True farm villages, on the other hand, did not at first have specialized craftsmen, as the farmer could produce most of what he needed and could get the rest on the markets. It seems that only at a later period, villages also usually contained some men who produced some of the tools the farmers needed.

When these cities grew, the food produced in the neighbourhood of the towns no longer sufficed for their inhabitants. This led to the building of roads, which also facilitated the transport of supplies for great armies. These roads mainly radiated from the centre of consumption into the surrounding country, and they were less in use for communication between one administrative centre and another. For long journeys the rivers were of more importance, since transport by wagon was always expensive owing to the shortage of draught animals. Thus we see in this period the first important construction of canals and a development of communications. With the canal construction was connected the construction of irrigation and drainage systems, which further promoted agricultural production. The cities were places in which great luxury often developed; music, dance, and other refinements were cultivated. We know that already at the time of Confucius the lords who invited other lords or ambassadors from other lords to their cities for the conclusion of treaties, entertained such guests not only with big dinners, but also had female dancers and musicians at hand, who, if we interpret Confucius's reaction correctly, influenced the guests by their charms. Similarly, the parties which the merchants gave and during which they discussed business, were enlivened by the presence of prostitutes. It is said that a statesman before the time of Confucius in the state of Ch'i opened the first houses of prostitution and drew profits from taxes imposed on these houses. We get the impression that the inmates of these houses were wives and daughters of convicted and executed criminals as well as prisoners of war while other unfortunate females were employed in state spinning and weaving factories and produced the technically superior silks of the time.

The life of the commoners in these cities was regulated by laws; the first codes are mentioned in 536 B.C. By the end of the fourth century B.C. a large body of criminal law existed, supposedly collected by Li K'uei, which became the foundation of all later Chinese law. It is interesting to remark that the use of minted coins as well as the formulation of laws begins in China later, but not much later than in the Near East, as recent research seems to have shown that the so-called codes of Sumer and Babylon were not applied by judges to actual cases, but in fact they were regarded as guidelines only.

So far nothing has been said in these chapters about China's foreign policy. Since the central ruling house was completely powerless, and the feudal lords were virtually independent rulers, little can be said, of course, about any 'Chinese' foreign policy. Some statelets which had existed in the North, along the zone in which farming was possible but marginal, had meanwhile been absorbed into the larger states of this time and fights with tribes of non-Chinese inside and outside the states continued. The important new development comes around 300 B.C. when, for the first time, a number of tribes of Turkish and/or Mongol type concluded a federation which took 'Hsiung-nu' as its name; the names of individual tribes at that time is not known, only later such names begin to be recorded. It is known that these northern peoples had mastered the technique of horseback warfare and were far ahead of the Chinese, although the Chinese imitated their methods. The peasants of China, as they penetrated farther and farther north, had to be protected by their rulers against the northern peoples, and since the rulers needed their armed forces for their struggles within China, a beginning was made with the building of frontier walls, to prevent sudden raids of the northern peoples against the peasant settlements. Thus came into existence the early forms of the 'Great Wall of China'. This provided for the first time a visible frontier between Chinese and non-Chinese. Along this frontier, just as by the walls of towns, great markets were held at which Chinese peasants bartered their produce to non-Chinese nomads. Both partners in this trade became accustomed to it and drew very substantial profits from it. We even know the names of several great horse-dealers who bought horses from the nomads and sold them within China.

3 Cultural changes

Together with the economic and social changes in this period, there came cultural changes. New ideas sprang up in exuberance, as would seem entirely natural, because in times of change and crisis men always come forward to offer solutions for pressing problems. We shall refer here only briefly to the principal philosophers of the period.

Mencius (c. 372–289 B.C.) and Hsün Tzŭ (c. 298–238 B.C.) both belonged to the so-called 'scholars', and both lived in the present Shantung, that is to say, in eastern China. Both elaborated the ideas of Confucius, but neither of them achieved personal success. Mencius (Meng Tzŭ) recognized that the removal of the ruling house of the Chou no longer presented any difficulty. The difficult question for him was when a change of ruler would be justified. And how could it be ascertained whom Heaven had destined as successor if the existing dynasty was brought down? Mencius replied that the voice of the 'people', that is to say of the upper class and its following, would declare the right man, and that this man would then be Heaven's nominee. This theory persisted throughout the history of China, but never led to the emergence of democracy. Every rebel claimed that Heaven had destined him to be the new legitimate ruler. If he was successful, he was right; if not, he was simply an impostor who deserved his death.

Hsün Tzŭ's chief importance lies in the fact that he recognized that the 'laws' of nature are unchanging but that man's fate is determined not by nature alone but, in addition, by his own activities. Man's nature is basically bad, but by working on himself within the framework of society, he can change his nature and can develop. Thus, Hsün Tzŭ's philosophy contains a dynamic element, fit for a dynamic period of history.

In the strongest contrast to these thinkers was the school of Mo Ti (at some time between 479 and 381 B.C.). The Confucian school held fast to the old feudal order of society, and was only ready to agree to a few superficial changes. The school of Mo Ti proposed to alter the fundamental principles of society. Family ethics must no longer be retained; the principles of family love must be extended to the whole upper class, which Mo Ti called the 'people'. One must love another member of the upper class just as much as one's own father. Then the friction between individuals and between states would cease. Instead of families, large groups of people friendly to one another must be created. Further one should live frugally and not expend endless money on effete rites, as the Confucianists demanded. The expenditure on weddings and funerals under the Confucianist ritual consumed so much money that many families fell into debt and, if they were unable to pay off the debt, sank from the upper into the lower class. In order to maintain the upper class, therefore, there must be more frugality. Mo Ti's teaching won great influence. He and his successors surrounded themselves with a private army of supporters which was rigidly organized and which could be brought into action at any time as its leader wished. Thus the Mohists came forward everywhere with an approach entirely different from that of the isolated Confucians. When the Mohists offered their assistance to a ruler, they brought with them a group of technical and military experts who had been trained on the same principles. In consequence of its great influence this teaching was naturally hotly opposed by the Confucianists.

We see clearly in Mo Ti's and his followers' ideas the influence of the changed times. His principle of 'universal love' reflects the breakdown of the clans and the general weakening of family bonds which had taken place. His ideal of social organization resembles organizations of merchants and craftsmen which we know only from later periods. His stress upon frugality, too, reflects a line of thought which is typical of businessmen. The rationality which can also be seen in his metaphysical ideas and which has induced modern Chinese scholars to call him an early materialist is fitting to an age in which a developing money economy and expanding trade required a cool, logical approach to the affairs of this world.

A similar mentality can be seen in another school which appeared from the fifth century B.C. on, the 'dialecticians'. Here are a number of names to mention: the most important are Kung-sun Lung and Hui Tzŭ, who are comparable with the ancient Greek dialecticians and Sophists. They saw their main task in the development of logic. Since, as we have mentioned, many 'scholars' journeyed from one princely court to another, and other people came forward, each recommending his own method to the prince for the increase of his power, it was of great importance to be able to talk convincingly, so as to defeat a rival in a duel of words on logical grounds.

Unquestionably, however, the most important school of this period was that of the so-called Legalists, whose most famous representative was Shang Yang (or Shang Tzŭ, died 338 B.C.). The supporters of this school came principally from old princely families that had lost their feudal possessions, and not from among the so-called scholars. They were people belonging to the upper class who possessed political experience and now offered their knowledge to other princes who still reigned. These men had entirely given up the old conservative traditions of Confucianism; they were the first to make their peace with the new social order. They recognized that little or nothing remained of the old upper class of feudal lords and their following.

The last of the feudal lords collected around the heads of the last remaining princely courts, or lived quietly on the estates that still remained to them. Such a class, with its moral and economic strength broken, could no longer lead. The Legalists recognized, therefore, only the ruler and next to him, as the really active and responsible man, the chancellor; under these there were to be only the common people, consisting of the richer and poorer peasants; the people's duty was to live and work for the ruler, and to carry out without question whatever orders they received. They were not to discuss or think, but to obey. The chancellor was to draft laws which came automatically into operation. The ruler himself was to have nothing to do with the government or with the application of the laws. He was only a symbol, a representative of the equally inactive Heaven. Clearly these theories were much the best suited to the conditions of the break-up of feudalism about 300 B.C. Thus they were first adopted by the state in which the old idea of the feudal state had been least developed, the state of Ch'in, in which alien peoples were most strongly represented. Shang Yang became the actual organizer of the state of Ch'in. His ideas were further developed by Han Fei Tzŭ (died 233 B.C.). The mentality which speaks out of his writings has closest similarity to the famous Indian Arthashastra which originated slightly earlier; both books exhibit a 'Machiavellian' spirit. It must be observed that these theories had little or nothing to do with the ideas of the old cult of Heaven or with family allegiance; on the other hand, the soldierly element, with the notion of obedience, was well suited to the militarized peoples of the west. The population of Ch'in, organized throughout on these principles, was then in a position to remove one opponent after another. In the middle of the third century B.C. the greater part of the China of that time was already in the hands of Ch'in, and in 256 B.C. the last emperor of the Chou dynasty was compelled, in his complete impotence, to abdicate in favour of the ruler of Ch'in.

Apart from these more or less political speculations, there came into existence in this period, by no mere chance, a school of thought which never succeeded in fully developing in China, concerned with natural science and comparable with the Greek natural philosophy. We have already several times pointed to parallels between Chinese and Indian thoughts. Such similarities may be the result of mere coincidence. But recent findings in Central Asia indicate that direct connections between India, Persia, and China may have started at a time much earlier than we had formerly thought. Sogdian merchants who later played a great role in commercial contacts might have been active already from 400 B.C. on and might have been the transmitters of new ideas. The most important philosopher of this school was

Tsou Yen (flourished between 320 and 295 B.C.); he, as so many other Chinese philosophers of this time, was a native of Shantung, and the ports of the Shantung coast may well have been ports of entrance of new ideas from western Asia as were the roads through the Sinkiang basin into western China. Tsou Yen's basic ideas had their root in earlier Chinese speculations: the doctrine that all that exists is to be explained by the positive, creative, or the negative, passive action (Yang and Yin) of the five 'elements', wood, fire, earth, metal, and water (Wu hsing). But Tsou Yen also considered the form of the world, and was the first to put forward the theory that the world consists not of a single continent with China in the middle of it, but of nine continents. The names of these continents sound like Indian names, and his idea of a central world-mountain may well have come from India. The 'scholars' of his time were quite unable to appreciate this beginning of science, which actually led to the contention of this school, in the first century B.C., that the earth was of spherical shape. Tsou Yen himself was ridiculed as a dreamer; but very soon, when the idea of the reciprocal destruction of the 'elements' was applied, perhaps by Tsou Yen himself, to politics, namely when, in connection with the astronomical calculations much cultivated by this school and through the identification of dynasties with the five elements, the attempt was made to explain and to calculate the duration and the supersession of dynasties, strong pressure began to be brought to bear against this school. For hundreds of years its books were distributed and read only in secret, and many of its members were executed as revolutionaries. Thus, this school, instead of becoming the nucleus of a school of natural science, was driven underground.

The secret societies which started to arise clearly from the first century B.C. on, but which may have been in existence earlier, adopted the politico–scientific ideas of Tsou Yen's school. Such secret societies have existed in China down to the present time. They all contained a strong religious, but heterodox element which can often be traced back to influences from a foreign religion. In times of peace they were centres of a true, emotional religiosity. In times of stress, a 'messianic' element tended to become prominent: the world is bad and degenerating; morality and a just social order have decayed, but the coming of a saviour is close; the saviour will bring a new, fair order and destroy those who are wicked. Tsou Yen's philosophy seemed to allow them to calculate when this new order would start; later secret societies contained ideas from Iranian Mazdaism, Manichaeism and Buddhism, mixed with traits from the popular religions and often couched in terms taken from the Taoists. The members of such societies were, typically, ordinary farmers who here found an emotional outlet for their frustrations in daily life. In times of stress, members of the leading élite often but not always established contacts with these societies, took over their leadership and led them to open rebellion.

The fate of Tsou Yen's school did not mean that the Chinese did not develop in the field of sciences. At about Tsou Yen's lifetime, the first mathematical handbook was written. From these books it is obvious that the interest of the government in calculating the exact size of fields, the content of measures for grain, and other fiscal problems stimulated work in this field, just as astronomy developed from the interest of the government in the fixation of the calendar. Science kept on developing in other fields, too, but mainly as a hobby of scholars and in the shops of craftsmen, if it did not have importance for the administration and especially taxation and budget calculations.

CHAPTER FIVE

Military Rule
(250–200 B.C.)

1 *Towards the unitary state*

In 256 B.C. the last ruler of the Chou dynasty abdicated in favour of the feudal lord of the state of Ch'in. Some people place the beginning of the Ch'in dynasty in that year, 256 B.C.; others prefer the date 221 B.C., because it was only in that year that the remaining feudal states came to their end and Ch'in really ruled all China.

The territories of the state of Ch'in, the present Shensi and eastern Kansu, were from a geographical point of view transit regions, closed off in the north by steppes and deserts and in the south by almost impassable mountains. Only between these barriers, along the rivers Wei (in Shensi) and T'ao (in Kansu), is there a rich cultivable zone which is also the only means of transit from east to west. All traffic from and to Central Asia had to take this route. It is believed that strong relations with Central Asia allowed the state of Ch'in to make big profits from such 'foreign trade'. We have reasons to believe that traders from a foreign country had first to offer their merchandise to the ruler, and could sell only what was left over to the populace. The population was growing through immigration from the east which the government encouraged. This growing population with its increasing means of production, especially the great new irrigation systems, provided a welcome field for trade which was also furthered by the roads, though these were actually built for military purposes.

The state of Ch'in had never been so closely associated with the feudal communities of the rest of China as the other feudal states. A great part of its population, including the ruling class, was not purely Chinese but contained an admixture of Turks and Tibetans. The other Chinese even called Ch'in a 'barbarian state', and the foreign influence was, indeed, unceasing. This was a favourable soil for the overcoming of feudalism, and the process was furthered by the factors mentioned in the preceding chapter, which were leading to a change in the social structure of China. Especially the recruitment of the whole population, including the peasantry, for war was entirely in the interest of the influential nomad fighting peoples within the state. About 250 B.C., Ch'in was not only one of the economically strongest among the feudal states, but had already made an end of its own feudal system.

Every feudal system harbours some seeds of a bureaucratic system of administration: feudal lords have their personal servants who are not recruited from the nobility, but who by their easy access to the lord can easily gain importance. They may, for instance, be put in charge of estates, workshops, and other properties of the lord and thus acquire experience in administration and an efficiency which are obviously of advantage to the lord. When Chinese lords of the preceding period, with the help of their sub-lords of the nobility, made wars, they tended to put the newly conquered areas not into the hands of newly enfeoffed noblemen, but to keep them as their property and to put their administration into the hands of efficient servants; these were the first bureaucratic officials. Thus, in the course of the later Chou period, a bureaucratic system of administration had begun to develop, and terms like 'district' or 'prefecture' began to appear, indicating that areas under a bureaucratic administration existed beside and inside areas under feudal rule. This process had gone furthest in Ch'in and was sponsored by the representatives of the Legalist School, which was best adapted to the new economic and social situation.

A son of one of the concubines of the penultimate feudal ruler of Ch'in was living as a hostage in the neighbouring state of Chao, in what is now northern Shansi. There he made the acquaintance of an unusual man, the merchant Lü Pu-wei, a man of education. Lü Pu-wei persuaded the feudal ruler of Ch'in to declare this son his successor. He also sold a girl to the prince to be his wife, and the son of this marriage was to be the famous and notorious Shih Huang-ti. Lü Pu-wei came with his protégé to Ch'in, where he became his Prime Minister, and after the prince's death in 247 B.C. Lü Pu-wei became the regent for his young son Shih Huang-ti (then called Cheng). For the first time in Chinese history a merchant, a commoner, had reached one of the highest positions in the state. It is not known what sort of trade Lü Pu-wei had carried on, but probably he dealt in horses, the principal export of the state of Chao. As horses were an absolute necessity for the armies of that time, it is easy to imagine that a horse-dealer might gain great political influence.

Soon after Shih Huang-ti's accession Lü Pu-wei was dismissed, and a new group of advisers, strong supporters of the Legalist school, came into power. These new men began an active policy of conquest instead of the peaceful course which Lü Pu-wei had pursued. One campaign followed another in the years from 230 to 222, until all the feudal states had been conquered, annexed, and brought under Shih Huang-ti's rule.

2 *Centralization in every field*

The main task of the now gigantic realm was the organization of administration. One of the first acts after the conquest of the other feudal states was to deport all the ruling families and other important nobles to the capital of Ch'in; they were thus deprived of the basis of their power, and their land could be sold. These upper-class families supplied to the capital a class of consumers of luxury goods which attracted craftsmen and businessmen and changed the character of the capital from that of a provincial town to a centre of arts and crafts. It was decided to set up the uniform system of administration throughout the realm, which had already been successfully introduced in Ch'in: the realm was split up into provinces and the provinces into prefectures; and an official was placed in charge of each province or prefecture. Originally the prefectures in Ch'in had been placed directly under the central administration, with an official, often a merchant, being responsible for the collection of taxes; the provinces, on the other hand, formed a sort of military command area, especially in the newly conquered frontier territories. With the growing militarization of Ch'in, greater importance was assigned to the provinces, and the prefectures were made subordinate to them. Thus the officials of the provinces were originally army officers but now, in the reorganization of the whole realm, the distinction between civil and military administration was abolished. At the head of the province were a civil and also a military governor, and both were supervised by a controller directly responsible to the emperor. Since there was naturally a continual struggle for power between these three officials, none of them was supreme and none could develop into a sort of independent lord. In this system we can see the essence of the later Chinese administration.

Owing to the centuries of division into independent feudal states, the various parts of the country had developed differently. Each province spoke a different dialect which also contained many words borrowed from the language of the indigenous population; and as these earlier populations sometimes belonged to different races with different languages, in each state different words had found their way into the Chinese dialects. This caused divergences not only in the spoken but in the written language, and even in the characters in use for writing. There were two possibilities: one could write a word from such a local language or dialect by using a word which in the language of the court had a definite meaning, and a sound similar to the local one. This is a technique used down to the present time if Cantonese want to write local dialect or slang words. Or one could invent new characters, not existing in standard Chinese. We have found documents written in this way which are only partially under- standable today. There exist to this day dictionaries in which the borrowed words of that time are indicated, and keys to the various old forms of writing also exist. Thus difficulties arose if, for instance, a man from the old territory of Ch'in was to be transferred as an official to the east: he could not properly understand the language and could not read the borrowed words, if he could read at all! For a large number of the officials of that time, especially the officers who became military governors, were certainly unable to read. The government therefore ordered that the language of the whole country should be unified, and that a definite style of writing should be gener- ally adopted. The words to be used were set out in lists, so that the first lexicography came into existence simply through the needs of practical administration, as had happened much earlier in Babylonia. From Ch'in times on, all characters found on Chinese documents are easily readable, because they are written in the standardized script, and all words used are found in dictionaries. We know now that all classical texts of pre-Ch'in time as we have them today, have been rewritten in this standardized script in the second century B.C.: we do not know which words they actually contained at the time when they were composed, nor how these words were actually pro- nounced, a fact which makes the reconstruction of Chinese language before Ch'in very difficult.

The next requirement for the carrying on of the administration was the unification of weights and measures and, a surprising thing to us, of the gauge of the tracks for wagons. In the various feudal states there had been different weights and measures in use, and this had led to great difficulties in the centralization of the collection of taxes. The centre of administration, that is to say the new capital of Ch'in, had grown through the transfer of nobles and through the enormous size of the administrative staff into a thickly populated city with very large requirements of food. The fields of the former state of Ch'in alone could not feed the city; and the grain supplied in payment of taxation had to be brought in from far around, partly by cart. The only roads then existing consisted of deep cart-tracks. If the axles were not of the same length for all carts, the roads were simply unusable for many of them. Accordingly a fixed length was laid down for axles. The advocates of all these reforms were also their beneficiaries, the merchants.

The first principle of the Legalist school, a principle which had been applied in Ch'in and which was to be extended to the whole realm, was that of the training of the population in discipline and obedience, so that it should become a convenient tool in the hands of the officials. This requirement was best met by a people composed as far as possible only of industrious, uneducated, and tax-paying peasants. Scholars and philosophers were not wanted, in so far as they were not directly engaged in work commissioned by the state. The Confucianist writings came under special attack because they kept alive the memory of the old feudal conditions, preaching the ethic of the old feudal class which had just been destroyed and must not be allowed to rise again if the state was not to suffer fresh dissolution or if the central administration was not to be weakened. In 213 B.C. there took place the great holocaust of books which destroyed the Confucianist writings with the exception of one copy of each work for the State Library. Books on practical subjects were not affected. In the fighting at the end of the Ch'in dynasty the State Library was burnt down, so that many of the old works have only come down to us in an imperfect state and with doubtful accuracy. Some of the damage which Chinese literature suffered from this persecution, may be remedied in the near future: recently, some texts were found in tombs which may allow us to reconstruct some important texts. One of the most important ones is the 'Art of War' by Sun Tzŭ ('Sun Tzŭ ping-fa'), a book still used by leaders of the present regime. We know now that our text is a combination of two, originally independent books. Tradition, written down later by Confucianists, also reports that the emperor buried alive hundreds of famous scholars. This may not really be true, but it may give us to think that in 1974 the present regime fought a campaign against Confucius and in favour of Shih Huang-ti. At a time when writing was not very widely spread, and where books consisted of bundles of bamboo slips, it was easy to confiscate all books; it also was easy to bring scholars to silence, but the real loss to Chinese culture arose from the fact that the new generation was little interested in the Confucianist literature, so that when, fifty years later, the effort was made to restore some texts from the oral tradition, there no longer existed any scholars who really knew them by heart, as had been customary in the past.

In 221 B.C. Shih Huang-ti had become emperor of all China. The judgements passed on him vary greatly: the official Chinese historiography rejects him entirely—naturally, for he tried to exterminate Confucianism, while every later historian was himself a Confucian. As with other prominent figures in Chinese history, his real personality remains unknown to us. It is interesting to see that this great military organizer was, on the other hand, a mystic. He built a palace which was constructed according to astronomical and magical principles. His tomb, later, was a copy of the universe. He believed that far away in the eastern ocean there was an island of the immortals and he sent an expedition to this island, which never returned. The emissaries, most of whom were young boys, probably drowned. Others think that they may have reached Japan. He believed that he was the first emperor of a series of ten thousand emperors of his own dynasty (Shih Huang-ti means 'first emperor'), though his empire like that of other dictators came to an end already under his successor. The basic principles of his administration had been laid down long before his time by the philosophers of the Legalist school, and were given effect by his Chancellor Li Ssŭ. Li Ssŭ was the really great personality of that period. The Legalists taught that the ruler must do as little as possible himself. His Ministers were there to act for him. He himself was to be regarded as a symbol of Heaven. In that capacity Shih Huang-ti undertook periodical journeys into the various parts of the empire, less for any practical purpose of inspection than for purposes of public worship. They corresponded to the course of the sun, and this indicates that Shih Huang-ti had adopted a notion derived from the older northern culture. Within the palace the emperor continually changed his residential quarters, probably not only from fear of assassination but also for astral reasons.

We cannot expect that this period brought forth a blossoming of literature. However, one aspect should be mentioned. Some time before Shih Huang-ti's time there lived in the state of Ch'u a member of the upper class, Ch'ü Yüan, who, according to tradition, was an adviser of his king. When the king did not listen to the advice he left the court and in despair threw himself into a river and drowned. Before his death he wrote a long poem in which he expressed his mood, the 'Li-sao', regarded as a poem with political undertones, although some Chinese scholars think it was a poem praising homosexuality. There are other poems attributed to him, and today he is praised as the first great poet of China, at least the first one whose name is known to us. The style of his poems, often called 'elegies', soon became a court style, used by poets who glorified their rulers and their actions in a flowery, very rich and complex, but beautiful language, very different from that kind of poetry which was incorporated into songs sung by female entertainers and dancers at the courts. We do not know whether this style of the 'elegy' was already used at the court of Shih Huang-ti, though we know that Ch'ü's descendants were among those upper class families which were deported by the emperor and resettled near the capital.

3 Frontier defence. Internal collapse

When the empire had been unified by the destruction of the feudal states, the central government became responsible for the protection of the frontiers from attack from without. In the south there were only peoples in a very low state of civilization, who could offer no serious menace to the Chinese. The trading colonies that gradually extended to Canton and still farther south served as Chinese administrative centres for provinces and prefectures, with small but adequate armies of their own, so that in case of need they could defend themselves. In the north the position was much more difficult. In addition to their conquest within China, the rulers of Ch'in had pushed their frontier far to the north. The nomad tribes had been pressed back and deprived of their best pasturage, namely the Ordos region. Here, the new tribal federation of the Hsiung-nu got its first leader known by name to us, T'ou-man. This first realm of the Hsiung-nu was not yet extensive, but its ambitious and warlike attitude made it a danger to Ch'in. It was therefore decided to maintain a large permanent army in the north. In addition to this, the frontier walls already existing in the mountains were rebuilt and made into a single great system. Thus came into existence in 214 B.C., out of the blood and sweat of countless pressed labourers, the famous Great Wall. Down to the present, folk ballads still sing about the cruel emperor and the sufferings of the people. The Great Wall as we can admire it today, is not the old one of Shih Huang-ti. In the course of centuries and again not many years ago, the wall was again and again repaired, first because it still served as a military bastion, today because it became a symbol of China and an attraction for tourists who do not think of the thousands who died there. Plate 5 shows a part of the wall as it was in 1935. Since then it has been repaired again.

On one of his periodical journeys the emperor fell ill and died. His death was the signal for the rising of many rebellious elements. Nobles rose in order to regain power and influence: generals rose because they objected to the permanent pressure from the central administration and their supervision by controllers; men of the people rose as popular leaders because the people were more tormented than ever, doing forced labour, generally at a distance from their homes. Within a few months there were six different rebellions and six different 'rulers'.

A court intrigue caused the death of the young and apparently capable heir to the throne. He was replaced by an adolescent who was controlled by eunuchs. Assassinations became the order of the day; the young heir to the throne was removed in this way and replaced by another young prince. But as early as 206 B.C. one of the rebels, Liu Chi (also called Liu Pang), entered the capital and dethroned the nominal emperor. Liu Chi at first had to retreat and was involved in hard fighting with a rival, but gradually he succeeded in gaining the upper hand and defeated not only his rival but also the other eighteen states that had been set up anew in China in those years. This brought an end to a military dictatorship and became the beginning of a new period of Chinese social history.

CHAPTER SIX

The Early Gentry Society (200 B.C.-A.D. 250)

1 *Development of the gentry-state*

In 206 B.C. Liu Chi assumed the title of Emperor and gave his dynasty the name of the Han Dynasty. After his death he was given as emperor the name of Kao Tsu. (From then on, every emperor was given after his death an official name as emperor, under which he appears in the Chinese sources. We have adopted the original or the official name according to which of the two has come into the more general use in Western books.) The period of the Han dynasty may be described as the beginning of the Chinese Middle Ages, while that of the Ch'in dynasty represents the transition from antiquity to the Middle Ages; for under the Han dynasty we meet in China with a new form of state, the 'gentry state'. The feudalism of ancient times has come definitely to its end.

In recent times, Chinese have adopted the name of the new dynasty to designate 'the Chinese race' (Han-jen) in distinction from minority ethnic groups inside the political frontiers of China. Our name 'China' may come from the Ch'in dynasty's name, though this is contested, and seems to have spread from India to the Mediterranean and Europe.

Emperor Kao Tsu came from eastern China, from a lowly family. He was the leader of a small band of soldiers who mutinied against the government because they had to fear punishment for neglect of orders. Other, similar groups, joined him. After his destruction of his strongest rival, the removal of the kings who had made themselves independent in the last years of the Ch'in dynasty was a relatively easy task for the new autocrat, although these struggles occupied the greater part of his reign. A much more difficult question, however, faced him: How was the empire to be governed? Kao Tsu's old friends and fellow-countrymen, who had helped him into power, had been rewarded by appointment as generals or high officials. Gradually he got rid of those who had been his best comrades, as so many upstart rulers have done before and after him in every country in the world. An emperor does not like to be reminded of a very humble past, and he is liable also to fear the rivalry of men who formerly were his equals. It is evident that little attention was paid to theories of administration; policy was determined mainly by practical considerations. Kao Tsu allowed many laws and regulations to remain in force, including the prohibition of Confucianist writings. On the other hand, he reverted to the allocation of fiefs, though not to old noble families but to his relatives and some of his closest adherents, generally men of inferior social standing. Thus a mixed administration came into being: part of the empire was governed by new feudal princes, and another part split up into provinces and prefectures and placed directly under the central power through its officials.

But whence came the officials? Kao Tsu and his supporters, as farmers from eastern China, looked down upon the trading population to which farmers always regard themselves as superior. The merchants were ignored as potential officials although they had often enough held official appointments under the former dynasty. The second group from which officials had been drawn under the Ch'in was that of the army officers, but their military functions had now, of course, fallen to Kao Tsu's soldiers. The emperor had little faith, however, in the loyalty of officers, even of his own, and apart from that he would have had first to create a new administrative organization for them. Accordingly he turned to another class which had come into existence, the class which we like to call 'gentry' in spite of important differences between the Chinese gentry and the English gentry.

The term 'gentry' has no direct parallel in Chinese texts; the later terms 'shen-shih' and 'chin-shen' do not quite cover this concept. The basic unit of the gentry class are families, not individuals. Such families often derive their origin from branches of the Chou nobility. But other gentry families were of different and more recent origin in respect to land ownership. Some late Chou and Ch'in officials of non-noble origin had become wealthy and had acquired land; the same was true for wealthy merchants and finally, some non-noble farmers who were successful in one or another way, bought additional land reaching the size of large holdings. All 'gentry' families owned substantial estates in the provinces which they leased to tenants on a kind of contract basis. The tenants, therefore, cannot be called 'serfs' although their factual position often was not different from the position of serfs. The rents of these tenants, usually about half the gross produce, are the basis of the livelihood of the gentry. One part of a gentry family normally lives in the country on a small home farm in order to be able to collect the rents. If the family can acquire more land and if this new land is too far away from the home farm to make collection of rents easy, a new home farm is set up under the control of another branch of the family. But the original home remains to be regarded as the real family centre.

In a typical gentry family, another branch of the family is in the capital or in a provincial administrative centre in official positions. These officials at the same time are the most highly educated members of the family and are often called the 'literati'. There are also always individual family members who are not interested in official careers or who failed in their careers and live as free 'literati' either in the big cities or on the home farms. It seems, to judge from much later sources, that the families assisted their most able members to enter the official careers, while those individuals who were less able were used in the administration of the farms, This system in combination with the strong familism of the Chinese, gave a double security to the gentry families. If difficulties arose in the estates either by attacks of bandits or by war or other catastrophes, the family members in official positions could use their influence and power to restore the property in the provinces. If, on the other hand, the family members in official positions lost their positions or even their lives by displeasing the court, the home branch could always find ways to remain untouched and could, in a generation or two, recruit new members and regain power and influence in the government. Thus, as families, the gentry was secure, although failures could occur to individuals. There are many gentry families who remained in the ruling élite for many centuries, some over more than a thousand years, weathering all vicissitudes of life. Some authors believe that Chinese leading families generally pass through a three- or four-generation cycle: a family member by his official position is able to acquire much land, and his family moves upward. He is able to give the best education and other facilities to his sons who lead a good life. But either these sons or the grandsons are spoiled and lazy; they begin to lose their property and status. The family moves downward, until in the fourth or fifth generation a new rise begins. Actual study of families seems to indicate that this is not true. The main branch of the family retains its position over centuries, if necessary by adopting intelligent children into the family from another branch. Of course, individuals within the main branch may turn out to be failures. Some of the other branch families, created by less able family members and often endowed with the less desirable pieces of landed property, may start on a lower level and not be able to move up again.

This system developed several typical traits. First, it is clear from the above that a gentry family should be interested in having a fair number of children. The more sons they have, the more positions of power the family can occupy and thus, the more secure it will be; the more daughters they have, the more 'political' marriages they can conclude, i.e. marriages with sons of other gentry families in positions of influence. Therefore, gentry families in China tend to be, on the average, larger than ordinary families, while in our Western countries the leading families usually were smaller than the lower-class families. This means that gentry families produced more children than was necessary to replenish the available leading positions; or, looking at this from the other side, gentry families, by their higher standard of living were able to keep more children alive, than the lower-class families. Down to this century, an average mother had nine pregnancies, but fewer than four children grew up to maturity. If a group produces more children than are needed to fill the positions which their parents had, necessarily some family members had to get into lower positions and had to lose status. In view of this situation it was very difficult for lower-class families to achieve access into this gentry group. In European countries the leading élite did not quite replenish their ranks in the next generation, so that there was always some chance for the lower classes to move up into leading ranks. The gentry society was, therefore, a comparably stable society with little upward social mobility but with some downward mobility. As a whole and for reasons of gentry self-interest, the gentry stood for stability and against change.

Second, if a gentry family had no sons and, therefore, felt forced to adopt a boy in order to continue the position and tradition of the family, they adopted only sons from one of the other branches of the family with the same family name, because any son of another family might later turn against the adopting family and return to his native family. This rule has, in general, continued to the present time, though the middle and lower classes developed some other devices because they could not always find a suitable nephew. Third, down to the present time, biographies of Chinese do not mention the place where the person actually was born. This is not important. Important is the place where the family home, the country seat is. Thus, when we hear that a man comes from Nanking, this does not mean that he was born there; in fact, he may never have been there in his life.

Fourth, because the gentry preferred 'political marriages', the position of women was relatively high. Behind them was the power and wealth of their own family, and if the husband needed their support, he had to treat his wife well. Thus, women in the early gentry period play an important role in society. They could remarry, when widowed, could participate in ceremonies, and we know of

71

some women who were poetesses, and one even who was a historian in a semi-official position.

The gentry members in the bureaucracy collaborated closely with one another because they were tied together by bonds of blood or marriage. It was easy for them to find good tutors for their children, because a pupil owed a debt of gratitude to his teacher and a child from a gentry family could later on nicely repay this debt; often, these teachers themselves were members of other gentry families. It was easy for sons of the gentry to get into official positions, because the people who had to recommend them for office were often related to them or knew the position of their family. In Han time, local officials had the duty to recommend young able men; if these men turned out to be good, the officials were rewarded, if not they were blamed or even punished. An official took less of a chance, if he recommended a son of an influential family, and he obliged such a candidate so that he could later count on his help if he himself should come into difficulties. When, towards the end of the second century B.C., a kind of examination system was introduced, this attitude was not basically changed.

The country branch of the family by the fact that it controlled large tracts of land, supplied also the logical tax collectors: they had the standing and power required for this job. Even if they were appointed in areas other than their home country (a rule which later was usually applied), they knew the gentry families of the other district or were related to them and got their support by appointing their members as their assistants.

Gentry society continued from Kao Tsu's time to the early twentieth century, but it went through a number of phases of development and changed considerably in time. We will later outline some of the most important changes. In general the number of politically leading gentry families was around one hundred (texts often speak of 'the hundred families' in this time) and they were concentrated in the capital; the most important home seats of these families in Han time were close to the capital and east of it or in the plains of eastern China, at that time the main centre of grain production.

Recently, Chinese historians have tended to describe this social system as an exploitatory one; earlier historians took a different view. They saw that a large society needs administrators who cannot be expected to earn their living by producing material goods. They need leisure time to develop new ideas. They may live in luxury, but this demand for luxury goods after all was responsible for all that we and present-day Chinese admire in Chinese culture and art. No agrarian society in history which did not have a well-defined upper class has developed into a higher society. Only an agro-industrial society of modern type has perhaps different possibilities. But Chinese thinkers recognized always that privileges also include obligations, and have always criticized and condemned men who did not live up to their obligations.

2 Situation of the Hsiung-nu empire; its relation to the Han empire. Incorporation of south China

In the time of the Ch'in dynasty there had already come into unpleasant prominence north of the Chinese frontier the tribal union, then relatively small, of the Hsiung-nu. Since then, the Hsiung-nu empire had destroyed the federation of Yüeh-chih tribes in the west, partly in the western sections of the present province of Kansu, and incorporated their people into their own federation. Some of the Yüeh-chih tribes seem to have been of Indo-European language stock. The Hsiung-nu also had conquered the less-well-organized eastern pastoral tribes, the Tung-hu and thus had become a formidable power. Everything goes to show that it had close relations with the territories of northern China. Many Chinese seem to have migrated to the Hsiung-nu empire, where they were welcome as artisans and probably also as farmers; but above all they were needed for the staffing of a new state administration. The scriveners in the newly introduced state secretariat were Chinese and wrote Chinese, for at that time the Hsiung-nu apparently had no written language. There were Chinese serving as administrators and court officials, and even as instructors in the army administration, teaching the art of warfare, against non-nomads. But what was the purpose of all this? Mao Tun, the second ruler of the Hsiung-nu, and his first successors undoubtedly intended ultimately to conquer China, exactly as many other northern peoples after them planned to do, and a few of them did. The main purpose of this was always to bring large numbers of peasants under the rule of the nomad rulers and so to solve, once for all, the problem of the provision of additional winter food. Everything that was needed, and everything that seemed to be worth trying to get as they grew more civilized, would thus be obtained better and more regularly than by raids or by tedious commercial negotiations. But if China was to be conquered and ruled there must exist a state organization of equal authority to hers; the Hsiung-nu ruler must himself come forward as Son of Heaven and develop a court ceremonial similar to that of a Chinese emperor. Thus the basis of the organization of the Hsiung-nu state lay in its rivalry with the neighbouring China; but the details naturally corresponded to the special nature of the Hsiung-nu social system. The young Hsiung-nu feudal state differed from the ancient Chinese feudal state not only in depending on a nomad economy with only supplementary agriculture, but also in possessing, in addition to a whole class of nobility and another of commoners, a stratum of slavery to be analysed further below. Similar to the Chou state, the Hsiung-nu state contained, especially around the ruler, an element of court bureaucracy which, however, never developed far enough to replace the basically feudal character of administration.

Thus Kao Tsu was faced in Mao Tun not with a mere nomad chieftain but with the most dangerous of enemies, and Kao Tsu's policy had to be directed to preventing any interference of the Hsiung-nu in north Chinese affairs, and above all to preventing alliances between Hsiung-nu and Chinese. Hsiung-nu alone, with their technique of horsemen's warfare, would scarcely have been equal to the permanent conquest of the fortified towns of the north and the Great Wall, although they controlled a population which may have been in excess of 2,000,000 people. But they might have succeeded with Chinese aid. Actually a Chinese opponent of Kao Tsu had already come to terms with Mao Tun, and in 200 B.C. Kao Tsu was very near suffering disaster in northern Shansi, as a result of which China would have come under the rule of the Hsiung-nu. But it did not come to that, and Mao Tun made no further attempt, although the opportunity came several times. Apparently the policy adopted by his court was not imperialistic but national, in the un-corrupted sense of the word. It was realized that a country so thickly populated as China could only be administered from a centre within China. The Hsiung-nu would thus have had to abandon their home territory and rule in China itself. That would have meant abandoning the flocks, abandoning nomad life, and turning into Chinese. The main supporters of the national policy, the first principle of which was loyalty to the old ways of life, seem to have been the tribal chieftains. Mao Tun fell in with their view, and the Hsiung-nu maintained their state as long as they adhered to that principle—for some seven hundred years. Other nomad peoples, Toba, Mongols, and Manchus, followed the opposite policy, and before long they were caught in the mechanism of the much more highly developed Chinese economy and culture, and each of them disappeared from the political scene in the course of a century or so.

The national line of policy of the Hsiung-nu did not at all mean an end of hostilities and raids on Chinese territory, so that Kao Tsu declared himself ready to give the Hsiung-nu the foodstuffs and clothing materials they needed if they would make an end of their raids. A treaty to this effect was concluded, and sealed by the marriage of a Chinese princess with Mao Tun. This was the first international treaty in the Far East between two independent powers mutually recognized as equals, and the forms of international diplomacy developed in this time remained the standard forms for the next thousand years. The agreement was renewed at the accession of each new ruler, but was never adhered to entirely by either side. The needs of the Hsiung-nu increased with the expansion of their empire and the growing luxury of their court; the Chinese, on the other hand, wanted to give as little as possible, and no doubt they did all they could to cheat the Hsiung-nu. Even the princesses they sent were never real daughters of the emperor. Thus, in spite of the treaties the Hsiung-nu raids went on. With China's progressive consolidation, the voluntary immigration of Chinese into the Hsiung-nu empire came to an end, and the Hsiung-nu actually began to kidnap Chinese subjects. These were the main features of the relations between Chinese and Hsiung-nu almost until 100 B.C.

In the extreme south, around the present-day Canton, another independent empire had been formed in the years of transition, under the leadership of a Chinese. The narrow basis of this realm was no doubt provided by the trading colonies, but the indigenous population of Yüeh tribes was not sufficiently organized for the building up of a state that could have maintained itself against China. Kao Tsu sent a diplomatic mission to the ruler of this state, and invited him to place himself under Chinese suzerainty (196 B.C.). The ruler realized that he could offer no serious resistance, while the existing circumstances guaranteed him virtual independence and he yielded to Kao Tsu without a struggle.

3 *Brief feudal reaction. Consolidation of the gentry*

Kao Tsu died in 195 B.C. From then to 179 the actual ruler was his widow, the empress Lü, while children were officially styled emperors. The empress tried to remove all members of her husband's family, the Liu, and to replace them with members of the Lü family. She met, however, with strong resistance from the remnants of the Liu family and their supporters who already in many cases belonged to the new gentry and controlled much of the land.

Chinese historians have depicted empress Lü in the darkest colours, and after her the two other women who rose to the highest power. Their objection was not only that the 'son of heaven' should be a man, but also that the empresses naturally had to try to remove the family of their husbands from power and put their own family in. This, in the view of the historians, violated the principle of legitimacy. Thus, we do not know whether empress Lü was as wicked as the texts show her.

On the death of the empress her opponents rose, under the leadership of Kao Tsu's family. Every member of the empress's family was exterminated, and a son of Kao Tsu, known later under the name of

75

Wen Ti (Emperor Wen), came to the throne. He reigned from 179 to 157 B.C. Under him there were still many fiefs, but with the limitation which the emperor Kao Tsu had laid down shortly before his death: only members of the imperial family should receive fiefs, to which the title of King was attached. Thus all the more important fiefs were in the hands of the imperial family, though this did not mean that rivalries came to an end.

On the whole, Wen Ti's period of rule passed in comparative peace. For the first time since the beginning of Chinese history, great areas of continuous territory were under unified rule, without unending internal warfare such as had existed under Shih Huang-ti and Kao Tsu. The creation of so extensive a region of peace produced great economic advance. The burdens that had lain on the peasant population were reduced, especially since under Wen Ti the court was very frugal. The population grew and cultivated fresh land, so that production increased. This may not all be the consequence of peace and good government. Recent research seems to indicate that China experienced a period of warmer weather from the late second century B.C. on to the third or fourth century A.D.

Already in the early years of the Eastern Chou dynasty local rulers had begun to interfere with the economy by manipulating taxes and money. Now, we enter a period in which economics were seriously studied. One of the important economic moves of emperor Wen was the abandonment of restrictions on the minting of copper coin, in order to prevent deflation through insufficiency of payment media. As a consequence more taxes were brought in, partly in kind, partly in coin, and this increased the power of the central government. The new gentry streamed into the towns, their standard of living rose, and they made themselves more and more into a class apart from the general population. As people free from material cares, they were able to devote themselves to scholarship. They went back to the old writings and studied them once more. They began to identify themselves with the nobles of feudal times. A member of the gentry also wanted to be a gentleman, and the Confucian books gave them the directions. We have to assume that in this period of early Han time there were small Confucian schools in which specialists in the books taught a selected group of pupils. On the other hand, we know that already in the time before the Han, there was a kind of examination for applicants for state jobs. Probably, such examinations consisted mainly of tests as to whether the men could read and write. Now, the Confucian schools also became training grounds for future government officials, for men who could read and write and who also knew the rules of social grace and behaviour. Around 100 B.C. a kind of official examination system arose, a system which underwent many

3 Bronze plaque representing two horses fighting each other.
Ordos region, animal style.

(From V. Griessmaier, 'Sammlung Baron Eduard von der
Heydt', Vienna, 1936, illustration No. 6.)

4 Hunting scene: detail from the reliefs in the tombs
at Wu-liang-tz'u.

(From a rubbing in the author's possession.)

5 Part of the 'Great Wall'.
(Photo Eberhard.)

changes, but remained in operation in principle until 1904. The object of examinations was not to test job qualification or job efficiency but command of the ideals of the gentry and knowledge of the literature inculcating them. A man trained in this way would be able to analyse every problem and to find the right solution; if not, he could ask his advisers, hear their arguments and then make his decisions. We find a similar concept in the early English civil service system which trained 'gentlemen' and not 'specialists' or 'technicians', and again today in the People's Republic, we see this in the discussion about 'Red' versus 'Expert'.

In theory this path to training of character and to admission to the state service was open to every 'respectable' citizen. Of the traditional four 'classes' of Chinese society, only the first two officials, (*shih*) and farmers (*nung*) were always regarded as fully 'respectable' (*liang-min*). Members of the other two classes, artisans (*kung*) and merchants (*shang*), were under numerous restrictions. Below these were classes of 'lowly people' (*chien-min*) and below these the slaves which were not part of society proper. The privileges and obligations of these categories were soon legally fixed. In practice, during the first thousand years of the existence of the examination system no peasant had a chance to become an official by means of the examinations. In the Han period, special state schools were created for the sons of officials, who, thus, had an easier start than others. It is interesting to note that there were, again and again, complaints about the low level of instruction in these schools. Nevertheless, through these schools all sons of officials, whatever their capacity or lack of capacity, could become officials in their turn. In spite of its weaknesses, the system had its good side. It inoculated a class of people with ideals that were unquestionably of high ethical value. The Confucian moral system gave a Chinese official or any member of the gentry a spiritual attitude and an outward bearing which in their best representatives has always commanded respect, an integrity that has always preserved its possessors, and in consequence Chinese society as a whole, from moral collapse, from spiritual nihilism, and has thus contributed to the preservation of Chinese cultural values in spite of all foreign conquerors.

In the time of Wen Ti and especially of his successors, the revival at court of the Confucianist ritual and of the earlier Heaven-worship proceeded steadily. The sacrifices supposed to have been performed in ancient times, the ritual supposed to have been prescribed for the emperor in the past, all this was reintroduced. Obviously much of it was spurious: much of the old texts had been lost, and when fragments were found they were arbitrarily completed. Moreover, the old writing was difficult to read and difficult to understand; thus various things were read into the texts without justification. The new Confucians who came forward as experts in the moral code were very different men from their predecessors; above all, like all their contemporaries, they were strongly influenced by the astrological speculations developed in the late Chou and Ch'in times.

Wen Ti's reign had brought economic advance and prosperity; intellectually it had been a period of renaissance, but like every such period it did not simply resuscitate what was old, but filled the ancient moulds with an entirely new content. This is seen most clearly in the field of law. In the time of the Legalists the first steps had been taken in the codification of the criminal law. They clearly intended these laws to serve equally for all classes of the people. The Ch'in code which was supposedly Li K'uei's code, was used in the Han period, and was extensively elaborated by Hsiao Ho (died 193 B.C.) and others. This code consisted of two volumes of the chief laws for grave cases, one of mixed laws for the less serious cases, and six volumes on the imposition of penalties. In the Han period 'decisions' were added, so that about A.D. 200 the code had grown to 26,272 paragraphs with over 17,000,000 words. The collection then consisted of 960 volumes. This colossal code has been continually revised, abbreviated, or expanded, and under its last name of 'Collected Statutes of the Manchu Dynasty' it retained its validity down to the present century.

Alongside this collection there was another book that came to be regarded and used as a book of precedences. The great Confucianist philosopher Tung Chung-shu (179–104 B.C.), a firm supporter of the ideology of the new gentry class, declared that the classic Confucianist writings, and especially the book 'Ch'un-ch'iu', 'Annals of Spring and Autumn', attributed to Confucius himself, were essentially books of legal decisions. They contained 'cases' and Confucius's decisions of them. Consequently any case at law that might arise could be decided by analogy with the cases contained in 'Annals of Spring and Autumn'. Only an educated person, of course, a member of the gentry, could claim that his action should be judged by the decisions of Confucius and not by the code compiled for the common people, for Confucius had expressly stated that his rules were intended only for the upper class. Thus, right down to modern times an educated person could be judged under regulations different from those applicable to the common people, or if judged on the basis of the laws, he had to expect a special treatment. The principle of the 'equality before the law' which the Legalists had advocated and which fitted well into the absolutistic, totalitarian system of the Ch'in, had been attacked by the feudal nobility at that time and was attacked by the new gentry of the Han time. Legalist thinking remained an important undercurrent for many centuries to come, but application of the equalitarian principle was from now on never seriously considered.

This 'double law' does not a priori mean that officials could get away with crimes for which the others were harshly punished, though in fact that often happened. We can also find many cases in which officials were exposed to 'double jeopardy', comparable to the disciplinary courts for officials in the old German system and the special treatment of party officials in one-party systems. The offender was first judged according to Confucian rules, and this could mean that he was judged to be unfit and deprived of his status. Afterwards, he was again judged according to criminal law.

Discussing Chinese written law, we should always keep in mind that it was basically criminal and administrative law. Large areas which fall into civil law, or trade law were never codified. Cases of this type were solved by processes of arbitration or mediation between the partners or, more often, between the families involved.

Against the growing influence of the officials belonging to the gentry there came a last reaction. It came as a reply to the attempt of a representative of the gentry to deprive the feudal princes of the whole of their power. In the time of Wen Ti's successor a number of feudal kings formed an alliance against the emperor, and even invited the Hsiung-nu to join them. The Hsiung-nu did not do so, because they saw that the rising had no prospect of success, and it was quelled. After that the feudal princes were steadily deprived of rights. They were divided into two classes, and only privileged ones were permitted to live in the capital, the others being required to remain in their domains. At first, the area was controlled by a 'minister' of the prince, an official of the state; later the area remained under normal administration and the feudal prince kept only an empty title; the tax income of a certain number of families of an area was assigned to him and transmitted to him by normal administrative channels. Often, the number of assigned families was fictional in that actual income was from far fewer families. This system differs from the Near Eastern system in which also no actual enfeoffment took place, but where deserving men were granted the right to collect themselves the taxes of a certain area with certain numbers of families.

Soon after this the whole government was given the shape which it continued to have until A.D. 220, and which formed the point of departure for all later forms of government. At the head of the state was the emperor, in theory the holder of absolute power in the state restricted only by his responsibility towards 'Heaven', i.e. he had to follow and to enforce the basic rules of morality, otherwise 'Heaven' would withdraw its 'mandate', the legitimation of the emperor's rule, and would indicate this withdrawal by sending natural catastrophes. Time and again we find emperors publicly accusing themselves for their faults when such catastrophes occurred; and to draw the emperor's attention to actual or made-up calamities or celestial irregularities was one way to criticize an emperor and to force him to change his behaviour. There are two other indications which show that Chinese emperors—excepting a few individual cases—at least in the first ten centuries of gentry society were not despots: it can be proved that in some fields the responsibility for governmental action did not lie with the emperor but with some of his ministers. Second, the emperor was bound by the law code: he could not change it nor abolish it. We know of cases in which the ruler disregarded the code, but then tried to 'defend' his arbitrary action. Each new dynasty developed a new law code, usually changing only details of the punishment, not the basic regulations. Rulers could issue additional 'regulations', but these, too, had to be in the spirit of the general code and the existing moral norms. This situation has some similarity to the situation in Muslim countries. At the ruler's side were three counsellors who had, however, no active functions. The real conduct of policy lay in the hands of the 'chancellor', or of one of the 'nine ministers'. Unlike the practice with which we are familiar in the West, the activities of the ministries (one of them being the court secretariat) were concerned primarily with the imperial palace. As, however, the court secretariat (*Shang-shu*), one of the nine ministries, was at the same time a sort of imperial statistical office, in which all economic, financial, and military statistical material was assembled, decisions on issues of critical importance for the whole country could and did come from it. The court, through the Ministry of Supplies, operated mines and workshops in the provinces and organized the labour service for public constructions. The court also controlled centrally the conscription for the general military service. Beside the ministries there was an extensive administration of the capital with its military guards. The various parts of the country, including the lands given as fiefs to princes, had a local administration, entirely independent of the central government and more or less elaborated according to their size. The regional administration was loosely associated with the central government through a sort of ministry of the interior, and similarly the Chinese representatives in the protectorates, that is to say the foreign states which had submitted to Chinese 'protective' overlordship, were loosely united with a sort of foreign ministry in the central government. When a rising or a local war broke out, that was the affair of the officer of the region concerned. If the regional troops were insufficient, those of the adjoining regions were drawn upon; if even these were insufficient, a real 'state of war' came into being; that is to say, the emperor appointed eight generals-in-chief, mobilized the imperial troops, and intervened. This imperial army then had authority over the regional and feudal troops, the troops of the protectorates, the guards of the capital, and those of the imperial palace. At the end of the war the imperial army was demobilized and the generals-in-chief were transferred to other posts.

In all this there gradually developed a division into civil and military administration. A number of regions would make up a province with a military governor, who was in a sense the representative of the imperial army, and who was supposed to come into activity only in the event of war.

This administration of the Han period lacked the tight organization that would make precise functioning possible. On the other hand, an extremely important institution had already come into existence in a primitive form. As central statistical authority, the court secretariat had a special position within the ministries and supervised the administration of the other offices. Thus there existed alongside the executive a means of independent supervision of it, and the resulting rivalry enabled the emperor or the chancellor to detect and eliminate irregularities. Later, in the system of the T'ang period (A.D. 618–906), this institution developed into an independent censorship, and the system was given a new form as a 'State and Court Secretariat', in which the whole executive was comprised and unified. Towards the end of the T'ang period the permanent state of war necessitated the permanent commissioning of the imperial generals-in-chief and of the military governors, and as a result there came into existence a 'Privy Council of State', which gradually took over functions of the executive. The system of administration in the Han and in the T'ang period is shown in the following table:

Han epoch	T'ang epoch
1. Emperor	1. Emperor
2. Three counsellors to the emperor (with no active functions)	2. Three counsellors and three assistants (with no active functions)
3. Eight supreme generals (only appointed in time of war)	3. Generals and governors-general (only appointed in time of war; but in practice continuously in office)
4. ———	4. (a) State secretariat 　　(1) Central secretariat 　　(2) Secretariat of the Crown 　　(3) Secretariat of the Palace and imperial historical commission

Han epoch	T'ang epoch
	(b) Emperor's secretariat
	(1) Private archives
	(2) Court adjutants' office
	(3) Harem administration
5. Court administration (Ministries)	5. Court administration (Ministries)
(1) Ministry for state sacrifices	(1) Ministry for state sacrifices
(2) Ministry for imperial coaches and horses	(2) Ministry for imperial coaches and horses
(3) Ministry for justice at court	(3) Ministry for justice at court
(4) Ministry for receptions	(4) Ministry for receptions (i.e. foreign affairs)
(5) Ministry for ancestors' temples	(5) Ministry for ancestors' temples
(6) Ministry for supplies to the court	(6) Ministry for supplies to the court
(7) Ministry for the harem	(7) Economic and financial Ministry
(8) Ministry for the palace guards	(8) Ministry for the payment of salaries
(9) Ministry for the court (state secretariat)	(9) Ministry for armament and magazines
6. Administration of the capital:	6. Administration of the capital:
(1) Crown prince's palace	(1) Crown prince's palace
(2) Security service for the capital	(2) Palace guards and guards' office
(3) Capital administration:	(3) Arms production department
(a) Guards of the capital	
(b) Guards of the city gates	
(c) Building department	
	(4) Labour service department
	(5) Building department
	(6) Transport department
	(7) Department for education (of sons of officials!)
7. Ministry of the Interior (Provincial administration)	7. Ministry of the Interior (Provincial administration)
8. Foreign Ministry	8. ——————————
	9. Censorship (Audit council)

There is no denying that according to our standard this whole system was still elementary and 'personal', that is to say, attached to the emperor's person—though it should not be overlooked that we ourselves are not yet far from a similar phase of development. To this day the titles of not a few of the highest officers of state—the Lord Privy Seal, for instance—recall that in the past their offices were conceived as concerned purely with the personal service of the monarch. In one point, however, the Han administrative set-up was quite modern: it already had a clear separation between the emperor's private treasury and the state treasury; laws determined which of the two received certain taxes and which had to make certain payments. This separation, which in Europe occurred not until the late Middle Ages, in China was abolished at the end of the Han dynasty.

The picture changes considerably to the advantage of the Chinese as soon as we consider the provincial administration. The governor of a province, and each of his district officers or prefects, had a staff often of more than a hundred officials. These officials were drawn from the province or prefecture and from the personal friends of the administrator, and they were appointed by the governor or the prefect. The staff was made up of officials responsible for communications with the central or provincial administration (private secretary, controller, finance officer), and a group of officials who carried on the actual local administration. There were departments for transport, finance, education, justice, medicine (hygiene), economic and military affairs, market control, and presents (which had to be made to the higher officials at the New Year and on other occasions). In addition to these offices, organized in a quite modern style, there was an office for advising the governor and another for drafting official documents and letters.

The interesting feature of this system is that the provincial administration was de facto independent of the central administration, and that the governor and even his prefects could rule like kings in their regions, appointing and discharging as they chose. This was a vestige of feudalism, but on the other hand it was a healthy check against excessive centralization. It is thanks to this system that even the collapse of the central power or the cutting off of a part of the empire did not bring the collapse of the country. In a remote frontier town like Tunhuang, on the border of Sinkiang, the life of the local Chinese went on undisturbed whether communication with the capital was maintained or was broken through invasions by foreigners.

Governors or other local officials (such as magistrates) were liable to be transferred from time to time. Many dynasties had certain normal periods of service. The local official was, therefore, unable in times of order to accumulate sufficient power to become a threat to the central government. On the other hand, being a stranger in his district, he could not rely on local people. Thus, he brought with him his own trusted friends, and in addition hired local people who knew the local situation and could help the official to collect the taxes he had to forward to the capital. By having such a staff which was antagonistic to one another, a good official had some ways to check upon them and to retain personal power.

In theory, the officials of the various offices or Ministries were appointed under the state examination system, but they had no special professional training; only for the more important subordinate posts were there specialists, such as jurists, physicians, and so on. A change came towards the end of the T'ang period, when a Department of Commerce and Monopolies was set up; only specialists were appointed to it, and it was placed directly under the emperor. Except for this, any official could be transferred from any ministry to any other without regard to his experience. Thus, professionalization and professional careers are a relatively late development. Within the central administration the officials were classified according to ranks, defined by salary classification. Most Chinese administrations had nine ranks, generally subdivided into eighteen ranks, and promotion meant a rise in rank. The official lists of the state system never do give us a full list of all ranks. There were always some ranks lower than the official ones; men in these classes were not regarded as members of the privileged class. Often men were assigned a specific rank and an appropriate title. Men could have concurrently numerous titles. This then did not necessarily mean that they exercised several different jobs; they may have had only one job, while the other titles expressed rank. And rank did not only mean salary, but also the right to appear at court and to have a specific place assigned in official ceremonies. We have in Western administrations similar posts which have no function but give rank; and the court ceremonials at the remaining kingdoms are regulated by the level of the rank the officials have, not by the title of their jobs.

4 *Central Asia policy. End of the Hsiung-nu empire*

In the two decades between 160 and 140 B.C. there had been further trouble with the Hsiung-nu, though there was no large-scale fighting. There was a fundamental change of policy under the next emperor, Wu (or Wu Ti, 141–86 B.C.). The Chinese entered for the first time upon an active policy against the Hsiung-nu. There seem to have been several reasons for this policy, and several objectives. The raids of the Hsiung-nu from the Ordos region and from northern Shansi had shown themselves to be a direct menace to the capital and to its extremely important hinterland. Northern Shansi is mountainous, with deep ravines. A considerable army on horseback could penetrate some distance to the south before attracting attention. Northern Shensi and the Ordos region are steppe country, in which there were few Chinese settlements and through which an army of horsemen could advance very quickly. It was therefore determined to push back the Hsiung-nu far enough to remove this threat. It was also of importance to break the power of the Hsiung-nu in the province of Kansu, and to separate them as far as possible from the Tibetans living in that region, to prevent any union of those two dangerous adversaries. A third point of importance was the safeguarding of caravan routes. The state, and especially the capital, had grown rich through Wen Ti's policy. Goods streamed into the capital from all quarters. Commerce with Central Asia had particularly increased, bringing the products of the Middle East to China. The caravan routes passed through western Shensi and Kansu to Sinkiang, but at that time the Hsiung-nu dominated the approaches to Sinkiang and were in a position to divert the trade to themselves or cut it off. The commerce brought profit not only to the caravan traders, most of whom were probably foreigners, but to the officials in the provinces and prefectures through which the routes passed. Thus the officials in western China were interested in the trade routes being brought under direct control, so that the caravans could arrive regularly and be immune from robbery. Finally, the Chinese government may well have regarded it as little to its honour to be still paying dues to the Hsiung-nu and sending princesses to their rulers, now that China was incomparably wealthier and stronger than at the time when that policy of appeasement had begun.

The first active step taken was to try, in 133 B.C., to capture the head of the Hsiung-nu state, who was called a *shan-yü*; but the *shan-yü* saw through the plan and escaped. There followed a period of continuous fighting until 119 B.C. The Chinese made countless attacks, without lasting success. But the Hsiung-nu were weakened, one sign of this being that there were dissensions after the death of the *shan-yü* Chün-ch'en, and in 127 B.C. his son went over to the Chinese. Finally the Chinese altered their tactics, advancing in 119 B.C. with a strong army of cavalry, which suffered enormous losses but inflicted serious loss on the Hsiung-nu. After that the Hsiung-nu withdrew farther to the north, and the Chinese settled peasants in the important region of Kansu.

Meanwhile, in 125 B.C., the famous Chang Ch'ien had returned. He had been sent in 138 to conclude an alliance with the Yüeh-chih against the Hsiung-nu. The Yüeh-chih had formerly been neighbours of the Hsiung-nu as far as the Ala Shan region, but owing to defeat by the Hsiung-nu their remnants had migrated to western Turkestan (i.e. roughly what is now Soviet Central Asia). Chang Ch'ien had followed them. Politically he had had no success, but he brought back accurate information about the countries in the far west, concerning which nothing had been known beyond the vague reports of merchants. Now it was learnt whence the foreign goods came and whither the Chinese goods went. Chang Ch'ien's reports (which are one of the principal sources for the history of Central Asia at that remote time) strengthened the desire to enter into direct and assured commercial relations with those distant countries. The government

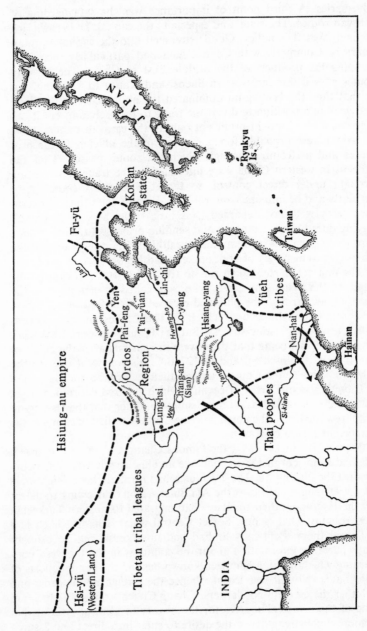

MAP 3   *China in the struggle with the Huns or Hsiung-nu (roughly 128–100 B.C.)*

evidently thought of getting this commerce into its own hands. The way to do this was to impose 'tribute' on the countries concerned. The idea was that the missions bringing the annual 'tribute' would be a sort of state bartering commission. The state laid under tribute must supply specified goods at its own cost, and received in return Chinese produce, the value of which was to be roughly equal to the 'tribute'. Thus Chang Ch'ien's reports had the result that, after the first successes against the Hsiung-nu, there was increased interest in a central Asian policy. The greatest military success were the campaigns of General Li Kuang-li to Ferghana in 104 and 102 B.C. The result of the campaigns was to bring under tribute all the small states in the Tarim basin and some of the states of western Turkestan. From now on not only foreign consumer goods came freely into China, but with them a great number of other things, notably plants such as grape, peach, pomegranate.

In 108 B.C. the western part of Korea was also conquered. At this time, Korea was no more a primitive country. Korean tradition claims that a sage of the end of Shang time left China and migrated to Korea, becoming the culture hero of the country. This is probably a myth, but it is true that Korea had a population closely related to that which at the time lived in the area of Peking, while the other, northern, parts of the country were inhabited by relatives of Tungus tribes and the southern tip by relatives of the Ryukyu and perhaps even people related to those in Taiwan and the Philippines. There were several small states in Korea, when the Chinese attacked. The attack gave the Chinese control over trade with the Japanese islands. Although the conquest represented a peril to the eastern flank of the Hsiung-nu, it did not by any means mean that they were conquered. The Hsiung-nu while weakened evaded the Chinese pressure, but in 104 B.C. and again in 91 they inflicted defeats on the Chinese. The Hsiung-nu were indirectly threatened by Chinese foreign policy, for the Chinese concluded an alliance with old enemies of the Hsiung-nu, the Wu-sun, in the north of the Tarim basin. This made the Tarim basin secure for the Chinese, and threatened the Hsiung-nu with a new danger in their rear. Finally the Chinese did all they could through intrigue, espionage, and sabotage to promote disunity and disorder within the Hsiung-nu, though it cannot be seen from the Chinese accounts how far the Chinese were responsible for the actual conflicts and the continual changes of *shan-yü*. One of the most interesting documents of Han literature is an essay, attributed to Chia I, but probably written later, in which in detail a whole strategy of propaganda and sabotage was outlined. It is not the earliest text of this type, but the first one in which techniques of mass persuasion applied to enemies were described. Hostilities against the

Hsiung-nu continued incessantly, after the death of Wu Ti, under his successor, so that the Hsiung-nu were further weakened. In consequence of this it was possible to rouse against them other tribes who until then had been dependent on them—the Ting-ling in the north and the Wu-huan in the east. The internal difficulties of the Hsiung-nu increased further.

Wu Ti's active policy had not been directed only against the Hsiung-nu. After heavy fighting he brought southern China, with the region round Canton, and the south-eastern coast, firmly under Chinese dominion—in this case again on account of trade interests. No doubt there were already considerable colonies of foreign merchants in Canton and other coastal towns, trading in Indian and Middle East goods. The traders seem often to have been Sogdians. We believe that the knowledge of glass and glassmaking came from the Mediterranean (Egypt?) via Canton to China, and Roman coins were found in Vietnam and South China.

The southern wars gave Wu Ti the control of the revenues from this commerce. He tried several times to advance through Yünnan in order to secure a better land route to India, but these attempts failed. Nevertheless, Chinese influence became stronger in the south-west.

In spite of his long rule, Wu Ti did not leave an adult heir, as the crown prince was executed, with many other persons, shortly before Wu Ti's death. The crown prince had been implicated in an alleged attempt by a large group of people to remove the emperor by various sorts of magic. It is difficult to determine today what lay behind this affair; probably it was a struggle between two cliques of the gentry. Thus a regency council had to be set up for the young heir to the throne; it included a member of a Hsiung-nu tribe. The actual government was in the hands of a general and his clique until the death of the heir to the throne and the beginning of his successor's reign.

At this time came the end of the Hsiung-nu empire—a foreign event of the utmost importance. As a result of the continual disastrous wars against the Chinese, in which not only many men but, especially, large quantities of cattle fell into Chinese hands, the livelihood of the Hsiung-nu was seriously threatened; their troubles were increased by plagues and by a few severe winters. To these troubles were added political difficulties, including unsettled questions in regard to the succession to the throne. The result of all this was that the Hsiung-nu could no longer offer effective military resistance to the Chinese. There were a number of *shan-yü* ruling contemporaneously as rivals, and one of them had to yield to the Chinese in 58 B.C.; in 51 he came as a vassal to the Chinese court. The collapse of the Hsiung-nu empire was complete. After 58 B.C.

the Chinese were freed from all danger from that quarter and were able, for a time, to impose their authority in Central Asia.

5 Impoverishment. Cliques. End of the dynasty

In other respects the Chinese were not doing as well as might have been assumed. The wars carried on by Wu Ti and his successors had been ruinous. The maintenance of large armies of occupation in the new regions also meant a permanent drain on the national funds. There was a special need for horses, for the people of the steppes could only be fought by means of cavalry. As the Hsiung-nu were supplying no horses, and the campaigns were not producing horses enough as booty, the peasants had to rear horses for the government. Additional horses were bought at very high prices, and apart from this the general financing of the wars necessitated increased taxation of the peasants, a burden on agriculture no less serious than was the enrolment of many peasants for military service. Finally, the new external trade did not by any means bring the economic advantages that had been hoped for. The tribute missions brought tribute but, to begin with, this meant an obligation to give presents in return; moreover, these missions had to be fed and housed in the capital, often for months, as the official receptions took place only on New Year's Day. Their maintenance entailed much expense, and meanwhile the members of the missions traded privately with the inhabitants and the merchants of the capital, buying things they needed and selling things they had brought in addition to the tribute. The tribute itself consisted mainly of 'precious articles', which meant strange or rare things of no practical value. The emperor made use of them as elements of personal luxury, or made presents of some of them to deserving officials. The gifts offered by the Chinese in return consisted mainly of silk. Silk was received by the government as a part of the tax payments and formed an important element of the revenue of the state. It now went abroad without bringing in any corresponding return. The private trade carried on by the members of the missions was equally unserviceable to the Chinese. It, too, took from them goods of economic value, silk and gold, which went abroad in exchange for luxury articles of little or no economic importance, such as glass, precious stones, or luxury horses, which in no way benefited the general population. Thus in this last century B.C. China's economic situation deteriorated. The peasants, more heavily taxed than ever, were impoverished, and yet the exchequer became not fuller but emptier, so that gold began even to be no longer available for payments. Wu Ti was aware of the situation and called different groups together to discuss the problems of economics. Under the name 'Discussions on Salt and Iron' ('Yen-t'ieh-lun') the gist of these talks is preserved and shows that one group under the leadership of Sang Hung-yang (143–80 B.C.) was business-oriented and thinking in economic terms, while their opponents, mainly Confucianists, regarded the situation mainly as a moral crisis. Sang proposed an 'equable transportation' and a 'standardization' system and favoured other state monopolies and controls; these ideas were taken up later and continued to be discussed, again and again.

Already under Wu Ti there had been signs of a development which now appeared constantly in Chinese history. Among the new gentry, families entered into alliances with each other, sealed their mutual allegiance by matrimonial unions, and so formed large cliques. Each clique made it its concern to get the most important government positions into its hands, so that it should itself control the government. Under Wu Ti, for example, almost all the important generals had belonged to a certain clique, which remained dominant under his two successors. Two of the chief means of attaining power were for such a clique to give the emperor a girl from its own ranks or any other beautiful girl. Such gifts were nothing unusual in the course of Chinese history. Governors as well as other important persons always felt obliged to present gifts to the emperor when they came to court, and from later texts we know that the parents of daughters in whole provinces trembled for fear that their daughter might be ordered to be presented to the ruler. It could mean glory, if the emperor ever spent a night with her and if she bore him a son, but it normally meant misery and loneliness. But if she gained the emperor's favour, if not love, she could (and felt morally forced to) bring as many of her relatives or of the family members of the man who presented her to the court, into office as she could. The eunuchs at court who watched over the harem and served the emperor personally, came usually from the poorer classes; they, too, were often presented to the emperor by the members of the great cliques, and could gain great influence because they could see the emperor in private. Some of the Han eunuchs were even homosexual lovers of the ruler.

The chief influence of the cliques lay, however, in the selection of officials. It is not surprising that the officials recommended only sons of people in their own clique—their family or its closest associates. On top of all this, the examiners were in most cases themselves members of the same families to which the provincial officials belonged. Thus it was made doubly certain that only those candidates who were to the liking of the dominant group among the gentry should pass.

Surrounded by these cliques, the emperors easily became powerless figureheads. At times energetic rulers were able to play off various cliques against each other, and so to acquire personal power;

but the weaker emperors found themselves entirely in the hands of cliques. Not a few emperors in China were removed by cliques which they had attempted to resist; and various dynasties were brought to their end by the cliques; this was the fate of the Han dynasty.

The beginning of its fall came with the activities of the widow of the emperor Yüan Ti. She virtually ruled in the name of her eighteen-year-old son, the emperor Ch'eng Ti (32–7 B.C.), and placed all her brothers, and also her nephew, Wang Mang, in the principal government posts. They succeeded at first in either removing the strongest of the other cliques or bringing them into dependence. Within the Wang family the nephew Wang Mang steadily advanced, securing direct supporters even in some branches of the imperial family; these personages declared their readiness to join him in removing the existing line of the imperial house. When Ch'eng Ti died without issue, a young nephew of his (Ai Ti, 6–1 B.C.) was placed on the throne by Wang Mang, and during this period the power of the Wangs and their allies grew further, until all their opponents had been removed and the influence of the imperial family very greatly reduced. When Ai Ti died, Wang Mang placed an eight-year-old boy on the throne, himself acting as regent; four years later the boy fell ill and died, probably with Wang Mang's aid. Wang Mang now chose a one-year-old baby, but soon after he felt that the time had come for officially assuming the rulership. In A.D. 8 he dethroned the baby, ostensibly at Heaven's command, and declared himself emperor and first of the Hsin ('new') dynasty. All the members of the old imperial family in the capital were removed from office and degraded to commoners, with the exception of those who had already been supporting Wang Mang. Only those members who held unimportant posts at a distance remained untouched.

Wang Mang's 'usurpation' is unusual from two points of view. First, he paid great attention to public opinion and induced large masses of the population to write petitions to the court asking the Han ruler to abdicate; he even fabricated 'heavenly omina' in his own favour and against the Han dynasty in order to get wide support even from intellectuals. Second, he inaugurated a formal abdication ceremony, culminating in the transfer of the imperial seal to himself. This ceremony became standard for the next centuries. The seal was made of a precious stone, once presented to the Ch'in dynasty ruler before he ascended the throne. From now on, the possessor of this seal was the legitimate ruler.

6 *The pseudo-socialistic dictatorship. Revolt of the 'Red Eyebrows'*
Wang Mang's dynasty lasted only from A.D. 9 to 23; but it was one of the most stirring periods of Chinese history. It is difficult to

evaluate Wang Mang, because all we know about him stems from sources hostile towards him. Yet we gain the impression that some of his innovations, such as the legalization of enthronement through the transfer of the seal, the changes in the administration of provinces and in the bureaucratic set-up in the capital, and even some of his economic measures, were so highly regarded that they were retained or reintroduced, although this happened in some instances centuries later and without mentioning Wang Mang's name. But most of his policies and actions were certainly neither accepted nor acceptable. He made use of every conceivable resource in order to secure power to his clique. As far as possible he avoided using open force, and resorted to a high-level propaganda. Confucianism, the philosophic basis of the power of the gentry, served him as a bait; he made use of the so-called 'old character school' for his purposes. When, after the holocaust of books, it was desired to collect the ancient classics again, texts were found under strange circumstances in the walls of Confucius's house; they were written in an archaic script. The people who occupied themselves with these books were called the old character school. The texts came under suspicion; most scholars had little belief in their genuineness. Wang Mang, however, and his creatures energetically supported the cult of these ancient writings. The texts were edited and issued, and in the process, as can now be seen, certain things were smuggled into them that fitted in well with Wang Mang's intentions. He even had other texts reissued with falsifications. He now represented himself in all his actions as a man who did with the utmost precision the things which the books reported of rulers or ministers of ancient times. As regent he had declared that his model was the brother of the first emperor of the Chou dynasty; as emperor he took for his exemplar one of the mythical emperors of ancient China; of his new laws he claimed that they were simply revivals of decrees of the golden age. In all this he appealed to the authority of literature that had been tampered with to suit his aims. Actually, such laws had never before been customary; either Wang Mang completely misinterpreted passages in an ancient text to suit his purpose, or he had dicta that suited him smuggled into the text. There can be no question that Wang Mang and his accomplices began by deliberately falsifying and deceiving. However, as time went on, he probably began to believe in his own frauds.

Wang Mang's great series of certain laws has brought him the name of 'the first Socialist on the throne of China'. But closer consideration reveals that these measures, ostensibly and especially aimed at the good of the poor, were in reality devised simply in order to fill the imperial exchequer and to consolidate the imperial power.

When we read of the turning over of great landed estates to the state, do we not imagine that we are faced with a modern land reform? But this applied only to the wealthiest of all the landowners, who were to be deprived in this way of their power. The prohibition of private slave-owning had a similar purpose, the state reserving to itself the right to keep slaves. We know that still in later times the state, i.e. the ruler, could give state male and female slaves to persons he favoured. Landless farmers were supposed to receive land to till, at the expense of expropriated landlords. As far as we can see, this was never seriously attempted. To help the farmers, a system of state credits for peasants was set up, but the aim of this measure seems to have been to increase the revenue, in spite of supposedly reduced interest rates. The peasants had never been in a position to pay back their private debts together with the usurious interest, but there were at least opportunities of coming to terms with a private usurer, whereas the state proved a merciless creditor. It could dispossess the peasant, and either turn his property into a state farm, convey it to another owner, or make the peasant a state slave. Thus this measure worked against the interest of the peasants, as did the state monopoly of the exploitation of mountains and lakes. 'Mountains and lakes' meant the uncultivated land around settlements, the 'village commons', where people collected firewood or went fishing. They now had to pay money for fishing rights and for the right to collect wood, money for the emperor's exchequer. The same purpose lay behind the wine, salt, and iron tool monopolies. Enormous revenues came to the state from the monopoly of minting coin, when old metal coin of full value was called in and exchanged for debased coin. Another modern-sounding institution, that of the 'equalization offices', was supposed to buy cheap goods in times of plenty in order to sell them to the people in times of scarcity at similarly low prices, so preventing want and also preventing excessive price fluctuations. In actual fact these state offices formed a new source of profit, buying cheaply and selling as dearly as possible.

Thus the character of these laws was in no way socialistic; nor, however, did they provide an El Dorado for the state finances, for Wang Mang's officials turned all the laws to their private advantage. The revenues rarely reached the capital; they vanished into the pockets of subordinate officials. We have reasons to assume that members of the clique which was related or connected with the Han dynasty were still in power in the provinces and thus in a position to sabotage the new laws. But Wang Mang had great need of money, because he attached importance to display and because he was planning a new war. He aimed at the final destruction of the Hsiung-nu, so that access to Central Asia should no longer be precarious and it should thus be possible to reduce the expense of the military administration of Central Asia. The war would also distract popular attention from the troubles at home. By way of preparation for war, Wang Mang sent a mission to the Hsiung-nu with dishonouring proposals, including changes in the name of the Hsiung-nu and in the title of the *shan-yü*. The name Hsiung-nu was to be given the insulting change of Hsiang-nu, meaning 'subjugated slaves'. The result was that risings of the Hsiung-nu took place, whereupon Wang Mang commanded that the whole of their country should be partitioned among fifteen *shan-yü* and declared the country to be a Chinese province. Since this declaration had no practical result, it robbed Wang Mang of the increased prestige he had sought and only further infuriated the Hsiung-nu. Wang Mang concentrated a vast army on the frontier. Meanwhile he lost the whole of the possessions in Central Asia. We have no way of knowing why Wang Mang made these moves. It seems to be possible to assume that already at that time he had lost contact with reality.

Before Wang Mang's campaign against the Hsiung-nu could begin, the difficulties at home grew steadily worse. In A.D. 12 Wang Mang felt obliged to abrogate all his reform legislation. There were continual risings, which culminated in A.D. 18 in a great popular insurrection, a genuine revolutionary rising of the peasants, whose distress had grown beyond bearing through Wang Mang's ill-judged measures. The rebels called themselves 'Red Eyebrows'; they had painted their eyebrows red by way of a badge and in order to bind their members indissolubly to their movement. The nucleus of this rising was a secret society. Such secret societies are usually harmless, but may, in emergency situations, become an immensely effective instrument in the hands of the rural population. The secret societies then organize the peasants, in order to achieve a forcible settlement of the matter in dispute. Occasionally, however, the movement grows far beyond its leaders' original objective and becomes a popular movement directed against the whole establishment. Like other similar movements in later times, this one finally failed. Their own leaders did not have the ability to unite masses of people with different backgrounds. In some popular rebellions, members of the old upper class joined the rebels and took over the command—but then, though chances for success became greater, after the victory a new regime was set up which was not different from the old one, perhaps less corrupt.

Vast swarms of peasants marched to the capital, killing all officials and people of position on their way. The troops sent against them by Wang Mang either went over to the Red Eyebrows or copied them, plundering wherever they could and killing officials. Owing to the appalling mass murders and the fighting, the forces placed by Wang Mang along the frontier against the Hsiung-nu received no reinforcements and, instead of attacking the Hsiung-nu, themselves went over to plundering, so that ultimately the army simply disintegrated. Fortunately for China, the *shan-yü* of the time did not take advantage of his opportunity, perhaps because his position within the Hsiung-nu empire was too insecure.

Scarcely had the popular rising begun when descendants of the deposed Han dynasty appeared and tried to secure the support of the upper class. They came forward as fighters against the usurper Wang Mang and as defenders of the old social order against the revolutionary masses. The armies which these Han princes were able to collect were no better than those of the other sides. They, too, consisted of poor and hungry peasants, whose aim was to get money or goods by robbery; they, too, plundered and murdered more than they fought.

However, one prince by the name of Liu Hsiu gradually gained the upper hand. The basis of his power was the district of Nanyang in Honan, one of the wealthiest agricultural centres of China at that time and also the centre of iron and steel production. The big landowners, the gentry of Nanyang, joined him, and the prince's party conquered the capital. Wang Mang, placing entire faith in his sanctity, did not flee; he sat in his robes in the throne-room and recited the ancient writings, convinced that he would overcome his adversaries by the power of his words. But a soldier cut off his head (A.D. 22). The skull was kept for two hundred years in the imperial treasury. The fighting, nevertheless, went on. Various branches of the prince's party fought one another, and all of them fought the Red Eyebrows. In those years millions of men came to their end. Finally, in A.D. 24, Liu Hsiu prevailed, becoming the first emperor of the second Han dynasty, also called the Later Han dynasty; his name as emperor was Kuang-wu Ti (A.D. 25–57).

7 Reaction and restoration: the Later Han dynasty

Within the country the period that followed was one of reaction and restoration. The massacres of the preceding years had so reduced the population that there was land enough for the peasants who remained alive. Moreover, their lords and the money-lenders of the towns were generally no longer alive, so that many peasants had become free of debt. The government was transferred from Sian to Loyang, in the present province of Honan. This brought the capital nearer to the great wheat-producing regions, so that the transport of grain and other taxes in kind to the capital was cheapened. Soon this cleared foundation was covered by a new stratum, a very sparse one, of great landowners who were supporters and members of the new imperial house, largely descendants of the landowners of the earlier Han period. At first they were not much in evidence, but they gained power more and more rapidly. In spite of this, the first half-century of the Later Han period was one of good conditions on the land and economic recovery.

8 Hsiung-nu policy

In foreign policy the first period of the Later Han dynasty was one of extraordinary success, both in the extreme south and in the question of the Hsiung-nu. During the period of Wang Mang's rule and the fighting connected with it, there had been extensive migration to the south and south-west. Considerable regions of Chinese settlement had come into existence in Yünnan and even in Annam and Tonking, and a series of campaigns under General Ma Yüan (14 B.C.–A.D. 49) now added these regions to the territory of the empire. These wars were carried on with relatively small forces, as previously in the Canton region, the natives being unable to offer serious resistance owing to their inferiority in equipment and civilization. The hot climate, however, to which the Chinese soldiers were unused, was hard for them to endure.

The Hsiung-nu, in spite of internal difficulties, had regained considerable influence in Sinkiang during the reign of Wang Mang. But the king of the city state of Yarkand had increased his power by shrewdly playing off Chinese and Hsiung-nu against each other, so that before long he was able to attack the Hsiung-nu. The small states in Sinkiang, however, regarded the overlordship of the distant China as preferable to that of Yarkand or the Hsiung-nu both of whom, being nearer, were able to bring their power more effectively into play. Accordingly many of the small states appealed for Chinese aid. Kuang-wu Ti met this appeal with a blank refusal, implying that order had only just been restored in China and that he now simply had not the resources for a campaign in Sinkiang. Thus, the king of Yarkand was able to extend his power over the remainder of the small states of Sinkiang, since the Hsiung-nu had been obliged to withdraw. Kuang-wu Ti had had several frontier wars with the Hsiung-nu without any decisive result. But in the years around A.D. 45 the Hsiung-nu had suffered several severe droughts and also great plagues of locusts, so that they had lost a large part of their cattle. They were no longer able to assert themselves in Sinkiang and at the same time to fight the Chinese in the south and the Hsien-pi and the Wu-huan in the east. These two peoples, apparently largely of Mongol origin, had been subject in the past to Hsiung-nu overlordship. They had spread steadily in the territories bordering Manchuria and Mongolia, beyond the eastern frontier of the Hsiung-nu empire. Living there in relative peace and at the same time in possession of very fertile pasturage, these two peoples had grown in strength. And since the great political collapse of 58 B.C. the Hsiung-nu had not only lost their best pasturage in the north of the provinces of Shensi and Shansi, but had largely grown used to living in co-operation with the Chinese. They had become much more accustomed to trade with China, exchanging animals for textiles and grain, than to warfare, so that in the end they were defeated by the Hsien-pi and Wu-huan, who had held to the older form of purely war-like nomad life. Weakened by famine and by the wars against Wu-huan and Hsien-pi, the Hsiung-nu split into two, one section withdrawing to the north.

The southern Hsiung-nu were compelled to submit to the Chinese in order to gain security from their other enemies. Thus the Chinese were able to gain a great success without moving a finger: the Hsiung-nu, who for centuries had shown themselves again and again to be the most dangerous enemies of China, were reduced to political insignificance. About a hundred years earlier the Hsiung-nu empire had suffered defeat; now half of what remained of it became part of the Chinese state. Its place was taken by the Hsien-pi and Wu-huan, but at first they were of much less importance.

In spite of the partition, the northern Hsiung-nu attempted in the years between A.D. 60 and 70 to regain a sphere of influence in Sinkiang; this seemed the easier for them since the king of Yarkand had been captured and murdered, and Sinkiang was more or less in a state of confusion. The Chinese did their utmost to play off the northern against the southern Hsiung-nu and to maintain a political balance of power in the west and north. So long as there were a number of small states in Sinkiang, of which at least some were friendly to China, Chinese trade caravans suffered relatively little disturbance on their journeys. Independent states in Sinkiang had proved more profitable for trade than when a large army of occupation had to be maintained there. When, however, there appeared to be the danger of a new union of the two parts of the Hsiung-nu as a restoration of a large empire also comprising all Sinkiang, the Chinese trading monopoly was endangered. Any great power would secure the best goods for itself, and there would be no good business remaining for China.

For these reasons a great Chinese campaign was undertaken against Central Asia in A.D. 73 under Tou Ku. Mainly owing to the ability of the Chinese deputy commander Pan Ch'ao, the whole of Sinkiang was quickly conquered. Meanwhile the emperor Ming Ti (A.D. 58–75) had died, and under the new emperor Chang Ti (76–88) the 'isolationist' party gained the upper hand against the clique of Tou Ku and Pan Ch'ao: the danger of the restoration of a Hsiung-nu empire, the isolationists contended, no longer existed; Central Asia should be left to itself; the small states would favour trade with China of their own accord. Meanwhile, a considerable part of Sinkiang had fallen away from China, for Chang Ti sent neither money nor troops to hold the conquered territories. Pan Ch'ao nevertheless remained in Sinkiang (at Kashgar and Khotan) where he held on amid countless difficulties. Although he reported (A.D. 78) that the troops could feed themselves and needed neither supplies nor money from home, no reinforcements of any importance were sent; only a few hundred or perhaps a thousand men, mostly released criminals, reached him. Not until A.D. 89 did the Pan Ch'ao clique return to power when the mother of the young emperor Ho Ti (89–105) took over the government during his minority; she was a member of the family of Tou Ku. She was interested in bringing to a successful conclusion the enterprise which had been started by members of her family and its followers. In addition, it can be shown that a number of other members of the 'war party' had direct interests in the west, mainly in the form of landed estates. Accordingly, a campaign was started in 89 under her brother against the northern Hsiung-nu, and it decided the fate of Sinkiang in China's favour. Sinkiang remained firmly in Chinese possession until the death of Pan Ch'ao in 102. Shortly afterwards heavy fighting broke out again: the Tanguts advanced from the south in an attempt to cut off Chinese access to Sinkiang. The Chinese drove back the Tanguts (a political unit related to the Tibetans) and maintained their hold on Sinkiang, though no longer absolutely.

9 Economic situation. Rebellion of the 'Yellow Turbans'. Collapse of the Han dynasty

The economic results of the Sinkiang trade in this period were not so unfavourable as in the earlier Han period. The army of occupation was incomparably smaller, and under Pan Ch'ao's policy the soldiers were fed and paid in Sinkiang itself, so that the cost to China remained small. Moreover, the drain on the national income was no longer serious because, in the intervening period, regular Chinese settlements had been planted at the eastern borders of Sinkiang including Chinese merchants, so that the trade no longer remained entirely in the hands of foreigners.

In spite of the economic consolidation at the beginning of the Later Han dynasty, and in spite of the more balanced trade, the political situation within China steadily worsened from A.D. 80 onwards. Although the class of great landowners was small, a number of cliques formed within it, and their mutual struggle for power soon went beyond the limits of court intrigue. New actors now came upon the state, namely the eunuchs. With the economic improvement there had been a general increase in the luxury at the court of the Han emperors, and the court steadily increased in size. The many hundred wives and concubines in the palace made necessary a great army of eunuchs. As they had the ear of the emperor and so could influence him, the eunuchs formed an important political factor. For a time the main struggle was between the group of eunuchs and the group of scholars. The eunuchs served a particular clique to which some of the emperor's wives belonged. The scholars, that is to say the ministers, together with members of the ministries and the administrative staff, served the interests of another clique. The struggles grew more and more sanguinary in the middle of the second century A.D. It soon proved that the group with the firmest hold in the provinces had the advantage, because it was not easy to control the provinces from a distance. The result was that, from about A.D. 150, events at court steadily lost importance, the lead being taken by the generals commanding the provincial troops. It would carry us too far to give the details of all these struggles. The provincial generals were at first Ts'ao Ts'ao, Lü Pu, Yüan Shao, and Sun Ts'ê; later came Liu Pei. All were striving to gain control of the government, and all were engaged in mutual hostilities from about 180 onwards. Each general was also trying to get the emperor into his hands. Several times the last emperor of the Later Han dynasty, Hsien Ti (190–220), was captured by one or another of the generals. As the successful general was usually unable to maintain his hold on the capital, he dragged the poor emperor with him from place to place until he finally had to give him up to another general. The point of this chase after the emperor was that according to the idea introduced earlier by Wang Mang the first ruler of a new dynasty had to receive the imperial seals from the last emperor of the previous dynasty. The last emperor must abdicate in proper form. Accordingly, each general had to get possession of the emperor to begin with, in order at the proper time to take over the seals.

By about A.D. 200 the new conditions had more or less crystallized. There remained only three great parties. The most powerful was that of Ts'ao Ts'ao, who controlled the north and was able to keep permanent hold of the emperor. In the west, in the province of Szechwan, Liu Pei had established himself, and in the south-east Sun Ts'ê's brother.

But we must not limit our view to these generals' struggles. At this time there were two other series of events of equal importance with those. The incessant struggles of the cliques against each other continued at the expense of the people, who had to fight them, whose harvests were confiscated and whose houses were destroyed. Orderly government broke down, and a new popular movement broke out, that of the so-called 'Yellow Turbans'. This was the first of the two important events. This popular movement had a characteristic which from now on became typical of many such uprisings. The intellectual leaders of the movement, Chang Ling and others, were members of a particular religious sect. This sect was, it seems, influenced by Iranian Mazdaism on the one side and by certain ideas from Lao Tzŭ on the other side; and these influences were superimposed on popular rural as well as, perhaps, local tribal religious beliefs. The sect had roots along the coastal settlements of Eastern China, where it seems to have gained the support of the peasantry and their local priests. These priests of the people were opposed to the representatives of the official religion, that is to say the officials drawn from the gentry. In small towns and villages the temples of the gods of the fruits of the field, of the soil, and so on, were administered by authorized local officials, and these officials also carried out the prescribed sacrifices and were thus integrated into the 'state cult'. As we have many edicts of the Han period which order the destruction of what the texts call 'wild temples', i.e. unauthorized temples, we may conclude that we had a situation which continued until this century. People had their own cults. Souls of people who had died without descendants, animals which seemed to have shown extraordinary powers, even trees and stones could develop into deities who were cared for by men and occasionally women, whom we for convenience usually call shamans. These priests built small places of worship which sometimes developed into regular temples and took care of the deities which, in turn, answered prayers, healed the sick, gave children to unfertile women. The educated regarded such cults as pure superstition; the gentry watched them and when they felt that the cult developed too strongly and might become a centre of power and unrest, they had the temples destroyed. In times of weak government this was not always done, and suffering peasants flocked ever more to them, regarding their unauthorized priests as their natural leaders against the gentry and against gentry forms of religion. One branch, probably the main branch of this movement, developed a stronghold in eastern Szechwan province, where its members succeeded to create a state of their own which retained its independence for a while. It is the only group which developed real religious communities in which men and women participated, extensive welfare schemes existed and class differences were discouraged. It had a real church organization with dioceses, communal friendship meals and a confession ritual: in short, real piety developed as it could not develop in the official religions. After the annihilation of this state, remnants of the organization can be traced through several centuries, mainly in central and south China. At least one later religious-political movement can be directly traced back to the Yellow Turbans. There is also the possibility that this movement grew up from a common religious background which we later call in Tibet the Bhon religion and in Burma the Nat religion and find under other names in south China. We also must mention that books belonging to such societies are rarely preserved; the government did all it could to destroy them. But the 'Book of the Great Peace' ('T'ai-p'ing ching') of the Yellow Turbans is, at least in fragments, preserved and has later been used by other societies.

The rising of the Yellow Turbans began in 184; all parties, cliques and generals alike, were equally afraid of them, since these were a threat to the gentry as such, and so to all parties. Consequently a combined army of considerable size was got together and sent against the rebels. The Yellow Turbans were beaten.

During these struggles it became evident that Ts'ao Ts'ao with his troops had become the strongest of all the generals. His troops seem to have consisted not of Chinese soldiers alone, but also of Hsiung-nu. It is understandable that the annals say nothing about this, and it can only be inferred. It appears that in order to reinforce their armies the generals recruited not only Chinese but foreigners. The generals operating in the region of the present-day Peking had soldiers of the Wu-huan and Hsien-pi, and even of the Ting-ling; Liu Pei, in the west, made use of Tanguts, and Ts'ao Ts'ao clearly went farthest of all in this direction; he seems to have been responsible for settling nineteen tribes of Hsiung-nu in the Chinese province of Shansi between 180 and 200, in return for their armed aid. In this way Ts'ao Ts'ao gained permanent power in the empire by means of these troops, so that immediately after his death his son Ts'ao P'i, with the support of powerful allied families, was able to force the emperor to abdicate and to found a new dynasty, the Wei dynasty (A.D. 220).

This meant, however, that a part of China which for several centuries had been Chinese was given up to the Hsiung-nu. This was not, of course, what Ts'ao Ts'ao had intended; he had given the Hsiung-nu some area of pasturage in Shansi with the idea that they should be controlled and administered by the officials of the surrounding district. His plan had been similar to what the Chinese had often done with success: aliens were admitted into the territory of the empire in a body, but then the influence of the surrounding administrative centres was steadily extended over them, until the immigrants completely lost their own nationality and became

Chinese. The nineteen tribes of Hsiung-nu, however, were much too numerous, and after the prolonged struggles in China the provincial administration proved much too weak to be able to carry out the plan. Thus there came into existence here, within China, a small Hsiung-nu realm ruled by several *shan-yü*. This was the second major development, and it became of the utmost importance to the history of the next four centuries.

10 *Culture, literature, and art*

After so much politics, we have to come back to discussing culture. One of the typical fields of culture of the Han seems to be directly in connection with the political development. With the emergence of a unified China under a ruler like Wu Ti, who came closer than others before him to make himself an all-powerful autocrat, the thinkers made attempts to unify the social world with the cosmos. Steps in this direction go back to the time of Tsou Yen, but Han thinkers went much farther still. On the basis of the theory of the 'five elements' each dynasty was assigned a specific number; the numbers again were associated with the five directions (four directions and centre), the directions with the five colours and with the basic tones of the five-tone scale. This then meant, for instance, that each dynasty developed its own ceremonial music based on the appropriate scale; the court dresses had the appropriate colour; the calendar was based on this number, as were all the measures. When Wang Mang set up his own regime, he changed everything to the new 'element' which, for instance, has the consequence that the calendar of his dynasty was not as exact as that of the Han dynasty. 'Progress' was subordinated to 'ideology'. Of course, the human body, too, was dominated by the five elements, the seasons expressed the elements, so that Chinese medicine of the time was dominated by these ideas, so that the 'science' of geomancy developed which attempted to calculate the good and bad luck of the living or their descendants from the position of tombs and houses in nature. While we tend to regard geomancy as a pseudo-science it cannot be denied that in practice many buildings are ecologically ideally placed, even down to our century. As the five elements also corresponded to the five planets, attempts were made to bring their movements in harmony with the social world. This had its influence on the one hand on the development of astronomy but also on the development of astrology. In its basic assumptions Chinese astrology shows parallels to Mesopotamian and Western astrology, but it is certainly an independent development. In both systems we find a zodiac, though the Chinese one is a cycle of twelve animals which also dominate a cycle of twelve years and give each year its special character. For all such developments this period has sometimes been called an age of magic and superstition, but we would hardly join in such an evaluation. In any case, the books on astrology and geomancy, and also the basic medical texts were written down, if not composed, during the Han time. At least the medical books are still today regarded as 'classics' of Chinese medicine. In Han time also the fundamental text on arithmetics was written down. Here, we can clearly see how mathematics was needed on the one hand to measure exactly the size of fields, so as to make land transactions and taxation easy, and on the other hand to develop rock-throwing machines which could shoot exactly at distant aims.

Excavations have brought forth bamboo slips with texts from military stations along China's north-western borders. They show us that indeed military conscription was relatively effective, so that soldiers from almost all parts of China were moved to the frontiers, but that they often remained there much longer than they should have. We see that the army had registers about their soldiers, describing them. We know that there were population registers and we have reasons to believe that the first reported census made between A.D. 1–2 was relatively accurate. It gave a population of over 57 million. From then on to the present, we have census reports. Some were incomplete, others complete; but none of them counted all citizens. Some censuses left out non-taxpayers, others minorities or other groups. In spite of this, with some skill, our demographers can get valuable information from these documents, such as the age of marriage, the number of children who survived the first years of life, the life expectancy of persons over fourteen, and the density of population in different areas. The Han also had information about food production and calculated the average food consumption of an adult, the cost of transportation of food; we even have calculations of how much labour had to be used for a certain building project and how much this would cost.

One point these materials clearly show: there were now many people who could read and write and do arithmetic. The spread of writing brought forth the development of encyclopaedias. Encyclopaedias convey knowledge in an easily grasped and easily found form. The first compilation of this sort dates from the third century B.C. It was the work of Lü Pu-wei, the merchant who was prime minister and regent during the minority of Shih Huang-ti. It contains general information concerning ceremonies, customs, historic events, and other things the knowledge of which was part of a general education. Soon afterwards other encyclopaedias appeared, of which the best known is the 'Book of the Mountains and Seas' ('Shan Hai Ching'). This book, arranged according to regions of the world, contains everything known at the time about geography, natural philosophy, and the animal and plant world, and also about popular myths. This tendency to systemization is shown also in the historical works. The famous 'Shih Chi', one of our main sources for Chinese history, is the first historical work of the modern type, that is to say, built up on a definite plan, and it was also the model for all later official historiography. Its author, Ssŭ-ma Ch'ien (born 135 B.C.), and his father, made use of the material in the state archives and of private documents, old historical and philosophical books, inscriptions, and the results of their own travels. The philosophical and historical books of earlier times (with the exception of those of the nature of chronicles) consisted merely of brief essays or sayings, attributed to thinkers. The 'Shih Chi' is a compendium of a mass of source-material. The documents were abbreviated, but the text of the extracts was altered as little as possible, so that the general result retains in a sense the value of an original source. In its arrangement the 'Shih Chi' became a model for all later historians: the first part is in the form of annals, and there follow tables concerning the occupants of official posts and fiefs, and then biographies of various important personalities, though the type of the comprehensive biography did not appear till later. We miss in those biographies which the history books contain a stress on the individual characteristics of the person. The biography describes him (or her) in his (or her) role in society and evaluates actions in terms of Confucian morality. We do not learn how they looked, what their personal life was, often not even whether they had daughters and one or more than one wife. They remain figures to us, not warm human beings. But Chinese history did not want to imitate individuals—this was left to the novels. The 'Shih Chi' also, like later historical works, contains many monographs dealing with particular fields of knowledge, such as astronomy, the calendar, music, economics, official dress at court, and much else. The whole type of construction differs fundamentally from such works as those of Thucydides or Herodotus. The Chinese historical works have the advantage that the section of annals gives at once the events of a particular year, the monographs describe the development of a particular field of knowledge, and the biographical section offers information concerning particular personalities. The mental attitude is that of the gentry: shortly after the time of Ssŭ-ma Ch'ien an historical department was founded, in which members of the gentry worked as historians upon the documents prepared by representatives of the gentry in the various government offices.

In addition to encyclopaedias and historical works, many books of philosophy were written in the Han period, but most of them offer no fundamentally new ideas and only three of them are of importance. One is the work of Tung Chung-shu, already mentioned. The second is a book by Liu An called 'Huai-nan Tzŭ'. Prince Liu An occupied himself with Taoism and allied problems, gathered around him scholars of different schools, and carried on discussions with them. Many of his writings are lost, but enough is extant to show that he was one of the earliest Chinese alchemists.

When we hear of alchemy or read books about it we should always keep in mind that many of these books can also be read as books of sex; in a similar way, books on the art of war, too, can be read as books on sexual relations. The first real sex book was probably also written in Han time, the 'Book of the Plain Girl' ('Su Nü Ching'), is still printed today and contains valuable observations and advice.

The third important book of the Han period was the 'Lun Hêng' ('Critique of Opinions') of Wang Ch'ung (born A.D. 27). Wang Ch'ung advocated rational thinking and tried to pave the way for a free natural science, in continuation of the beginnings which the natural philosophers of the later Chou period had made. The book analyses reports in ancient literature and customs of daily life, and shows how much they were influenced by superstition and by ignorance of the facts of nature. It had little impact in its time, but has recently been highly praised by Chinese scholars; to us it is also a rich source of beliefs and attitudes.

There were great literary innovations in the field of poetry. The splendour and elegance at the new imperial court of the Han dynasty attracted many poets who sang the praises of the emperor and his court and were given official posts and dignities. These praises were in the form of grandiloquent, overloaded poetry, full of strange similes and allusions, but with little real feeling. This style of describing poetry ultimately has its source in the poetry of Ch'ü Yüan and his successors. Indeed, the luxury of the court was overwhelming. The palaces of the emperor had galleries with paintings of heroes of history. In addition to the main palace, the rulers had their hunting parks (the word which we use to describe the 'paradise' originally meant 'emperor's hunting preserve') which were stocked with rare animals sent by local governors or foreign ambassadors—and in line with more than two millennia of history, an American president coming to Communist China like the tribute-bringing kings of old, brought a rare animal to the ruler of the country.

In the tombs have been found reliefs whose technique is generally intermediate between simple outline engraving and intaglio. The lining-in is most frequently executed in scratched lines. The representations, mostly in strips placed one above another, are of lively historical scenes, scenes from the life of the dead, great ritual ceremonies, or adventurous scenes from mythology. Bronze vessels have representations in inlaid gold and silver, mostly of animals. The most important documents of the painting of the Han period have also been found in tombs. We see especially ladies and gentlemen of society, with richly ornamented, elegant, expensive clothing that is very reminiscent of the clothing customary to this day in Japan. We also see fantastic beings or deities which in only a very few cases can be identified with the beasts and demons in the 'Shan Hai Ching'. However, when recently in a magnificent tomb a corpse was found completely clothed in a dress made of jade plates, sewn togther with gold wire, it was found that actually such a custom had been mentioned in a book of the Han period, but the reference had been neglected, probably because it sounded too unbelievable. Jade is a very hard mineral and it takes an enormous amount of time to shape a single plate, not to speak of a whole dress.

The tombs also revealed numerous vessels made of lacquer—a typically Chinese material to the present time. Lacquer caskets and bowls show artistic representations of human figures and scenes which, in some cases, we knew from literary works. We see here the court parties in which women enlivened the meal with music and dancing. These women, mostly slaves from southern China, introduced at the court southern Chinese forms of song and poem, which were soon adopted and elaborated by poets. Poems and dance songs were composed which belonged to the finest that Chinese poetry can show—full of natural feeling, simple in language, moving in content. Other scenes show us jugglers and acrobats. As these performances were called 'Hunnic plays', we have reason to assume that they were inspired by Central Asian or western Asian performances; if not the performers themselves were in some cases foreigners. Some scholars have been tempted to regard some of the scenes on the walls of Han tombs as showing theatre plays, not real life scenes. If this does not mean that there must be a standard text, spoken or sung to be called a 'theatre' play, it is quite possible that mimic religious plays were known and were early forms of the later Chinese theatres.

In Han time, Chinese still used to sit and to sleep on mats on the floor; however, the first kind of bed, a wooden frame with a network of strings, is mentioned, as well as a kind of light chair. The still typical north Chinese 'oven-bed', a brick or mud platform which could be heated from below, was probably a Korean invention and spread to China proper only later.

We know that in Han time silk was used as a writing material at court, and some of the painting was also on silk, but almost nothing has yet been found of it. Paper had meanwhile been invented in the second century A.D., according to tradition, but most likely earlier. At first fibres of textiles were used in a technique similar to that used in making bark-cloth and felt. Later bamboo fibres became the common material. Ink, made of the soot of specific wood, seems to have been known already in the beginning of history, and the brush, too, seems to be very old.

The persons who painted the walls of tombs or of palaces were regarded as craftsmen, because they did not belong to the gentry, though we would call many of their products works of art. In Han time, representations of human beings, probably even true portraits, were common. When painting became also an occupation of the gentry and then an 'art', the human being begins to fade more and more into the background, though it never fully disappeared. The gentry painted as a social pastime, just as they assembled together for poetry, discussion, or performances of song and dance; they painted as an aesthetic pleasure and rarely as a means of earning. We find philosophic ideas or greetings, emotions, and experiences represented by paintings—paintings with fanciful or ideal landscapes; paintings representing the life and environment of the cultured class in idealized form, never naturalistic either in fact or in intention. Until recently it was an indispensable condition in the Chinese view that an artist must be 'cultured' and be a member of the gentry—distinguished, unoccupied, wealthy. A man who was paid for his work, for instance for a portrait for the ancestral cult, was until late time regarded as a craftsman, not as an artist. Yet these, 'craftsmen' have produced in Han time and even earlier, many works which, in our view, undoubtedly belong to the realm of art.

In contrast to ancient Greece, sculpture did not count as 'art'; it was a craft only. We mentioned that the Shang produced sculptures, but then we do not know much about sculpture until the coming of Buddhism, and certainly for a long time Buddhist sculptures, even if made by Chinese craftsmen, were artistically determined by rules developed in India.

We mentioned above a possible influence of Mazdaism, an Iranian religion developed probably at the time of Confucius, characterized by a strong dualism, which is expressed as an unending fight of the forces of the light against those of the dark, of good against evil. We find in Han time a set of seven planets, i.e. the old five together with sun and moon—the set of names which in the West became the names of the seven days of the week. Later texts even mention the foreign words for the Iranian days of the week. But the Chinese never accepted our concept of a week. There is also a set of nine planets which originated in the West, the seven enlarged by two imagined counterparts to the moon; as nine is an important number in Chinese numerical speculation (the square of three, which is a male number), this cycle got some distribution in China.

More important than Mazdaism and Manichaeism, which developed centuries after the end of Han, was Buddhism. According to Chinese legend, it came to China in A.D. 65, as a consequence of a dream of emperor Ming. According to our present knowledge, Buddhism entered China from the south coast and through Central Asia at latest in the first century B.C.; it came with foreign merchants from India or Central Asia. According to Indian customs, Brahmans, the Hindu caste providing all Hindu priests, could not leave their their homes. As merchants on their trips, which lasted often several years, did not want to go without religious services, they turned to Buddhist priests as well as to priests of Near Eastern religions. These priests were not prevented from travelling and used this opportunity for missionary purposes. Thus, for a long time after the first arrival of Buddhists, the Buddhist priests in China were foreigners who served foreign merchant colonies. Buddhism brought something to China which was new. Chinese philosophers had never speculated about the origin of mankind and about man's fate on earth. There had been among the people a vague belief that the souls of dead people would gather somewhere around mountains; that some souls could change into dangerous, evil demons and ghosts, others into gods. Buddhism brought the new idea that our present fate is conditioned by acts done by ourselves in a previous existence, and that our present actions influence our next reincarnation. In a period of unrest and misery, as the second century A.D. was, Buddhism attracted members of the lower classes into its arms, while the parts of Indian science which these monks brought with them from India aroused some interest in certain educated circles. Buddhism, therefore, undeniably exercised an influence at the end of the Han dynasty, although no Chinese were priests and few, if any, gentry members were adherents of the religious teachings.

With the end of the Han period a further epoch of Chinese history comes to its close. The Han period was that of the final completion and consolidation of the social order of the gentry. The period that followed was that of the conflicts of the Chinese with the populations on their northern borders.

6 Sun Ch'üan, ruler of Wu.
(From a painting by Yen Li-pen, c. 640-680.)

7 General view of the Buddhist cave-temples of Yün-kang. In the foreground, the present village; in the background, the rampart.
(Photo H. Hammer-Morrisson.)

CHAPTER SEVEN

The Epoch of the First Division of China (A.D. 220–580)

(A) THE THREE KINGDOMS (A.D. 220–265)

1 *Social, intellectual, and economic problems during the first division*
The end of the Han period was followed by the three and a half centuries of the first division of China into several kingdoms, each with its own dynasty. In fact, once before during the period of the Contending States, China had been divided into a number of states, but at least in theory they had been subject to the Chou dynasty, and none of the contending states had made the claim to be the legitimate ruler of all China. In this period of the 'first division' several states claimed to be legitimate rulers, and later Chinese historians tried to decide which of these had 'more right' to this claim. At the outset (220–280) there were three kingdoms (Wei, Wu, Shu Han); then came an unstable reunion during twenty-seven years (280–307) under the rule of the Western Chin. This was followed by a still sharper division between north and south: while a wave of non-Chinese nomad dynasties poured over the north, in the south one Chinese clique after another seized power, so that dynasty followed dynasty until finally, in 580, a united China came again into existence, adopting the culture of the north and the traditions of the gentry.

In some ways, the period from 220 to 580 can be compared with the period of the coincidentally synchronous breakdown of the Roman Empire: in both cases there was no great increase in population, although in China perhaps no over-all decrease in population as in the Roman Empire; decrease occurred, however, in the population of the great Chinese cities, especially of the capital; furthermore we witness, in both empires, a disorganization of the monetary system, i.e. in China the reversal to a predominance of natural economy after almost 400 years of an economy in which prices were calculated in terms of money. As in the West, gold disappears almost completely. It is possible, though not too likely, that much of China's gold went into the gilding of millions of large and small Buddha statues; it seems more likely that it left China and the Roman Empire as well and came together in Central Asia or India.

Yet this period cannot be simply dismissed as a transition period, as was usually done by the older European works on China. The social order of the gentry, whose birth and development inside China we followed, had for the first time to defend itself against views and systems entirely opposed to it; for the Turkish and Mongol peoples who ruled northern China brought with them their traditions of a feudal nobility with privileges of birth and all that they implied. Thus this period, socially regarded, is especially that of the struggle between the Chinese gentry and the northern nobility, the gentry being excluded at first as a direct political factor in the northern and more important part of China. In the south the gentry continued in the old style with a constant struggle between cliques, the only difference being that the class assumed a sort of 'colonial' character through the formation of gigantic estates and through association with the merchant class.

To throw light on the scale of events, we need to have figures of population. There are no figures for the years around A.D. 220, and we must make do with those of 140; but in order to show the relative strength of the three states it is the ratio between the figures that matters. In 140 the regions which later belonged to Wei had roughly 29,000,000 inhabitants; those later belonging to Wu had 11,700,000; those which belonged later to Shu Han had a bare 7,500,000. (The figures take no account of the non-Chinese native population, which was not yet included in the taxation lists.) The Hsiung-nu formed only a small part of the population, as there were only the nineteen tribes which had abandoned one of the parts, already reduced, of the Hsiung-nu empire. The whole Hsiung-nu empire may never have counted more than some 3,000,000. At the time when the population of what became the Wei territory totalled 29,000,000 the capital with its immediate environment had over a million inhabitants. The figure is exclusive of most of the officials and soldiers, as these were taxable in their homes and so were counted there. It is clear that this was a disproportionate concentration round the capital.

It was at this time that both south and north China felt the influence of Buddhism, which until A.D. 220 had no more real effect on China than had, for instance, the penetration of European civilization between 1580 and 1842. Buddhism offered new notions, new ideals, foreign science, and many other elements of culture, with which the old Chinese philosophy and science had to contend. At the same time there came with Buddhism the first direct knowledge of the great civilized countries west of China. Until then China had regarded

110

herself as the only existing civilized country, and all other countries had been regarded as barbaric, for a civilized country was then taken to mean a country with urban industrial crafts and agriculture. In our present period, however, China's relations with the Middle East and with southern Asia were so close that the existence of civilized countries outside China had to be admitted. Consequently, when alien dynasties ruled in northern China and a new high civilization came into existence there, it was impossible to speak of its rulers as barbarians any longer. Even the theory that the Chinese emperor was the Son of Heaven and enthroned at the centre of the world was no longer tenable. Thus a vast widening of China's intellectual horizon took place.

Economically, our present period witnessed an adjustment in south China between the Chinese way of life, which had penetrated from the north, and that of the natives of the south. Large groups of Chinese had to turn over from wheat culture in dry fields to rice culture in wet fields, and from field culture to market gardening. In north China the conflict went on between Chinese agriculture and the cattle breeding of Central Asia. Was the will of the ruler to prevail and north China to become a country of pasturage, or was the country to keep to the agrarian tradition of the people under this rule? Only by attention to this problem shall we be in a position to explain why the rule of the Turkish peoples did not last, why these peoples were gradually absorbed and disappeared.

2 Status of the two southern kingdoms

When the last emperor of the Han period had to abdicate in favour of Ts'ao P'i and the Wei dynasty began, China was in no way a unified realm. Almost immediately, in 221, two other army commanders, who had long been independent, declared themselves emperors. In the south-west of China, in the present province of Szechwan, the Shu Han dynasty was founded in this way, and in the south-east, in the region of the present Nanking, the Wu dynasty.

The situation of the southern kingdom of Shu Han (221–263) corresponded more or less to that of the Chungking regime in the Second World War. West of it the high Tibetan mountains towered up; there was very little reason to fear any major attack from that direction. In the north and east the realm was also protected by difficult mountain country. The south lay relatively open, but at that time there were few Chinese living there, only natives with a relatively low civilization. The kingdom could only be seriously attacked from two corners—through the north-west, where there was a negotiable plateau, between the Ch'in-ling mountains in the north and the Tibetan mountains in the west, a plateau inhabited by fairly highly developed Tibetan tribes; and secondly through the south-east corner, where it would be possible to penetrate up the Yangtze. There was in fact incessant fighting at both these dangerous corners.

Economically, Shu Han was not in a bad position. The country had long been part of the Chinese wheat lands, and had a fairly large Chinese peasant population in the well-irrigated plain of Ch'engtu. There was also a wealthy merchant class, supplying grain to the surrounding mountain peoples and buying medicaments and other profitable Tibetan products. And there were trade routes from here through the present province of Yünnan to India.

Shu Han's difficulty was that its population was not large enough to be able to stand against the northern state of Wei; moreover, it was difficult to carry out an offensive from Shu Han, though the country could defend itself well. The first attempt to find a remedy was a campaign against the native tribes of the present Yünnan. The purpose of this was to secure man-power for the army and also slaves for sale; for the south-west had for centuries been a main source for traffic in slaves. Finally it was hoped to gain control over the trade to India. All these things were intended to strengthen Shu Han internally, but in spite of certain military successes they produced no practical result, as the Chinese were unable in the long run to endure the climate or to hold out against the guerrilla tactics of the natives. Shu Han tried to buy the assistance of the Tibetans and with their aid to carry out a decisive attack on Wei, whose dynastic legitimacy was not recognized by Shu Han. The ruler of Shu Han claimed to be a member of the imperial family of the deposed Han dynasty, and therefore to be the rightful, legitimate ruler over China. His descent, however, was a little doubtful, and in any case it depended on a link far back in the past. Against this the Wei of the north declared that the last ruler of the Han dynasty had handed over to them with all due form the seals of the state and therewith the imperial prerogative. The controversy was of no great practical importance, but it played a big part in the Chinese Confucianist school until the twelfth century, and contributed largely to a revision of the old conceptions of legitimacy.

The political plans of Shu Han were well considered and far-seeing. They were evolved by the premier, a man from Shantung named Chu-ko Liang; but the ruler died in 226 and his successor was still a child. Chu-ko Liang lived only for a further eight years, and after his death in 234 the decline of Shu Han began. Its political leaders no longer had a sense of what was possible. Thus Wei inflicted several defeats on Shu Han, and finally subjugated it in 263.

The situation of the state of Wu was much less favourable than that of Shu Han, though this second southern kingdom lasted from

221 to 280. Its country consisted of marshy plains or mountains with narrow valleys. Here Thai peoples had long cultivated their rice, while in the mountains Yao tribes lived by hunting and by simple agriculture. Peasants immigrating from the north found that their wheat and pulse did not thrive here, and they had to gain familiarity with rice cultivation. They were also compelled to give up their sheep and cattle and in their place to breed pigs and water buffaloes, as was done by the former inhabitants of the country. The lower class of the population was mainly non-Chinese; above it was an upper class of Chinese, at first relatively small, consisting of officials, soldiers, and merchants in towns and administrative centres. The country was poor, and its only important economic asset was the trade in metals, timber, and other southern products; soon there came also a growing over-seas trade with India and the Middle East, bringing revenues to the state in so far as the goods were re-exported from Wu to the north.

Wu never attempted to conquer the whole of China, but endea-voured to consolidate its own difficult territory with a view to building up a state on a firm foundation. In general, Wu played mainly a passive part in the incessant struggles between the three kingdoms, though it was active in diplomacy. The Wu kingdom entered into relations with a man who in 232 had gained control of the present South Manchuria and shortly afterwards assumed the title of king. This new ruler of 'Yen', as he called his kingdom had determined to attack the Wei dynasty, and hoped, by putting pressure on it in association with Wu, to overrun Wei from north and south. Wei answered this plan very effectively by recourse to diplomacy and it began by making Wu believe that Wu had reason to fear an attack from its western neighbour Shu Han. A mission was also dispatched from Wei to negotiate with Japan. Japan was then emerging from its stone age and introducing metals; there were countless small princi-palities and states, of which the state of Yamato, then ruled by a queen, was the most powerful. Recently a debate has arisen: tradi-tional sources claim that Yamato already at this time had control over a piece of southern Korea; others believe that a massive emigra-tion from this part of Korea turned to Japan, and that, for some time the emigrants retained contact with the motherland. In any case, Wei offered Yamato the prospect of gaining the whole of Korea if it would turn against the state of Yen in south Manchuria. Wu, too, had turned to Japan, but the negotiations came to nothing, since Wu, as an ally of Yen, had nothing to offer. The queen of Yamato accordingly sent a mission to Wei; she had already decided in favour of that state. Thus Wei was able to embark on war against Yen, which it annihilated in 237. This wrecked Wu's diplomatic projects, and no more was heard of any ambitious plans of the kingdom of Wu.

The two southern states had a common characteristic: both were condottiere states, not built up from their own population but conquered by generals from the north and ruled for a time by those generals and their northern troops. Natives gradually entered these northern armies and reduced their percentage of northerners, but a gulf remained between the native population, including its gentry, and the alien military rulers. This reduced the striking power of the southern states.

On the other hand, this period had its positive element. For the first time there was an emperor in south China, with all the organization that implied. A capital full of officials, eunuchs, and all the satellites of an imperial court provided incentives to economic advance, because it represented a huge market. The peasants around it were able to increase their sales and grew prosperous. The increased demand resulted in an increase of tillage and a thriving trade. Soon the transport problem had to be faced, as had happened long ago in the north, and new means of transport, especially ships, were provided, and new trade routes opened which were to last far longer than the three kingdoms; on the other hand, the costs of transport involved fresh taxation burdens for the population. The skilled staff needed for the business of administration came into the new capital from the surrounding districts, for the conquerors and new rulers of the territory of the two southern dynasties had brought with them from the north only uneducated soldiers and almost equally uneducated officers. The influx of scholars and administrators into the chief cities produced cultural and economic centres in the south, a circumstance of great importance to China's later development.

3 The northern state of Wei

The situation in the north, in the state of Wei (220–265) was anything but rosy. Wei ruled what at that time were the most important and richest regions of China, the plain of Shensi in the west and the great plain east of Loyang, the two most thickly populated areas of China. But the events at the end of the Han period had inflicted great economic injury on the country. The southern and south-western parts of the Han empire had been lost, and though parts of Central Asia still gave allegiance to Wei, these, as in the past, were economically more of a burden than an asset, because they called for incessant expenditure. At least the trade caravans were able to travel undisturbed from and to China through Sinkiang. Moreover, the Wei kingdom, although much smaller than the empire of the Han, maintained a completely staffed court at great expense, because the rulers, claiming to rule the whole of China, felt bound to display more magnificence than the rulers of the southern dynasties. They had also to reward the nineteen tribes of the Hsiung-nu in the north for their military aid, not only with cessions of land but with payments of money. Finally, they would not disarm but maintained great armies for the continual fighting against the southern states. The Wei dynasty did not succeed, however, in closely subordinating the various army commanders to the central government. Thus the commanders, in collusion with groups of the gentry, were able to enrich themselves and to secure regional power. The inadequate strength of the central government of Wei was further undermined by the rivalries among the dominant gentry. The imperial family (Ts'ao P'i, who reigned from 220 to 226, had taken as emperor the name of Wen Ti) was descended from one of the groups of great landowners that had formed in the later Han period. The nucleus of that group was a family named Ts'ui, of which there is mention from the Han period onward and which maintained its power down to the tenth century; but it remained in the background and at first held entirely aloof from direct intervention in high policy. Another family belonging to this group was the Hsia-hou family which was closely united to the family of Wen Ti by adoption; and very soon there was also the Ssŭ-ma family. Quite naturally Wen Ti, as soon as he came into power, made provision for the members of these powerful families, for only thanks to their support had he been able to ascend the throne and to maintain his hold on the throne. Thus we find many members of the Hsia-hou and Ssŭ-ma families in government positions. The Ssŭ-ma family especially showed great activity, and at the end of Wen Ti's reign their power had so grown that a certain Ssŭ-ma I was in control of the government, while the new emperor Ming Ti (227–233) was completely powerless. This virtually sealed the fate of the Wei dynasty, so far as the dynastic family was concerned. The next emperor was installed and deposed by the Ssŭ-ma family; dissensions arose within the ruling family, leading to members of the family assassinating one another. In 264 a member of the Ssŭ-ma family declared himself king; when he died and was succeeded by his son Ssŭ-ma Yen, the latter, in 265, staged a formal act of renunciation of the throne of the Wei dynasty and made himself the first ruler of the new Chin dynasty. There is nothing to gain by detailing all the intrigues that led up to this event: they all took place in the immediate environment of the court and in no way affected the people, except that every item of expenditure, including all the bribery, had to come out of the taxes paid by the people.

With such a situation at court, with the bad economic situation in the country, and with the continual fighting against the two southern states, there could be no question of any far-reaching foreign policy. Parts of eastern Sinkiang still showed some measure of allegiance to Wei, but only because at the time it had no stronger opponent. The Hsiung-nu beyond the frontier were suffering from a period of depression which was at the same time a period of reconstruction. It seems that some of their tribes went farther to the west, joined other tribes there and reappeared in western Asia and Europe as the feared Huns. Thus, the western Huns and the eastern Hsiung-nu seem to some, as yet undetermined, degree to be related. Other Hsiung-nu tribes were beginning slowly to form a new unit, together with Mongol tribes, the Juan-juan; but at this time, the new federation was still politically unimportant. We see here a typical process: after the breakdown of a tribal federation, the remaining tribes or fragments of tribes, join other tribal groups and form a new federation under a new name—thus, we often cannot easily recognize them in the new conglomerate. The nineteen tribes within north China held more and more closely together as militarily organized nomads, but did not yet represent a military power and remained loyal to the Wei. The only important element of trouble seems to have been furnished by the Hsien-pi tribes, who had joined with Wu-huan tribes and apparently also with vestiges of the Hsiung-nu in eastern Mongolia, and who made numerous raids over the frontier into the Wei empire. The state of Yen, in southern Manchuria, had already been destroyed by Wei in 238 thanks to Wei's good relations with Japan. Loose diplomatic relations were maintained with Japan in the period that followed; in that period many elements of Chinese civilization found their way into Japan and there, together with settlers from many parts of China, helped to transform the culture of ancient Japan.

This period is not a time of flourishing literature and art. On the contrary, we find here for the first time an intelligentsia which turned away from working with the government. Groups of scholars came together for what is called 'clean discussion' (ch'ing-t'an), consisting of short verbal exchanges or 'bons mots', brilliant remarks, sometimes combined with philosophical insights, often with exercises in logic. These men were no more imbued with Confucian ethics, often knew philosophical Taoism well, and, slightly later, Buddhism too. Their products, collected in part in the famous 'Shih-shuo hsin-yü', are not great or deep, but give us better insight into the spirit of the time and the character of the intelligentsia than any document from earlier time gives. The movement seems to have begun already before A.D. 200, though Wang Pi (226–249) is regarded as their leader. Wang Pi was also one of the important commentators of the book of Lao Tzŭ. Others went further and rejected social life as it was defined for the governing class completely. We hear of men who were drunk all the time, others who walked around in the nude—considering the modesty of Chinese at all times, an extreme act of rejection. Some scholars are of the belief that this was a real period of drug use, though they have not been able to tell us which drug was used. Chinese knew the effects of hemp (which is related to marijuana); opium and its derivates, however, were not yet known.

(B) THE WESTERN CHIN DYNASTY (A.D. 265–317)

1 *Internal situation in the Chin empire*

The change of dynasty in the state of Wei did not bring any turn in China's internal history. Ssŭ-ma Yen, who as emperor was called Wu Ti (265–289), had come to the throne with the aid of his clique and his extraordinarily large and widely ramified family. To these he had to give offices as reward. There began at court once more the same spectacle as in the past, except that princes of the new imperial family now played a greater part than under the Wei dynasty, whose ruling house had consisted of a small family. It was now customary, in spite of the abolition of the feudal system, for the imperial princes to receive large regions to administer, the fiscal revenues of which represented their income. The princes were not, however, to exercise full authority in the style of the former feudal lords: their courts were full of imperial control officials. In the event of war it was their duty to come forward, like other governors, with an army in support of the central government. The various Chin princes succeeded, however, in making other governors, beyond the frontiers of their regions, dependent on them. Also, they collected armies of their own independently of the central government and used those armies to pursue personal policies. The members of the families allied with the ruling house, for their part, did all they could to extend their own power. Thus the first ruler of the dynasty was tossed to and fro between the conflicting interests and was himself powerless. But though intrigue was piled on intrigue, the ruler who, of course, himself had come to the head of the state by means of intrigues, was more watchful than the rulers of the Wei dynasty had been, and by shrewd counter-measures he repeatedly succeeded in playing off one party against another, so that the dynasty remained in power. Numerous widespread and furious risings nevertheless took place, usually led by princes. Thus during this period the history of the dynasty was of an extraordinarily dismal character.

In spite of this, the Chin troops succeeded in overthrowing the second southern state, that of Wu (A.D. 280), and in so restoring the unity of the empire, the Shu Han realm having been already conquered by the Wei. After the destruction of Wu there remained no external enemy that represented a potential danger, so that a general disarmament was decreed (280) in order to restore a healthy economic and financial situation. This disarmament applied, of course, to the troops directly under the orders of the dynasty, namely the troops of the court and the capital and the imperial troops in the provinces. Disarmament could not, however, be carried out in the princes' regions, as the princes declared that they needed personal guards. The dismissal of the troops was accompanied by a decree ordering the surrender of arms. It may be assumed that the government proposed to mint money with the metal of the weapons surrendered, for coin (the old coin of the Wei dynasty) had become very scarce; as we indicated previously, money had largely been replaced by goods so that, for instance, grain and silks were used for the payment of salaries. China, from c. A.D. 200 on until the eighth century, remained in a period of such partial 'natural economy'.

Naturally the decree for the surrender of weapons remained a dead-letter. The discharged soldiers kept their weapons at first and then preferred to sell them. A large part of them was acquired by the Hsiung-nu and the Hsien-pi in the north of China; apparently they usually gave up land in return. In this way many Chinese soldiers, though not all by any means, went as peasants to the regions in the north of China and beyond the frontier. They were glad to do so, for the Hsiung-nu and the Hsien-pi had not the efficient administration and rigid tax collection of the Chinese; and above all, they had no great landowners who could have organized the collection of taxes. For their part, the Hsiung-nu and the Hsien-pi had no reason to regret this immigration of peasants, who could provide them with the farm produce they needed. And at the same time they were receiving from them large quantities of the most modern weapons.

This ineffective disarmament was undoubtedly the most pregnant event of the period of the Western Chin dynasty. The measure was intended to save the cost of maintaining the soldiers and to bring them back to the land as peasants (and taxpayers); but the discharged men were not given land by the government. The disarmament achieved nothing, not even the desired increase in the money in circulation; what did happen was that the central government lost all practical power, while the military strength both of the dangerous princes within the country and also of the frontier people was increased. The results of these mistaken measures became evident at once and compelled the government to arm anew.

2 *Effect on the frontier peoples*

Four groups of frontier peoples drew more or less advantage from the demobilization law—the people of the Toba, the Tibetans, and the Hsien-pi in the north, and the nineteen tribes of the Hsiung-nu within the frontiers of the empire. In the course of time all sorts of complicated relations developed among those ascending peoples as well as between them and the Chinese.

The Toba (T'o-po, Tabgaç) formed a small group in the north of the present province of Shansi, north of the city of Tat'ungfu, and they were about to develop their small state. They were probably of Turkish origin, but had absorbed many tribes of the older Hsiung-nu and the Hsien-pi. In considering the ethnic relationships of all these northern peoples we must rid ourselves of our present-day notions of national unity. Among the Toba there were many Turkish tribes, but also Mongols, and probably a Tungus tribe, as well as perhaps others whom we cannot yet analyse. These tribes may even have spoken different languages, much as later not only Mongol but also Turkish was spoken in the Mongol empire. The political units they formed were tribal unions, not national states.

Such a union or federation can be conceived of, structurally, as a cone. At the top point of the cone there was the person of the ruler of the federation. He was a member of the leading family or clan of the leading tribe (the two top layers of the cone). If we speak of the Toba as of Turkish stock, we mean that according to our present knowledge, their leading tribe (a) spoke a language belonging to the Turkish language family and (b) exhibited a pattern of culture which belonged to the type described above in Chapter One as 'north-western Culture'. The next layer of the cone represented the 'inner circle of tribes', i.e. such tribes as had joined with the leading tribe at an early moment. The leading family of the leading tribe often took their wives from the leading families of the 'inner tribes', and these leaders served as advisers and councillors to the leader of the federation. The next lower layer consisted of the 'outer tribes', i.e. tribes which had joined the federation only later, often under strong pressure; their number was always much larger than the number of the 'inner tribes', but their political influence was much weaker. Every layer below that of the 'outer tribes' was regarded as inferior and more or less 'unfree'. There was many a tribe which, as a tribe, had to serve a free tribe; and there were others who, as tribes, had to serve the whole federation. In addition, there were individuals who had quit or had been forced to quit their tribe or their home and had joined the federation leader as his personal 'bondsmen'; further, there were individual slaves and, finally, there were the large masses of agriculturists who had been conquered by the federation. When such a federation was dissolved, by defeat or inner dissent, individual tribes or groups of tribes could join a new federation or could resume independent life.

119

Typically, such federations exhibited two tendencies. In the case of the Hsiung-nu we indicated previously that the leader of the federation repeatedly attempted to build up a kind of bureaucratic system, using his bondsmen as a nucleus. A second tendency was to replace the original tribal leaders by members of the family of the federation leader. If this initial step, usually first taken when 'outer tribes' were incorporated, was successful, a reorganization was attempted: instead of using tribal units in war, military units on the basis of 'Groups of Hundred', 'Groups of Thousand', etc., were created and the original tribes were dissolved into military regiments. In the course of time, and especially at the time of the dissolution of a federation, these military units had gained social coherence and appeared to be tribes again; we are probably correct in assuming that all 'tribes' which we find from this time on were already 'secondary' tribes of this type. A secondary tribe often took its name from its leader, but it could also revive an earlier 'primary tribe' name.

The Toba, whom we will soon discuss in detail, represented a good example of this 'cone' structure of pastoral society. Also the Hsiung-nu of this time seem to have had a similar structure. Incidentally, we will from now on call the Hsiung-nu 'Huns' because Chinese sources begin to call them 'Hu', a term which also had a more general meaning (all non-Chinese in the north and west of China) as well as a more special meaning (non-Chinese in Central Asia and India).

The Tibetans fell apart into two sub-groups, the Ch'iang and the Ti. Both names appeared repeatedly as political conceptions, but the Tibetans, like all other state-forming groups of peoples, sheltered in their realms countless alien elements. In the course of the third and second centuries B.C. the group of the Ti, mainly living in the territory of the present Szechwan, had mixed extensively with remains of the Yüeh-chih; the others, the Ch'iang, were northern Tibetans or so-called Tanguts; that is to say, they contained Turkish and Mongol elements. In A.D. 296 there began a great rising of the Ti, whose leader Ch'i Wan-nien took on the title emperor. The Ch'iang rose with them, but it was not until later, from 312, that they pursued an independent policy. The Ti State, however, though it had a second emperor, very soon lost importance, so that we shall be occupied solely with the Ch'iang.

As the tribal structure of Tibetan groups was always weak and as leadership developed among them only in times of war, their states always show a military rather than a tribal structure, and the continuation of these states depended strongly upon the personal qualities of their leaders. Incidentally, Tibetans fundamentally were sheep-breeders and not horse-breeders and, therefore, they always showed inclination to incorporate infantry into their armies. Thus, Tibetan

120

states differed strongly from the aristocratically organized 'Turkish' states as well as from the tribal, non-aristocratic 'Mongol' states of that period.

The Hsien-pi, according to our present knowledge, were under 'Mongol' leadership, i.e. we believe that the language of the leading group belonged to the family of Mongolian languages and that their culture belonged to the type described above as 'northern culture'. They had, in addition, a strong admixture of Hunnic tribes. Throughout the period during which they played a part in history, they never succeeded in forming any great political unit, in strong contrast to the Huns, who excelled in state formation. The separate groups of the Hsien-pi pursued a policy of their own; very frequently Hsien-pi fought each other, and they never submitted to a common leadership. Thus their history is entirely that of small groups. As early as the Wei period there had been small-scale conflicts with the Hsien-pi tribes, and at times the tribes had had some success. The campaigns of the Hsien-pi against north China now increased, and in the course of them the various tribes formed firmer groupings, among which the Mu-jung tribes played a leading part. In 281, the year after the demobilization law, this group marched south into China, and occupied the region round Peking. After fierce fighting, in which the Mu-jung section suffered heavy losses, a treaty was signed in 289, under which the Mu-jung tribe of the Hsien-pi recognized Chinese overlordship. The Mu-jung were driven to this step mainly because they had been continually attacked from southern Manchuria by another Hsien-pi tribe, the Yü-wen, the tribe most closely related to them. The Mu-jung made use of the period of their so-called subjection to organize their community in north China.

South of the Toba were the nineteen tribes of the Hsiung-nu or Huns, as we are now calling them. Their leader in A.D. 287, Liu Yüan, was one of the principal personages of this period. His name is purely Chinese, but he was descended from the Hun *shan-yü*, from the family and line of Mao Tun. His membership of that long-famous noble line and old ruling family of Huns gave him a prestige which he increased by his great organizing ability.

3   Struggles for the throne

We shall return to Liu Yüan later; we must now cast another glance at the official court of the Chin. In that court a family named Yang had become very powerful, a daughter of this family having become empress. When, however, the emperor died, the wife of the new emperor Hui Ti (290–306) secured the assassination of the old empress Yang and of her whole family. Thus began the rule at court of the Chia family. In 299 the Chia family got rid of the heir to the throne, to whom they objected, assassinating this prince and another one. This event became the signal for large-scale activity on the part of the princes, each of whom was supported by particular groups of families. The princes had not complied with the disarmament law of 280 and so had become militarily supreme. The generals newly appointed in the course of the imperial rearmament at once entered into alliance with the princes, and thus were quite unreliable as officers of the government. Both the generals and the princes entered into agreements with the frontier peoples to assure their aid in the struggle for power. The most popular of these auxiliaries were the Hsien-pi, who were fighting for one of the princes whose territory lay in the east. Since the Toba were the natural enemies of the Hsien-pi, who were continually contesting their hold on their territory, the Toba were always on the opposite side to that supported by the Hsien-pi, so that they now supported generals who were ostensibly loyal to the government. The Huns, too, negotiated with several generals and princes and received tempting offers. Above all, all the frontier peoples were now militarily well equipped, continually receiving new war material from the Chinese who from time to time were co-operating with them.

In A.D. 300 Prince Lun assassinated the empress Chia and removed her group. In 301 he made himself emperor, but in the same year he was killed by the prince of Ch'i. This prince was killed in 302 by the prince of Ch'ang-sha, who in turn was killed in 303 by the prince of Tung-hai. The prince of Ho-chien rose in 302 and was killed in 306; the prince of Ch'engtu rose in 303, conquered the capital in 305, and then, in 306, was himself removed. I mention all these names and dates only to show the disunion within the ruling groups.

4 *Migration of Chinese*

All these struggles raged round the capital, for each of the princes wanted to secure full power and to become emperor. Thus the border regions remained relatively undisturbed. Their population suffered much less from the warfare than the unfortunate people in the neighbourhood of the central government. For this reason there took place a mass migration of Chinese from the centre of the empire to its periphery. This process, together with the shifting of the frontier peoples, is one of the most important events of that epoch. A great number of Chinese migrated especially into the present province of Kansu, where a governor who had originally been sent there to fight the Hsien-pi had created a sort of paradise by his good administration and maintenance of peace. The territory ruled by this Chinese, first as governor and then in increasing independence, was surrounded by Hsien-pi, Tibetans, and other peoples, but thanks to the great immigration of Chinese and to its situation on the main caravan route to Sinkiang, it was able to hold its own, to expand, and to become prosperous.

Other groups of Chinese peasants migrated southward into the territories of the former state of Wu. A Chinese prince of the house of the Chin was ruling there, in the present Nanking. His purpose was to organize that territory, and then to intervene in the struggles of the other princes. We shall meet him again at the beginning of the Hun rule over north China in 317, as founder and emperor of the first south Chinese dynasty, which was at once involved in the usual internal and external struggles. For the moment, however, the southern region was relatively at peace, and was accordingly attracting settlers.

Finally, many Chinese migrated northward, into the territories of the frontier peoples, not only of the Hsien-pi but especially of the Huns. These alien peoples, although in the official Chinese view they were still barbarians, at least maintained peace in the territories they ruled, and they left in peace the peasants and craftsmen who came to them, even while their own armies were involved in fighting inside China. Not only peasants and craftsmen came to the north but more and more educated persons. Members of families of the gentry that had suffered from the fighting, people who had lost their influence in China, were welcomed by the Huns and appointed teachers and political advisers of the Hun nobility.

5 Victory of the Huns. The Hun Han dynasty
(later renamed the Earlier Chao dynasty)

With its self-confidence thus increased, the Hun council of nobles declared that in future the Huns should no longer fight now for one and now for another Chinese general or prince. They had promised loyalty to the Chinese emperor, but not to any prince. No one doubted that the Chinese emperor was a complete nonentity and no longer played any part in the struggle for power. It was evident that the murders would continue until one of the generals or princes overcame the rest and made himself emperor. Why should not the Huns have the same right? Why should not they join in this struggle for the Chinese imperial throne?

There were two arguments against this course, one of which was already out of date. The Chinese had for many centuries set down the Huns as uncultured barbarians; but the inferiority complex thus engendered in the Huns had virtually been overcome, because in the course of time their upper class had deliberately acquired a Chinese education and so ranked culturally with the Chinese. Thus the ruler

123

Liu Yüan, for example, had enjoyed a good Chinese education and was able to read all the classical texts. The second argument was provided by the rigid conceptions of legitimacy to which the Turkish-Hunnic aristocratic society adhered. The Huns asked themselves: 'Have we, as aliens, any right to become emperors and rulers in China, when we are not descended from an old Chinese family?' On this point Liu Yüan and his advisers found a good answer. They called Liu Yüan's dynasty the 'Han dynasty', and so linked it with the most famous of all the Chinese dynasties, pointing to the pact which their ancestor Mao Tun had concluded five hundred years earlier with the first emperor of the Han dynasty and which had described the two states as 'brethren'. They further recalled the fact that the rulers of the Huns were closely related to the Chinese ruling family, because Mao Tun and his successors had married Chinese princesses. Finally, Liu Yüan's Chinese family name, Liu, had also been the family name of the rulers of the Han dynasty. Accordingly the Han Lius came forward not as aliens but as the rightful successors in continuation of the Han dynasty, as legitimate heirs to the Chinese imperial throne on the strength of relationship and of treaties.

Thus the Hun Liu Yüan had no intention of restoring the old empire of Mao Tun, the empire of the nomads; he intended to become emperor of China, emperor of a country of farmers. In this lay the fundamental difference between the earlier Hun empire and this new one. The question whether the Huns should join in the struggle for the Chinese imperial throne was therefore decided among the Huns themselves in 304 in the affirmative, by the founding of the 'Hun Han dynasty'. All that remained was the practical question of how to hold out with their small army of 50,000 men if serious opposition should be offered to the 'barbarians'.

Meanwhile Liu Yüan provided himself with court ceremonial on the Chinese model, in a capital which, after several changes, was established at P'ing-ch'êng in southern Shansi. He attracted more and more of the Chinese gentry, who were glad to come to this still rather barbaric but well-organized court. In 309 the first attack was made on the Chinese capital, Loyang. Liu Yüan died in the following year, and in 311, under his successor Liu Ts'ung (310–318), the attack was renewed and Loyang fell. The Chin emperor, Huai Ti, was captured and kept a prisoner in P'ing-ch'êng until in 313 a conspiracy in his favour was brought to light in the Hun empire, and he and all his supporters were killed. Meanwhile the Chinese clique of the Chin dynasty had hastened to make a prince emperor in the second capital, Ch'ang-an (Min Ti, 313–316) while the princes' struggles for the throne continued. Nobody troubled about the fate of the unfortunate emperor in his capital. He received no reinforcements, so that he was helpless in face of the next attack of the Huns, and in 316 he was compelled to surrender like his predecessor. Now the Hun Han dynasty held both capitals, which meant virtually the whole of the western part of north China, and the so-called 'Western Chin dynasty' thus came to its end. Its princes and generals and many of its gentry became landless and homeless and had to flee into the south.

(C) THE ALIEN EMPIRES IN NORTH CHINA, DOWN TO THE TOBA (A.D. 317–385)

1 *The Later Chao dynasty in eastern north China (Hun; 329–352)* At this time the eastern part of north China was entirely in the hands of Shih Lo, a former follower of Liu Yüan. Shih Lo had escaped from slavery in China and had risen to be a military leader among de-tribalized Huns. In 310 he had not only undertaken a great campaign right across China to the south, but had slaughtered more than 100,000 Chinese, including forty-eight princes of the Chin dynasty, who had formed a vast burial procession for a prince. This achieve-ment added considerably to Shih Lo's power, and his relations with Liu Ts'ung, already tense, became still more so. Liu Yüan had tried to organize the Hun state on the Chinese model, intending in this way to gain efficient control of China; Shih Lo rejected Chinese methods, and held to the old warrior-nomad tradition, making raids with the aid of nomad fighters. He did not contemplate holding the territories of central and southern China which he had conquered; he withdrew, and in the two years 314–315 he contented himself with bringing considerable expanses in north-eastern China, especially territories of the Hsien-pi, under his direct rule, as a base for further raids. Many Huns in Liu Ts'ung's dominion found Shih Lo's method of rule more to their taste than living in a state ruled by officials, and they went over to Shih Lo and joined him in breaking entirely with Liu Ts'ung. There was a further motive for this: in states founded by nomads, with a federation of tribes as their basis, the personal qualities of the ruler played an important part. The chiefs of the various tribes would not give unqualified allegiance to the son of a dead ruler unless the son was a strong personality or gave promise of becoming one. Failing that, there would be independence move-ments. Liu Ts'ung did not possess the indisputable charisma of his predecessor Liu Yüan; and the Huns looked with contempt on his court splendour, which could only have been justified if he had con-quered all China. Liu Ts'ung had no such ambition; nor had his successor Liu Yao (319–329), who gave the Hun Han dynasty retro-actively, from its start with Liu Yüan, the new name of 'Earlier Chao

dynasty' (304–320). Many tribes then went over to Shih Lo, and the remainder of Liu Yao's empire was reduced to a precarious existence. In 329 the whole of it was annexed by Shih Lo.

Although Shih Lo had long been much more powerful than the emperors of the 'Earlier Chao dynasty', until their removal he had not ventured to assume the title of emperor. The reason for this seems to have lain in the conceptions of nobility held by the Turkish peoples in general and the Huns in particular, according to which only those could become *shan-yü* (or, later, emperor) who could show descent from the Tu-ku tribe, the rightful *shan-yü* stock. In accordance with this conception, all later Hun dynasties deliberately disowned Shih Lo. For Shih Lo, after his destruction of Liu Yao, no longer hesitated: ex-slave as he was, and descended from one of the non-noble stocks of the Huns, he made himself emperor of the 'Later Chao dynasty' (329–352).

Shih Lo was a forceful army commander, but he was a man without statesmanship, and without the culture of his day. He had no Chinese education; he hated the Chinese and would have been glad to make north China a grazing ground for his nomad tribes of Huns. Accordingly he had no desire to rule all China. The part already subjugated, embracing the whole of north China with the exception of the present province of Kansu, sufficed for his purpose.

The governor of that province was a loyal subject of the Chinese Chin dynasty, a man famous for his good administration, and himself a Chinese. After the execution of the Chin emperor Huai Ti by the Huns in 313, he regarded himself as no longer bound to the central government; he made himself independent and founded the 'Earlier Liang dynasty', which was to last until 376. This mainly Chinese realm was not very large, although it had admitted a broad stream of Chinese emigrants from the dissolving Chin empire; but economically the Liang realm was very prosperous, so that it was able to extend its influence as far as Central Asia. During the earlier struggles Central Asia had been virtually in isolation, but now new contacts began to be established. Many traders from Central Asia set up branches in Liang. In the capital there were whole quarters inhabited only by aliens from western and eastern Central Asia and from India. With the traders came Buddhist monks; trade and Buddhism seemed to be closely associated everywhere. In the trading centres monasteries were installed in the form of blocks of houses within strong walls that successfully resisted many an attack. Consequently the Buddhists were able to serve as bankers for the merchants, who deposited their money in the monasteries, which made a charge for its custody; the merchants also warehoused their goods in the monasteries. Sometimes the process was reversed, a trade centre being formed around an existing monastery. In this case the monastery also served as a hostel for the merchants. Economically this Chinese state in Kansu was much more like a Sinkiang city state that lived by commerce than the agrarian states of the Far East, although agriculture was also pursued under the Earlier Liang.

From this trip to the remote west we will return first to the Hun capital. From 329 onward Shih Lo possessed a wide empire, but an unstable one. He himself felt at all times insecure, because the Huns regarded him, on account of his humble origin, as a 'revolutionary'. He exterminated every member of the Liu family, that is to say the old *shan-yü* family, of whom he could get hold, in order to remove any possible pretender to the throne; but he could not count on the loyalty of the Hun and other Turkish tribes under his rule. During this period not a few Huns went over to the small realm of the Toba; other Hun tribes withdrew entirely from the political scene and lived with their herds as nomad tribes in Shansi and in the Ordos region. The general insecurity undermined the strength of Shih Lo's empire. He died in 333, and there came to the throne, after a short interregnum, another personality of a certain greatness, Shih Hu (334–349). He transferred the capital to the city of Yeh, in northern Honan, where the rulers of the Wei dynasty had reigned. There are many accounts of the magnificence of the court of Yeh. Foreigners, especially Buddhist monks, played a greater part there than Chinese. On the one hand, it was not easy for Shih Hu to gain the active support of the educated Chinese gentry after the murders of Shih Lo and, on the other hand, Shih Hu seems to have understood that foreigners without family and without other relations to the native population, but with special skills, are the most reliable and loyal servants of a ruler. Indeed, his administration seems to have been good, but the regime remained completely parasitic, with no support of the masses or the gentry. After Shih Hu's death there were fearful combats between his sons; ultimately a member of an entirely different family of Hun origin seized power, but was destroyed in 352 by the Hsien-pi, bringing to an end the Later Chao dynasty.

2 *Earlier Yen dynasty in the north-east (proto-Mongol; 352–370), and the Earlier Ch'in dynasty in all north China (Tibetan; 351–394)*
In the north, proto-Mongol Hsien-pi tribes had again made themselves independent; in the past they had been subjects of Liu Yüan and then of Shih Lo. A man belonging to one of these tribes, the tribe of the Mu-jung, became the leader of a league of tribes, and in 337 founded the state of Yen. This proto-Mongol state of the Mu-jung, which the historians call the 'Earlier Yen' state, conquered parts of southern Manchuria and also the state of Kao-li in Korea,

and there began then an immigration of Hsien-pi into Korea, which became noticeable at a later date. The conquest of Korea, which was still, as in the past, a Japanese market and was very wealthy, enormously strengthened the state of Yen. Not until a little later, when Japan's trade relations were diverted to central China, did Korea's importance begin to diminish. Although this 'Earlier Yen dynasty' of the Mu-jung officially entered on the heritage of the Huns, and its regime was therefore dated only from 352 (until 370), it failed either to subjugate the whole realm of the 'Later Chao' or effectively to strengthen the state it had acquired. This old Hun territory had suffered economically from the anti-agrarian nomad tendency of the last of the Hun emperors; and unremunerative wars against the Chinese in the south had done nothing to improve its position. In addition to this, the realm of the Toba was dangerously gaining strength on the flank of the new empire. But the most dangerous enemy was in the west, on former Hun soil, in the province of Shensi —Tibetans, who finally came forward once more with claims to dominance. These were Tibetans of the P'u family, which later changed its name to Fu. The head of the family had worked his way up as a leader of Tibetan auxiliaries under the 'Later Chao', gaining more and more power and following. When under that dynasty the death of Shih Hu marked the beginning of general dissolution, he gathered his Tibetans around him in the west, declared himself independent of the Huns, and made himself emperor of the 'Earlier Ch'in dynasty' (351–394). He died in 355, and was followed after a short interregnum by Fu Chien (357–385), who was unquestionably one of the most important figures of the fourth century. This Tibetan empire ultimately defeated the 'Earlier Yen dynasty' and annexed the realm of the Mu-jung. Thus the Mu-jung Hsien-pi came under the dominion of the Tibetans; they were distributed among a number of places as garrisons or mounted troops.

The empire of the Tibetans was organized quite differently from the empires of the Huns and the Hsien-pi tribes. The Tibetan organization was purely military and had nothing to do with tribal structure. This had its advantages, for the leader of such a formation had no need to take account of tribal chieftains; he was answerable to no one and possessed considerable personal power. Nor was there any need for him to be of noble rank or descended from an old family. The Tibetan ruler Fu Chien organized all his troops, including the non-Tibetans, on this system, without regard to tribal membership.

Fu Chien's state showed another innovation: the armies of the Huns and the Hsien-pi had consisted entirely of cavalry, for the nomads of the north were, of course, horsemen; to fight on foot was in their eyes not only contrary to custom but contemptible. So long as a state consisted only of a league of tribes, it was simply out of the question to transform part of the army into infantry. Fu Chien, however, with his military organization that paid no attention to the tribal element, created an infantry in addition to the great cavalry units, recruiting for it large numbers of Chinese. The infantry proved extremely valuable, especially in the fighting in the plains of north China and in laying siege to fortified towns. Fu Chien thus very quickly achieved military predominance over the neighbouring states. As we have seen already, he annexed the 'Earlier Yen' realm of the proto-Mongols (370), but he also annihilated the Chinese 'Earlier Liang' realm (376) and in the same year the small Turkish Toba realm. This made him supreme over all north China and stronger than any alien ruler before him. He had in his possession both the ancient capitals, Ch'ang-an and Loyang; the whole of the rich agricultural regions of north China belonged to him; he also controlled the routes to Sinkiang. He himself had had a Chinese education, and he attracted Chinese to his court; he protected the Buddhists; and he tried in every way to make the whole country culturally Chinese. As soon as Fu Chien had all north China in his power, as Liu Yüan and his Huns had done before him, he resolved, like Liu Yüan, to make every effort to gain the mastery over all China, to become emperor of China. Liu Yüan's successors had not had the capacity for which such a venture called; Fu Chien was to fail in it for other reasons. Yet, from a military point of view, his chances were not bad. He had far more soldiers under his command than the Chinese 'Eastern Chin dynasty' which ruled the south, and his troops were undoubtedly better. In the time of the founder of the Tibetan dynasty, the southern empire had been utterly defeated by his troops (354), and the south Chinese were no stronger now.

Against them the north had these assets: the possession of the best northern tillage, the control of the trade routes, and 'Chinese' culture and administration. At the time, however, these represented only potentialities and not tangible realities. It would have taken ten to twenty years to restore the capacities of the north after its devastation in many wars, to reorganize commerce, and to set up a really reliable administration, and thus to interlock the various elements and consolidate the various tribes. But as early as 383 Fu Chien started his great campaign against the south, with an army of something like a million men. At first the advance went well. The horsemen from the north, however, were men of the mountain country, and in the soggy plains of the Yangtze region, cut up by hundreds of water-courses and canals, they suffered from climatic and natural conditions to which they were unaccustomed. Their main strength was still in cavalry; and they came to grief. The supplies and rein-forcements for the vast army failed to arrive in time; units did not reach the appointed places at the appointed dates. The southern troops under the supreme command of Hsieh Hsüan, far inferior in numbers and militarily of no great efficiency, made surprise attacks on isolated units before these were in regular formation. Some they defeated, others they bribed; they spread false reports. Fu Chien's army was seized with widespread panic, so that he was compelled to retreat in haste. As he did so it became evident that his empire had no inner stability: in a very short time it fell into fragments. The south Chinese had played no direct part in this, for in spite of their victory they were not strong enough to advance far to the north.

3 The fragmentation of north China

The first to fall away from the Tibetan ruler was a noble of the Mu-jung, a member of the ruling family of the 'Earlier Yen dynasty', who withdrew during the actual fighting to pursue a policy of his own. With the vestiges of the Hsien-pi who followed him, mostly cavalry, he fought his way northwards into the old homeland of the Hsien-pi and there, in central Hopei, founded the 'Later Yen dynasty' (384–409), himself reigning for twelve years. In the remaining thirteen years of the existence of that dynasty there were no fewer than five rulers, the last of them a member of another family. The history of this Hsien-pi dynasty, as of its predecessor, is an unedifying succession of intrigues; no serious effort was made to build up a true state.

In the same year 384 there was founded, under several other Mu-jung princes of the ruling family of the 'Earlier Yen dynasty', the 'Western Yen dynasty' (384–394). Its nucleus was nothing more than a detachment of troops of the Hsien-pi which had been thrown by Fu Chien into the west of his empire, in Shensi, in the neighbourhood of the old capital Ch'ang-an. There its commanders, on learning the news of Fu Chien's collapse, declared their independence. In western China, however, far removed from all liaison with the main body of the Hsien-pi, they were unable to establish themselves, and when they tried to fight their way to the north-east they were dispersed, so that they failed entirely to form an actual state.

There was a third attempt in 384 to form a state in north China. A Tibetan who had joined Fu Chien with his followers declared himself independent when Fu Chien came back, a beaten man, to Shensi. He caused Fu Chien and almost the whole of his family to be assassinated, occupied the capital, Ch'ang-an, and actually entered into the heritage of Fu Chien. This Tibetan dynasty is known as the 'Later Ch'in dynasty' (384–417). It was certainly the strongest of those founded in 384, but it still failed to dominate any considerable part of China and remained of local importance, mainly confined to the present province of Shensi. Fu Chien's empire nominally had three further rulers, but they did not exert the slightest influence on events.

With the collapse of the state founded by Fu Chien, the tribes of Hsien-pi who had left their homeland in the third century and migrated to the Ordos region proceeded to form their own state: a man of the Hsien-pi tribe of the Ch'i-fu founded the so-called 'Western Ch'in dynasty' (385–431). Like the other Hsien-pi states, this one was of weak construction, resting on the military strength of a few tribes and failing to attain a really secure basis. Its territory lay in the east of the present province of Kansu, and so controlled the eastern end of the western Asian caravan route, which might have been a source of wealth if the Ch'i-fu had succeeded in attracting commerce by discreet treatment and in imposing taxation on it. Instead of this, the bulk of the long-distance traffic passed through the Ordos region, a little farther north, avoiding the Ch'i-fu state, which seemed to the merchants to be too insecure. The Ch'i-fu depended mainly on cattle-breeding in the remote mountain country in the south of their territory, a region that gave them relative security from attack; on the other hand, this made them unable to exercise any influence on the course of political events in western China.

Mention must be made of one more state that rose from the ruins of Fu Chien's empire. It lay in the far west of China, in the western part of the present province of Kansu, and was really a continuation of the Chinese 'Earlier Liang' realm, which had been annexed ten years earlier (376) by Fu Chien. A year before his great march to the south, Fu Chien had sent the Tibetan Lü Kuang into the 'Earlier Liang' region in order to gain influence over Sinkiang. As mentioned previously, after the great Hun rulers Fu Chien was the first to make a deliberate attempt to secure cultural and political overlordship over the whole of China. Although himself a Tibetan, he never succumbed to the temptation of pursuing a 'Tibetan' policy; like an entirely legitimate ruler of China, he was concerned to prevent the northern peoples along the frontier from uniting with the Tibetan peoples of the west for political ends. The possession of Sinkiang would avert that danger, which had shown signs of becoming imminent of late: some tribes of the Hsien-pi had migrated as far as the high mountains of Tibet and had imposed themselves as a ruling class on the still very primitive Tibetans living there. From this symbiosis there began to be formed a new people, the so-called T'u-yü-hun, a hybridization of Mongol and Tibetan stock with a slight Turkish admixture. Lü Kuang had had success in Sinkiang; he had brought

131

considerable portions of eastern Sinkiang under Fu Chien's sovereignty and administered those regions almost independently. When the news came of Fu Chien's end, he declared himself an independent ruler, of the 'Later Liang' dynasty (386–403). Strictly speaking, this was simply a trading State, like the city-states of Central Asia: its basis was the transit traffic that brought it prosperity. For commerce brought good profit to the small states that lay right across the caravan route, whereas it was of doubtful benefit, as we know, to agrarian China as a whole, because the luxury goods which it supplied to the court were paid for out of the production of the general population.

This 'Later Liang' realm was inhabited not only by a few Tibetans and many Chinese, but also by Hsien-pi and Huns. These heterogeneous elements with their divergent cultures failed in the long run to hold together in this long but extremely narrow strip of territory, which was almost incapable of military defence. As early as 397 a group of Huns in the central section of the country made themselves independent, assuming the name of the 'Northern Liang' (397–439). These Huns quickly conquered other parts of the 'Later Liang' realm, which then fell entirely to pieces. Chinese again founded a state, 'West Liang' (400–421) in western Kansu, and the Hsien-pi founded 'South Liang' (379–414) in eastern Kansu. Thus the 'Later Liang' fell into three parts, more or less differing ethnically, though they could not be described as ethnically unadulterated states.

4 Sociological analysis of the two great alien empires

The two great empires of north China at the time of its division had been founded by non-Chinese—the first by the Hun Liu Yüan, the second by the Tibetan Fu Chien. Both rulers went to work on the same principle of trying to build up truly 'Chinese' empires, but the traditions of Huns and Tibetans differed, and the two experiments turned out differently. Both failed, but not for the same reasons and not with the same results. The Hun Liu Yüan was the ruler of a league of feudal tribes, which was expected to take its place as an upper class above the unchanged Chinese agricultural population with its system of officials and gentry. But Liu Yüan's successors were national reactionaries who stood for the maintenance of the nomad life against that new plan of transition to a feudal class of urban nobles ruling an agrarian population. Liu Yüan's more far-seeing policy was abandoned, with the result that the Huns were no longer in a position to rule an immense agrarian territory, and the empire soon disintegrated. For the various Hun tribes this failure meant falling back into political insignificance, but they were able to maintain their national character and existence.

Fu Chien, as a Tibetan, was a militarist and soldier, in accordance with the past of the Tibetans. Under him were grouped Tibetans without tribal chieftains; the great mass of Chinese; and dispersed remnants of tribes of Huns, Hsien-pi, and others. His organization was militaristic and, outside the military sphere, a militaristic bureaucracy. The Chinese gentry, so far as they still existed, preferred to work with him rather than with the feudalist Huns. These gentry probably supported Fu Chien's southern campaign, for, in consequence of the wide ramifications of their families, it was to their interest that China should form a single economic unit. They were, of course, equally ready to work with another group, one of southern Chinese, to attain the same end by other means, if those means should prove more advantageous: thus the gentry were not a reliable asset, but were always ready to break faith. Among other things, Fu Chien's southern campaign was wrecked by that faithlessness. When an essentially military state suffers military defeat, it can only go to pieces. This explains the disintegration of that great empire within a single year into so many diminutive states, as already described.

5 Sociological analysis of the petty states

The states that took the place of Fu Chien's empire, those many diminutive states (the Chinese speak of the period of the Sixteen Kingdoms), may be divided from the economic point of view into two groups—trading states and warrior states; sociologically they also fall into two groups, tribal states and military states.

The small states in the west, in Kansu (the Later Liang and the Western, Northern, and Southern Liang), were trading states: they lived on the earnings of transit trade with Sinkiang. The eastern states were warrior states, in which an army commander ruled by means of an armed group of non-Chinese and exploited an agricultural population. It is only logical that such states should be short-lived, as in fact they all were.

Sociologically regarded, during this period only the Southern and Northern Liang were still tribal states. In addition to these came the young Toba realm, which began in 385 but of which mention has not yet been made. The basis of that state was the tribe, not the family or the individual; after its political disintegration the separate tribes remained in existence. The other states of the east, however, were military states, made up of individuals with no tribal allegiance but subject to a military commandant. But where there is no tribal association, after the political downfall of a state founded by ethnic groups, those groups sooner or later disappear as such. We see this in the years immediately following Fu Chien's collapse: the

Tibetan ethnic group to which he himself belonged disappeared entirely from the historical scene. The two Tibetan groups that outlasted him, also forming military states and not tribal states, similarly came to an end shortly afterwards for all time. The Hsien-pi groups in the various fragments of the empire, with the exception of the petty states in Kansu, also continued only as tribal fragments led by a few old ruling families. They, too, after brief and undistinguished military rule, came to an end; they disappeared so completely that thereafter we no longer find the term Hsien-pi in history. Not that they had been exterminated. When the social structure and its corresponding economic form fall to pieces, there remain only two alternatives for its individuals. Either they must go over to a new form, which in China could only mean that they became Chinese; many Hsien-pi in this way became Chinese in the decades following 384. Or, they could retain their old way of living in association with another stock of similar formation; this, too, happened in many cases. Both these courses, however, meant the end of the Hsien-pi as an independent ethnic unit. We must keep this process and its reasons in view if we are to understand how a great people can disappear once and for all.

The Huns, too, so powerful in the past, were suddenly scarcely to be found any longer. Among the many petty states there were many Hsien-pi kingdoms, but only a single, quite small Hun state, that of the Northern Liang. The disappearance of the Huns was, however, only apparent; at this time they remained in the Ordos region and in Shansi as separate nomad tribes with no integrating political organization; their time had still to come.

6 Culture and religion

According to the prevalent Chinese view, nothing of importance was achieved during this period in north China in the intellectual sphere; there was no culture in the north, only in the south. This is natural: for a Confucian this period, the fourth century, was one of degeneracy in north China, for no one came into prominence as a celebrated Confucian. Nothing else could be expected, for in the north the gentry, which had been the class that maintained Confucianism since the Han period, had largely been destroyed; from political leadership especially it had been shut out during the periods of alien rule. Nor could we expect to find Taoists in the true sense, that is to say followers of the teaching of Lao Tzŭ, for these, too, had been dependent since the Han period on the gentry. Until the fourth century, these too had remained the dominant philosophies.

What could take their place? The alien rulers had left little behind them. Most of them had been unable to write Chinese, and in so far as they were warriors they had no interest in literature or in political philosophy, for they were men of action. As far as we know, none of these foreigners as yet had developed a script of their own. We have, naturally, also to keep in mind that what has been written about the culture of the northern foreigners, was written by basically hostile Chinese for whom the tribal rulers, even if they lived in a luxury prepared for them by their Chinese employees and slaves, remained 'barbarians'. Few songs and poems of theirs remain extant in translations from their language into Chinese, but these preserve a strong alien flavour in their mental attitude and in their diction. They are the songs of fighting men, songs that were sung on horseback, songs of war and its sufferings. These songs have nothing of the excessive formalism and aestheticism of the Chinese, but give expression to simple emotions in unpolished language with a direct appeal. The epic of the Turkish peoples had clearly been developed already, but Chinese sources do not mention it. We find songs which we call 'ballads'. We have many early ballads which are clearly Chinese, but should assume that the tribal rulers, too, had ballads of their own. With very few exceptions, Chinese scholars found ballads 'vulgar' and did not write them down for us. Even today, there are still in all parts of China traditional ballads, often written down in local dialect, yet just as with genuine folk songs, nobody—except a small group of Chinese and foreign folklorists—seems to be interested in them.

The actual literature, however, and the philosophy of this period are Buddhist. How can we explain that Buddhism had gained such influence? If we look into the Buddhist canon as it exists now, compiled many centuries after our period, we see many elements of Buddhism which Chinese must have detested. A real Buddhist is a monk, and a monk must 'leave the family' and live in the artificial family of his monastery. To leave one's family is still one of the most serious breaches of filial piety, China's highest ethical ideal to this century. A real Buddhist must give up sex, and Buddhist texts designed for the layman, describe sexual life in most disgusting terms. For Chinese, sex life was a natural part of life, necessary in order to preserve the family. When a Chinese saw a statue of Buddha, modelled after Indian standards of beauty, laid down in Buddhist texts, they found the figure extremely ugly and strange; they abhorred Buddha's dress which, leaving one shoulder open, was regarded as immodest. Numerous Buddhist texts and sects, spreading in these and the following centuries, preached that our world is irreal, the result of our imaginations, an idea which for the down-to-earth Chinese has remained strange to this day. Finally, the idea of sin and punishment was strange. But it had some attraction to the lower classes.

135

This doctrine was in a certain sense revolutionary: it declared that all the high officials and superiors who treated the people so unjustly and who so exploited them, would in their next reincarnation be born in poor circumstances or into inferior rank and would have to suffer punishment for all their ill deeds. The poor who had to suffer undeserved evils would be born in their next life into high rank and would have a good time. This doctrine brought a ray of light, a promise, to the country people who had suffered so much since the later Han period of the second century A.D. Of course, the doctrine was also utilized by the élite: people who are poor are suffering the just punishment for sins committed in a prior existence.

But Buddhism still had other attractions for the unsophisticated 'common man'. Chinese ancestral worship had no way to take care of people who died without children, who died far away from their home, of children or daughters who died before maturity or marriage. These beings could change into demons and become a menace to the people. Buddhists, many of whom in the first centuries were foreigners, were a different breed, they lived in a pseudo-family and thus, could take others into their houses, errant souls. They would provide masses for them and pacify them. They were also outside the Chinese circle of purity and pollution, so they could handle the dead, the corpses. Thus, to the present time, Buddhism has functioned as an institution which filled a hole in Chinese beliefs and rituals of the lower classes. These men and women knew very little of philosophical Buddhism, or even of ordinary texts. To the present time, only a few sections of some texts are generally known and recited. Ritual is more important than the word.

The merchants made use of the Buddhist monasteries as banks and warehouses. Thus they, too, were well inclined towards Buddhism and gave money and land for its temples. The temples were able to settle peasants on this land as their tenants. In those times a temple was a more reliable landlord than an individual alien, and the poorer peasants readily became temple tenants; this increased their inclination towards Buddhism.

The Indian, Sogdian, and Sinkiang monks were readily allowed to settle by the alien rulers of China, who had no national prejudice against other aliens. The monks were educated men and brought some useful knowledge from abroad. Educated Chinese were scarcely to be found, for the gentry retired to their estates, which they protected as well as they could from their alien ruler. So long as the gentry had no prospect of regaining control of the threads of political life that extended throughout China, they were not prepared to provide a class of officials and scholars for the anti-Confucian foreigners, who showed interest only in fighting and trading. Thus educated persons were needed at the courts of the alien rulers, and Buddhists were therefore engaged. These foreign Buddhists had all the important Buddhist writings translated into Chinese, and so made use of their influence at court for religious propaganda.

Big translation bureaux were set up for the preparation of these translations into Chinese, in which many copyists simultaneously took down from dictation a translation made by a 'master' with the aid of a few native helpers. The translations were not literal but were paraphrases, most of them greatly reduced in length, glosses were introduced when the translator thought fit for political or doctrinal reasons, or when he thought that in this way he could better adapt the texts to Chinese feeling.

This does not mean that every text was translated from Indian languages; especially in the later period many works appeared which came not from India but from Sogdia or Sinkiang, or had even been written in China by Sogdians or other natives of Sinkiang, and were then translated into Chinese. In Sinkiang, Khotan in particular became a centre of Buddhist culture. Buddhism was influenced by vestiges of indigenous cults, so that Khotan developed a special religious atmosphere of its own; deities were honoured there (for instance, the king of Heaven of the northerners) to whom little regard was paid elsewhere. This 'Khotan Buddhism' had special influence on the Buddhist Turkish peoples.

Buddhism, quite apart from the special case of 'Khotan Buddhism', underwent extensive modification on its way across Central Asia. Its main Indian form (Hinayana) was a purely individualistic religion of salvation without a God—related in this respect to genuine Taoism —and based on a concept of two classes of people: the monks who could achieve salvation and, second, the masses who fed the monks but could not achieve salvation. This religion did not gain a footing in China; only traces of it can be found in some Buddhistic sects in China. Mahayana Buddhism, on the other hand, developed into a true popular religion of salvation. It did not interfere with the indigenous deities and did not discountenance life in human society; it did not recommend Nirvana at once, but placed before it a hereafter with all the joys worth striving for. In this form Buddhism was certain of success in Asia. On its way from India to China it divided into countless separate streams, each characterized by a particular book. We commonly speak of Buddhist 'sects' which is a wrong term. There are philosophical differences between Buddhist sects in China, but the important point is that each Master teaches 'his' text to his disciples; when a priest is asked about his qualifications, he will give the name of his Master and his Master's Masters and transmit this wisdom, this book, to an endless chain of Masters. He would not regard a school which reads a different book with a different philosophy as 'heretic'.

The Chinese state cult, the cult of Heaven saturated with Confucianism, was another living form of religion. The alien rulers, in turn, had brought their own mixture of worship of Heaven and shamanism. Their worship of Heaven was their official 'representative' religion; their shamanism the private religion of the individual in his daily life. The alien rulers, accordingly, showed interest in the Chinese shamans as well as in shamanistic aspects of Mahayana Buddhism.

Here was an area of conflict. The folk religion which we have mentioned in an earlier chapter also contained many elements which we would call shamanistic. The folk priests resented the competition of Buddhist priests who also could work miracles. Moreover, the Buddhists, when they had to translate strange Indian terms into Chinese, had extensively used Taoist terminology, so that in the eyes of the less sophisticated, both religions were similar. The foreign rulers have often exploited this antagonism: they called in priests of both religions and let them compete in the production of miracles or simply in scholarly discussions. Some of these discussions (contained in the 'Hung-ming-chi') belong to the most fascinating pieces of early Chinese literature, such as for instance the discussion as to whether a soul exists or not. We can compare such courtly 'diversions' with similar disputes arranged by rulers in India and the West, and in all these cases, the defeated party could lose more than just an argument.

(D) THE TOBA EMPIRE IN NORTH CHINA (A.D. 385–550)

1 *The rise of the Toba state*

On the collapse of Fu Chien's empire one more state made its appearance; it has not yet been dealt with, although it was the most important one. This was the empire of the Toba, in the north of the present province of Shansi. Fu Chien had brought down the small old Toba state in 376, but had not entirely destroyed it. Its territory was partitioned, and part was placed under the administration of a Hun: in view of the old rivalry between Toba and Huns, this seemed to Fu Chien to be the best way of preventing any revival of the Toba. However, a descendant of the old ruling family of the Toba succeeded, with the aid of related families, in regaining power and forming a small new kingdom. Very soon many tribes which still lived in north China and which had not been broken up into military units, joined him. Of these there were ultimately 119, including many Hun tribes from Shansi and also many Hsien-pi tribes.

Thus the question who the Toba were is not easy to answer. The leading tribe itself had migrated southward in the third century from the frontier territory between northern Mongolia and northern Manchuria. After this migration the first Toba state, the so-called Tai state, was formed (338–376); not much is known about it. The tribes that, from 385 after the break-up of the Tibetan empire, grouped themselves round this ruling tribe, were both Turkish and Mongol; but from the culture and language of the Toba we think that the Turkish element seems to have been stronger than the Mongolian.

Thus the new Toba kingdom was a tribal state, not a military state. But the tribes were no longer the same as in the time of Liu Yüan a hundred years earlier. Their total population must have been quite small; we must assume that they were but the remains of 119 tribes rather than 119 full-sized tribes. Only part of them were still living the old nomad life; others had become used to living alongside Chinese peasants and had assumed leadership among the peasants. These Toba now faced a difficult situation. The country was arid and mountainous and did not yield much agricultural produce. For the many people who had come into the Toba state from all parts of the former empire of Fu Chien, to say nothing of the needs of a capital and a court which since the time of Liu Yüan had been regarded as the indispensable entourage of a ruler who claimed imperial rank, the local production of the Chinese peasants was not enough. All the government officials, who were Chinese, and all the slaves and eunuchs needed grain to eat. Attempts were made to settle more Chinese peasants round the new capital, but without success; something had to be done. It appeared necessary to embark on a campaign to conquer the fertile plain of eastern China. In the course of a number of battles the Hsien-pi of the 'Later Yen' were annihilated and eastern China conquered (409).

Now a new question arose: what should be done with all those people? Nomads used to enslave their prisoners and use them for watching their flocks. Some tribal chieftains had adopted the practice of establishing captives on their tribal territory as peasants. There was an opportunity now to subject the millions of Chinese captives to servitude to the various tribal chieftains in the usual way. But those captives who were peasants could not be taken away from their fields without robbing the country of its food; therefore it would have been necessary to spread the tribes over the whole of eastern China, and this would have added immensely to the strength of the various tribes and would have greatly weakened the central power. Furthermore almost all Chinese officials at the court had come originally from the territories just conquered. They had come from there about a hundred years earlier and still had all their relatives in the east. If the eastern territories had been placed under the rule of separate tribes, and the tribes had been distributed in this way, the gentry in those territories would have been destroyed and reduced to the position of enslaved peasants. The Chinese officials accordingly persuaded the Toba emperor not to place the new territories under the tribes, but to leave them to be administered by officials of the central administration. These officials must have a firm footing in their territory, for only they could extract from the peasants the grain required for the support of the capital. Consequently the Toba government did not enslave the Chinese in the eastern territory, but made the local gentry into government officials, instructing them to collect as much grain as possible for the capital. This Chinese local gentry worked in close collaboration with the Chinese officials at court, a fact which determined the whole fate of the Toba empire.

The Hsien-pi of the newly conquered east no longer belonged to any tribe, but only to military units. They were transferred as soldiers to the Toba court and placed directly under the government, which was thus notably strengthened, especially as the millions of peasants under their Chinese officials were also directly responsible to the central administration. The government now proceeded to convert also its own Toba tribes into military formations. The tribal men of noble rank were brought to the court as military officers, and so were separated from the common tribesmen and the slaves who had to remain with the herds. This change, which robbed the tribes of all means of independent action, was not carried out without bloodshed. There were revolts of tribal chieftains which were ruthlessly suppressed. The central government had triumphed, but it realized that more reliance could be placed on Chinese than on its own people, who were used to independence. Thus the Toba were glad to employ more and more Chinese, and the Chinese pressed more and more into the administration. In this process the differing social organizations of Toba and Chinese played an important part. The Chinese have patriarchal families with often hundreds of members. When a member of a family obtains a good position, he is obliged to make provision for the other members of his family and to secure good positions for them too; and not only the members of his own family but those of allied families and of families related to it by marriage. In contrast the Toba had a patriarchal nuclear family system; as nomad warriors with no fixed abode, they were unable to form extended family groups. Among them the individual was much more independent; each one tried to do his best for himself. No Toba thought of collecting a large clique around himself; everybody should be the artificer of his own fortune. Thus, when a Chinese obtained an

8 Detail from the Buddhist cave-reliefs of Lung-men.
(From a rubbing in the author's possession.)

9 Statue of Mi-lo (Maitreya, the next future Buddha), in the 'Great Buddha Temple' at Chengting (Hopei).

(Photo H. Hammer-Morrisson.)

official post, he was followed by countless others; but when a Toba had a position he remained alone, and so the sinification of the Toba empire went on incessantly.

2 *The Hun kingdom of the Hsia (407–431)*

At the rebuilding of the Toba empire, however, a good many Hun tribes withdrew westward into the Ordos region beyond the reach of the Toba, and there they formed the Hun 'Hsia' kingdom. Its ruler, Ho-lien P'o-p'o, belonged to the family of Mao Tun and originally, like Liu Yüan, bore the sinified family name Liu; but he altered this to a Hun name, taking the family name of Ho-lien. This one fact alone demonstrates that the Hsia rejected Chinese culture and were nationalistic Hun. Thus there were now two realms in north China, one undergoing progressive sinification, the other falling back to the old traditions of the Huns.

3 *Rise of the Toba to a great power*

The present province of Szechwan, in the west, had belonged to Fu Chien's empire. At the break-up of the Tibetan state, that province passed to the southern Chinese empire and gave the southern Chinese access, though it was very difficult access, to the caravan route leading to Central Asia. The small states in Kansu, which dominated the route, now passed on the traffic along two routes, one northward to the Toba and the other alien states in north China, the other through north-west Szechwan to south China. In this way the Kansu states were strengthened both economically and politically, for they were able to direct the commerce either to the northern states or to south China as suited them. When the south Chinese saw the break-up of Fu Chien's empire into numberless fragments, Liu Yü, who was then all-powerful at the south Chinese court, made an attempt to conquer the whole of western China. A great army was sent from south China into the province of Shensi, where the Tibetan empire of the 'Later Ch'in' was situated. The Ch'in appealed to the Toba for help, but the Toba were themselves too hotly engaged to be able to spare troops. They also considered that south China would be unable to maintain these conquests, and that they themselves would find them later an easy prey. Thus in 417 the state of 'Later Ch'in' received a mortal blow from the south Chinese army. Large numbers of the upper class fled to the Toba. As had been foreseen, the south Chinese were unable to maintain their hold over the conquered territory, and it was annexed with ease by the Hun Ho-lien P'o-p'o. But why not by the Toba?

Towards the end of the fourth century, vestiges of Hun, Hsien-pi, and other tribes had united in Mongolia to form the new people of

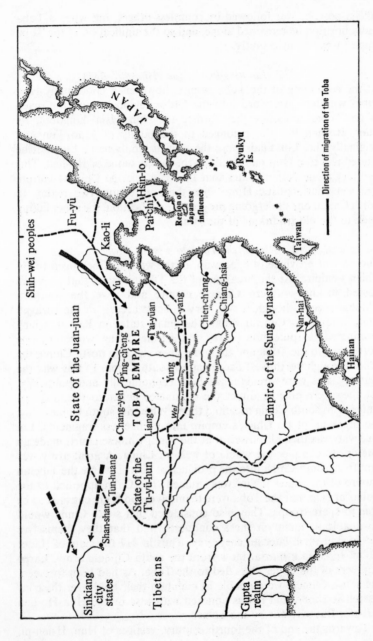

MAP 4   *The Toba empire (about A.D. 500)*

the Juan-juan (also called Ju-juan or Jou-jan). Scholars disagree as to whether the Juan-juan were Turks or Mongols; European investigators believe them to have been identical with the Avars who appeared in the Near East in 558 and later in Europe, and are inclined, on the strength of a few vestiges of their language, to regard them as Mongols. Investigations concerning the various tribes, however, show that among the Juan-juan there were both Mongol and Turkish tribes, and that the question cannot be decided in favour of either group. Some of the tribes belonging to the Juan-juan had formerly lived in China. Others had lived farther north or west and came into the history of the Far East now for the first time.

This Juan-juan people threatened the Toba in the rear, from the north. It made raids into the Toba empire for the same reasons for which the Huns in the past had raided agrarian China; for agriculture had made considerable progress in the Toba empire. Consequently, before the Toba could attempt to expand southward, the Juan-juan peril must be removed. This was done in the end, after a long series of hard and not always successful struggles. That was why the Toba had played no part in the fighting against south China, and had been unable to take immediate advantage of that fighting.

After 429 the Juan-juan peril no longer existed, and in the years that followed the whole of the small states of the west were destroyed, one after another, by the Toba—the 'Hsia kingdom' in 431, bringing down with it the 'Western Ch'in', and the 'Northern Liang' in 439. The non-Chinese elements of the population of those countries were moved northward and served the Toba as soldiers; the Chinese also, especially the remains of the Kansu 'Western Liang' state (conquered in 420), were enslaved, and some of them transferred to the north. Here again, however, the influence of the Chinese gentry made itself felt after a short time. As we know, the Chinese of 'Western Liang' in Kansu had originally migrated there from eastern China. Their eastern relatives who had come under Toba rule through the conquest of eastern China and who through their family connections with Chinese officials of the Toba empire had found safety, brought their influence to bear on behalf of the Chinese of Kansu, so that several families regained office and social standing.

Their expansion into Kansu gave the Toba control of the commerce with Sinkiang, and there are many mentions of tribute missions to the Toba court in the years that followed, some even from India. The Toba also spread in the east. And finally there was fighting with south China (430–431), which brought to the Toba empire a large part of the province of Honan with the old capital, Loyang. Thus about 440 the Toba must be described as the most powerful state in the Far East, ruling the whole of north China.

4 *Economic and social conditions*

The internal changes of which there had only been indications in the first period of the Toba empire now proceeded at an accelerated pace. There were many different factors at work. The whole of the civil administration had gradually passed into Chinese hands, the Toba retaining only the military administration. But the wars in the south called for the services of specialists in fortification and in infantry warfare, who were only to be found among the Chinese. The growing influence of the Chinese was further promoted by the fact that many Toba families were exterminated in the revolts of the tribal chieftains, and others were wiped out in the many battles. Thus the Toba lost ground also in the military administration.

The wars down to A.D. 440 had been large-scale wars of conquest, lightning campaigns that had brought in a great deal of booty. With their loot the Toba developed great magnificence and luxury. The campaigns that followed were hard and long-drawn-out struggles, especially against south China, where there was no booty, because the enemy retired so slowly that they could take everything with them. The Toba therefore began to be impoverished, because plunder was the main source of their wealth. In addition to this, their herds gradually deteriorated, for less and less use was made of them; for instance, horses were little required for the campaign against south China, and there was next to no fighting in the north. In contrast with the impoverishment of the Toba, the Chinese gentry grew not only more powerful but more wealthy.

The Toba seem to have tried to prevent this development by introducing the famous 'land equalization system' (*chün-t'ien*), one of their most important innovations. We must admit, however, that already before the Toba period, attempts had been made to give 'land to the tiller'. The direct purposes of this measure were to resettle uprooted farm population; to prevent further migrations of farmers; and to raise production and taxes. The founder of this system was Li An-shih, member of a Toba family and later husband of an imperial princess. The plan was basically accepted in 477, put into action in 485, and remained the land law until c. 750. Every man and every woman had a right to receive a certain amount of land for their lifetime. After their death, the land was redistributed. In addition to this 'personal land' there was so-called 'mulberry land' on which farmers could plant mulberries for silk production; but they also could plant other crops under the trees. This land could be inherited from father to son and was not redistributed. Incidentally we know many similar regulations for trees in the Near East and Central Asia. As the tax was levied upon the personal land in form of grain, and on the tree land in form of silk, this regulation stimulated the cultivation of diversified crops on the tree land which then was not taxable. The basic idea behind this law was, that all land belonged to the state, a concept for which the Toba could point to the ancient Chou but which also fitted well for a dynasty of conquest. The new *chün-t'ien* system required a complete land and population survey which was done in the next years. We know from much later census fragments that the government tried to enforce this equalization law, but did not always succeed; we read statements such as 'X has so and so much land; he has a claim on so and so much land and, therefore, has to get so and so much'; but there are no records that X ever received the land due to him.

One consequence of the new land law was a legal fixation of the social classes. Already during Han time (and perhaps even earlier) a distinction had been made between 'free burghers' (*liang-min*) and 'commoners' (*chien-min*). This distinction had continued as informal tradition until, now, it became a legal concept. Only 'burghers', i.e. gentry and free farmers, were real citizens with all rights of a free man. The 'commoners' were completely or partly unfree and fell under several heads. Ranking as the lowest class were the real slaves (*nu*), divided into state and private slaves. By law, slaves were regarded as pieces of property, not as members of human society. They were, however, forced to marry and thus, as a class, were probably reproducing at a rate similar to that of the normal population, while slaves in Europe reproduced at a lower rate than the population. The next higher class were serfs (*fan-hu*), hereditary state servants, usually descendants of state slaves. They were obliged to work three months during the year for the state and were paid for this service. They were not registered in their place of residence but under the control of the Ministry of Agriculture which distributed them to other offices, but did not use them for farm work. Similar in status to them were the private bondsmen (*pu-ch'ü*), hereditarily attached to gentry families. These serfs received only 50 per cent of the land which a free burgher received under the land law. Higher than these were the service families (*tsa-hu*), who were registered in their place of residence, but had to perform certain services; here we find 'tomb families' who cared for the imperial tombs, 'shepherd families', postal families, kiln families, soothsayer families, medical families, and musician families. Each of these categories of commoners had its own laws, each had to marry within the category. No intermarriage or adoption was allowed. It is interesting to observe that a similar fixation of the social status of citizens occurred in the Roman Empire from c. A.D. 300 on.

Thus in the years between 440 and 490 there were great changes not only in the economic but in the social sphere. The Toba declined in number and influence. Many of them married into rich families of the Chinese gentry and regarded themselves as no longer belonging to the Toba. In the course of time the court was completely sinified.

The Chinese at the court now formed the leading element, and they tried to persuade the emperor to claim dominion over all China, at least in theory, by installing his capital in Loyang, the old centre of China. This transfer had the advantage for them personally that the territories in which their properties were situated were close to that capital, so that the grain they produced found a ready market. And it was indeed no longer possible to rule the great Toba empire, now covering the whole of north China from north Shansi. The administrative staff was so great that the transport system was no longer able to bring in sufficient food. For the present capital did not lie on a navigable river, and all the grain had to be carted, an expensive and unsafe mode of transport. Ultimately, in 493–4, the Chinese gentry officials secured the transfer of the capital to Loyang. In the years 490 to 499 the Toba emperor Wen Ti (471–499) took further decisive steps required by the stage reached in internal development. All aliens were prohibited from using their own language in public life. Chinese became the official language. Chinese clothing and customs also become general. The system of administration which had largely followed a pattern developed by the Wei dynasty in the early third century, was changed and took a form which became the model for the T'ang dynasty in the seventh century. It is important to note that in this period, for the first time, an office for religious affairs was created which dealt mainly with Buddhistic monasteries. While after the Toba such a special office for religious affairs disappeared again, this idea was taken up later by Japan when Japan accepted a Chinese-type of administration.

Owing to his bringing up, the emperor no longer regarded himself as Toba but as Chinese; he adopted the Chinese culture, acting as he was bound to do if he meant to be no longer an alien ruler in North China. Already he regarded himself as emperor of all China, so that the south Chinese empire was looked upon as a rebel state that had to be conquered. While, however, he succeeded in everything else, the campaign against the south failed except for some local successes.

The transfer of the capital to Loyang was a blow to the Toba nobles. Their herds became valueless, for animal products could not be carried over the long distance to the new capital. In Loyang the Toba nobles found themselves parted from their tribes, living in an unaccustomed climate and with nothing to do, for all important posts were occupied by Chinese. The government refused to allow them to return to the north. Those who did not become Chinese by finding their way into Chinese families grew visibly poorer and poorer.

It is understandable that in this period of constant warfare and of great movements, the examination system by which the best qualified men should be selected for state service did not function. In the third century, a new system was developed which continued to be used for centuries, especially under the Toba. The government at first set up a system of nine ranks for families. Each family of the upper class was classified and a definite rank was assigned to them. According to that rank, the family members could move into one of the (usually) nine official ranks, i.e. the positions in the administration. The basic idea behind this was, that some families had a higher level of culture (or of social status) and were, therefore, automatically qualified. This system eliminated the recommendation system of the Han period. It led to the development of a strong feeling for family genealogy: each high-class family tried to keep their genealogy up, so that their claims to positions could not be doubted; they were proud of their status and preferred marriages between families of equal rank. The Toba nobility, of course, could easily be fitted into this system, and as conquerors, they occupied the top ranks. It seems that this system was also introduced into Japan; the complicated rank system of Japanese upper-class families of the seventh century is most easily explained, it seems, by reference to the Toba system. In fact, it seems that many traits in Japanese society and culture which were regarded as loans from the T'ang dynasty, were in fact loans from the Toba. Perhaps the Japanese rulers, whom the real Chinese always regarded as 'barbarians' felt closer to the Toba who also were 'barbarians'.

5 *Victory and retreat of Buddhism*

What we said in regard to the religious position of the other alien peoples applied also to the Toba, As soon, however, as their empire grew, they, too, needed an 'official' religion of their own. For a few years they had continued their old sacrifices to Heaven; then another course opened to them. The Toba, together with many Chinese living in the Toba empire, were all captured by Buddhism, and especially by its shamanist element. One element in their preference of Buddhism was certainly the fact that Buddhism accepted all foreigners alike—both the Toba and the Chinese were 'foreign' converts to an essentially Indian religion; whereas the Confucianist Chinese always made the non-Chinese feel that in spite of all their attempts they were still 'barbarians' and that only real Chinese could be real Confucianists.

Second, it can be assumed that the Toba rulers by fostering Buddhism intended to break the power of the Chinese gentry. A few centuries later, Buddhism was accepted by the Tibetan kings to break the power of the native nobility, by the Japanese to break the power of a federation of noble clans, and still later by the Burmese kings for the same reason. The acceptance of Buddhism by rulers in the Far East always meant also an attempt to create a more autocratic, absolutistic regime. Mahayana Buddhism, as an ideal, desired a society without clear-cut classes under one enlightened ruler; in such a society all believers could strive to attain the ultimate goal of salvation.

Throughout the early period of Buddhism in the Far East, the question had been discussed of what should be the relations between the Buddhist monks and the emperor, whether they were subject to him or not. This was connected, of course, with the fact that to the early fourth century the Buddhist monks were foreigners who, in the view prevalent in the Far East, owed only a limited allegiance to the ruler of the land. The Buddhist monks at the Toba court now submitted to the emperor, regarding him as a reincarnation of Buddha. Thus the emperor became protector of Buddhism and a sort of god. This combination was a good substitute for the old Chinese theory that the emperor was the Son of Heaven; it increased the prestige and the splendour of the dynasty. At the same time the old shamanism was legitimized under a Buddhist reinterpretation. Thus Buddhism became a sort of official religion. The emperor appointed a Buddhist monk as head of the Buddhist state church, and through this 'Pope' he conveyed endowments on a large scale to the church. T'an-yao, head of the state church since 460, induced the state to attach state slaves, i.e. enslaved family members of criminals, and their families to state temples. They were supposed to work on temple land and to produce for the upkeep of the temples and monasteries. Thus, the institution of 'temples slaves' was created, an institution which existed in South Asia and Burma for a long time, and which greatly strengthened the economic position of Buddhism.

Like all Turkish peoples, the Toba possessed a myth according to which their ancestors came into the world from a sacred grotto. The Buddhists took advantage of this conception to construct, with money from the emperor, the vast and famous cave-temple of Yünkang, in northern Shansi. If we come from the bare plains into the green river valley, we may see to this day hundreds of caves cut out of the steep cliffs of the river bank. Here monks lived in their cells, worshipping the deities of whom they had thousands of busts and reliefs sculptured in stone, some of more than life-size, some diminutive. The majestic impression made today by the figures does not correspond to their original effect, for they were covered with a layer of coloured stucco.

148

We know only few names of the artists and craftsmen who made these objects. Probably some at least were foreigners from Sinkiang, for in spite of the predominantly Chinese character of these sculptures, some of them are reminiscent of works in Sinkiang and even in the Near East. In the past the influences of the Near East on the Far East—influences traced back in the last resort to Greece—were greatly exaggerated; it was believed that Greek art, carried through Alexander's campaign as far as the present Afghanistan, degenerated there in the hands of Indian imitators (the so-called Gandhara art) and ultimately passed on in more and more distorted forms to China. Actually, however, some eight hundred years lay between Alexander's campaign and the Toba period sculptures at Yün-kang and, owing to the different cultural development, the contents of the Greek and the Toba-period art were entirely different. We may say, therefore, that suggestions came from the centre of the Greco-Bactrian culture (in the present Afghanistan) and were worked out by the Toba artists; old forms were filled with a new content, and the elements in the reliefs of Yün-kang that seem to us to be non-Chinese were the result of this synthesis of Western inspiration and Turkish initiative. It is interesting to observe that all steppe rulers showed special interest in sculpture and, as a rule, in architecture; after the Toba period, sculpture flourished in China in the T'ang period, the period of strong cultural influence from Turkish peoples, and there was a further advance of sculpture and of the cave-dwellers' worship in the period of the 'Five Dynasties' (906–960; three of these dynasties were Turkish) and in the Mongol period.

But not all Buddhists joined the 'Church', just as not all Taoists had joined the Church of Chang Ling's Taoism. Some Buddhists remained unorganized in the small towns and villages and suffered oppression from the central Church. These village Buddhist monks soon became instigators of a considerable series of attempts at revolution. Their Buddhism was of the so-called 'Maitreya school', which promised the appearance on earth of a new Buddha who would do away with all suffering and introduce a Gold Age. The Chinese peasantry, exploited by the gentry, came to the support of these monks whose Messianism gave the poor a hope in this world. The nomad tribes also, abandoned by their nobles in the capital and wandering in poverty with their now worthless herds, joined these monks. We know of many revolts of Hun and Toba tribes in this period, revolts that had a religious appearance but in reality were simply the result of the extreme impoverishment of these remaining tribes.

In addition to these conflicts between state and popular Buddhism, clashes between Buddhists and representatives of organized

Taoism occurred. Such fights, however, reflected more the power struggle between cliques than between religious groups. The most famous incident was the action against the Buddhists in 446 which brought destruction to many temples and monasteries and death to many monks. Here, a mighty Chinese gentry faction under the leadership of the Ts'ui family had united with the Taoist leader K'ou Ch'ien-chih against another faction under the leadership of the crown prince.

With the growing influence of the Chinese gentry, however, Confucianism gained ground again, until with the transfer of the capital to Loyang it gained a complete victory, taking the place of Buddhism and becoming once more as in the past the official religion of the state. This process shows us once more how closely the social order of the gentry was associated with Confucianism.

(E) SUCCESSION STATES OF THE TOBA (A.D. 550–580): NORTHERN CH'I DYNASTY, NORTHERN CHOU DYNASTY

1 Reasons for the splitting of the Toba empire

Events now pursued their logical course. The contrast between the central power, now become entirely Chinese, and the remains of the tribes who were with their herds mainly in Shansi and the Ordos region and were hopelessly impoverished, grew more and more acute. From 530 onward the risings became more and more formidable. A few Toba who still remained with their old tribes placed themselves at the head of the rebels and conquered not only the whole of Shansi but also the capital, where there was a great massacre of Chinese and pro-Chinese Toba. The rebels were driven back; in this a man of the Kao family distinguished himself, and all the Chinese and pro-Chinese gathered round him. The Kao family, which may have been originally a Hsien-pi family, had its estates in eastern China and so was closely associated with the eastern Chinese gentry, who were the actual rulers of the Toba State. In 534 this group took the impotent emperor of their own creation to the city of Yeh in the east, where he reigned *de jure* for a further sixteen years. Then he was deposed, and Kao Yang made himself the first emperor of the Northern Ch'i dynasty (550–577).

The national Toba group, on the other hand, found another man of the imperial family and established him in the west. After a short time this puppet was removed from the throne and a man of the Yü-wen family made himself emperor, founding the 'Northern Chou dynasty' (557–580). The Hsien-pi family of Yü-wen was a branch of the Hsien-pi, but was closely connected with the Huns and probably of Turkish origin. All the still existing remains of Toba tribes who had eluded sinification moved into this western empire.

The splitting of the Toba empire into these two separate realms was the result of the policy embarked on at the foundation of the empire. Once the tribal chieftains and nobles had been separated from their tribes and organized militarily, it was inevitable that the two elements should have different social destinies. The nobles could not hold their own against the Chinese; if they were not actually eliminated in one way or another, they disappeared into Chinese families. The rest, the people of the tribe, became destitute and were driven to revolt. The northern peoples had been unable to perpetuate either their tribal or their military organization, and the Toba had been equally unsuccessful in their attempt to perpetuate the two forms of organization alongside each other.

These social processes are of particular importance because the ethnic disappearance of the northern peoples in China had nothing to do with any racial inferiority or with any particular power of assimilation; it was a natural process resulting from the different economic, social, and cultural organizations of the northern peoples and the Chinese.

2 *Appearance of the (Gök) Turks*

The Toba had liberated themselves early in the fifth century from the Juan-juan peril. None of the fighting that followed was of any great importance. The Toba resorted to the old means of defence against nomads—they built great walls. Apart from that, after their move southward to Loyang, their new capital, they were no longer greatly interested in their northern territories. When the Toba empire split into the Ch'i and the Northern Chou, the remaining Juan-juan entered into treaties first with one realm and then with the other: each realm wanted to secure the help of the Juan-juan against the other.

Meanwhile there came unexpectedly to the fore in the north a people grouped round a nucleus tribe of Huns, the tribal union of the 'T'u-chüeh', that is to say the Gök Turks, who began to pursue a policy of their own under their khan. In 546 they sent a mission to the western empire, then in the making, of the Northern Chou, and created the first bonds with it, following which the Northern Chou became allies of the Turks. The eastern empire, Ch'i, accordingly made terms with the Juan-juan, but in 552 the latter suffered a crushing defeat at the hands of the Turks, their former vassals. The remains of the Juan-juan either fled to the Ch'i state or went reluctantly into the land of the Chou. Soon there was friction between the Juan-juan and the Ch'i, and in 555 the Juan-juan in that state were annihilated. In response to pressure from the Turks, the Juan-juan in the western empire of the Northern Chou were delivered up to them and killed in the same year. The Juan-juan then disappeared from the history of the Far East. They broke up into their several tribes, some of which were admitted into the Turks' tribal league. A few years later the Turks also annihilated the Ephthalites, who had been allied with the Juan-juan; this made the Turks the dominant power in Central Asia. The Ephthalites (Yet-ha, Haytal) were a mixed group which contained elements of the old Yüeh-chih and spoke an Indo-European language. Some scholars regard them as a branch of the Tocharians of Central Asia. One menace to the northern states of China had disappeared—that of the Juan-juan. Their place was taken by a much more dangerous power, the Turks.

3 The Northern Ch'i dynasty; the Northern Chou dynasty

In consequence of this development the main task of the Northern Chou state consisted in the attempt to come to some settlement with its powerful Turkish neighbours, and meanwhile to gain what it could from shrewd negotiations with its other neighbours. By means of intrigues and diplomacy it intervened with some success in the struggles in south China. One of the pretenders to the throne was given protection; he was installed in the present Hanko was a quasi-feudal lord depending on Chou, and there he founded the 'Later Liang dynasty' (555–587). In this way Chou had brought the bulk of south China under its control without itself making any real contribution to that result.

Unlike the Chinese state of Ch'i, Chou followed the old Toba tradition. Old customs were revived, such as the old sacrifice to Heaven and the lifting of the emperor on to a carpet at his accession to the throne; family names that had been sinified were turned into Toba names again, and even Chinese were given Toba names; but in spite of this the inner cohesion had been destroyed. After two centuries it was no longer possible to go back to the old nomad, tribal life. There were also too many Chinese in the country, with whom close bonds had been forged which, in spite of all attempts, could not be broken. Consequently there was no choice but to organize a state essentially similar to that of the great Toba empire.

There is just as little of importance that can be said of the internal politics of the Ch'i dynasty. The rulers of that dynasty were thoroughly repulsive figures, with no positive achievements of any sort to their credit. Confucianism had been restored in accordance with the Chinese character of the state. It was a bad time for Buddhists, and especially for the followers of the popularized Taoism. In spite of this, about A.D. 555 great new Buddhist cave-temples were created in Lung-men, near Loyang, in imitation of the famous temples of Yün-kang.

The fighting with the western empire, the Northern Chou state, still continued, and Ch'i was seldom successful. In 563 Chou made preparations for a decisive blow against Ch'i, but suffered defeat because the Turks, who had promised aid, gave none and shortly afterwards began campaigns of their own against Ch'i. In 571 Ch'i had some success in the west against Chou, but then it lost parts of its territory to the south Chinese empire, and finally in 576-7 it was defeated by Chou in a great counter-offensive. Thus for some three years all north China was once more under a single rule, though of nothing approaching the strength of the Toba at the height of their power. For in all these campaigns the Turks had played an important part, and at the end they annexed further territory in the north of Ch'i, so that their power extended far into the east.

Meanwhile intrigue followed intrigue at the court of Chou; the mutual assassinations within the ruling group were as incessant as in the last years of the great Toba empire, until the real power passed from the emperor and his Toba entourage to a Chinese family, the Yang. Yang Chien's daughter was the wife of a Chou emperor; his son was married to a girl of the Hun family Tu-ku; her sister was the wife of the father of the Chou emperor. Amid this tangled relationship in the imperial house it is not surprising that Yang Chien should attain great power. The Tu-ku were a very old family of the Hun nobility, originally the name belonged to the Hun house from which the *shan-yü* had to be descended. This family still observed the traditions of the Hun rulers, and relationship with it was regarded as an honour even by the Chinese. Through their centuries of association with aristocratically organized foreign peoples, some of the notions of nobility had taken root among the Chinese gentry; to be related with old ruling houses was a welcome means of evidencing or securing a position of special distinction among the gentry. Yang Chien gained useful prestige from his family connections. After the leading Chinese cliques had regained predominance in the Chou empire, much as had happened before in the Toba empire, Yang Chien's position was strong enough to enable him to massacre the members of the imperial family and then, in 581, to declare himself emperor. Thus began the Sui dynasty, the first dynasty that was once more to rule all China.

But what had happened to the Toba? With the ending of the Chou empire they disappeared for all time, just as the Juan-juan had done a little earlier. So far as the tribes did not entirely disintegrate, the people of the tribes seem during the last years of Toba and Chou to have joined Turkish and other tribes. In any case, nothing more is heard of them as a people, and they themselves lived on under the name of the tribe that led the new tribal league.

Most of the Toba nobility, on the other hand, became Chinese. This process can be closely followed in the Chinese annals. The tribes that had disintegrated in the time of the Toba empire broke up into families of which some adopted the name of the tribe as their family name, while others chose Chinese family names. During the centuries that followed, in some cases indeed down to modern times, these families continue to appear, often playing an important part in Chinese history.

(F) THE SOUTHERN EMPIRES

1 *Economic and social situation in the south*

During the 260 years of alien rule in north China, the picture of south China also was full of change. When in 317 the Huns had destroyed the Chinese Chin dynasty in the north, a Chin prince who normally would not have become heir to the throne declared himself, under the name Yüan Ti, the first emperor of the 'Eastern Chin dynasty' (317–419). The capital of this new southern empire adjoined the present Nanking. Countless members of the Chinese gentry had fled from the Huns at that time and had come into the southern empire. They had not done so out of loyalty to the Chinese dynasty or out of national feeling, but because they saw little prospect of attaining rank and influence at the courts of the alien rulers, and because it was to be feared that the aliens would turn the fields into pasturage, and also that they would make an end of the economic and monetary system which the gentry had evolved for their own benefit.

But the south was, of course, not uninhabited. There were already two groups living there—the old autochthonous population, consisting of Yao, Tai and Yüeh, and the earlier Chinese immigrants from the north, who had mainly arrived in the time of the Three Kingdoms, at the beginning of the third century A.D. The countless new immigrants now came into sharp conflict with the old-established earlier immigrants. Each group looked down on the other and abused it. The two immigrant groups in particular not only spoke different dialects but had developed differently in respect to manners and customs. A look for example at Taiwan in the first years after 1948 will certainly help in an understanding of this situation: analogous tensions developed between the new refugees, the old Chinese immigrants, and the native Taiwanese population. But let us return to the southern empires.

The two immigrant groups also differed economically and socially: the old immigrants were firmly established on the large properties

154

they had acquired, and dominated their tenants, who were largely autochthones; or they had engaged in large-scale commerce. In any case, they possessed capital, and more capital than was usually possessed by the gentry of the north. Some of the new immigrants, on the other hand, were military people. They came with empty hands, and they had no land. They hoped that the government would give them positions in the military administration and so provide them with means; they tried to gain possession of the government and to exclude the old settlers as far as possible. The tension was increased by the effect of the influx of Chinese in bringing more land into cultivation, thus producing a boom period such as is produced by the opening up of colonial land. Everyone was in a hurry to grab as much land as possible. There was yet a further difference between the two groups of Chinese: the old settlers had long lost touch with the remainder of their families in the north. For them, south China was the home; here were the temples of their ancestors. Their economic interests lay in the south. We also can assume that many families had intermarried with the indigenous population. For the wealthier among them, it was easy to get a beautiful native girl as a concubine, because they were able to pay a higher bridal price than the native man could pay. For the poorer ones, sometimes marriage with an indigenous woman was the only way to find an acceptable wife—the bridal price was always lower than that for a Chinese wife. Such intermarriages created ties between both groups which often turned out to be economically profitable for the Chinese. The new immigrants had left part of their families in the north under alien rule. Their interests still lay to some extent in the north. They were working for the reconquest of the north by military means; at times individuals or groups returned to the north, while others persuaded the rest of their relatives to come south. It would be wrong to suppose that there was no inter-communication between the two parts into which China had fallen. As soon as the Chinese gentry were able to regain any footing in the territories under alien rule, the official relations, often those of belligerency, proceeded alongside unofficial intercourse between individual families and family groupings, and these latter were, as a rule, in no way belligerent.

The lower stratum in the south consisted mainly of the remains of the original non-Chinese population, particularly in border and southern territories which had been newly annexed from time to time. In the centre of the southern state the way of life of the non-Chinese was very quickly assimilated to that of the Chinese, so that the aborigines were soon indistinguishable from Chinese. The remaining part of the lower class consisted of Chinese peasants. This whole lower section of the population rarely took any active and visible part in politics, except at times in the form of great popular risings.

Until the third century, the south had been of no great economic importance, in spite of the good climate and the extraordinary fertility of the Yangtze valley. The country had been too thinly settled, and the indigenous population had not become adapted to organized trade. After the move southward of the Chin dynasty the many immigrants had made the country of the lower Yangtze more thickly populated, but not over-populated. The top-heavy court with more than the necessary number of officials (because there was still hope for a reconquest of the north which would mean many new jobs for administrators) was a great consumer; prices went up and stimulated local rice production. The estates of the southern gentry yielded more than before, and naturally much more than the small properties of the gentry in the north where, moreover, the climate is far less favourable. Thus the southern landowners were able to acquire great wealth, which ultimately made itself felt in the capital.

One very important development was characteristic in this period in the south, although it also occurred in the north. Already in pre-Han times, some rulers had gardens with fruit trees. The Han emperors had large hunting parks which were systematically stocked with rare animals; they also had gardens and hot-houses for the production of vegetables for the court. These 'gardens' (*yüan*) were often called 'manors' (*pieh-yeh*) and consisted of fruit plantations with luxurious buildings. We hear soon of water-cooled houses for the gentry, of artificial ponds for pleasure and fish breeding, artificial water-courses, artificial mountains, bamboo groves, and parks with parrots, ducks, and large animals. Here, the wealthy gentry of both north and south, relaxed from government work, surrounded by their friends and by women. These manors grew up in the hills, on the 'village commons' where formerly the villagers had collected their firewood and had grazed their animals. Thus, the village commons begin to disappear. The original farmland was taxed, because it produced one of the two products subject to taxation, namely grain or mulberry leaves for silk production. But the village common had been and remained tax-free because it did not produce taxable things. While land-holdings on the farmland were legally restricted in their size, the 'gardens' were unrestricted. Around A.D. 500 the ruler allowed high officials to have manors of three hundred *mou* size, while in the north a family consisting of husband and wife and children below fifteen years of age were allowed a farm of sixty *mou* only; but we hear of manors which were many times larger than the allowed size of three hundred. These manors began to play an important economic role, too: they were cultivated by tenants and produced fish, vegetables, fruit and bamboo for the market, thus they gave more income than ordinary rice or wheat land.

With the creation of manors the total amount of land under cultivation increased, though not the amount of grain-producing land. We gain the impression that from about the third century A.D. on to the eleventh century the intensity of cultivation was generally lower than in the period before.

The period from c. A.D. 300 on also seems to be the time of the second change in Chinese dietary habits. The first change occurred probably between 400 and 100 B.C. when the meat-eating Chinese reduced their meat intake greatly, gave up eating beef and mutton and changed over to some pork and dog meat. This first change was the result of increase of population and decrease of available land for pasturage. Cattle breeding in China was then reduced to the minimum of one cow or water-buffalo per farm for ploughing. Wheat was the main staple for the masses of the people. Between A.D. 300 and 600 rice became the main staple in the southern states although, theoretically, wheat could have been grown and some wheat probably was grown in the south. The vitamin and protein deficiencies which this change from wheat to rice brought forth, were made up by higher consumption of vegetables, especially beans, and partially also by eating of fish and sea food. In the north, rice became the staple food of the upper class, while wheat remained the main food of the lower classes. However, new forms of preparation of wheat, such as dumplings of different types, were introduced. The foreign rulers consumed more meat and milk products. Chinese never in their history used milk, except during periods of foreign rule, when milk products like yoghurt were sometimes used. It seems that to this day, many Chinese lack the enzyme which is necessary for an adult in order to digest milk. A change seems to be beginning now, when the consumption of ice-cream has greatly increased and when children are given milk after the weaning period and into adolescence. In most cases, the enzyme then continues to be produced. This trait, which has often been regarded as a genetic particularity seems, after all, to be socially conditioned.

2 Struggles between cliques under the Eastern Chin dynasty (A.D. 317–419)

The officials immigrating from the north regarded the south as colonial country, and so as more or less uncivilized. They went into its provinces in order to get rich as quickly as possible, and they had no desire to live there for long: they had the same dislike of a provincial existence as had the families of the big landowners. Thus as a rule the bulk of the families remained in the capital, close to the court. Thither the products accumulated in the provinces were sent, and they found a ready sale, as the capital was also a great and long-established trading centre with a rich merchant class. Thus in the capital there was every conceivable luxury and every refinement of civilization. The people of the gentry class, who were maintained in the capital by relatives serving in the provinces as governors or senior officers, themselves held offices at court, though these gave them little to do. They had time at their disposal, and made use of it—in much worse intrigues than ever before, but also in music and poetry and in the social life of the harems. There is no question at all that the highest refinement of the civilization of the Far East between the fourth and the sixth century was to be found in south China, but the accompaniments of this over-refinement were terrible.

We cannot enter into all the intrigues recorded at this time. The details are, indeed, historically unimportant. They were concerned only with the affairs of the court and its entourage. Not a single ruler of the Eastern Chin dynasty possessed personal or political qualities of any importance. The rulers' power was extremely limited because, with the exception of the founder of the state, Yüan Ti, who had come rather earlier, they belonged to the group of the new immigrants, and so had no firm footing and were therefore caught at once in the net of the newly regrouping gentry class.

To the present time, cliques have existed, but as the period of the southern dynasties is perhaps the period of Chinese history in which cliques were best developed and most powerful, it may be the place to discuss briefly their structure. Basically, they consist of members of two classes. Their leaders are of the gentry. One strong family with a material background and an intelligent head, begins to form his clique. He does this once by contracting marriages for his sons and daughters. The sons have to get brides from other families who the father thinks will join him in the struggle for power and who are already of importance or wealth. The daughters are given to families who are already close to the leader. If possible and necessary, several marriage bonds with these families are created in order to fasten the ties. These families then form the 'inner circle' of the forming clique. They, in turn, have already marriage relations with a circle of other families, and they may be induced to join the clique. The next step then is, to bring as many sons, cousins, nephews and in-laws into position in the government. We can assume that at the time of the formation of the clique, the leading family at least, already had several members in the government. An important move then is to give the emperor a daughter, or if there is no suitable one available, to give him a girl from a lower-class family, which in turn depends upon the gentry family, as concubine. These women bring into the palace their servants, and these again may act as spies, reporting on the activities of the emperor and other officials; they may also directly influence the emperor. And if they gained the favour of the ruler and had a son from him, their influence would be very strong. The lower-class members of the clique consisted of bondsmen, servants, advisers, teachers of the leading families. They could contact persons of the same status within the families belonging to the clique, but could also do more secret jobs, such as offer bribes to influential persons whose favours were needed; they could, if necessary, kill enemies of the clique. They had, in general, to do the 'dirty jobs' for their masters. The aim of all these cliques was to gain power, if possible supreme power, and to keep power. The wider the network of a clique was, the safer it was; if a political move failed, they could still save at least the lives of most of their members, and always some part of their wealth, so that a resuscitation in the future was possible, if the other members of the clique remained faithful. Within the clique, there were, of course, also fights for power, and such fights could break up the clique. Thus, not all cliques had a long life.

In later centuries, the constitution of cliques changed: not all members were related to one another or tied to one another by intrigues which they had started in common. Now, clique members could be persons who had been together in school, or persons who lived in the same hometown and had properties in the same area. It seems that these changes made the later cliques less long-living and more changeable.

When today Chinese discuss politics, they still regard the cliques as the most important factor and first try to find out who belongs to which clique and what are his ties to the leader of the clique. From this basis they try to analyse their political moves. That means, they do not pay much attention to the proclaimed ideological or other goals of those in power or aiming at power, in contrast to Western observers who take the proclamations much more seriously and tend to believe that political actions were taken because of an ideological, economic or other goal which is to be realized in the future.

The emperor Yüan Ti lived to see the first great rising. This rising (under Wang Tun) started in the region of the present Hankow, a region that today is one of the most important in China; it was already a centre of special activity. To it lead all the trade routes from the western provinces of Szechwan and Kweichow and from the central provinces of Hupei, Hunan, and Kiangsi. Normally the traffic from those provinces comes down the Yangtze, and thus in practice this region is united with that of the lower Yangtze, the environment of Nanking, so that Hankow might just as well have been the capital as Nanking. For this reason, in the period with which we are now concerned the region of the present Hankow was several times the place of origin of great risings whose aim was to gain control of the whole of the southern empire.

Wang Tun had grown rich and powerful in this region; he also had near relatives at the imperial court; so he was able to march against the capital. The emperor in his weakness was ready to abdicate but died before that stage was reached. His son, however, defeated Wang Tun with the aid of General Yü Liang (A.D. 323). Yü Liang was the empress's brother; he, too, came from a northern family. Yüan Ti's successor also died early, and the young son of Yü Liang's sister came to the throne as Emperor Ch'eng (326–342); his mother ruled as regent, but Yü Liang carried on the actual business of government. Against this clique rose Su Chün, another member of the northern gentry, who had made himself leader of a bandit gang in A.D. 300 but had then been given a military command by the dynasty. In 328 he captured the capital and kidnapped the emperor, but then fell before the counterthrust of the Yü Liang party. The domination of Yü Liang's clique continued after the death of the twenty-one-year-old emperor. His twenty-year-old brother was set in his place; he, too, died two years later, and his two-year-old son became emperor (Mu Ti, 345–361).

Meanwhile this clique was reinforced by the very important Huan family. This family came from the same city as the imperial house and was a very old gentry family of that city. One of the family attained a high post through personal friendship with Yü Liang: on his death his son Huan Wen came into special prominence as military commander.

Huan Wen, like Wang Tun and others before him, tried to secure a firm foundation for his power, once more in the west. In 347 he reconquered Szechwan and deposed the local dynasty. Following this, Huan Wen and the Yü family undertook several joint campaigns against northern states—the first reaction of the south against the north, which in the past had always been the aggressor. The first fighting took place directly to the north, where the collapse of the 'Later Chao' seemed to make intervention easy. The main objective was the regaining of the regions of eastern Honan, northern Anhwei and Kiangsu, in which were the family seats of Huan's and the emperor's families, as well as that of the Hsieh family which also formed an important group in the court clique. The purpose of the northern campaigns was not, of course, merely to defend private interests of court cliques: the northern frontier was the weak spot of the southern empire, for its plains could easily be overrun. It was then observed that the new 'Earlier Ch'in' state was trying to spread from the north-west eastward into this plain, and Ch'in was attacked in an attempt to gain a more favourable frontier territory. These expeditions brought no important practical benefit to the south; and they were not embarked on with full force, because there was only the one court clique at the back of them, and that not whole-heartedly, since it was too much taken up with the politics of the court.

Huan Wen's power steadily grew in the period that followed. He sent his brothers and relatives to administer the regions along the upper Yangtze, those fertile regions were the basis of his power. In 371 he deposed the reigning emperor and appointed in his place a frail old prince who died a year later, as required, and was replaced by a child. The time had now come when Huan Wen might have ascended the throne himself, but he died. None of his family could assemble as much power as Huan Wen had done. The equality of strength of the Huan and the Hsieh saved the dynasty for a time.

In 383 came the great assault of the Tibetan Fu Chien against the south. As we know, the defence was carried out more by the methods of diplomacy and intrigue than by military means, and it led to the disaster in the north already described. The successes of the southern state especially strengthened the Hsieh family, whose generals had come to the fore. The emperor (Hsiao Wu Ti, 373–396), who had come to the throne as a child, played no part in events at any time during his reign. He occupied himself occasionally with Buddhism, and otherwise only with women and wine. He was followed by his five-year-old son. At this time there were some changes in the court clique. In the Huan family Huan Hsüan, a son of Huan Wen, came especially into prominence. He parted from the Hsieh family, which had been closest to the emperor, and united with the Wang (the empress's) and Yin families. The Wang, an old Shansi family, had already provided two empresses, and was therefore strongly represented at court. The Yin had worked at first with the Hsieh, especially as the two families came from the same region, but afterwards the Yin went over to Huan Hsüan. At first this new clique had success, but later one of its generals, Liu Lao-chih, went over to the Hsieh clique, and its power declined. Wang Kung was killed, and Yin Chung-k'an fell away from Huan Hsüan and was killed by him in 399. Huan Hsüan himself, however, held his own in the regions loyal to him. Liu Lao-chih had originally belonged to the Hsieh clique, and his family came from a region not far from that of the Hsieh. He was very ambitious, however, and always took the side which seemed most to his own interest. For a time he joined Huan Hsüan; then he went over to the Hsieh, and finally returned to Huan Hsüan in 402 when the latter reached the height of his power. At that moment Liu Lao-chih was responsible for the defence of the capital from Huan Hsüan, but instead he passed over to him. Thus Huan Hsüan conquered the capital, deposed the emperor, and began a dynasty of his own. Then came the reaction, led by an earlier subordinate of Liu Lao-chih, Liu Yü. It may be assumed that these two army commanders were in some way related, though the two branches of their family must have been long separated. Liu Yü had distinguished himself especially in the suppression of a great popular rising which, around the year 400, had brought wide stretches of Chinese territory under the rebels' power, beginning with the southern coast. This rising was the first in the south. It was led by members of a secret society which was a direct continuation of the 'Yellow Turbans' of the latter part of the second century A.D. and of organized church-Taoism. The whole course of this rising of the exploited and ill-treated lower classes was very similar to that of the popular rising of the 'Yellow Turbans'. The movement spread as far as the neighbourhood of Canton, but in the end it was suppressed, mainly by Liu Yü.

Through these achievements Liu Yü's military power and political influence steadily increased; he became the exponent of all the cliques working against the Huan clique. He arranged for his supporters to dispose of Huan Hsüan's chief collaborators; and then, in 404, he himself marched on the capital. Huan Hsüan had to flee, and in his flight he was killed in the upper Yangtze region. The emperor was restored to his throne, but he had as little to say as ever, for the real power was Liu Yü's.

Before making himself emperor, Liu Yü began his great northern campaign, aimed at the conquest of the whole of western China. The Toba had promised to remain neutral, and in 415 he was able to conquer the 'Later Ch'in' in Shensi. The first aim of this campaign was to make more accessible the trade routes to Central Asia, which up to now had led through the difficult mountain passes of Szechwan; to this end treaties of alliance had been concluded with the states in Kansu against the 'Later Ch'in'. In the second place, this war was intended to increase Liu Yü's military strength to such an extent that the imperial crown would be assured to him; and finally he hoped to cut the claws of pro-Huan Hsüan elements in the 'Later Ch'in' kingdom who, for the sake of the link with Sinkiang, had designs on Szechwan.

3 The Liu-Sung dynasty (A.D. 420–478) and the Southern Ch'i dynasty (479–501)

After his successes in 416–417 in Shensi, Liu Yü returned to the capital, and shortly after he lost the chief fruits of his victory to Ho-lien P'o-p'o, the Hun ruler in the north, while Liu Yü himself was occupied with the killing of the emperor (419) and the installation of a puppet. In 420 the puppet had to abdicate and Liu Yü became emperor. He called his dynasty the Sung dynasty, but to distinguish it from another and more famous Sung dynasty of later time his dynasty is also called the Liu-Sung dynasty.

The struggles and intrigues of cliques against each other continued as before. We shall pass quickly over this period after a glance at the nature of these internal struggles.

Part of the old imperial family and its following fled northwards from Liu Yü and surrendered to the Toba. There they agitated for a campaign of vengeance against south China, and they were supported at the court of the Toba by many families of the gentry with landed interests in the south. Thus long-continued fighting started between Sung and Toba, concerned mainly with the domains of the deposed imperial family and its following. This fighting brought little success to south China, and about 450 it produced among the Toba an economic and social crisis that brought the wars to a temporary close. In this pause the Sung turned to the extreme south, and tried to gain influence there and in Annam. The merchant class and the gentry families of the capital who were allied with it were those chiefly interested in this expansion.

About 450 began the Toba policy of shifting the central government to the region of the Yellow river, to Loyang; for this purpose the frontier had to be pushed farther south. Their great campaign brought the Toba in 450 down to the Yangtze. The Sung suffered a heavy defeat; they had to pay tribute, and the Toba annexed parts of their northern territory.

The Sung emperors who followed were as impotent as their predecessors and personally much more repulsive. Nothing happened at court but drinking, licentiousness, and continual murders.

From 460 onward there were a number of important risings of princes; in some of them the Toba had a hand. They hoped by supporting one or another of the pretenders to gain overlordship over the whole of the southern empire. In these struggles in the south the Hsiao family, thanks mainly to General Hsiao Tao-ch'eng, steadily gained in power, especially as the family was united by marriage with the imperial house. In 477 Hsiao Tao-ch'eng finally had the emperor killed by an accomplice, the son of a shamaness; he set a boy on the throne and made himself regent. Very soon after this the boy emperor and all the members of the imperial family were murdered, and Hsiao Tao-ch'eng created the 'Southern Ch'i' dynasty (479–501). Once more the remaining followers of the deposed dynasty fled northward to the Toba, and at once fighting between Toba and the south began again.

This fighting ended with a victory for the Toba and with the final establishment of the Toba in the new capital of Loyang. South China was heavily defeated again and again, but never finally conquered. There were intervals of peace. In the years between 480 and 490 there was less disorder in the south, at all events in internal affairs. Princes were more often appointed to governorships, and the influence of the cliques was thus weakened. In spite of this, a stable regime was not built up, and in 494 a prince rose against the youthful emperor. This prince, with the help of his clique including the Ch'en family, which later attained importance, won the day, murdered the emperor, and became emperor himself. All that is recorded about him is that he fought unsuccessfully against the Toba, and that he had the whole of his own family killed out of fear that one of its members might act exactly as he had done. After his death there were conflicts between the emperor's few remaining relatives; in these the Toba again had a hand. The victor was a person named Hsiao Yen; he removed the reigning emperor in the usual way and made himself emperor. Although he belonged to the imperial family, he altered the name of the dynasty, and reigned from 502 as the first emperor of the 'Liang dynasty'.

4 *The Liang dynasty (A.D. 503–556)*

The fighting with the Toba continued until 515. As a rule the Toba were the more successful, not least through the aid of princes of the deposed 'Southern Ch'i dynasty' and their followers. Wars began also in the west, where the Toba tried to cut off the access of the Liang to the caravan routes to Sinkiang. In 507, however, the Toba suffered an important defeat. The southern states had tried at all times to work with the Kansu states against the northern states; the Toba now followed suit and allied themselves with a large group of native chieftains of the south, whom they incited to move against the Liang. This produced great native unrest, especially in the provinces by the upper Yangtze. The natives, who were steadily pushed back by the Chinese peasants, were reduced to migrating into the mountain country or to working for the Chinese in semi-servile conditions; and they were ready for revolt and very glad to work with the Toba. The result of this unrest was not decisive, but it greatly reduced the strength of the regions along the upper Yangtze. Thus the main strength of the southern state was more than ever confined to the Nanking region.

The first emperor of the Liang dynasty, who assumed the name Wu Ti (502–549), became well known in the Western world owing to his love of literature and of Buddhism. After he had come to the throne with the aid of his followers, he took no further interest in politics; he left that to his court clique. From now on, however, the political initiative really belonged to the north. At this time there began in the Toba empire the risings of tribal leaders against the government which we have fully described above. One of these leaders, Hou Ching, who had become powerful as a military leader in the north, tried in 547 to conclude a private alliance with the Liang to strengthen his own position. At the same time the ruler of the northern state of the 'Northern Ch'i', then in process of formation, himself wanted to negotiate an alliance with the Liang, in order to be able to get rid of Hou Ching. There was indecision in Liang. Hou Ching, who had been getting into difficulties, now negotiated with a dissatisfied prince in Liang, invaded the country in 548 with the prince's aid, captured the capital in 549, and killed Emperor Wu. Hou Ching now staged the usual spectacle: he put a puppet on the imperial throne, deposed him eighteen months later and made himself emperor.

This man of the Toba on the throne of south China was unable, however, to maintain his position; he had not sufficient backing. He was at war with the new rulers in the northern empire, and his own army, which was not very large, melted away; above all, he proceeded with excessive harshness against the helpers who had gained access for him to the Liang, and thereafter he failed to secure a following from among the leading cliques at court. In 552 he was driven out by a Chinese army led by one of the princes and was killed.

The new emperor had been a prince in the upper Yangtze region, and his closest associates were engaged there. They did not want to move to the distant capital, Nanking, because their private financial interests would have suffered. The emperor therefore remained in the city now called Hankow. He left the eastern territory in the hands of two powerful generals, one of whom belonged to the Ch'en family, which he no longer had the strength to remove. In this situation the generals in the east made themselves independent, and this naturally produced tension at once between the east and the west of the Liang empire; this tension was now exploited by the leaders of the Chou state then in the making in the north. On the invitation of a clique in the south and with its support, the Chou invaded the present province of Hupei and in 555 captured the Liang emperor's capital. They were now able to achieve their old ambition: a prince of the Chou dynasty was installed as a feudatory of the north, reigning until 587 in the present Hankow. He was permitted to call his quasi-feudal territory a kingdom and his dynasty, as we know already, the 'Later Liang dynasty'.

5 The Ch'en dynasty (A.D. 557–588) and its ending by the Sui

The more important of the independent generals in the east, Ch'en Pa-hsien, installed a shadow emperor, forced him to abdicate, and made himself emperor. The Ch'en dynasty which thus began was even feebler than the preceding dynasties. Its territory was confined to the lower Yangtze valley. Once more cliques and rival pretenders were at work and prevented any sort of constructive home policy. Abroad, certain advantages were gained in north China over the Northern Ch'i dynasty, but none of any great importance.

Meanwhile in the north, Yang Chien had brought into power the Chinese Sui dynasty. It began by liquidating the quasi-feudal state of the 'Later Liang'. Then followed, in 588–589, the conquest of the Ch'en empire, almost without any serious resistance. This brought all China once more under united rule, and a period of 360 years of division was ended.

6 Cultural achievements of the south

For nearly three hundred years the southern empire had witnessed unceasing struggles between powerful cliques, making impossible any peaceful development within the country. Culturally, however, the period was rich in achievement. The court and the palaces of wealthy members of the gentry attracted scholars and poets, and the gentry themselves had time for artistic occupations. A large number of the best-known Chinese poets appeared in this period, and their works plainly reflect the conditions of that time: they are poems for the small circle of scholars among the gentry and for cultured patrons, spiced with quotations and allusions, elaborate in metre and construction, masterpieces of aesthetic sensitivity—but unintelligible except to highly educated members of the aristocracy. The works were of the most artificial type, far removed from all natural feeling.

An exception is T'ao Ch'ien (T'ao Yüan-ming, 372?–427), who retreated to his villa after a rather unsuccessful career and composed poems which are simple and full of a real appreciation of landscape and nature. Modern historians of literature praise him highly as a precursor of modern poetry. He is also credited with a collection of short stories about miraculous or curious happenings, the continuation of an earlier similar collection by Kan Pao. Such collections, which later became more and more common, are valuable sources of folk traditions and beliefs, for the Chinese reader they serve as entertainment. Some collections of this period have a Buddhist tinge and tell of ghosts who take revenge for wrongs they had suffered during their human life, and of the punishment of others for sins committed. As in all Chinese literature, the moral tone is strong, but they still provided a diversion, as we today may feel when reading a detective story. In this period, there was a feverish activity of Buddhists in translating holy texts from Indian or Central Asian sources. Some of these texts were highly sophisticated and brought to China the fundamentals of the Indian system of logic and philology. Others had a different purpose. The so-called 'Jataka' are entertaining stories, usually stories of the past in which Buddha and/or some of his disciples in an earlier incarnation play the main role. These stories, too, are moralistic, but highly entertaining, because they introduced into China famous folktales and fables of India.

As in other Buddhist countries, the stories were used by monks to make their sermons more interesting or to illuminate a moral rule by a story. It is very interesting that many animal tales—for which India is famous—came to China, but in the course of time were eliminated again, so that today China has few animal tales, i.e. tales in which animals interact with other animals (not with humans). The reason for this seems to be that for a Chinese animals cannot talk; thus, such stories are untrue, and one should not tell children lies. If an animal talks to a man, the animal then is not a real animal but a ghost or spirit, and ghosts and spirits are believed to exist and to be able to speak in human language.

Ideologically, the gentry of the south was still Confucian, in the sense that they claimed to adhere to the rules of behaviour that were expected, and that they performed the ceremonies prescribed. But they were much more fascinated by Buddhism. While the so-called 'Mahayana' schools of Buddhism were most widely spread, in the south 'Hinayana' schools flourished, and a special importance was gained by the meditative schools which we later call with the Japanese name of Zen (Chinese: Ch'an). These meditative schools were close ideologically to the original Taoism, highly individualistic, not interested in society or life in society, only in the perfection of the self and the attainment of higher levels of insight.

Others took to the more common schools and tried to make up for their evil deeds by rich gifts to the monasteries. Many emperors in this period, especially Wu Ti of the Liang dynasty, inclined to Buddhism. Wu Ti turned to it especially in his old age, when he was shut out entirely from the tasks of a ruler and was no longer satisfied with the usual pleasures of the court. Several times he instituted Buddhist ceremonies of purification on a large scale in the hope of so securing forgiveness for the many murders he had committed.

Music, too, was never so assiduously cultivated as at this time. But the old Chinese music disappeared in the south as in the north, where dancing troupes and women musicians in the Sodgian commercial colonies of the province of Kansu established the music of Central Asia. Here in the south, native courtesans brought the aboriginal, non-Chinese music to the court; Chinese poets wrote songs in Chinese for this music, and so the old Chinese music became unfashionable and was forgotten.

Although, as we have mentioned, houses of prostitution existed, the gentry did not visit them and—during many periods of China's history—were not allowed to visit them. Instead, they bought courtesans from slave markets or houses of prostitution and kept them not as concubines but as house entertainers to enliven their parties.

Principal dynasties of north and south China

North and south

Western Chin dynasty (A.D. 265–317)

North		South	
1. Earlier Chao (Hsiung-nu)	304–329	1. Eastern Chin (Chinese)	
2. Later Chao (Hsiung-nu)	328–329		317–419
3. Earlier Ch'in (Tibetans)	351–394		
4. Later Ch'in (Tibetans)	384–417		
5. Western Ch'in (Hsiung-nu)			
	385–431		
6. Earlier Yen (Hsien-pi)	352–370		
7. Later Yen (Hsien-pi)	384–409		
8. Western Yen (Hsien-pi)	384–395		
9. Southern Yen (Hsien-pi)	398–410		
10. Northern Yen (Hsien-pi)	409–436		
11. Tai (Toba)	338–376		
12. Earlier Liang (Chinese)	313–376		
13. Northern Liang (Hsiung-nu)			
	397–439		
14. Western Lian (Chinese?)	400–421		
15. Later Liang (Tibetans)	386–403		
16. Southern Liang (Hsien-pi)	379–414		
17. Hsia (Hsiung-nu)	407–431		
18. Toba (Turks)	385–550		
		2. Liu-Sung	420–478
		3. Southern Ch'i	479–501
19. Northern Ch'i (Chinese?)	550–576	4. Liang	502–556
20. Northern Chou (Toba)	557–579	5. Ch'en	557–588
21. Sui (Chinese)	580–618	6. Sui	580–618

CHAPTER EIGHT

Climax and Downfall of the Imperial Gentry (A.D. 580–950)

These 370 years brings us to the most glorious period of China's history, the time when China reached its greatest extension before the eighteenth century, when China became known to the Western world as a centre of civilization. To this day, Chinese in some parts of the world still call themselves 'T'ang-jen', people of the T'ang (dynasty). This is at the same time the climax of gentry society. The rule of northern tribal federations with their strong ideas of aristocracy and nobility, had its influence upon the Chinese gentry and we will see this in the following chapters. But after three hundred years of glory, a new world began to emerge, in which the gentry as we knew it disintegrated and disappeared to make room for a gentry of different type and a different society. It is always somewhat arbitrary to cut history into periods, and the last seventy or so years of this period can be and have been regarded as the period of the emergence of the new society or as the end of the old one.

(A) THE SUI DYNASTY (A.D. 580–618)

1 Internal situation in the newly unified empire

The last of the northern dynasties, the Northern Chou, had been brought to an end by Yang Chien: rapid campaigns had made an end of the remaining petty states, and thus the Sui dynasty had come into power. China, reunited after 360 years, was again under Chinese rule. This event brought about a new epoch in the history of the Far East. But the happenings of 360 years could not be wiped out by a change of dynasty. The short Sui period can only be described as a period of transition to unified forms.

In the last resort the union of the various parts of China proceeded from the north. The north had always, beyond question, been militarily superior, because its ruling class had consisted of warlike peoples. Yet it was not a northerner who had united China but a Chinese who was closely related to the northern peoples. His wife, the jealous empress, was from the Tu-ku family, the noble family from which tribal leaders had come again and again. The rule, however, of the actual northern peoples was at an end. The start of the Sui dynasty, while the Chou still held the north, was evidence, just like the emergence in the north-east some thirty years earlier of the Northern Ch'i dynasty, that the Chinese gentry with their land-owning basis had gained the upper hand over the warrior nomads.

The Chinese gentry had not come unchanged out of that struggle. Culturally they had taken over many things from the foreigners, beginning with music and the style of their clothing, in which they had entirely adopted the northern pattern, and including other elements of daily life. Among the gentry were now many formerly alien families who had gradually become entirely Chinese. On the other hand, the foreigners' feudal outlook had influenced the gentry, so that a sense of distinctions of rank had developed among them. There were Chinese families who regarded themselves as superior to the rest, just as had been the case among the northern peoples, and who married only among themselves or with the ruling house and not with ordinary families of the gentry. They paid great attention to their genealogies, had the state keep records of them and insisted that the dynastic histories mentioned their families and their main family members. Lists of prominent gentry families were set up which mentioned the home of each clan, so that pretenders could easily be detected. Genealogies, all over the world, are documents to the glory of a family; they are not strictly honest. Misbegotten sons were omitted—daughters and wives seldom mentioned at all; if a family member was punished for a crime and banished, the fact was either not mentioned or couched in special, unclear language. Yet, for the research in Chinese social history, they are, if used with caution, one of the most important 'unofficial', i.e. not government-sponsored, sources. The rules of giving personal names were changed so that it became possible to identify a person's genealogical position within the family. At the same time the contempt of the military underwent modification; the gentry were even ready to take over high military posts, and also to profit by them.

The new Sui empire found itself faced with many difficulties. During the three and a half centuries of division, north and south had developed in different ways. They no longer spoke the same language in everyday life (we distinguish to this day between a Nanking and Peking 'High Chinese', to say nothing of dialects). The social and economic structures were very different in the two parts of the country. How could unity be restored in these things?

170

Then there was the problem of population. The north-eastern plain had always been thickly populated; it had early come under Toba rule and had been able to develop further. The region round the old northern capital Ch'ang-an, on the other hand, had suffered greatly from the struggles before the Toba period and had never entirely recovered. Meanwhile, in the south the population had greatly increased in the region north of Nanking, while the regions south of the Yangtze and the upper Yangtze valley were more thinly peopled. The real south, i.e. the modern provinces of Fukien, Kwangtung and Kwangsi, was still underdeveloped, mainly because of the malaria there. In the matter of population the north unquestionably remained prominent.

The founder of the Sui dynasty, known by his reign name of Wen Ti (589–604), came from the west, close to Ch'ang-an. There he and his following had their extensive domains. Owing to the scanty population there and the resulting shortage of agricultural labourers, these properties were very much less productive than the small properties in the north-east. This state of things was well known in the south, and it was expected, with good reason, that the government would try to transfer parts of the population to the north-west, in order to settle a peasantry round the capital for the support of its greatly increasing staff of officials, and to satisfy the gentry of the region. This produced several revolts in the south.

As an old soldier who had long been a subject of the Toba, Wen Ti had no great understanding of theory: he was a practical man. He was anti-intellectual and emotionally attached to Buddhism; he opposed Confucianism for emotional reasons and believed that it could give him no serviceable officials of the sort he wanted. He demanded from his officials the same obedience and sense of duty as from his soldiers; and he was above all thrifty, almost miserly, because he realized that the finances of his state could only be brought into order by the greatest exertions. The budget had to be drawn up for the vast territory of the empire without any possibility of saying in advance whether the revenues would come in and whether the transport of dues to the capital would function.

This cautious calculation was entirely justified, but it aroused great opposition. Both east and south were used to a much better style of living; yet the gentry of both regions were now required to cut down their consumption. On top of this they were excluded from the conduct of political affairs. In the past, under the Northern Ch'i empire in the north-east and under the Ch'en empire in the south, there had been thousands of positions at court in which the whole of the gentry could find accommodation of some kind. Now the central government was far in the west, and other people were its administrators.

171

In the past the gentry had had a profitable and easily accessible market for their produce in the neighbouring capital; now the capital was far away, entailing long-distance transport at heavy risk with little profit.

The dissatisfied circles of the gentry in the north-east and in the south incited Prince Kuang to rebellion. The prince and his followers murdered the emperor and set aside the heir-apparent; and Kuang came to the throne, assuming the name of Yang Ti. His first act was to transfer the capital back to the east, to Loyang, close to the grain-producing regions. His second achievement was to order the construction of great canals, to facilitate the transport of grain to the capital and to provide a valuable new market for the producers in the north-east and the south. It was at this time that the first fore-runner of the famous 'Imperial Canal' was constructed, the canal that connects the Yangtze with the Yellow river. Small canals, connecting various streams, had long been in existence, so that it was possible to travel from north to south by water, but these canals were not deep enough or broad enough to take large freight barges. There are records of lighters of 500 and even 800 tons capacity! These are dimensions unheard of in the West in those times. In addition to a serviceable canal to the south, Yang Ti made another that went north almost to the present Peking.

Hand in hand with these successes of the north-eastern and southern gentry went strong support for Confucianism, and a reor-ganization of the Confucian examination system. As a rule, however, the examinations were a mere formality; the various governors were ordered each to send annually to the capital three men with the required education, for whose quality they were held personally responsible; merchants and artisans were expressly excluded.

2 Relations with the Turks and with Korea

In foreign affairs an extraordinarily fortunate situation for the Sui dynasty had come into existence. The T'u-chüeh, the Turks, much the strongest people of the north, had given support now to one and now to another of the northern kingdoms, and this, together with their many armed incursions, had made them the dominant political factor in the north. But in the first year of the Sui period (581) they split into two sections, so that the Sui had hopes of gaining influence over them. At first both sections of the Turks had entered into alli-ance with China, but this was not a sufficient safeguard for the Sui, for one of the Turkish khans was surrounded by Toba who had fled from the vanished state of the Northern Chou, and who now tried to induce the Turks to undertake a campaign for the reconquest of north China. The leader of this agitation was a princess of the Yü-

10 Ladies of the court: clay models which accompanied the dead
person to the grave. T'ang period.
(In the collection of the Museum für Völkerkunde, Berlin.)

11 Distinguished founder: a temple banner found
at Khotcho, Sinkiang.
(Museum für Völkerkunde, Berlin, No. 1B 4524,
illustration B 408.)

wen family, the ruling family of the Northern Chou. The Chinese fought the Turks several times; but much more effective results were gained by their diplomatic missions, which incited the eastern against the western Turks and vice versa, and also incited the Turks against the Toba clique. In the end one of the sections of Turks accepted Chinese overlordship, and some tribes of the other section were brought over to the Chinese side; so, fresh disunion was sown among the Turks.

Under the emperor Yang Ti, P'ei Chü carried this policy further. He induced the Tölös tribes to attack the T'u-yü-hun, and then himself attacked the latter, so destroying their power. The T'u-yü-hun were a people living in the extreme north of Tibet, under a ruling class apparently of Hsien-pi origin; the people were largely Tibetan. The purpose of the conquest of the T'u-yü-hun was to safeguard access to Central Asia. An effective Central Asia policy was, however, impossible so long as the Turks were still a formidable power. Accordingly, the intrigues that aimed at keeping the two sections of Turks apart were continued. In 615 came a decisive counter-attack from the Turks. Their khan, Shih-pi, made a surprise assault on the emperor himself, with all his following, in the Ordos region, and succeeded in surrounding them. They were in just the same desperate situation as when, eight centuries earlier, the Chinese emperor had been beleaguered by Mao Tun. But the Chinese again saved themselves by a trick. The young Chinese commander, Li Shih-min, succeeded in giving the Turks the impression that large reinforcements were on the way; a Chinese princess who was with the Turks spread the rumour that the Turks were to be attacked by another tribe—and Shih-pi raised the siege, although the Chinese had been entirely defeated.

In the Sui period the Chinese were faced with a further problem. Korea or, rather, the most important of three states in Korea, had generally been on friendly terms with the southern state during the period of China's division, and for this reason had been more or less protected from its north Chinese neighbours. After the unification of China, Korea had reason for seeking an alliance with the Turks, in order to secure a new counterweight against China.

A Turco-Korean alliance would have meant for China a sort of encirclement that might have grave consequences. The alliance might be extended to Japan, who had certain interests in Korea. Accordingly the Chinese determined to attack Korea, though at the same time negotiations were set on foot. The fighting, which lasted throughout the Sui period, involved technical difficulties, as it called for combined land and sea attacks; in general it brought little success.

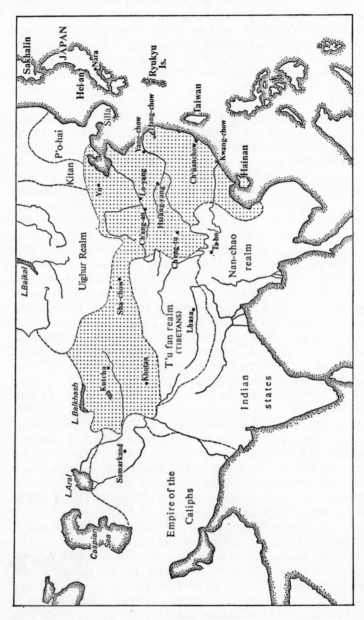

MAP 5   *The T'ang realm (about A.D. 750)*

3   *Reasons for collapse*

The continual warfare entailed great expense, and so did the intrigues, because they depended for their success on bribery. Still more expensive were the great canal works. In addition to this, the emperor Yang Ti, unlike his father, was very extravagant. He built enormous palaces and undertook long journeys throughout the empire with an immense following. All this wrecked the prosperity which his father had built up and had tried to safeguard. The only productive expenditure was that on the canals, and they could not begin to pay in so short a period. The emperor's continual journeys were due, no doubt, in part simply to the pursuit of pleasure, though they were probably intended at the same time to hinder risings and to give the emperor direct control over every part of the country. But the empire was too large and too complex for its administration to be possible in the midst of journeying. The whole of the chancellery had to accompany the emperor, and all the transport necessary for the feeding of the emperor and his government had continually to be diverted to wherever he happened to be staying. Later Chinese historians regard these travels as mere amusement trips made by an emperor whose main interest was in sexual adventures. A whole novel, written around 1600, is devoted to this aspect of Yang Ti's life, and the end of his dynasty is attributed to it. We are not sure whether he was really such a playboy or whether the breakdown of the Sui was not caused by his attempt to create a new type of administration. In any case, the gentry, who at first had so strongly supported the emperor and had been able to obtain anything they wanted from him, now began to desert him and set up pretenders. From 615 onward, after the defeat at the hands of the Turks, rising broke out everywhere. The emperor had to establish his government in the south, where he felt safer. There, however, in 618, he was assassinated by conspirators led by Toba of the Yü-wen family. Everywhere now independent governments sprang up, and for five years China was split up into countless petty states.

(B) THE T'ANG DYNASTY (A.D. 618–906)

1   *Reforms and decentralization*

The hero of the Turkish siege, Li Shih-min, had allied himself with the Turks in 615–616. There were special reasons for his ability to do this. In his family it had been a regular custom to marry women belonging to Toba families, so that he naturally enjoyed the confidence of the Toba party among the Turks. There are various theories as to the origin of his family, the Li. The family itself claimed to be descended from the ruling family of the Western Liang. It is doubtful whether that family was purely Chinese, and in any case Li Shih-min's descent from it is a matter of doubt. It is possible that his family was a sinified Toba family, or at least came from a Toba region. There was again a marriage with a woman from the Tu-ku family.

Li Shih-min continued the policy which had been pursued since the beginning of the Sui dynasty by the members of the deposed Toba ruling family of the Northern Chou—the policy of collaboration with the Turks in the effort to remove the Sui. The nominal leadership in the rising that now began lay in the hands of Li Shih-min's father, Li Yüan; in practice Li Shih-min saw to everything. At the end of 617 he was outside the first capital of the Sui, Ch'ang-an, with a Turkish army that had come to his aid on the strength of the treaty of alliance. After capturing Ch'ang-an he installed a puppet emperor there, a grandson of Yang Ti. In 618 the puppet was dethroned and Li Yüan, the father, was made emperor, in the T'ang dynasty. Internal fighting went on until 623, and only then was the whole empire brought under the rule of the T'ang.

Great reforms then began. A new land law aimed at equalizing ownership, so that as far as possible all peasants should own the same amount of land and the formation of large estates be prevented. The law aimed also at protecting the peasants from the loss of their land. The law was, however, nothing but a modification of the Toba land law (chün-t'ien), and it was hoped that now it would provide a sound and solid economic foundation for the empire. Census reports, found in Tun-huang, note the amount of land an individual family should receive, and, in many cases, how much they actually did receive. We may then conclude that the measures were in fact effective, though few farmers seem to have received as much as they were legally entitled to. Soon, however, loopholes in the laws began to influence the situation: members of the gentry who were connected with the imperial house were given a privileged position; then officials were excluded from the prohibition of leasing, so that there continued to be tenant farmers in addition to the independent peasants. Moreover, the temples enjoyed special treatment, and were also exempted from taxation. All these exceptions brought grist to the mills of the gentry, and so did the failure to carry into effect many of the provisions of the law. Before long a new gentry had been formed, consisting of the old gentry together with those who had directly aided the emperor's ascent to the throne. From the beginning of the eighth century there were repeated complaints that peasants were 'disappearing'. In at least some cases, the gentry by direct pressure or by giving credit to farmers and, when they could not repay the debt, taking over their land and treating them as tenants, succeeded in controlling much more land than they were entitled to. Due to the privileged position of the gentry in regard to taxation, the revenue sank in proportion as the number of independent peasants decreased. One of the reasons for the flight of farmers may have been the corvée laws connected with the 'equal land' system: small families were much less affected by the corvée obligation than larger families with many sons. It may be, therefore, that large families or at least sons of the sons in large families moved away in order to escape these obligations. In order to prevent irregularities, the T'ang renewed the old *pao-chia* system, as a part of a general reform of the administration in 624. In this system groups of five families were collectively responsible for the payment of taxes, the corvée, for crimes committed by individuals within one group, and for loans from state agencies. Such a system is attested for pre-Christian times already; it was reactivated in the eleventh century and again from time to time, down to the present.

Thus the system of land equalization soon broke down and was abolished officially around A.D. 780. But the classification of citizens into different classes, first legalized under the Toba, was retained and even more refined.

As early as in the Han period there had been a dual administration—the civil and, independent of it, the military administration. One and the same area would belong to a particular administrative prefecture (*chün*) and at the same time to a particular military prefecture (*chou*). This dual organization had persisted during the Toba period and, at first, remained unchanged in the beginning of the T'ang.

The backbone of the military power in the seventh century was the militia, 574 units of an average of a thousand men, recruited from the general farming population for short-term service: one month in five in the areas close to the capital. These men formed a part of the emperor's protection and were under the command of members of the Shensi gentry. This system, which had its direct parallels in the Han time and evolved out of a Toba system, broke down when short offensive wars were no longer fought. The sixteen units of imperial guards were staffed with young sons of the gentry who were stationed in the most delicate parts of the palaces. The emperor T'ai-Tsung had his personal bodyguard, a part of his own army of conquest, consisting of his former bondsmen (*pu-ch'ü*). The ranks of the Army of conquest were later filled by descendants of the original soldiers and by orphans.

In the provinces, the armies of the military prefectures gradually lost their importance when wars became longer and militiamen proved insufficient. Many of the soldiers here were convicts and exiles. It is interesting to note that the title of the commander of these armies, *tu-tu*, in the fourth century meant a commander in the church-Taoist organization; it was used by the Toba and from the seventh century on became widely accepted as a title among the Uighurs, Tibetans, Sogdians, Turks and Khotanese.

The wars of conquest which the T'ang conducted led to the creation of frontier armies with permanent commanders and a corresponding weakening of the prefectural armies and the militia (from 678 on). A similar institution had existed among the Toba, but they had greatly reduced these armies after 500. The commanders of these new T'ang armies soon became more important than the civil administrators, because they commanded a number of districts making up a whole province. This assured a better functioning of the military machine, but put the governors-general in a position to pursue a policy of their own, even against the central government. In addition to this, the financial administration of their commands was put under them, whereas in the past it had been in the hands of the civil administration of the various provinces. The civil administration was also reorganized (see the table on pages 81–2).

Towards the end of the T'ang period the state secretariat was set up in two parts: it was in possession of all information about the economic and political affairs of the empire, and it made the actual decisions. Moreover, a number of technical departments had been created—in all, a system that might compare favourably with European systems of the eighteenth century. At the end of the T'ang period there was added to this system a section for economic affairs, working quite independently of it and directly under the emperor; it was staffed entirely with economic or financial experts, while for the staffing of the other departments no special qualification was demanded besides the passing of the state examinations. In addition to these, at the end of the T'ang period a new department was in preparation, a sort of Privy Council, a mainly military organization, probably intended to control the generals (section 3 of the table on page 81), just as the state secretariat controlled the civil officials. The Privy Council became more and more important in the tenth century and especially in the Mongol epoch. Its absence in the early T'ang period gave the military governors much too great freedom, ultimately with baneful results.

We now have to look into the social stratification of the upper class. There was a 'super-gentry', divided into four regional groups which were often in competition with one another. First, the Lung-hsi gentry, from the area of the present province of Kansu. The imperial house of T'ang came from this group, as had the Sui house. This gentry was highly mixed with non-Chinese, Toba and Turkish elements and therefore was looked down upon by the Shantung gentry which, together with the Kiangsu gentry regarded themselves as the banner-carriers of old Chinese traditions. It is, for instance, the Ts'ui family which expressed the attitude that a marriage with the imperial house was a mismarriage. The fourth gentry group consisted of remnants of Toba and Turkish tribal leaders who had, in time, been assimilated and become 'Chinese'. Their influence tended to diminish with time.

Below this 'super-gentry' there was a provincial gentry, locally important, but only rarely able to play a role at the capital. The gentry created lists, comparable to the European 'Gotha calendar' in which, area by area, the gentry families were enumerated as a guide for marriages.

For the relatives of the emperor, moves into positions of great power were easiest. Members of the super-gentry could get into office simply as being sons of officials (the so-called 'yin' privilege), others had to pass one state examination. The road to success was through state schools. Two of the three state schools took only sons of officials, the third one occasionally also took some others. Prefectural officials could 'recommend' able men, but only if these men already belonged to gentry families of power did they have a chance to get into office. Men who came from provincial gentry families and passed the examination usually got into advisory jobs, advising the emperor on questions of ethics, after a career in low prefectural administrative positions. They could also, without taking an examination, move into one of the nine ranks of clerical jobs at the court, and after ten years of service take an examination and become regular officials of low rank with little hope of advancement. Similarly, they could enter the imperial guards, and after ten years take an examination and then become low regular officials in the civil administration.

Thus, the posts of political importance were taken almost exclusively by the members of the super-gentry, the clerical and military jobs usually by members of the provincial gentry. For men from ordinary families, the only chance was to enter the armies of frontier generals in the hope of being promoted by them.

During the seventh century the reforms of A.D. 624 worked well. The administration showed energy, and taxes flowed in. In the middle of the eighth century the annual budget of the state included the following items: over a million tons of grain for the consumption of the capital and the palace and for salaries of civil and military officials; twenty-seven million pieces of textiles, also for the consumption of capital and palace and army, and for supplementary purchases of grain; two million strings of money (a string nominally held a thousand copper coins) for salaries and for the army. This was much more than the state budget of the Han period. The population of the empire had also increased; it seems to have amounted to some fifty million. The capital grew enormously, at times containing two million people. Ch'ang-an, before its destruction in 881 had 110 wards. Each ward, like a ghetto, was surrounded by a wall with gates; at night the gates were closed. There was a special prostitution quarter, not too far from the centre of the city. Members of the gentry often secretly went there, though it was not allowed, and ate and drank and played games with the ladies. Many of China's best poets created their poems there in the company of ladies and friends. Typically, a Chinese poet does not write poems at home, in his studio, but in a group in which one member may propose a theme and a rhyme pattern. Then each member of the party may add a line or two; or each may create a whole poem, parallel to that of his predecessor. The ladies also were famous musicians and dancers, many of them from Central Asia, with their own local dances and their own music. Among the many imports of musical instruments and tunes, the import of the bow for string instruments at the end of the T'ang time is important because it changed the style of music. If the guests of the amusement quarter wanted to have more than just entertainment, they ordered the ladies to their houses. Of course, many of the more official parties took place in the houses of the gentry and entertainers were invited to enliven these parties. For those who retired from the bustle of the capital to work on their estates and to enjoy the society of their friends, there was time to occupy themselves with Taoism and Buddhism, especially meditative Buddhism. Everyone, of course, was Confucian, as was fitting for a member of the gentry, but Confucianism was so taken for granted that it was not discussed. It was the basis of morality for the gentry, but held no problems. It no longer contained anything of interest.

In addition to the actual capital, Ch'ang-an, there was the second capital, Loyang, in no way inferior to the other in importance; and the great towns in the south also played their part as commercial and cultural centres that had developed in the 360 years of division between north and south. There the local gentry gathered to lead a cultivated life, though not quite in the grand style of the capital. If an official was transferred to the Yangtze, it no longer amounted to a punishment as in the past; he would not meet only uneducated people, but a society resembling that of the capital. The institution of governors-general further promoted this decentralization: the governor-general surrounded himself with a little court of his own, drawn from the local gentry and the local intelligentsia. This placed the whole edifice of the empire on a much broader foundation, with lasting results.

2 *Turkish policy*

The foreign policy of this first period of the T'ang, lasting until about 690, was mainly concerned with the Turks and Sinkiang. There were still two Turkish realms in the Far East, both of considerable strength but in keen rivalry with each other. The T'ang had come into power with the aid of the eastern Turks, but they admitted the leader of the western Turks to their court; he had been at Ch'ang-an in the time of the Sui. He was murdered, however, by Chinese at the instigation of the eastern Turks. The next khan of the eastern Turks nevertheless turned against the T'ang, and gave his support to a still surviving pretender to the throne representing the Sui dynasty; the khan contended that the old alliance of the eastern Turks had been with the Sui and not with the T'ang. The T'ang therefore tried to come to terms once more with the western Turks, who had been affronted by the assassination; but the negotiations came to nothing in face of an approach made by the eastern Turks to the western, and of the distrust of the Chinese with which all the Turks were filled. About 624 there were strong Turkish invasions, carried right up to the capital. Suddenly, however, for reasons not disclosed by the Chinese sources, the Turks withdrew, and the T'ang were able to conclude a fairly honourable peace. This was the time of the maximum power of the eastern Turks. Soon afterwards disturbances broke out (627), under the leadership of Turkish Uighurs and their allies. The Chinese took advantage of these disturbances, and in a great campaign in 629–630 succeeded in overthrowing the eastern Turks; the khan was taken to the imperial court in Ch'ang-an, and the Chinese emperor made himself 'Heavenly Khan' of the Turks. In spite of the protest of many of the ministers, who pointed to the result of the settlement policy of the Later Han dynasty, the eastern Turks were settled in the bend of the upper Hwang-ho and placed more or less under the protectorate of two governors-general. Their leaders were admitted into the Chinese army, and the sons of their nobles lived at the imperial court. No doubt it was hoped in this way to turn the Turks into Chinese, as had been done with the Toba, though for entirely different reasons. More than a million Turks were settled in this way, and some of them actually became Chinese later and gained important posts.

In general, however, this in no way broke the power of the Turks. The great Turkish empire, which extended as far as Byzantium, continued to exist. The Chinese success had done no more than safeguard the frontier from a direct menace and frustrate the efforts of the supporters of the Sui dynasty and the Toba dynasty, who had been living among the eastern Turks and had built on them. The power of the western Turks remained a lasting menace to China, especially if they should succeed in co-operating with the Tibetans. After the annihilation of the T'u-yü-hun by the Sui at the very beginning of the seventh century, a new political unit had formed in northern Tibet, the T'u-fan, who also seem to have had an upper class of Turks and Mongols and a Tibetan lower class. Just as in the Han period, Chinese policy was bound to be directed to preventing a union between Turks and Tibetans. This, together with commercial interests, seems to have been the political motive of the Chinese Central Asian policy under the T'ang.

3 Conquest of Central Asia and Korea. Summit of power

The Central Asian wars began in 639 with an attack on the city-state of Kao-ch'ang (Khocho). This state had been on more or less friendly terms with north China since the Toba period, and it had succeeded again and again in preserving a certain independence from the Turks. Now, however, Kao-ch'ang had to submit to the western Turks, whose power was constantly increasing. China made that submission a pretext for war. By 640 the whole basin of Sinkiang was brought under Chinese dominance. The whole campaign was really directed against the western Turks, to whom Sinkiang had become subject. The western Turks had been crippled by two internal events, to the advantage of the Chinese: there had been a tribal rising, and then came the rebellion and the rise of the Uighurs (640–650). These events belong to Turkish history, and we shall confine ourselves here to their effects on Chinese history. The Chinese were able to rely on the Uighurs; above all, they were furnished by the Tölös Turks with a large army, with which they turned once more against Sinkiang in 647–648, and now definitely established their rule there.

The active spirit at the beginning of the T'ang rule had not been the emperor but his son Li Shih-min, who was not, however, named as heir to the throne because he was not the eldest son. The result of this was tension between Li Shih-min and his father and brothers, especially the heir to the throne. When the brothers learned that Li Shih-min was claiming the succession, they conspired against him, and in 626, at the very moment when the western Turks had made a rapid incursion and were once more threatening the Chinese capital, there came an armed collision between the brothers, in which Li Shih-min was the victor. The brothers and their families were exterminated, the father compelled to abdicate, and Li Shih-min became emperor, assuming the name T'ai Tsung (627–649). His reign marked the zenith of the power of China and of the T'ang dynasty. Their inner struggles and the Chinese penetration of Central Asia had weakened the position of the Turks; the reorganization of the administration and of the system of taxation, the improved transport resulting from the canals constructed under the Sui, and the useful results of the creation of great administrative areas under strong military control, had brought China inner stability and in consequence external power and prestige. The reputation which she then obtained as the most powerful state of the Far East endured when her inner stability had begun to deteriorate. Thus in 638 the Sassanid ruler Jedzgerd sent a mission to China asking for her help against the Arabs. Three further missions came at intervals of a good many years. The Chinese declined, however, to send a military expedition to such a distance; they merely conferred on the ruler the title of a Chinese governor; this was of little help against the Arabs, and in 675 the last ruler, Peruz, fled to the Chinese court.

The last years of T'ai Tsung's reign were filled with a great war against Korea, which represented a continuation of the plans of the Sui emperor Yang Ti. This time Korea came firmly into Chinese possession. In 661, under T'ai Tsung's son, the Korean fighting was resumed, this time against Japanese who were defending their interests in Korea. This was the period of great Japanese enthusiasm for China. The Chinese system of administration was copied, and Buddhism was adopted, together with every possible element of Chinese culture. This meant increased trade with Japan, bringing in large profits to China, and so the Korean middleman was to be eliminated.

T'ai Tsung's son, Kao Tsung (650–683), merely carried to a conclusion what had been begun. Externally China's prestige continued at its zenith. The caravans streamed into China from western and Central Asia, bringing great quantities of luxury goods. At this time, however, the foreign colonies were not confined to the capital but were installed in all the important trading ports and inland trade centres. The whole country was covered by a commercial network; foreign merchants who had come overland to China met others who had come by sea. The foreigners set up their own counting-houses and warehouses; whole quarters of the capital were inhabited entirely by foreigners who lived as if they were in their own country. They brought with them their own religions: Manichaeism, Mazdaism, and Nestorian Christianity. The first Jews came into China, apparently as dealers in fabrics, and the first Arabian Mohammedans made their appearance. In China the foreigners bought silkstuffs and collected everything of value that they could find, especially precious metals. Culturally this influx of foreigners enriched China; economically, as in earlier periods, it did not; its disadvantages were only compensated for a time by the very beneficial results of the trade with Japan, and this benefit did not last long.

The pressure of the western Turks had been greatly weakened in this period, especially as their attention had been diverted to the west, where the advance of Islam and of the Arabs was a new menace for them. On the other hand, from 650 onward the Tibetans gained immensely in power, and pushed from the south into the Tarim basin. In 678 they inflicted a heavy defeat on the Chinese, and it cost the T'ang decades of diplomatic effort before they attained, in 699, their aim of breaking up the Tibetans' realm and destroying their power. In the last year of Kao Tsung's reign, 683, came the first of the wars of liberation of the northern Turks, known until then as the western Turks, against the Chinese.

4 The reign of the empress Wu: Buddhism and capitalism

With the end of Kao Tsung's reign began the decline of the T'ang regime. Most of the historians attribute it to a woman, the later empress Wu. She had been a concubine of T'ai Tsung, and after his death had become a Buddhist nun—a frequent custom of the time—until Kao Tsung fell in love with her and made her a concubine of his own. In the end he actually divorced the empress and made the concubine empress (655). She gained more and more influence, being placed on a par with the emperor and soon entirely eliminating him in practice; in 680 she removed the rightful heir to the throne and put her own son in his place; after Kao Tsung's death in 683 she became regent for her son. Soon afterwards she dethroned him in favour of his twenty-two-year-old brother; in 690 she deposed him too and made herself empress in the 'Chou dynasty' (690–701). This officially ended the T'ang dynasty.

Matters, however, were not so simple as this might suggest. For otherwise on the empress's deposition there would not have been a mass of supporters moving heaven and earth to treat the new empress Wei (705–712) in the same fashion. There is every reason to suppose that behind the empress Wu there was a group opposing the ruling clique.

Communist Chinese historians like to praise her. First, as a woman; indeed, during the T'ang time, as a survival of Toba times, women were freer than in almost the next thousand years; they took part in official parties, accompanied their men on hunting expeditions. Second, Empress Wu is credited with progressive ideas. It is said that she stressed examinations and thus brought new men from families other than the super-gentry into the government. This seems to be incorrect. During her rule fewer examinations than before were held. The real point seems to have been a power struggle. In spite of everything, the T'ang government clique was very pro-Turkish, and many Turks and members of Toba families had government posts and, above all, important military commands. No campaign of that period was undertaken without Turkish auxiliaries. The fear seems to have been left in some quarters that this T'ang group might pursue a military policy hostile to the gentry. The T'ang group had its roots mainly in western China; thus the eastern Chinese gentry were inclined to be hostile to it. The first act of the empress Wu had been to transfer the capital to Loyang in the east. Thus, she tried to rely upon the co-operation of the eastern gentry which since the Northern Chou and Sui dynasties had been out of power. There were differences in education and outlook between both groups which continued long after the death of the empress. In addition, the eastern gentry, who supported the empress Wu and later the empress Wei, were closely associated with the foreign merchants of western Asia and the Buddhist organizations to which they adhered. In gratitude for help from the Buddhists, the empress Wu endowed them with enormous sums of money, and tried to make Buddhism a sort of state religion. A similar development had taken place in the Toba and also in the Sui period. Like these earlier rulers, the empress Wu seems to have aimed at combining spiritual leadership with her position as ruler of the empire.

In this epoch Buddhism helped to create the first beginnings of capitalism. In connection with the growing foreign trade, the monasteries grew in importance as repositories of capital; the temples bought more and more land, became more and more wealthy, and so gained increasing influence over economic affairs. They accumulated large quantities of metal, which they stored in the form of bronze figures of Buddha, and with these stocks they exercised controlling influence over the money market. There is a constant succession of records of the total weight of the bronze figures, as an indication of the money value they represented. It is interesting to observe that temples and monasteries also acquired shops and had rental income from them. They further operated many mills, as did the owners of private estates (now called *chuang*) and thus controlled the price of flour, and polished rice.

The cultural influence of Buddhism found expression in new and improved translations of countless texts, and in the passage of pilgrims along the caravan routes, helped by the merchants, as far as western Asia and India, like the famous Hsüan-tsang. Translations were made not only from Indian or other languages into Chinese, but also, for instance, from Chinese into the Uighur and other Turkish tongues, and into Tibetan, Korean, and Japanese.

The attitude of the Turks can only be understood when we realize that the background of events during the time of empress Wu was formed by the activities of groups of the eastern Chinese gentry. The

185

northern Turks, who since 630 had been under Chinese overlordship, had fought many wars of liberation against the Chinese; and through the conquest of neighbouring Turks they had gradually become once more, in the decade-and-a-half after the death of Kao Tsung, a great Turkish realm. In 698 the Turkish khan, at the height of his power, demanded a Chinese prince for his daughter—not, as had been usual in the past, a princess for his son. His intention, no doubt, was to conquer China with the prince's aid, to remove the empress Wu, and to restore the T'ang dynasty—but under Turkish overlordship! Thus, when the empress Wu sent a member of her own family, the khan rejected him and demanded the restoration of the deposed T'ang emperor. To enforce this demand, he embarked on a great campaign against China. In this the Turks must have been able to rely on the support of a strong group inside China, for before the Turkish attack became dangerous the empress Wu recalled the deposed emperor, at first as 'heir to the throne'; thus she yielded to the khan's principal demand.

In spite of this, the Turkish attacks did not cease. After a series of imbroglios within the country in which a group under the leadership of the powerful Ts'ui gentry family had liquidated the supporters of the empress Wu shortly before her death, a T'ang prince finally succeeded in killing empress Wei and her clique. At first, his father ascended the throne, but was soon persuaded to abdicate in favour of his son, now called emperor Hsüan Tsung (713–755), just as the first ruler of the T'ang dynasty had done. The practice of abdicating —in contradiction with the Chinese concept of the ruler as Son of Heaven and the duties of a son towards his father—seems to have impressed Japan where similar steps later became quite common. With Hsüan Tsung there began now a period of forty-five years, which the Chinese describe as the second blossoming of T'ang culture, a period that became famous especially for its painting and literature.

5 *Second blossoming of T'ang culture*

The T'ang literature shows the co-operation of many favourable factors. The ancient Chinese classical style of official reports and decrees which the Toba had already revived, now led to the clear prose style of the essayists, of whom Han Yü (768–825) and Liu Tsung-yüan (747–796) call for special mention. But entirely new forms of sentences make their appearance in prose writing, with new pictures and similes brought from India through the medium of the Buddhist translations. Poetry was also enriched by the simple songs that spread in the north under Turkish influence, and by southern influences. The great poets of the T'ang period adopted the rules of form laid down by the poetic art of the south in the fifth century; but while at that time the writing of poetry was a learned pastime, precious and formalistic, the T'ang poets brought to it genuine feeling. Widespread fame came to Li T'ai-po (701–762) and Tu Fu (712–770); in China two poets almost equal to these two in popularity were Po Chü-i (772–846) and Yüan Chen (779–831), who in their works kept as close as possible to the vernacular.

New forms of poetry rarely made their appearance in the T'ang period, but the existing forms were brought to the highest perfection. Not until the very end of the T'ang period did there appear the form of a 'free' versification, with lines of no fixed length. This form came from the indigenous folk-songs of south-western China, and was spread through the agency of the *filles de joie* in the houses. Before long it became the custom to string such songs together in a continuous series—the first step towards opera. For these song sequences were sung by way of accompaniment to the theatrical productions. Thus the Chinese theatre, with its union with music, should rather be called opera, although it offers a sort of pantomimic show. What amounted to a court conservatoire trained actors and musicians as early as in the T'ang period for this court opera. These actors and musicians were selected from the best-looking 'commoners', but they soon tended to become a special caste with a legal status just below that of 'burghers'.

The short-story, too, developed in T'ang times further by taking up episodes of normal life, rather than stressing the supernatural. Thus, the first short-stories of lightly erotic character, depicting love affairs, began to appear. Many of these short-stories later became the texts for operas down to the sixteenth century.

In plastic art there are fine sculptures in stone and bronze, and we have also technically excellent fabrics, the finest of lacquer, and remains of artistic buildings; but the principal achievement of the T'ang period lies undoubtedly in the field of painting. As in poetry, in painting there are strong traces of alien influences; even before the T'ang period, the painter Hsieh Ho laid down the six fundamental laws of painting, in all probability drawn from Indian practice. Foreigners were continually brought into China as decorators of Buddhist temples, since the Chinese could not know at first how the new gods had to be presented. The Chinese regarded these painters as craftsmen, but admired their skill and their technique and learned from them.

The most famous Chinese painter of the T'ang period is Wu Tao-tzǔ, who was also the painter most strongly influenced by Central Asian works. As a pious Buddhist he painted pictures for temples among others. Among the landscape painters, Wang Wei (721–729) ranks first; he was also a famous poet and aimed at uniting poem and painting into an integral whole. With him begins the great tradition of Chinese landscape painting, which attained its zenith later, in the Sung epoch.

Porcelain had been invented in China long ago. There was as yet none of the white porcelain that is preferred today; the inside was a brownish-yellow; but on the whole it was already technically and artistically of a very high quality. Since porcelain was at first produced only for the requirements of the court and of high dignitaries —mostly in state factories—a few centuries later the T'ang porcelain had become a great rarity. But in the centuries that followed, porcelain became an important new article of Chinese export. The Chinese prisoners taken by the Arabs in the great battle of Samarkand (751), the first clash between the world of Islam and China, brought to the West the knowledge of Chinese culture, of several Chinese crafts, of the art of papermaking, and also of porcelain.

The emperor Hsüan Tsung gave active encouragement to all things artistic. Poets and painters contributed to the elegance of his magnificent court ceremonial. As time went on he showed less and less interest in public affairs, and grew increasingly inclined to Taoism and mysticism in general—an outcome of the fact that the conduct of matters of state was gradually taken out of his hands. On the whole, however, Buddhism was pushed into the background in favour of a rather formalistic Confucianism, as a reaction against the unusual privileges that had been accorded to the Buddhists in the past fifteen years under the empress Wu.

6 Revolt of a military governor

At the beginning of Hsüan Tsung's reign the capital had been in the east at Loyang; then it was transferred once more to Ch'ang-an in the west due to pressure of the western gentry. The emperor soon came under the influence of the unscrupulous but capable and energetic Li Lin-fu, a distant relative of the ruler. Li was a virtual dictator at the court from 736 to 752, who had first advanced in power by helping the concubine Wu, a relative of the famous empress Wu, and by continually playing the eastern against the western gentry. After the death of the concubine Wu, he procured for the emperor a new concubine named Yang, of a western family. This woman, usually called 'Concubine Yang' (Yang Kui-fei), became the heroine of countless state-plays and stories and even films; all the misfortunes that marked the end of Hsüan Tsung's reign were attributed solely to her. This is incorrect, as she was but a link in the chain of influences that played upon the emperor. Naturally she found important official posts for her brothers and all her relatives; but more important than these was a military governor named An Lu-shan (703–757). His mother was a Turkish shamaness, his father a foreigner, probably of Sogdian origin. An Lu-shan succeeded in gaining favour with the Li clique, which hoped to make use of him for its own ends. Chinese sources describe him as a prodigy of evil, and it will be very difficult today to gain a true picture of his personality. In any case, he was certainly a very capable military officer. His rise started from a victory over the Kitan in 744. He spent some time establishing relations with the court and then went back to resume operations against the Kitan. He made so much of the Kitan peril that he was permitted a larger army than usual, and he had command of 150,000 troops in the neighbourhood of Peking. Meanwhile Li Lin-fu died. He had sponsored An as a counterbalance against the western gentry. When now, within the clique of Li Lin-fu, the Yang family tried to seize power, they turned against An Lu-shan. But he marched against the capital, Ch'ang-an, with 200,000 men; on his way he conquered Loyang and made himself emperor (756: Yen dynasty). T'ang troops were sent against him under the leadership of the Chinese Kuo Tzǔ-i, a Kitan commander, and a Turk, Ko-shu Han.

The first two generals had considerable success, but Ko-shu Han, whose task was to prevent access to the western capital, was quickly defeated and taken prisoner. The emperor fled betimes, and An Lu-shan captured Ch'ang-an. The emperor now abdicated; his son, emperor Su Tsung (756–762), also fled, though not with him into Szechwan, but into north-western Shensi. There he defended himself against An Lu-shan and his capable general Shih Ssǔ-ming (himself a Turk), and sought aid in Central Asia. A small Arab troop came from the caliph Abu-Jafar, and also small bands from Sinkiang; of more importance was the arrival of Uighur cavalry in substantial strength. At the end of 757 there was a great battle in the neighbourhood of the capital, in which An Lu-shan was defeated by the Uighurs; shortly afterwards he was murdered by one of his eunuchs. His followers fled; Loyang was captured and looted by the Uighurs. The victors further received in payment from the T'ang government 10,000 rolls of silk with a promise of 20,000 rolls a year; the Uighur khan was given a daughter of the emperor as his wife. An Lu-shan's general, the Turk Shih Ssǔ-ming, entered into An Lu-shan's heritage, and dominated so large a part of eastern China that the Chinese once more made use of the Uighurs to bring him down. The commanders in the fighting against Shih Ssǔ-ming this time were once more Kuo Tzǔ-i and the Kitan general, together with P'u-ku Huai-en, a member of a Tölös family that had long been living in China. At first Shih Ssǔ-ming was victorious, and he won back Loyang, but then he was murdered by his own son, and only by taking advantage

of the disturbances that now arose were the government troops able
to quell the dangerous rising.

In all this, two things seem interesting and important. To begin
with, An Lu-shan had been a military governor. His rising showed
that while this new office, with its great command of power, was of
value in attacking external enemies, it became dangerous, especially
if the central power was weak, the moment there were no external
enemies of any importance. An Lu-shan's rising was the first of many
similar ones in the later T'ang period. The gentry of eastern China
had shown themselves entirely ready to support An Lu-shan against
the government, because they had hoped to gain advantage as in the
past from a realm with its centre once more in the east. In the second
place, the important part played by aliens in events within China
calls for notice: not only were the rebels An Lu-shan and Shih Ssŭ-
ming non-Chinese, but so also were most of the generals opposed to
them. But they regarded themselves as Chinese, not as members of
another national group. The Turkish Uighurs brought in to help
against them were fighting actually against Turks, though they regarded those Turks as Chinese. We must not bring to the circumstances
of those times the present-day notions with regard to national feeling.

7 The role of the Uighurs. Confiscation of the capital of the monasteries

This rising and its sequels broke the power of the dynasty, and also
of the empire. The extremely sanguinary wars had brought fearful
suffering upon the population. During the years of the rising, no
taxes came in from the greater part of the empire, but great sums
had to be paid to the peoples who had lent aid to the empire. And
the looting by government troops and by the auxiliaries injured the
population as much as the war itself did.

When the emperor Su Tsung died, in 762, Tengri, the khan of the
Uighurs, decided to make himself ruler over China. The events of
the preceding years had shown him that China alone was entirely
defenceless. Part of the court clique supported him, and only by
the intervention of P'u-ku Huai-en, who was related to Tengri by
marriage, was his plan frustrated. Naturally there were countless
intrigues against P'u-ku Huai-en. He entered into alliance with the
Tibetan T'u-fan, and in this way the union of Turks and Tibetans,
always feared by the Chinese, had come into existence. In 763 the
Tibetans captured and burned down the western capital, while P'u-ku
Huai-en with the Uighurs advanced from the north. Undoubtedly
this campaign would have been successful, giving an entirely different
turn to China's destiny, if P'u-ku Huai-en had not died in 765 and
the Chinese under Kuo Tzŭ-i had not succeeded in breaking up the

alliance. The Uighurs now came over into an alliance with the Chinese, and the two allies fell upon the Tibetans and robbed them of their booty. China was saved once more.

Friendship with the Uighurs had to be paid for this time even more dearly. They crowded into the capital and compelled the Chinese to buy horses, in payment for which they demanded enormous quantities of silkstuffs. They behaved in the capital like lords, and expected to be maintained at the expense of the government. The system of military governors was adhered to in spite of the country's experience of them, while the difficult situation throughout the empire, and especially along the western and northern frontiers, facing the Tibetans and the more and more powerful Kitan, made it necessary to keep considerable numbers of soldiers permanently with the colours. This made the military governors stronger and stronger; ultimately they no longer remitted any taxes to the central government, but spent them mainly on their armies. Thus from 750 onward the empire consisted of an impotent central government and powerful military governors, who handed on their positions to their sons as a further proof of their independence. When in 781 the government proposed to interfere with the inheriting of the posts, there was a great new rising, which in 783 again extended as far as the capital; in 784 the T'ang government at last succeeded in overcoming it. A compromise was arrived at between the government and the governors, but it in no way improved the situation. Life became more and more difficult for the central government. In 780, the 'equal land' system was finally officially given up and with it a tax system which was based upon the idea that every citizen had the same amount of land and, therefore, paid the same amount of taxes. The new system tried to equalize the tax burden and the corvée obligation, but not the land. This change may indicate a step towards greater freedom for private enterprise. Yet it did not benefit the government, as most of the tax income was retained by the governors and was used for their armies and their own court.

In the capital, eunuchs ruled in the interests of various cliques. Several emperors fell victim to them or to the drinking of 'elixirs of long life'.

Abroad, the Chinese lost their dominion over Sinkiang, for which Uighurs and Tibetans competed. There is nothing to gain from any full description of events at court. The struggle between cliques soon became a struggle between eunuchs and literati, in much the same way as at the end of the second Han dynasty. Trade steadily diminished, and the state became impoverished because no taxes were coming in and great armies had to be maintained, though they did not even obey the government.

Events that exerted on the internal situation an influence not to be belittled were the break-up of the Uighurs (from 832 onward) the appearance of the Sha-t'o, and almost at the same time, the dissolution of the Tibetan empire (from 842). Many other foreigners had placed themselves under the Uighurs living in China, in order to be able to do business under the political protection of the Uighur embassy, but the Uighurs no longer counted, and the T'ang government decided to seize the capital sums which these foreigners had accumulated. It was hoped in this way especially to remedy the financial troubles of the moment, which were partly due to a shortage of metal for minting. As the trading capital was still placed with the temples as banks, the government attacked the religion of the Uighurs, Manichaeism, and also the religions of the other foreigners, Mazdaism, Nestorianism, and apparently also Islam. In 843 alien religions were prohibited; aliens were also ordered to dress like Chinese. This gave them the status of Chinese citizens and no longer of foreigners, so that Chinese justice had a hold over them. That this law abolishing foreign religions was aimed solely at the foreigners' capital is shown by the proceedings at the same time against Buddhism which had long become a completely Chinese Church. Four thousand, six hundred Buddhist temples, 40,000 shrines and monasteries were secularized, and all statues were required to be melted down and delivered to the government, even those in private possession. Two hundred and sixty thousand, five hundred monks were to become ordinary citizens once more. Until then monks had been free of taxation, as had millions of acres of land belonging to the temples and leased to tenants or some 150,000 temple slaves.

Thus the edict of 843 must not be described as concerned with religion at all times, down to the present, Chinese governments looked with suspicion at any organization other than the family (the basis of Chinese society to 1949), because such an organization could become a centre of power and thus a threat. In this case, the persecution was also a measure of compulsion aimed at filling the government coffers. All the property of foreigners and a large part of the property of the Buddhist Church came into the hands of the government. The law was not applied to Taoism, because the ruling gentry of the time were, as so often before, Confucianist and at the same time interested in applied Taoism. As early as 846 there came a reaction: with the new emperor, Confucians came into power who were at the same time Buddhists and who now evicted some of the Taoists. From this time one may observe closer co-operation between Confucianism and Buddhism; not only with meditative Buddhism (Zen) as at the beginning of the T'ang epoch and earlier, but with the main branch of Buddhism, monastery Buddhism (Vinaya). From now onward the Buddhist doctrines of transmigration and retribution, which had been really directed against the gentry and in favour of the common people, were turned into an instrument serving the gentry: everyone who was unfortunate in this life must show such amenability to the government and the gentry that he would have a chance of a better existence at least in the next life. Thus the revolutionary Buddhist doctrine of retribution became a reactionary doctrine that was of great service to the gentry. One of the Buddhist Confucians in whose works this revised version makes its appearance most clearly was Niu Seng-yu, who was at once summoned back to court in 846 by the new emperor. Three new large Buddhist sects came into existence in the T'ang period. One of them, the school of the Pure Land (*Ching-t'u tsung*) since 641 required of its mainly lower-class adherents only the permanent invocation of the Buddha Amithabha who would secure them a place in the 'Western Paradise' —a place without social classes and economic troubles. The cult of Maitreya, which was always more revolutionary, receded for a while.

8   *First successful peasant revolt. Collapse of the empire*
The chief sufferers from the continual warfare of the military governors, the sanguinary struggles between the cliques, and the universal impoverishment which all this fighting produced, were, of course, the common people. The Chinese annals are filled with records of popular risings, but not one of these had attained any wide extent, for want of organization. In 860 began the first great popular rising, a revolt caused by famine in the province of Chekiang. Government troops suppressed it with bloodshed. Further popular risings followed. In 874 began a great rising in the south of the present province of Hopei, the chief agrarian region.

The rising was led by a peasant, Wang Hsien-chih, together with Huang Ch'ao, a salt merchant, who had fallen into poverty and had joined the hungry peasants, forming a fighting group of his own. It is important to note that Huang was well educated. It is said that he failed in the state examination. Huang is not the first merchant who became rebel. An Lu-shan, too, had been a businessman for a while. It was pointed out that trade had greatly developed in the T'ang period; of the lower Yangtze region people it was said that 'they were so much interested in business that they paid no attention to agriculture'. Yet merchants were subject to many humiliating conditions. They could not enter the examinations, except by illegal means. In various periods, from the Han time on, they had to wear special dress. Thus, a law from c. A.D. 300 required them to wear a white turban on which name and type of business was written, and to wear one white and one black shoe, but we have reasons to doubt that these discriminatory measures were enforced. They were subject to various taxes, but were either not allowed to own land, or were allotted less land than ordinary citizens. Thus they could not easily invest in land, the safest investment at that time. Finally, the government occasionally resorted to the method which was often used in the Near East: when in 782 the emperor ran out of money, he requested the merchants of the capital to 'loan' him a large sum—a request which in fact was a special tax.

Wang and Huang both proved good organizers of the peasant masses, and in a short time they had captured the whole of eastern China, without the military governors being able to do anything against them, for the provincial troops were more inclined to show sympathy to the peasant armies than to fight them. The terrified government issued an order to arm the people of the other parts of the country against the rebels; naturally this helped the rebels more than the government, since the peasants thus armed went over to the rebels. Finally Wang was offered a high office. But Huang urged him not to betray his own people, and Wang declined the offer. In the end the government, with the aid of the troops of the Turkish and Sogdian Sha-t'o, defeated Wang and beheaded him (878). Huang Ch'ao now moved into the south-east and the south, where in 879 he captured and burned down Canton; according to an Arab source, over 120,000 foreign merchants lost their lives in addition to the Chinese. From Canton Huang Ch'ao returned to the north, laden with loot from that wealthy commercial city. His advance was held up again by the Sha-t'o troops; he turned away to the lower Yangtze, and from there marched north again. At the end of 880 he captured the eastern capital. The emperor fled from the western capital, Ch'ang-an, into Szechwan, and Huang Ch'ao now captured with ease the western capital as well, and removed every member of the ruling family on whom he could lay hands. He then made himself emperor, in a Ch'i dynasty. It was the first time that a peasant rising had succeeded against the gentry.

There was still, however, the greatest disorder in the empire. There were other peasant armies on the move, armies that had deserted their governors and were fighting for themselves; finally, there were still a few supporters of the imperial house and, above all, the Sha-t'o, who had a competent commander with the sinified name of Li K'o-yung. The Sha-t'o, who had remained loyal to the government, revolted the moment the government had been overthrown. They ran the risk, however, of defeat at the hands of an alien army of the Chinese government's, commanded by an Uighur, and they therefore fled to the Tatars. In spite of this, the Chinese entered again into relations with the Sha-t'o, as without them there could be no possibility of getting rid of Huang Ch'ao. At the end of 881 Li K'o-yung fell upon the capital; there was a fearful battle. Huang Ch'ao was able to hold out, but a further attack was made in 883 and he was defeated and forced to flee; in 884 he was killed by the Sha-t'o.

This popular rising, which had only been overcome with the aid of foreign troops, brought the end of the T'ang dynasty. In 885 the T'ang emperor was able to return to the capital, but the only question now was whether China should be ruled by the Sha-t'o under Li K'o-yung or by some other military commander. In a short time Chu Ch'üan-chung, a former follower of Huang Ch'ao, proved to be the strongest of the commanders. In 890 open war began between the two leaders. Li K'o-yung was based on Shansi; Chu Ch'üan-chung had control of the plains in the east. Meanwhile the governors of Szechwan in the west and Chekiang in the south-east made themselves independent. Both declared themselves kings or emperors and set up dynasties of their own (from 895).

Within the capital, the emperor was threatened several times by revolts, so that he had to flee and place himself in the hands of Li K'o-yung as the only leader on whose loyalty he could count. Soon after this, however, the emperor fell into the hands of Chu Ch'üan-chung, who killed the whole entourage of the emperor, particularly the eunuchs; after a time he had the emperor himself killed, set a puppet—as had become customary—on the throne, and at the beginning of 907 took over the rule from him, becoming emperor in the 'Later Liang dynasty'.

That was the end of the T'ang dynasty, at the beginning of which China had risen to unprecedented power. Its downfall had been brought about by the military governors, who had built up their power and had become independent hereditary satraps, exploiting the people for their own purposes, and by their continual mutual struggles undermining the economic structure of the empire. In addition to this, the empire had been weakened first by its foreign trade and then by the dependence on foreigners, especially Turks, into which it had fallen owing to internal conditions, A large part of the national income had gone abroad. Such is the explanation of the great popular risings which ultimately brought the dynasty to its end.

(C) THE SECOND DIVISION OF CHINA: THE FIVE DYNASTIES (A.D. 906–960)

1 Political situation in the tenth century

The Chinese call the period from 906 to 960 the 'period of the Five Dynasties' (*Wu Tai*). This is not quite accurate. It is true that there were five dynasties in rapid succession in north China; but at the same time there were ten other dynasties in south China. The ten southern dynasties, however, are regarded by Chinese historians as not legitimate. The south was much better off with its illegitimate dynasties than the north with the legitimate ones. The dynasties in the south (we may dispense with giving their names) were the realms of some of the military governors so often mentioned above. These governors had already become independent at the end of the T'ang epoch; they declared themselves kings or emperors and ruled particular provinces in the south, the chief of which covered the territory of the present provinces of Szechwan, Kwangtung and Chekiang. In these territories there was comparative peace and economic prosperity, since they were able to control their own affairs and were no longer dependent on a corrupt central government. They also made great cultural progress, and they did not lose their importance later when they were annexed in the period of the Sung dynasty.

As an example of these states one may mention the small state of Ch'u in the present province of Hunan. Here, Ma Yin, a former carpenter (died 931), had made himself a king. He controlled some of the main trade routes, set up a clean administration, bought up all merchandise which the merchants brought, but allowed them to export only local products, mainly tea, iron and lead. This regulation gave him a personal income of several millions every year, and in addition fostered the exploitation of the natural resources of this hitherto retarded area.

2 *Monopolistic trade in south China. Printing and paper money in the north*

The prosperity of the small states of south China was largely due to the growth of trade, especially the tea trade. The habit of drinking tea seems to have been an ancient Tibetan custom, which spread to south-eastern China in the third century A.D. Since then there had been two main centres of production, Szechwan and south-eastern China. Until the eleventh century, Szechwan had remained the leading producer, and tea had been drunk in the Tibetan fashion, mixed with flour, salt, and ginger. It then began to be drunk without admixture. In the T'ang epoch tea drinking spread all over China, and there sprang up a class of wholesalers who bought the tea from the peasants, accumulated stocks, and distributed them. From 783 date the first attempts of the state to monopolize the tea trade and to make it a source of revenue; but it failed in an attempt to make the cultivation a state monopoly. A tea commissariat was accordingly set up to buy the tea from the producers and supply it to traders in possession of a state licence. There naturally developed then a pernicious collaboration between state officials and the wholesalers.

The latter soon eliminated the small traders, so that they themselves secured all the profit; official support was secured by bribery. The state and the wholesalers alike were keenly interested in the prevention of tea smuggling, which was strictly prohibited.

The position was much the same with regard to salt. We have here for the first time the association of officials with wholesalers or even with a monopoly trade. This was of the utmost importance in all later times. Monopoly progressed most rapidly in Szechwan, where there had always been a numerous commercial community. In the period of political fragmentation Szechwan, as the principal tea-producing region and at the same time an important producer of salt, was much better off than any other part of China. Salt in Szechwan was largely produced by, technically, very interesting salt wells which had existed there since around the first century B.C. The importance of salt will be understood if we remember that a grown-up person in China uses an average of twelve pounds of salt per year. The salt tax was the top budget item around A.D. 900.

South-eastern China was also the chief centre of porcelain production, although china clay is found also in north China. The use of porcelain spread more and more widely. The first translucent porcelain made its appearance, and porcelain became an important article of commerce both within the country and for export. Already the Muslim rulers of Baghdad around 800 used imported Chinese porcelain, and by the end of the fourteenth century porcelain was known in Eastern Africa. Exports to South-East Asia and Indonesia, and also to Japan gained more and more importance in later centuries. Manufacture of high quality porcelain calls for considerable amounts of capital investment and working capital; small manufacturers produce too many second-rate pieces; thus we have here the first beginnings of an industry that developed industrial towns such as Ching-tê, in which the majority of the population were workers and merchants, with some 10,000 families alone producing porcelain. Yet, for many centuries to come, the state controlled the production and even the design of porcelain and appropriated most of the production for use at court or as gifts.

The third important new development to be mentioned was that of printing, which since c. 770 was known in the form of wood-block printing. The first reference to a printed book dated from 835, and the most important event in this field was the first printing of the Classics by the orders of Feng Tao (882–954) around 940. The first attempts to use movable type in China occurred around 1045, although this invention did not get general acceptance in China. It was more commonly used in Korea from the thirteenth century on and revolutionized Europe from 1538 on. It seems that from the middle of the twentieth century on, the West, too, shows a tendency to come back to the printing of whole pages, but replacing the wood blocks by photographic plates or other means. In the Far East, just as in Europe, the invention of printing had far-reaching consequences. Books, which until then had been very dear, because they had had to be produced by copyists, could not be produced cheaply and in quantity. It became possible for a scholar to accumulate a library of his own and to work in a wide field, where earlier he had been confined to a few books or even a single text. The results were the spread of education, beginning with reading and writing, among wider groups, and the broadening of education: a large number of texts were read and compared, and no longer only a few. Private libraries came into existence, so that the imperial libraries were no longer the only ones. Publishing soon grew in extent, and in private enterprise works were printed that were not so serious and politically important as the classic books of the past. Thus a new type of literature, the literature of entertainment, could come into existence. Not all these consequences showed themselves at once; some made their first appearance later, in the Sung period.

A fourth important innovation, this time in north China, was the introduction of prototypes of paper money. The Chinese copper 'cash' was difficult or expensive to transport, simply because of its weight. It thus presented great obstacles to trade. Occasionally a region with an adverse balance of trade would lose all its copper money, with the result of a local deflation. From time to time, iron money was introduced in such deficit areas; it had for the first time been used in Szechwan for a short time in the first century B.C., and was there extensively used in the tenth century. In the history of business and trade, this iron money was an important step. For the first time, China had a medium of exchange which did not have the value which the metal of the coin itself had. The drawback was, that iron money was still relatively heavy. Paper money is an even more important step in the direction of symbolic money. So long as there was an orderly administration, the government could send money, though at considerable cost; but if the administration was not functioning well, the deflation continued. For this reason some provinces prohibited the export of copper money from their territory at the end of the eighth century. As the provinces were in the hands of military governors, the central government could do next to nothing to prevent this. On the other hand, the prohibition automatically made an end of all external trade. The merchants accordingly began to prepare deposit certificates, and in this way to set up a sort of transfer system. Soon these deposit certificates entered into circulation as a sort of medium of payment at first again in Szechwan, and gradually this led to a banking system and the linking of wholesale trade with it. This made possible a much greater volume of trade. Towards the end of the T'ang period the government began to issue deposit certificates of its own: the merchant deposited his copper money with a government agency, receiving in exchange a certificate which he could put into circulation like money. Meanwhile the government could put out the deposited money at interest, or throw it into general circulation. The government's deposit certificates were now printed. They were the predecessors of the paper money used from the time of the Sung.

3 Political history of the Five Dynasties

The southern states were a factor not to be ignored in the calculations of the northern dynasties. Although the southern kingdoms were involved in a confusion of mutual hostilities, any one of them might come to the fore as the ally of Turks or other northern powers. The capital of the first of the five northern dynasties (once more a Liang dynasty, but not to be confused with the Liang dynasty of the south in the sixth century) was, moreover, quite close to the territories of the southern dynasties, close to the site of the present K'aifeng, in the fertile plain of eastern China with its good means of transport. Militarily the town could not be held, for its one and only defence was the Yellow river. The founder of this Later Liang dynasty, Chu Ch'üan-chung (906), was himself an eastern Chinese and, as will be remembered, a past supporter of the revolutionary Huang Ch'ao, but he had then gone over to the T'ang and had gained high military rank.

His northern frontier remained still more insecure than the southern, for Chu Ch'üan-chung did not succeed in destroying the Turkish general Li K'o-yung; on the contrary, the latter continually widened the range of his power. Fortunately he, too, had an enemy at his back—the Kitan (or Khitan), whose ruler had made himself emperor in 916, and so staked a claim to reign over all China. The first Kitan emperor held a middle course between Chu and Li, and so was able to establish and expand his empire in peace. The striking power of his empire, which from 937 onward was officially called the Liao empire, grew steadily, because the old tribal league of the Kitan was transformed into a centrally commanded military organization.

To these dangers from abroad threatening the Later Liang state internal troubles were added. Chu Ch'üan-chung's dynasty was one of the three Chinese dynasties that have ever come to power through a popular rising. He himself was of peasant origin, and so were a large part of his subordinates and helpers. Many of them had originally been independent peasant leaders; others had been under Huang

Ch'ao. All of them were opposed to the gentry, and the great slaughter of the gentry of the capital, shortly before the beginning of Chu's rule, had been welcomed by Chu and his followers. The gentry therefore would not co-operate with Chu and preferred to join the Turk Li K'o-yung. But Chu could not confidently rely on his old comrades. They were jealous of his success in gaining the place they all coveted, and were ready to join in any independent enterprise as opportunity offered. All of them, moreover, as soon as they were given any administrative post, busied themselves with the acquisition of money and wealth as quickly as possible. These abuses not only ate into the revenues of the state but actually produced a common front between the peasantry and the remnants of the gentry against the upstarts.

In 917, after Li K'o-yung's death, the Sha-t'o beat off an attack from the Kitan, and so were safe for a time from the northern menace. They then marched against the Liang state, where a crisis had been produced in 912 after the murder of Chu Ch'üan-chung by one of his sons. The Liang generals saw no reason why they should fight for the dynasty, and all of them went over to the enemy. Thus the 'Later T'ang dynasty' (923–936) came into power in north China, under the son of Li K'o-yung.

The dominant element at this time was quite clearly the Chinese gentry, especially in western and central China. The Sha-t'o themselves must have been extraordinarily few in number, probably little more than 100,000 men. Most of them, moreover, were politically passive, being simple soldiers. Only the ruling family and its following played any active part, together with a few families related to it by marriage. The whole state was regarded by the Sha-t'o rulers as a sort of family enterprise, members of the family being placed in the most important positions. As there were not enough of them, they adopted into the family large numbers of aliens of all nationalities. Military posts were given to faithful members of Li K'o-yung's or his successor's bodyguard, and also to domestic servants and other clients of the family. Thus, while in the Later Liang state elements from the peasantry had risen in the world, some of these neo-gentry reaching the top of the social pyramid in the centuries that followed, in the Sha-t'o state some of its warriors, drawn from the most various peoples, entered the gentry class through their personal relations with the ruler. But in spite of all this the bulk of the officials came once more from the Chinese. These educated Chinese not only succeeded in winning over the rulers themselves to the Chinese cultural ideal, but persuaded them to adopt laws that substantially restricted the privileges of the Sha-t'o and brought advantages only to the Chinese gentry. Consequently all the Chinese historians are

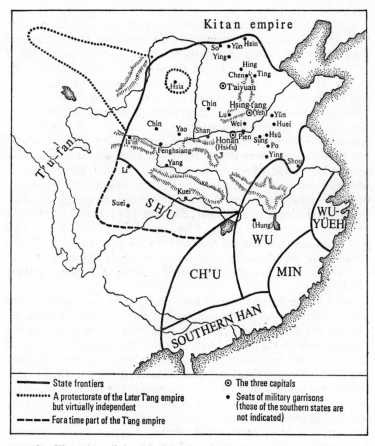

MAP 6   *The state of the Later T'ang dynasty (A.D. 923–935)*

enthusiastic about the 'Later T'ang', and especially about the emperor Ming Ti, who reigned from 927 onward, after the assassination of his predecessor. They also abused the Liang because they were against the gentry.

In 936 the Later T'ang dynasty gave place to the Later Chin dynasty (936–946), but this involved no change in the structure of the empire. The change of dynasty meant no more than that instead of the son following the father the son-in-law had ascended the throne. It was of more importance that the son-in-law, the Sha-t'o Turk Shih Ching-t'ang, succeeded in doing this by allying himself with the Kitan and ceding to them some of the northern provinces. The youthful successor, however, of the first ruler of this dynasty was soon made to realize that the Kitan regarded the founding of his dynasty as no more than a transition stage on the way to their annexation of the whole of north China. The old Sha-t'o nobles, who had not been sinified in the slightest, suggested a preventive war; the actual court group, strongly sinified, hesitated, but ultimately were unable to avoid war. The war was very quickly decided by several governors in eastern China going over to the Kitan, who had promised them the imperial title. In the course of 946–947 the Kitan occupied the capital and almost the whole of the country. In 947 the Kitan ruler proclaimed himself emperor of the Kitan and the Chinese.

The Chinese gentry seem to have accepted this situation because a Kitan emperor was just as acceptable to them as a Sha-t'o emperor; but the Sha-t'o were not prepared to submit to the Kitan regime, because under it they would have lost their position of privilege. At the head of this opposition group stood the Sha-t'o general Liu Chih-yüan, who founded the 'Later Han dynasty' (947–950). He was able to hold out against the Kitan only because in 947 the Kitan emperor died and his son had to leave China and retreat to the north; fighting had broken out between the empress dowager, who had some Chinese support, and the young heir to the throne. The new Turkish dynasty, however, was unable to withstand the internal Chinese resistance. Its founder died in 948, and his son, owing to his youth, was entirely in the hands of a court clique. In his effort to free himself from the tutelage of this group he made a miscalculation, for the men on whom he thought he could depend were largely supporters of the clique. So he lost his throne and his life, and a Chinese general, Kuo Wei, took his place, founding the 'Later Chou dynasty' (951–959).

A feature of importance was that in the years of the short-lived 'Later Han dynasty' a tendency showed itself among the Chinese military leaders to work with the states in the south. The increase in the political influence of the south was due to its economic advance while the north was reduced to economic chaos by the continual heavy fighting, and by the complete irresponsibility of the Sha-t'o ruler in financial matters: several times in this period the whole of the money in the state treasury was handed out to soldiers to prevent them from going over to some enemy or other. On the other hand, there was a tendency in the south for the many neighbouring states to amalgamate, and as this process took place close to the frontier of north China the northern states could not passively look on. During the 'Later Han' period there were wars and risings, which continued in the time of the 'Later Chou'.

On the whole, the few years of the rule of the second emperor of the 'Later Chou' (954–958) form a bright spot in those dismal fifty-five years. Sociologically regarded, that dynasty formed merely a transition stage on the way to the Sung dynasty that now followed: the Chinese gentry ruled under the leadership of an upstart who had risen from the ranks, and they ruled in accordance with the old principles of gentry rule. The Sha-t'o, who had formed the three preceding dynasties, had been so reduced that they were now a tiny minority and no longer counted. This minority had only been able to maintain its position through the special social conditions created by the 'Later Liang' dynasty: the Liang, who had come from the lower classes of the population, had driven the gentry into the arms of the Sha-t'o Turks. As soon as the upstarts, in so far as they had not fallen again or been exterminated, had more or less assimilated themselves to the old gentry, and on the other hand the leaders of the Sha-t'o had become numerically too weak, there was a possibility of resuming the old form of rule.

There had been certain changes in this period. The north-west of China, the region of the old capital Ch'ang-an, had been so ruined by the fighting that had gone on mainly there and farther north, that it was eliminated as a centre of power for a hundred years to come; it had been largely depopulated. The north was under the rule of the Kitan: its trade, which in the past had been with the Huang-ho basin, was now perforce diverted to Peking, which soon became the main centre of the power of the Kitan. The south, particularly the lower Yangtze region and the province of Szechwan, had made economic progress, at least in comparison with the north; consequently it had gained in political importance.

One other event of this time has to be mentioned: the great persecution of Buddhism in 955, but not only because 30,336 temples and monasteries were secularized and only some 2,700 with 61,200 monks were left. Although the immediate reason for this action seems to have been that too many men entered the monasteries in order to avoid being taken as soldiers, the effect of the law of 955 was that from now on the Buddhists were put under regulations which clarified once and for ever their position within the framework of a society which had as its aim to define clearly the status of each individual within each social class. Private persons were no more allowed to erect temples and monasteries. The number of temples per district was legally fixed. A person could become a monk only if the head of the family gave its permission. He had to be over fifteen years of age and had to know by heart at least one hundred pages of texts. The state took over the control of the ordinations which could be performed only after a successful examination. Each year a list of all monks had to be submitted to the government in two copies. Monks had to carry six identification cards with them, one of which was the ordination diploma for which a fee had to be paid to the government (already since 755). The diploma was, in the eleventh century, issued by the Bureau of Sacrifices, but the money was collected by the Ministry of Agriculture. It can be regarded as a payment in lieu of land tax. The price was in the eleventh century 130 strings, which represented the value of a small farm or the value of some 17,000 litres of grain. The price of the diploma went up to 220 strings in 1101, and the then government sold 30,000 diplomas per year in order to get still more cash. But as diplomas could be traded, a black market developed, on which they were sold for as little as twenty strings.

12 Ancient tiled pagoda at Chengting (Hopei).
(Photo H. Hammer-Morrisson.)

13 Horse-training. Painting by Li Lung-mien. Late Sung period.
(Manchu Imperial House Collection.)

CHAPTER NINE

Modern Times

(A) GENERAL CHARACTERISTICS

Any division into periods is arbitrary as changes do not happen from one year to the next. The first beginnings of the changes which led to the 'Modern Times' actually can be seen from the end of An Lu-shan's rebellion on, from c. A.D. 780 on. The period of the 'Five Dynasties' can be regarded as the end of the 'Middle Ages' or with about just as much justification, the beginning of a new age. In any case, the changes which went on in all parts of China, in all the different local governments, were very radical and deep-going, and only around A.D. 1000 was the transformation more or less completed.

If we want to characterize the 'Modern Times' by one concept, we would have to call this epoch the time of the emergence of a middle class, and it will be remembered that the growth of the middle class in Europe was also the decisive change between the Middle Ages and Modern Times in Europe. The parallelism should, however, not be overdone. The gentry continued to play a role in China during the Modern Times, much more than the aristocracy did in Europe. The middle class did not ever really get into power during the whole period. And yet, if we had no documents about China after the year 1300, we would probably have concluded that China entered the 'industrial age' shortly after that date. Probably we would also have predicted the development of a clear capitalistic system. It did not happen, and the reasons for this are not yet fully clear; different explanations have been proposed.

While we will discuss the individual developments later in some detail, a few words about the changes in general might be given already here. The wars which followed Huang Ch'ao's rebellion greatly affected the ruling gentry. A number of families were so strongly affected that they lost their importance and disappeared. Commoners from the followers of Huang Ch'ao or other armies succeeded in getting into power, acquiring property and entering the ranks of the gentry. At about A.D. 1000 almost half of the gentry families were new families of low origin. The state, often ruled by men who had just moved up, was no more interested in the aristocratic manners of the old gentry families, especially no more interested in their genealogies. When conditions began to improve after A.D. 1000, and when the new families felt themselves as real gentry families, they tried to set up a mechanism to protect the status of their families. In the eleventh century private genealogies began to be more generally kept, and such genealogies have often been preserved to the present day. Their function was on the one side to avoid mistakes in the ancestral worship by forgetting to honour one ancestor or by putting his ancestral tablet in a wrong place. Another function was that any claim against the clan could be checked. Clans set up rules of behaviour and procedure to regulate all affairs of the clan and its branches without the necessity of asking the state to interfere in case of conflict. Many such 'clan rules' exist in China and also in Japan, which took over this innovation. Clans often set apart special pieces of land as clan land; the income of this land was to be used to secure a minimum of support for every clan member and his own family, so that no member ever could fall into utter poverty. Clan schools which were run by income from special pieces of clan land were established to guarantee an education for the members of the clan, again in order to make sure that the clan would remain a part of the élite. Many clans set up special marriage rules for clan members, and after some time cross-cousin marriages between two or three families were legally allowed; such marriages tended to fasten bonds between clans and to prevent the loss of property by marriage. While on the one hand, a new 'clan consciousness' grew up among the gentry families in order to secure their power, tax and corvée legislation, especially in the eleventh century, induced many families to split up into small families.

It can be shown that over the next centuries, the power of the family head increased. He was now regarded as owner of the property, not only mere administrator of family property. He got power over the life and death of his children. The increase of power went together with a change of position of the ruler. The period of transition (until c. A.D. 1000) was followed by a period of 'moderate absolutism' (until 1278) in which emperors as persons played a greater role than before, and some emperors, such as Shen Tsung (in 1071), even declared that they regarded the welfare of the masses as more important than the profit of the gentry. After 1278, however, the personal influence of the emperors grew further towards absolutism and at times became pure despotism.

Individuals, especially family heads, gained more freedom in

'Modern Times'. Not only the period of transition, but also the following period was a time of much greater social mobility than existed in the Middle Ages. By various legal and/or illegal means people could move up into positions of power and wealth: we know of many merchants who succeeded in being allowed to enter the state examinations and thus got access to jobs in the administration. Large, influential gentry families in the capital protected sons from less important families and thus gave them a chance to move into the gentry. Thus, these families built up a clientele of lesser gentry families which assisted them and upon the loyalty of which they could count. The gentry can from now on be divided into two parts. First, there was a 'big gentry' which consisted of much fewer families than in earlier times and which directed the policy in the capital; and second, there was a 'small gentry' which was operating mainly in the provincial cities, directing local affairs and bound by ties of loyalty to big gentry families. Gentry cliques now extended into the provinces and it often became possible to identify a clique with a geographical area, which, however, usually did not indicate particularistic tendencies.

Individual freedom did not show itself only in greater social mobility. The restrictions which, for instance, had made the craftsmen and artisans almost into serfs, were gradually lifted. From the early sixteenth century on, craftsmen were free and no longer subject to forced labour services for the state. Only in the first decades of the eighteenth century did the 'outcast' groups acquire the status of citizens. Such 'outcasts' were small ethnic groups, living as minorities in areas now fully colonized by Chinese and performing 'dishonourable' professions, such as prostitution and music. Slavery, too, faded out slowly over the centuries. However, some of the larger ethnic groups living in areas where they still were the majority, remained under restrictions to the twentieth century.

To return to the craftsmen: most of them down to the nineteenth century still had their shops in one lane or street and lived above their shops, as they had done in the earlier period. But from now on, they began to organize in guilds of an essentially religious character, as similar guilds in other parts of Asia at the same time also did. They provided welfare services for their members, made some attempts towards standardization of products and prices, imposed taxes upon their members, kept their streets clean and tried to regulate salaries. Apprentices were initiated in a kind of semi-religious ceremony, and often meetings took place in temples. No guild, however, connected people of the same craft living in different cities. Thus, they did not achieve political power. Furthermore, each trade had its own guild; in Peking in the nineteenth century there existed over 420 different guilds. Thus, guilds failed to achieve political influence even within individual cities.

Probably at the same time, regional associations, the so-called *hui-kuan* originated. Such associations united people from one city or one area who lived in another city. People of different trades, but mainly businessmen, came together under elected chiefs and councillors. Sometimes, such regional associations could function as pressure groups, especially as they were usually financially stronger than the guilds. They often owned city property or farmland. Not all merchants, however, were so organized. Although merchants remained under humiliating restrictions as to the colour and material of their dress and the prohibition to ride a horse, they could more often circumvent such restrictions and in general had much more freedom in this epoch.

Trade, including overseas trade, developed greatly from now on. Soon we find in the coastal ports a special office which handled custom and registration affairs, supplied interpreters for foreigners, received them officially and gave good-bye dinners when they left. Down to the thirteenth century, most of this overseas trade was still in the hands of foreigners, mainly Indians. Entrepreneurs hired ships, if they were not ship-owners, hired trained merchants who in turn hired sailors mainly from the South-East Asian countries, and sold their own merchandise as well as took goods on commission. Wealthy Chinese families invested money in such foreign enterprises and in some cases even gave their daughters in marriage to foreigners in order to profit from this business.

While there was thus more freedom for men of the ranks below the gentry than ever before, there was a severe restriction of the freedom of women—all women. This may be a consequence of the greater powers of the family heads at this time. Remarriage of widows was now regarded as immoral: a widow had belonged to her husband in life, she still belonged to him or at least to his family after his death and could not simply go away and join another family. Women, with the exception of courtesans and musicians, could normally no more participate in parties. And, again with the exception of a small ethnic group, women did no more participate in the actual work on the land: their place was in the house where they were supposed to spin, weave, cook, and take care of the children.

We also see an emergence of industry from the eleventh century on. We find men who were running almost monopolistic enterprises, such as preparing charcoal for iron production and producing iron and steel at the same time; some of these men had several factories, operating under hired and qualified managers with more than 500 labourers. We find beginnings of a labour legislation and the first strikes (A.D. 782 the first strike of merchants in the capital; 1601 first strike of textile workers).

Some of these labourers were so-called 'vagrants', farmers who had secretly left their land or their landlord's land for various reasons, and had shifted to other regions where they did not register and thus did not pay taxes. Entrepreneurs liked to hire them for industries outside the towns where supervision by the government was not so strong; naturally, these 'vagrants' were completely at the mercy of their employers.

Since c. 780 the economy can again be called a money economy; more and more taxes were imposed in form of money instead of in kind. This pressure forced farmers out of the land and into the cities in order to earn there the cash they needed for their tax payments. These men provided the labour force for industries, and this in turn led to the strong growth of the cities, especially in central China where trade and industries developed most.

Wealthy people not only invested in industrial enterprises, but also began to make heavy investments in agriculture in the vicinity of cities in order to increase production and thus income. We find men who drained lakes in order to create fields below the water level for easy irrigation; others made floating fields on lakes and avoided land tax payments; still others combined pig and fish breeding in one operation.

The introduction of money economy and money taxes led to a need for more coinage. As metal was scarce and minting very expensive, iron coins were introduced, silver became more and more common as a means of exchange, and paper money was issued. As the relative value of these moneys changed with supply and demand, speculation became a flourishing business which led to further enrichment of people in business. Even the government became more money-minded: costs of operations and even of wars were carefully calculated in order to achieve savings; financial specialists were appointed by the government, just as clans appointed such men for the efficient administration of their clan properties.

Yet no real capitalism or industrialism developed until towards the end of this epoch, although at the end of the twelfth century almost all conditions for such a development seemed to be given.

(B) PERIOD OF MODERATE ABSOLUTISM

(1) The Northern Sung dynasty

1 *Southward expansion*

The founder of the Sung dynasty, Chao K'uang-yin (ruled 960–974), came of a Chinese military family living to the south of Peking.

He advanced from general to emperor, and so differed in no way from the emperors who had preceded him. But his dynasty did not disappear as quickly as the others; for this there were several reasons. To begin with, there was the simple fact that he remained alive longer than the other founders of dynasties, and so was able to place his rule on a firmer foundation. But in addition to this he followed a new course, which in certain ways smoothed matters for him and for his successors, in foreign policy.

This Sung dynasty, as Chao K'uang-yin named it, no longer turned against the northern peoples, particularly the Kitan, but against the south. This was not exactly an heroic policy: the north of China remained in the hands of the Kitan. There were frequent clashes, but no real effort was made to destroy the Kitan, whose dynasty was now called 'Liao'. The second emperor of the Sung was actually heavily defeated several times by the Kitan. But they, for their part, made no attempt to conquer the whole of China, especially since the task would have become more and more burdensome the farther south the Sung expanded. And very soon there were other reasons why the Kitan should refrain from turning their whole strength against the Chinese.

As we said, the Sung turned at once against the states in the south. Some of the many small southern states had made substantial economic and cultural advance, but militarily they were not strong. Chao K'uang-yin (named as emperor T'ai Tsu) attacked them in succession. Most of them fell very quickly and without any heavy fighting, especially since the Sung dealt mildly with the defeated rulers and their following. The gentry and the merchants in these small states could not but realize the advantages of a widened and well-ordered economic field, and they were therefore entirely in favour of the annexation of their country so soon as it proved to be tolerable. And the Sung empire could only endure and gain strength if it had control of the regions along the Yangtze and around Canton, with their great economic resources. The process of absorbing the small states in the south continued until 980. Before it was ended, the Sung tried to extend their influence in the south beyond the Chinese border, and secured a sort of protectorate over parts of North Vietnam (973). This sphere of influence was politically insignificant and not directly of any economic importance; but it fulfilled for the Sung the same functions which colonial territories fulfilled for Europeans, serving as a field of operation for the commercial class, who imported raw materials from it—mainly, it is true, luxury articles such as special sorts of wood, perfumes, ivory, and so on—and exported Chinese manufactures. As the power of the empire grew, this zone of influence extended as far as Indonesia: the process

210

had begun in the T'ang period. The trade with the south had not the deleterious effects of the trade with Central Asia. There was no sale of refined metals, and none of fabrics, as the natives produced their own textiles which sufficed for their needs. And the export of porcelain brought no economic injury to China, but the reverse.

This Sung policy was entirely in the interest of the gentry and of the trading community which was now closely connected with them. Undoubtedly it strengthened China. The policy of non-intervention in the north was endurable even when peace with the Kitan had to be bought by the payment of an annual tribute. From 1004 onward, 100,000 ounces of silver and 200,000 bales of silk were paid annually to the Kitan, amounting in value to about 270,000 strings of cash, each of 1,000 coins. The state budget amounted to some 20,000,000 strings of cash. In 1038 the payments amounted to 500,000 strings, but the budget was by then much larger. One is liable to get a false impression when reading of these big payments if one does not take into account what percentage they formed of the total revenues of the state. The tribute to the Kitan amounted to less than 2 per cent of the revenue, while the expenditure on the army accounted for 25 per cent of the budget. It cost much less to pay tribute than to maintain large armies and go to war. Financial considerations played a great part during the Sung epoch. The taxation revenue of the empire rose rapidly after the pacification of the south; soon after the beginning of the dynasty the state budget was double that of the T'ang. If the state expenditure in the eleventh century had not continually grown through the increase in military expenditure—in spite of everything! —there would have come a period of great prosperity in the empire.

2 Administration and army. Inflation

The Sung emperor, like the rulers of the transition period, had gained the throne by his personal abilities as military leader; in fact, he had been made emperor by his soldiers as had happened to so many emperors in later Imperial Rome. For the next 300 years we observe a change in the position of the emperor. On the one hand, if he was active and intelligent enough, he exercised much more personal influence than the rulers of the Middle Ages. On the other hand, at the same time, the emperors were much closer to their ministers as before. We hear of ministers who patted the ruler on the shoulders when they retired from an audience; another one fell asleep on the emperor's knee and was not punished for this familiarity. The emperor was called *kuan-chia* (Administrator) and even called himself so. And in the early twelfth century an emperor stated 'I do not regard the empire as my personal property; my job is to guide the people.' Financially-minded as the Sung dynasty was, the cost of

211

the operation of the palace was calculated, so that the emperor had a budget: in 1068 the salaries of all officials in the capital amounted to 40,000 strings of money per month, the armies 100,000, and the emperor's ordinary monthly budget was 70,000 strings. For festivals, imperial birthdays, weddings and burials extra allowances were made. Thus, the Sung rulers may be called 'moderate absolutists' and not despots.

One of the first acts of the new Sung emperor, in 963, was a fundamental reorganization of the administration of the country. The old system of a civil administration and a military administration independent of it was brought to an end and the whole administration of the country placed in the hands of civil officials. The gentry welcomed this measure and gave it full support, because it enabled the influence of the gentry to grow and removed the fear of competition from the military, some of whom did not belong by birth to the gentry. The generals by whose aid the empire had been created were put on pension, or transferred to civil employment, as quickly as possible. The army was demobilized, and this measure was bound up with the settlement of peasants in the regions which war had depopulated, or on new land. Soon after this the revenue noticeably increased. Above all, the army was placed directly under the central administration, and the system of military governors was thus brought to an end. The soldiers became mercenaries of the state, whereas in the past there had been conscription. In 975 the army had numbered only 378,000, and its cost had not been insupportable. Although the numbers increased greatly, reaching 912,000 in 1017 and 1,259,000 in 1045, this implied no increase in military strength; for men who had once been soldiers remained with the army even when they were too old for service. Moreover, the soldiers grew more and more exacting; when detachments were transferred to another region, for instance, the soldiers would not carry their baggage; an army of porters had to be assembled. The soldiers also refused to go to regions remote from their homes until they were given extra pay. Such allowances gradually became customary, and so the military expenditure grew by leaps and bounds without any corresponding increase in the striking power of the army.

The government was soon unable to meet the whole cost of the army out of taxation revenue. The attempt was made to cover the expenditure by coining fresh money. In connection with the increase in commercial capital described above, and the consequent beginning of an industry, China's metal production had greatly increased. In 1050 thirteen times as much silver, eight times as much copper, and fourteen times as much iron was produced as in 800. It is estimated that the production per year was perhaps around 2,120,000 tons. In part, this was made possible by the extensive use of coal instead of the predominant use of charcoal in earlier periods. Iron money remained in use in Szechwan and parts of Hunan, but copper remained the main currency. The cost of minting, however, amounted in China to about 75 per cent and often over 100 per cent of the value of the money coined.

To meet the increasing expenditure, an unexampled quantity of new money was put into circulation. The state budget increased from 22,200,000 in A.D. 1000 to 150,800,000 in 1021. The Kitan state coined a great deal of silver, and some of the tribute was paid to it in silver. The greatly increased production of silver led to its being put into circulation in China itself. And this provided a new field of speculation, through the variations in the rates for silver and for copper. Speculation was also possible with the deposit certificates, which were issued in quantities by the state from the beginning of the eleventh century, and to which the first true paper money was soon added. The paper money and the certificates were redeemable at a definite date, but at a reduction of at least 3 per cent of their value; this, too, yielded a certain revenue to the state.

The inflation that resulted from all these measures brought profit to the big merchants in spite of the fact that they had to supply directly or indirectly all non-agricultural taxes (in 1160 some 40,000,000 strings annually), especially the salt tax (50 per cent), wine tax (36 per cent), tea tax (7 per cent) and customs (7 per cent). Although the official economic thinking remained Confucian, i.e. anti-business and pro-agrarian, we find in this time insight in price laws, for instance, that peace times and/or decrease of population induce deflation. The government had always attempted to manipulate the prices by interference. Already in much earlier times, again and again, attempts had been made to lower the prices by the so-called 'ever-normal granaries' of the government which threw grain on the market when prices were too high and bought grain when prices were low. But now, in addition to such measures, we also find others which exhibit a deeper insight: in a period of starvation the scholar and official Fan Chung-yen, instead of officially reducing grain prices, raised the prices in his district considerably. Although the population got angry, merchants started to import large amounts of grain; as soon as this happened, Fan (himself a big landowner) reduced the price again. Similar results were achieved by others by just stimulating merchants to import grain into deficit areas.

It was in land that the newly formed capital was invested. Thus we see in the Sung period, and especially in the eleventh century, the greatest accumulation of estates that there had ever been up to then in China.

Many of these estates came into origin as gifts of the emperor to individuals or to temples, others were created on hillsides on land which belonged to the villages. From this time on, the rest of the village commons in China proper disappeared. Villagers could no longer use the top-soil of the hills as fertilizer, or the trees as firewood and building material. In addition, the hillside estates diverted the water of springs and creeks, thus damaging severely the irrigation works of the villagers in the plains. The estates (*chuang*) were controlled by appointed managers who often became hereditary managers. There is still a controversy as to what the tenants were. Some say they were serfs, while others regard them as tenants in the narrower definition of the word. Unfortunately, Chinese at the time had no clear terminology, and we probably have to assume that combinations of all kinds existed. Some tenants were probably the non-registered migrants, of whom we spoke above. As such, they depended upon the managers who could always denounce them to the authorities, which would lead to punishment, because nobody was allowed to leave his home without officially changing his registration. If such restriction of movement were typical of tenants only, we could properly call them serfs, but other citizens were under the same restrictions, officials excepted. Other scholars think that some tenants were freed slaves. It all depends upon the explanation of the term *k'o-hu* (guest families). As officials had 'office land' as source of income, and as the state had state land, we should probably assume that such land was tilled by tenants who were not allowed to leave, because officials were transferred quite often and would have a hard time to find new tenants every time they were transferred to a new post. The problem arises that our documents are often tendentious. Some make overstatements for political reasons, others talk about exceptional and regional situations, and the interpreters often have their own biases. Only in-depth studies of small areas over longer periods of time can be of help, and such studies are under way in Japan and the West. Certainly, there was not only a great diversity of rural labour organization, but also of farming itself. In Sung times, many tanks to store water for irrigation purposes were built; sluices to regulate the flow were built. We even hear that in addition to the treadmills and other implements to lift water into the fields, some windmills were in use. On the other hand, some farmers surrounded low-lying land by dykes and had fields below the water level ('polders', as they are called in Holland), while still others raised the level by excavating a part of their land, thus creating fields safe of floods, and ponds in which they could raise fish.

To return to the estates: some of them operated their own mills and even textile factories with non-registered weavers. It seems that in course of time, many such estates later became villages (recognizable by the syllable *-chuang* at the end of the village name) which were, from the beginning, not merely farming villages but also had some 'industries' in the village, in contrast to villages in other parts of Asia where villages house only farmers and no other professionals,

A new development in this period were the 'clan estates' (*i-chuang*). created by Fan Chung-yen (989–1052) in 1048. The incomes of these clan estates were used for the benefit of the whole clan, were controlled by clan-appointed managers and had tax-free status, guaranteed by the government which regarded them as welfare institutions. Technically, they might better be called corporations because they were similar in structure to some of our industrial corporations. Under the Chinese economic system, large-scale landowning always proved socially and politically injurious. Up to very recent times the peasant who rented his land paid 40–50 per cent of the produce to the landowner, who was responsible for payment of the normal land tax. The landlord, however, had always found means of evading payment. As each district had to yield a definite amount of taxation, the more the big landowners succeeded in evading payment the more had to be paid by the independent small farmers. These independent peasants could then either 'give' their land to the big landowner and pay rent to him, thus escaping from the attentions of the tax-officer, or simply leave the district and secretly enter another one where they were not registered. In either case the government lost taxes.

All this made itself felt especially in the south with its great estates of tax-evading landowners. Here the remaining small peasant-owners had to pay the new taxes or to become tenants of the landowners and lose their property, though some of them may have managed to survive by becoming part-tenant and part-owners. Still others seem to have managed by going into commercial farming or fruit-culture, fish-breeding, or doing labour services in transport business. The diversification of rural life is a typical trait of the Sung time. The agricultural boom which took place in spite of the pressure of taxation may, perhaps, at least in part be an effect of a new period of warmer climate (900–1100?).

Furthermore, we find now a significant difference between the northern and the southern parts of the Sung empire. The north was still suffering from the war-devastation of the tenth century. As the landlords were always the first sufferers from popular uprisings as well as from war, they had disappeared, leaving their former tenants as free peasants. From this period on, we have enough data to observe a social 'law': as the capital was the largest consumer, especially of high-priced products such as vegetables which could not be transported over long distances, the gentry always tried to control the land around the capital. Here, we find the highest concentration of landlords and tenants. Production in this inner circle shifted at least partly from rice and wheat to mulberry trees for silk, and vegetables grown under the trees. These urban demands resulted in the growth of an 'industrial' quarter on the outskirts of the capital, in which especially silk for the upper classes was produced. The next circle also contained many landlords, but production was more in staple foods such as wheat and rice which could be transported. Exploitation in this second circle was not much less than in the first circle, because of less close supervision by the authorities. In the third circle we find independent subsistence farmers. Some provincial capitals, especially in Szechwan, exhibited a similar pattern of circles. With each shift of the capital, a complete reorganization appeared: landlords and officials gave up their properties, cultivation changed, and a new system of circles began to form around the new capital. We find, therefore, the grotesque result that the thinly populated province of Shensi in the north-west yielded about a quarter of the total revenues of the state: it had no large landowners, no wealthy gentry, with their evasion of taxation, only a mass of newly settled small peasants' holdings. For this reason the government was particularly interested in that province, and closely watched the political changes in its neighbourhood. In 990 a man belonging to a sinified Toba family, living on the border of Shensi, had made himself king with the support of remnants of Toba tribes. In 1034 came severe fighting, and in 1038 the king proclaimed himself emperor, in the Hsia dynasty, and threatened the whole of north-western China. Tribute was now also paid to this state (250,000 strings), but the fight against it continued, to save that important province.

These were the main events in internal and external affairs during the Sung period until 1068. It will be seen that foreign affairs were of much less importance than developments in the country.

3 Reforms and welfare schemes

The situation just described was bound to produce a reaction. In spite of the inflationary measures the revenue fell, partly in consequence of the tax evasions of the great landowners. It fell from 150,000,000 in 1021 to 116,000,000 in 1065. Expenditure did not fall, and there was a constant succession of budget deficits. The young emperor Shen Tsung (1068–1085) became convinced that the policy followed by the ruling clique of officials and gentry was bad, and he gave his adhesion to a small group led by Wang An-shih (1021–1086). The ruling gentry clique represented especially the interests of the large tea producers and merchants in Szechwan and Kiangsi. It advocated a policy of laissez-faire in trade: it held that everything would adjust itself. Wang An-shih himself came from Kiangsi and was therefore supported at first by the government clique, within which the Kiangsi group was trying to gain predominance over the Szechwan group. But Wang An-shih came from a poor family, as did his supporters, for whom he quickly secured posts. They represented the interests of the small landholders and the small dealers. This group succeeded in gaining power, and in carrying out a number of reforms, all directed against the monopolist merchants. Credits for small peasants were introduced, and officials were given bigger salaries, in order to make them independent and to recruit officials who were not big landowners. The army was greatly reduced, and in addition to the paid soldiery a national militia was created. Special attention was paid to the province of Shensi, whose conditions were taken more or less as a model.

It seems that one consequence of Wang's reforms was a strong fall in the prices, i.e. a deflation; therefore, as soon as the first decrees were issued, the large owners and the merchants who were allied to them, offered furious opposition. A group of officials and landlords who still had large properties in the vicinity of Loyang—at that time a quiet cultural centre—also joined them. Even some of Wang An-shih's former adherents came out against him. After a few years the emperor was no longer able to retain Wang An-shih and had to abandon the new policy. How really political interests were here at issue may be seen from the fact that for many of the new decrees which were not directly concerned with economic affairs, such, for instance, as the reform of the examination system, Wang An-shih was strongly attacked though his opponents had themselves advocated them in the past and had no practical objection to offer to them. The contest, however, between the two groups was not over. The monopolistic landowners and their merchants had the upper hand from 1086 to 1102, but then the advocates of the policy represented by Wang again came into power for a short time. They had but little success to show, as they did not remain in power long enough and, owing to the strong opposition, they were never able to make their control really effective.

Basically, both groups were against allowing the developing middle class and especially the merchants to gain too much freedom, and whatever freedom they in fact gained, came through extra-legal or illegal practices. A proverb of the time said 'People hate their ruler as animals hate the net (of the hunter).' The basic laws of medieval times which had attempted to create stable social classes remained: down to the eighteenth century there were slaves, different classes of serfs, 'commoners', and free burghers. Craftsmen remained under work obligation. Merchants were second-class people. Each class had to wear dresses of special colour and material, so that the social status of a person, even if he were not an official and thus recognizable by his insignia, was immediately clear when one saw him. The houses of different classes differed from one another by the type of tiles, the decorations of the doors and gates; the size of the main reception room of the house was prescribed and was kept small for all non-officials; and even size and form of the tombs was prescribed in detail for each class. Once a person had a certain privilege, he and his descendants, even if they had lost their position in the bureaucracy, retained their elevated status in the community. All burghers were admitted to the examinations and thus there was a certain social mobility allowed within the leading class of the society, and a new 'small gentry' emerged. There is no doubt that in the Sung states (as opposed to the northern Liao and later Chin states) examinations became more and more the ladder to success. But this broadening of the basis of the 'upper class' also meant that in general, the power of the central gentry, i.e. those families whose members were in offices around the court, diminished, and in the countryside the dominant element now became the 'small gentry', whose status depended in part of the political situation at court, in part on the local situation: local fights between gentry families as well as severe floods or droughts could severely affect them. There was now a feeling of insecurity within the gentry. The eleventh and twelfth centuries were periods of extensive social legislation in order to give the lower classes some degree of security and thus prevent them from attempting to upset the status quo. In addition to the 'ever-normal granaries' of the state, 'social granaries' were revived, into which all farmers of a village had to deliver grain for periods of need. In 1098 a bureau for housing and care was created which created homes for the old and destitute; 1102 a bureau for medical care sent state doctors to homes and hospitals as well as to private homes to care for poor patients; from 1104 a bureau of burials took charge of the costs of burials of poor persons. Doctors as craftsmen were under corvée obligation and could easily be ordered by the state. Buddhist priests sometimes also took charge of medical care, burial costs and hospitalization. The state gave them premiums if they did good work. The Ministry of Civil Affairs made the surveys of cases and costs, while the Ministry of Finances paid the costs. We hear of state orphanages in 1247, a free pharmacy in 1248, state hospitals were reorganized in 1143. In 1167 the government gave low-interest loans to poor persons and (from 1159 on) sold cheap grain from state granaries. Fire protection services in large cities were organized. Finally, from 1141 on, the government opened up to twenty-three geisha houses for the entertainment of soldiers who were far from home in the capital and had no possibility for other amusements. Public baths had existed already some centuries ago; now Buddhist temples opened public baths as a social service.

Social services for the officials were also extended. Already from the eighth century on, offices were closed every tenth day and during holidays, a total of almost eighty days per year. Even criminals got some leave and exiles had the right of a home leave once every three years. The pensions for retired officials after the age of seventy which amounted to 50 per cent of the salary from the eighth century on, were again raised, though widows did not receive benefits.

All these data, however, should be treated with care: we really do not know how often free medicines were distributed, how many state hospitals there were, how they functioned and who actually was accepted as a patient. The same is the case with the above-mentioned 'sumptuary laws': to some degree, they were operating, but to what degree?

4 *Cultural situation* (*philosophy, religion, literature, painting*)
Culturally the eleventh century was the most active period China had so far experienced, apart from the fourth century B.C. As a consequence of the immensely increased number of educated people resulting from the invention of printing, circles of scholars and private schools set up by scholars were scattered all over the country. The various philosophical schools differed in their political attitude and in the choice of literary models with which they were politically in sympathy. Thus Wang An-shih and his followers preferred the rigid classic style of Han Yü (768–825) who lived in the T'ang period and had also been an opponent of the monopolistic tendencies of pre-capitalism. For the Wang An-shih group formed itself into a school with a philosophy of its own and with its own commentaries on the classics. As the representative of the small merchants and the small landholders, this school advocated policies of state control and specialized in the study and annotation of classical books which seemed to favour their ideas.

But the Wang An-shih school was unable to hold its own against the school that stood for monopolist trade capitalism, the new philosophy described as Neo-Confucianism or the Sung school. Here Confucianism and Buddhism were for the first time in a fruitful dialogue. In the last centuries, Buddhistic ideas had penetrated all of Chinese culture: the slaughtering of animals and the executions of criminals were allowed only on certain days, in accordance with Buddhist rules. Formerly, monks and nuns had to greet the emperor as all citizens had to do; now they were exempt from this rule. On the other hand, the first Sung emperor was willing to throw himself to the earth in front of the Buddha statues, but he was told he did not have to do it because he was the 'Buddha of the present time' and thus equal to the God. Buddhist priests participated in the celebrations on the emperor's birthday, and emperors from time to time gave free meals to large crowds of monks. Buddhist thought entered the field of justice: in Sung time we hear complaints that judges did not apply the laws and showed laxity, because they hoped to gain religious merit by sparing the lives of criminals. We have seen how the main current of Buddhism had changed from a revolutionary to a reactionary doctrine. The new gentry of the eleventh century adopted a number of elements of this reactionary Buddhism and incorporated them in the Confucianist system. This brought into Confucianism a metaphysic which it had lacked in the past, greatly extending its influence on the people and at the same time taking the wind out of the sails of Buddhism. The gentry never again placed themselves on the side of the Buddhist Church as they had done in the T'ang period. When they got tired of Confucianism, they interested themselves in Taoism or the politically innocent, escapist, meditative Buddhism.

Men like Chou Tun-i (1017–1073) and Chang Tsai (1020–1077) developed a cosmological theory which could measure up with Buddhistic cosmology and metaphysics. But perhaps more important was the attempt of the Neo-Confucianists to explain the problem of evil. Confucius and his followers had believed that every person could perfect himself by overcoming the evil in him. As the good persons should be the élite and rule the others, theoretically everybody who was a member of human society, could move up and become a leader. It was commonly assumed that human nature is good or indifferent, and that human feelings are evil and have to be tamed and educated. When in Han time, with the establishment of the gentry society and its social classes, the idea that any person could move up to become a leader if he only perfected himself, appeared to be too unrealistic, the theory of different grades of men was formed which found its clearest formulation by Han Yü: some people have a good, others a neutral, and still others a bad nature; therefore, not everybody can become a leader. The Neo-Confucianists, especially Ch'eng Hao (1032–1085) and Ch'eng I (1033–1107), tried to find the reasons for this inequality. According to them, nature is neutral; but physical form originates with the combination of Matter with Spiritual Force (*ch'i*). This combination produces individuals in whom there is a lack of balance or harmony. Man should try to transform physical form and recover original nature. The creative force by which such a transformation is possible is *jen*, love, the creative, life-giving quality of nature itself.

It should be remarked that Neo-Confucianism accepts an inequality of men, as early Confucianism did; and that *jen*, benevolence, i.e. humane behaviour of one of a higher status towards one in a lower status, in its practical application has to be channelled by *li*, the system of rules of behaviour. The *li*, however, always started from the idea of a stratified class society. Chu Hsi (1130–1200), the famous scholar and systematizer of Neo-Confucian thoughts, brought out rules of behaviour for those burghers who did not belong to the gentry and could not, therefore, be expected to perform all *li*; his 'simplified *li*' exercised a great influence not only upon contemporary China, but also upon Korea and Annam and there strengthened a hitherto looser patriarchal, patrilinear family system. By taking texts in the Classics seriously the freedom of women was now severely limited. Women began to disappear from the fields, from the streets and from social parties. They had to be virgins on the day of the wedding and were not supposed to marry again after divorce (by their husband) or after the husband's death. Still, we know of a good number of famous men in the eleventh century who married divorced women and did not seem to be against marrying a widow. However, the rules became more and more strict down to the nineteenth century.

The Neo-Confucianists also compiled great analytical works of history and encyclopaedias whose authority continued for many centuries. They interpreted in these works all history in accordance with their outlook; they issued new commentaries on all the classics in order to spread interpretations that served their purposes. In the field of commentary this school of thought was given perfect expression by Chu Hsi, who also wrote one of the chief historical works. Chu Hsi's commentaries became standard works for centuries, until the beginning of the twentieth century. Yet, although Chu became the symbol of conservatism, he was quite interested in science, and in this field he had an open eye for changes.

The Sung period is so important because it is also the time of the greatest development of Chinese science and technology. Many new theories, but also many practical new inventions were made. Medicine made substantial progress. About 1145 the first autopsy was made, on the body of a south Chinese captive. Sung medicine seems to be the highpoint of traditional Chinese medicine; afterwards, few developments of importance are noticeable. Most important was the attempt to bring medical knowledge about the human body, pharmacology, and general philosophy into one system, to unify in this area, too, the cosmos, nature, and man. We should keep in mind, that before the Sung, Chinese doctors did not know how organs which were called 'liver', 'heart', etc., looked and where

221

they were located in the body. It is important to observe that in Sung time detailed standards of professional ethics were laid down; the first attempts in this direction of a 'Hippocratic oath' were made in the sixth century. Further, it is interesting sociologically that Sung doctors were of the opinion that the bodies of upper-class people were finer than those of ordinary persons, and both classes of men should be treated differently and by different doctors. This is an application of the doctrine of the inequality of men, stressed so much in the eleventh century.

Another important field of development in Sung time was law. We find here for the first time theoretical discussions and legal rules concerning the interrogation of defendants, the right to appeal, the training of judges, the evaluation of testimony. If these rules were really applied in practical life, the judicial system of China can only be called very progressive and modern, if compared to Europe at the same time.

The Wang An-shih school of political philosophy had opponents also in the field of literary style, the so-called Shu Group (Shu means the present province of Szechwan), whose leaders were the famous Three Sus. The greatest of the three was Su Shih or Su Tung-p'o (1036–1101); the others were his father, Su Hsün, and his brother, Su Che. It is characteristic of these Shu poets, and also of the Kiangsi school associated with them, that they made as much use as they could of the vernacular. It had not been usual to introduce the phrases of everyday life into poetry, but Su Tung-p'o made use of the most everyday expressions, without diminishing his artistic effectiveness by so doing; on the contrary, the result was to give his poems much more genuine feeling than those of other poets. These poets were in harmony with the writings of the T'ang period poet Po Chü-i (772–846) and were supported, like Neo-Confucianism, by representatives of trade capitalism. Politically, in their conservatism they were sharply opposed to the Wang An-shih group. Midway between the two stood the so-called Loyang School, whose greatest leaders were the historian and poet Ssŭ-ma Kuang (1019–1086) and the philosopher-poet Shao Yung (1011–1077).

In addition to its poems, the Sung literature was famous for the so-called *pi-chi* or miscellaneous notes. These consist of short notes of the most various sort, notes on literature, art, politics, archaeology, all mixed together. The *pi-chi* are a treasure-house for the history of the culture of the time; they contain many details, often of importance, about China's neighbouring peoples. They were intended to serve as suggestions for learned conversation when scholars came together; they aimed at showing how wide was a scholar's knowledge. To this group we must add the accounts of travel, of which some of great value dating from the Sung period are still extant; they contain information of the greatest importance about the early Mongols and also about Sinkiang and south China.

Mainly through the *pi-chi* literature of the Sung period, we learn more about the folk literature and art. We hear that there were story-tellers, professionals who told their long stories for cash reward on the market places, as their descendants in this century still did. To judge from some titles we can assume that many of these stories were based upon official histories or travel accounts, but changed by the story-tellers into folk language and adorned with thrilling episodes and details. Thus, the story-tellers formed long stories which later were written down and became the early forms of novels. They also told ballads, performed shadow-plays and marionette plays. The shadow-play seems to have a long history in China, though we cannot believe a story according to which it was known already in the second century B.C. Marionette plays existed in two forms; in one, the figures were moved by strings from above; in the other by sticks moved from below. The figures which were manipulated by putting the hand into the body of the figure, the so-called 'bag plays', seem to be of later origin and have only a local distribution.

While these men performed in the open, behind screens or on temporary platforms, the upper class already could enjoy real theatre plays; some of these Sung period plays are still preserved today. There developed several local styles, which will be mentioned later. Another entertainment of the upper class was the dance. Here, some foreign influence remains, as in T'ang time. According to one theory, one style of dance consisted of dancing delicate patterns on carpets, according to the designs on the carpet. As the designs were small in size, the dancers danced on the tip of their toes, and this led to the development, it is said, of the custom of foot-binding, famous in China to the beginning of this century. It is certain that the custom at first developed at the court and later trickled down to the lower classes, so that it was finally widely spread even among the poor. The very painful custom, by which the foot was so deformed that the women could walk only with difficulty, kept women in the house and prevented their moving around or doing physical labour. Some Chinese men openly confessed that this custom made faithful and obedient wives. It is interesting that this custom was connected with an erotic cult of the foot; as soon as the custom disappeared the Chinese foot lost its erotic appeal.

Foreign influence played a role also in the music of the time. From Sung on, the seven-tone scale becomes dominant, displacing the old Chinese five-tone scale. The use of notation systems becomes more general.

All these performers: musicians, dancers, and actors belonged to the outcasts: they were regarded as the lowest members of society, allowed only to marry within their caste, excluded from other professions and from state service. Yet, the customers often were very attached to them, and rumours about sexual or homosexual relations circulated then as later.

While the Sung period was of perfection in all fields of art, painting undoubtedly gained its highest development in this time. We find now two main streams in painting: some painters preferred the decorative, pompous, but realistic approach, with great attention to detail. Men who belonged to this school of painting often were active court officials or painted for the court and for other representative purposes. One of the most famous among them, Li Lung-mien (c. 1040–1106), for instance painted the different breeds of horses in the imperial stables. He was also famous for his Buddhistic figures. Another school regarded painting as an intimate, personal expression. They tried to paint inner realities and not outer forms. They, too, were educated, but they did not paint for anybody. They painted in their country houses when they felt in the mood for expression. Their paintings did not stress details, but tried to give the spirit of a landscape, for in this field they excelled most. Best known of them is Mi Fei (c. 1051–1107), a painter as well as a calligrapher, art collector, and art critic. Typically, his paintings were not much liked by the emperor Hui Tsung (ruled 1101–1125) who was one of the greatest art collectors and whose catalogue of his collection became very famous. He created the Painting Academy, an institution which mainly gave official recognition to painters in form of titles which gave the painter access to and status at court. Ma Yüan (c. 1190–1224), member of a whole painter's family, and Hsia Kui (c. 1180–1230) continued the more 'impressionistic' tradition. Already in Sung time, however, many painters could and did paint in different styles, 'copying', i.e. painting in the way of T'ang painters, in order to express their changing emotions by changed styles, a fact which often makes the dating of Chinese paintings very difficult.

Finally, art craft has left us famous porcelains of the Sung period. The most characteristic production of that time is the green porcelain known as 'Celadon'. It consists usually of a rather solid paste, less like porcelain than stoneware, covered with a green glaze; decoration is incised, not painted, under the glaze. In the Sung period, however, came the first pure white porcelain with incised ornamentation under the glaze, and also with painting on the glaze. Not until near the end of the Sung period did the blue and white porcelain begin (blue painting on a white ground). The cobalt needed for this came from Asia Minor. In exchange for the cobalt, Chinese porcelain went to Asia Minor. This trade did not, however, grow greatly until the Mongol epoch; later really substantial orders were placed in China, the Chinese executing the patterns wanted in the West.

5 *Military collapse*

In foreign affairs the whole eleventh century was a period of diplomatic manoeuvring, with every possible effort to avoid war. There was long-continued fighting with the Kitan, and at times also with the Turco-Tibetan Hsia, but diplomacy carried the day: tribute was paid to both enemies, and the effort was made to stir up the Kitan against the Hsia and vice versa; the other parties also intrigued in like fashion. In 1110 the situation seemed to improve for the Sung in this game, as a new enemy appeared in the rear of the Liao (Kitan), the Tungusic Juchên (Jurchen), who in the past had been more or less subject to the Kitan. In 1114 the Juchên made themselves independent and became a political factor. The Kitan were crippled, and it became an easy matter to attack them. But this pleasant situation did not last long. The Juchên conquered Peking, and in 1125 the Kitan empire was destroyed; but in the same year the Juchên marched against the Sung. In 1126 they captured the Sung capital; the emperor and his art-loving father, who had retired a little earlier, were taken prisoner, and the Northern Sung dynasty was at an end. The report of the transport of the emperor towards the north is one of the most touching of Chinese literature. At first, he was still treated with some respect and allowed to keep some of his concubines, servants and maids in acceptable quarters. Step by step, everything was taken away from him, and in the end he died in a miserable hut, alone, totally degraded.

The collapse came so quickly because the whole edifice of security between the Kitan and the Sung was based on a policy of balance and of diplomacy. Neither state was armed in any way, and so both collapsed at the first assault from a military power.

(2) The Liao (Kitan) dynasty in the north (937–1125)

1 *Social structure. Claim to the Chinese imperial throne*

The Kitan, a league of tribes under the leadership of a Mongol tribe, had grown steadily stronger in north-eastern Mongolia during the T'ang epoch. They had gained the allegiance of many tribes in the west and also in Korea and Manchuria, and in the end, about A.D. 900, had become the dominant power in the north. The process of growth of this nomad power was the same as that of other nomad states, such as the Toba state, and therefore need not be described again in any detail here. When the T'ang dynasty was deposed, the Kitan were among the claimants to the Chinese throne, feeling fully justified in their claim as the strongest power in the Far East. Owing to the strength of the Sha-t'o, who themselves claimed leadership in China, the expansion of the Kitan empire slowed down. In the many battles the Kitan suffered several setbacks. They also had enemies in the rear, a state named Po-hai, ruled by Tunguses, in northern Korea, and the new Korean state of Kao-li, which liberated itself from Chinese overlordship in 919.

In 927 the Kitan finally destroyed Po-hai. This brought many Tungus tribes, including the Jurchen (Juchên), under Kitan dominance. Then, in 936, the Kitan gained the allegiance of the Turkish general Shih Ching-t'ang, and he was set on the Chinese throne as a feudatory of the Kitan. It was hoped now to secure dominance over China, and accordingly the Mongol name of the dynasty was altered to 'Liao dynasty' in 937, indicating the claim to the Chinese throne. Considerable regions of north China came at once under the direct rule of the Liao. As a whole, however, the plan failed: the feudatory Shih Ching-t'ang tried to make himself independent; Chinese fought the Liao; and the Chinese sceptre soon came back into the hands of a Sha-t'o dynasty (947). This ended the plans of the Liao to conquer the whole of China.

For this there were several reasons. A nomad people was again ruling the agrarian regions of north China. This time the representatives of the ruling class remained military commanders, and at the same time retained their herds of horses. As early as 1100 they had well over 10,000 herds, each of more than a thousand animals. The army commanders had been awarded large regions which they themselves had conquered. They collected the taxes in these regions, and passed on to the state only the yield of the wine tax. On the other hand, in order to feed the armies, in which there were now many Chinese soldiers, the frontier regions were settled, the soldiers working as peasants in times of peace, and peasants being required to contribute to the support of the army. Both processes increased the interest of the Kitan ruling class in the maintenance of peace. That class was growing rich, and preferred living on the income from its properties or settlements to going to war, which had become a more and more serious matter after the founding of the great Sung empire, and was bound to be less remunerative. The herds of horses were a further excellent source of income, for they could be sold to the Sung, who had no good horses. Then, from 1004 onward, came the tribute payments from China, strengthening the interest in the maintenance of peace. Thus great wealth accumulated in Peking, the capital of the Liao; in this wealth the whole Kitan ruling class participated, but the tribes in the north, owing to their remoteness, had no share in it. In 988 the Chinese began negotiations, as a move in their diplomacy, with the ruler of the later realm of the Hsia; in 990 the Kitan also negotiated with him, and they soon became a third partner in the diplomatic game. Delegations were continually going from one to another of the three realms, and they were joined by trade missions. Agreement was soon reached on frontier questions, on armament, on questions of demobilization, on the demilitarization of particular regions, and so on, for the last thing anyone wanted was to fight.

Then came the rising of the tribes of the north. They had remained military tribes; of all the wealth nothing reached them, and they were given no military employment, so that they had no hope of improving their position. The leadership was assumed by the tribe of the Juchên (1114). In a campaign of unprecedented rapidity they captured Peking, and the Liao dynasty was ended (1125), a year earlier, as we know, than the end of the Sung.

2 *The state of the Kara-Kitai*

A small troop of Liao, under the command of a member of the ruling family, fled into the west. They were pursued without cessation, but they succeeded in fighting their way through. After a few years of nomad life in the mountains of northern Sinkiang, they were able to gain the collaboration of a few more tribes, and with them they then invaded western Sinkiang. There they founded the 'Western Liao' state, or, as the western sources call it, the 'Kara-Kitai' state, with its capital at Balasagun. This state must not be regarded as a purely Kitan state. The Kitan formed only a very thin stratum, and the real power was in the hands of autochthonous Turkish tribes, to whom the Kitan soon became entirely assimilated in culture. Thus the history of this state belongs to that of western Asia, especially as the relations of the Kara-Kitai with the Far East were entirely broken off. In 1211 the state was finally destroyed.

(3) The Hsi-Hsia state in the north (1038–1227)

1 *Continuation of Toba traditions*

After the end of the Toba state in north China in 550, some tribes of the Toba, including members of the ruling tribe with the tribal name Toba, withdrew to the borderland between Tibet and China, where they ruled over Tibetan and Tangut tribes. At the beginning of the T'ang dynasty this tribe of Toba joined the T'ang. The tribal leader received in return, as a distinction, the family name of the T'ang dynasty, Li. His dependence on China was, however, only nominal and soon came entirely to an end. In the tenth century the tribe gained in strength. It is typical of the long continuance of old tribal traditions that a leader of the tribe in the tenth century married a woman belonging to the family to which the khans of the Hsiung-nu and all Turkish ruling houses had belonged since 200 B.C. With the rise of the Kitan in the north and of the Tibetan state in the south, the tribe decided to seek the friendship of China. Its first mission, in 982, was well received. Presents were sent to the chieftain of the tribe, he was helped against his enemies, and he was given the status of a feudatory of the Sung; in 988 the family name of the Sung, Chao, was conferred on him. Then the Kitan took a hand. They over-trumped the Sung by proclaiming the tribal chieftain king of Hsia (990). Now the small state became interesting. It was pampered by Liao and Sung in the effort to win it over or to keep its friendship. The state grew; in 1031 its ruler resumed the old family name of the Toba, thus proclaiming his intention to continue the Toba empire; in 1034 he definitely parted from the Sung, and in 1038 he proclaimed himself emperor in the Hsia dynasty, or, as the Chinese generally called it, the 'Hsi-Hsia', which means the Western Hsia. This name, too, had associations with the old Hun tradition; it recalled the state of Ho-lien P'o-p'o in the early fifth century. The state soon covered the present province of Kansu, small parts of the adjoining Tibetan territory, and parts of the Ordos region. It attacked the province of Shensi, but the Chinese and the Liao attached the greatest importance to that territory. Thus that was the scene of most of the fighting.

The Hsia state had a ruling group of Toba, but these Toba had become Tibetanized. The language of the country was Tibetan; the customs were those of the Tanguts. A script was devised, in imitation of the Chinese script. Only in recent years has it begun to be studied.

In 1125, when the Tungusic Juchên destroyed the Liao, the Hsia also lost large territories in the east of their country, especially the province of Shensi, which they had conquered; but they were still able to hold their own. Their political importance to China, however, vanished, since they were now divided from southern China and as partners were no longer of the same value to it. Not until the Mongols became a power did the Hsia recover some of their importance; but they were among the first victims of the Mongols: in 1209 they had to submit to them, and in 1227, the year of the death of Genghiz Khan, they were annihilated.

This section on the northern, non-Chinese dynasties, reports almost exclusively about the rulers and their fights. What about the people? Most of what we know about the Kitan and Juchên is written by Chinese; the Hsi-Hsia had their own script which is still not yet wholly deciphered, and Chinese do not report much about them. We hear of terrible suffering of the population under the 'barbarians', but we should be careful in assigning such statements great weight, as they are written by the enemy, the Chinese. The overwhelming majority of the population in these states, perhaps with the exception of Hsi-Hsia, was Chinese. Some of the Chinese upper class collaborated with the foreign rulers, some continued to compose essays and poems in almost the same style and content as their Sung colleagues. There is some indication that the lot of the common man was not much worse than on the other side. We know that under the Chin (Juchên) a new sect of Taoism (Cheng-i sect) developed to importance, a sect which still exists and supplies many of the priests who administer masses for the population in times of need or of death. Parallel to this, a Tantric sect of Buddhism gained more importance, although it had entered China, possibly from the area of Bengal, already in T'ang time. Tantric Buddhism, often called magic Buddhism, stresses the use of 'mantra', magic formulae; it also harbours a secret sub-sect which combines meditative techniques with sexual practices.

(4) The empire of the Southern Sung dynasty (1127–1279)

1 *Foundation*

In the disaster of 1126, when the Juchên captured the Sung capital and destroyed the Sung empire, a brother of the captive emperor escaped. He made himself emperor in Nanking and founded the 'Southern Sung' dynasty, whose capital was soon shifted to the present Hangchow. The foundation of the new dynasty was a relatively easy matter, and the new state was much more solid than the southern kingdoms of 800 years earlier, for the south had already been economically supreme, and the great families that had ruled the state were virtually all from the south. The loss of the north, i.e. the area north of the Yellow river and of parts of Kiangsu, was of no importance to this governing group and meant no loss of estates to it. Thus the transition from the Northern to the Southern Sung was not of fundamental importance. Consequently the Juchên had no chance of success when they arranged for Liu Yü, who came of a northern Chinese family of small peasants and had become an official to be proclaimed emperor in the 'Ch'i' dynasty in 1130. They hoped that this puppet might attract the southern Chinese, but seven years later they dropped him.

Many southern Chinese families today trace their genealogy back to the year in which the capital K'ai-feng fell to the Liao (Kitan), saying that their family originally was a northern one, but decided to leave when the 'barbarians' came. Especially the Hakka (K'o-chia), a fairly large minority in the present province of Kuangtung, southern Fukien, Taiwan and in the South-East Asian settlements of Chinese claim to be the 'original' Chinese, stemming from the home province of China, Honan. They assert that their dialect is closest to the old Chinese language, but their claims are quite doubtful and some scholars today believe that we have here a case which has numerous other parallels in China: a minority, in order to free itself from discrimination, claims to be in fact Chinese and not a minority. These scholars think it is possible that the Hakka are fully sinicized Yao. However, we can say with certainty that the twelfth and thirteenth centuries with their upheavals were periods in which many Chinese migrated into the south. There is hardly any Chinese family in the provinces of Fukien or Kuangtung and Kuangsi which can retrace its genealogy as a southern family beyond this period.

2 Internal situation

Perhaps we should here throw some light on the internal organization of the Sung, especially the rural administration. It has been estimated that the population of Southern Sung in the early twelfth century was somewhere between 30 and 50 million. These were ruled by a bureaucracy which was probably not much over 12,000 men. Of these 8,000 were in the capital, around the emperor. The country was divided into 170 larger units with an average of eight officials; these units controlled 800 districts (hsien) with, at most, three officials each. This was the whole staff of the administration on the government payroll, except, of course, the army.

In each district was a staff of clerks, scribes, gaolers; normally between 100 and 150 men. In certain periods, many of them were salaried, and this meant a heavy load on the payroll; in other periods they received no salary and we can assume that they had sufficient income from unofficial and/or illegal sources, because many of these posts became hereditary. Below the district were the villages with unpaid staff. Neither the district clerks and employees nor the village officials had the right to move up into the regular career. The village headman, li-chang, nominally a chief of a hundred households, was selected out of 'better' rural families and ordered to serve for a limited time, usually three years. Then another family's head took over. He had to collect taxes and was assisted by a 'household chief'. He also had one scribe to keep the records, and three 'elders' and 'stalwart men' who were responsible for law and order, the upkeep of roads and the building of bridges. This system, by which a very large state is governed by a small bureaucratic élite, assisted by small bureaucrats and helped by unpaid village workers lasted, with some changes, basically to the end of the monarchy. It was developed in Northern Sung time, and not much changed in Southern Sung. So, the countryside was not affected by the loss of the north.

Only the policy of diplomacy could not be pursued at once, as the Juchên were bellicose at first and would not negotiate. There were therefore several battles at the outset (in 1131 and 1134), in which the Chinese were actually the more successful, but not decisively. The Sung military group was faced as early as in 1131 with furious opposition from the greater gentry, led by Ch'in K'ui, one of the largest landowners of all. His estates were around Nanking, and so in the deployment region and the region from which most of the soldiers had to be drawn for the defensive struggle. Ch'in K'ui secured the assassination of the leader of the military party, General Yo Fei, in 1141, and was able to conclude peace with the Juchên. To this day, numerous Chinese operas show Ch'in K'ui as the model of a traitor, while a long, famous folk novel praises Yo Fei as the ideal patriot, and in many places on the mainland and in Taiwan temples were erected in his honour.

The Sung had to accept the status of vassals and to pay annual tribute to the Juchên. This was the situation that best pleased the greater gentry. They paid hardly any taxes (in many districts the greater gentry directly owned more than 30 per cent of the land, in addition to which they had indirect interests in the soil), and they were now free from the war peril that ate into their revenues. The tribute amounted only to 500,000 strings of cash.

In 1165 it was agreed between the Sung and the Juchên to regard each other as states with equal rights. It is interesting to note here that in the treaties during the Han time with the Hsiung-nu, the two countries called one another brothers—with the Chinese ruler as the older and thus privileged brother; but the treaties since the T'ang time with northern powers and with Tibetans used the terms father-in-law and son-in-law. The foreign power was the 'father-in-law', i.e. the older and, therefore, in a certain way the more privileged; the Chinese were the 'son-in-law', the representative of the paternal lineage and, therefore, in another respect also the more privileged! In spite of such agreements with the Juchên, fighting continued, but it was mainly of the character of frontier engagements. Not until 1204 did the military party, led by Han T'o-wei, regain power; it resolved upon an active policy against the north. In preparation for this a military reform was carried out. The campaign proved a disastrous failure, as a result of which large territories in the north were lost. The Sung sued for peace; Han T'o-wei's head was cut off and sent to the Juchên. In this way peace was restored in 1208. The old treaty relationship was now resumed, but the relations between the two states

remained tense. Meanwhile the Sung observed with malicious pleasure how the Mongols were growing steadily stronger, first destroying the Hsia state and then aiming the first heavy blows against the
Juchên. In the end the Sung entered into alliance with the Mongols
(1233) and joined them in attacking the Juchên, thus hastening the
end of the Juchên state.

The Sung now faced the Mongols, and were defenceless against
them. All the buffer states had gone. The Sung were quite without
adequate military defence. They hoped to stave off the Mongols in
the same way as they had met the Kitan and the Juchên. This time,
however, they misjudged the situation. In the great operations begun
by the Mongols in 1273 the Sung were defeated over and over again.
In 1276 their capital was taken by the Mongols and the emperor was
made prisoner. For three years longer there was a Sung emperor, in
flight from the Mongols, until the last emperor perished near Macao
in south China.

3 Cultural situation; reasons for the collapse

The Southern Sung period was again one of flourishing culture.
The imperial court was entirely in the power of the important families; several times the emperors, who personally do not deserve individual mention, were compelled to abdicate. They then lived on with
a court of their own, devoting themselves to pleasure in much the
same way as the 'reigning' emperor. Round them was a countless
swarm of poets and artists. Never was there a time so rich in poets,
though hardly one of them was in any way outstanding. The poets,
unlike those of earlier times, belonged to the lesser gentry who were
suffering from the prevailing inflation. Salaries bore no relation to
prices. Food was not dear, but the things which a man of the upper
class ought to have were far out of reach: a big house cost 2,000
strings of cash, a concubine 800 strings. Thus the lesser gentry and
the intelligentsia all lived on their patrons among the greater gentry
—with the result that they were entirely shut out of politics. This
explains why the literature of the time is so unpolitical, and also why
scarcely any philosophical works appeared. The writers took refuge
more and more in romanticism and flight from realities.

The greater gentry, on the other hand, led a very elegant life,
building themselves magnificent palaces in the capital. They also
speculated in every direction. They speculated in land, in money,
and above all in the paper money that was coming more and more
into use. In 1166 the paper circulation exceeded the value of
10,000,000 strings!

It seems that after 1127 a good number of farmers had left Honan
and the Yellow river plains when the Juchên conquered these places

and showed little interest in fostering agriculture; more left the border areas of Southern Sung because of permanent war threat. Many of these lived as tenants on the farms of the gentry between Nanking and Hangchow. By this time, the influence of the wealthy rural families had grown, because they succeeded in becoming appointed as village officers or even as Superior Guard Officers. These latter were the leaders of the local militia, but also functioned as local police, could influence the tax registers and therefore control the tax assessments of individual families. If they did not want to take over the office, they could appoint replacements, poorer villagers who did the work for them. As the village officers and Superior Guard Officers had obligations which included expenses, such as supplying food and lodging for travelling government officials, poorer rural families would not try to get appointed. Thus, the power of wealthy landowners and rural gentry increased in this period. There are some indications that wealthier merchants also became interested in the farmers. They began to give loans to poor farmers whose wives would then weave textiles, which the merchant would accept in the autumn as repayment of the loan. This is an early form of the putting-out system of later times.

The increase of the power of the wealthy landowners and of their control over tenants and free farmers soon became a serious problem for the finances of the state. At this stage, Chia Ssŭ-tao drafted a reform law. Chia had come to the court through his sister becoming the emperor's concubine, but he himself belonged to the lesser gentry. His proposal was that state funds should be applied to the purchase of land in the possession of the greater gentry over and above a fixed maximum. Peasants were to be settled on this land, and its yield was to belong to the state, which would be able to use it to meet military expenditure. In this way the country's military strength was to be restored. Chia's influence lasted just ten years, until 1275. He began putting the law into effect in the region south of Nanking, where the principal estates of the greater gentry were then situated. He brought upon himself, of course, the mortal hatred of the greater gentry, and paid for his action with his life. The emperor, in entering upon this policy, no doubt had hoped to recover some of his power, but the greater gentry brought him down. The gentry now openly played into the hands of the approaching Mongols, so hastening the final collapse of the Sung. The peasants and the lesser gentry would have fought the Mongols if it had been possible; but the greater gentry enthusiastically went over to the Mongols, hoping to save their property and so their influence by quickly joining the enemy. On a long view they had not judged badly. The Mongols removed the members of the gentry from all political posts, but left them their estates; and before long the greater gentry reappeared in political life. And when, later, the Mongol empire in China was brought down by a popular rising, the greater gentry showed themselves to be the most faithful allies of the Mongols!

(5) The empire of the Juchên in the north (1115–1234)

1 *Rapid expansion from northern Korea to the Yangtze*
The Juchên in the past had been only a small league of Tungus tribes, whose name is preserved in that of the present Tungus tribe of the Jurchen, which came under the domination of the Kitan after the collapse of the state of Po-hai in northern Korea. We have already briefly mentioned the reasons for their rise. After their first successes against the Kitan (1114), their chieftain at once proclaimed himself emperor (1115), giving his dynasty the name 'Chin' (The Golden). The Chin quickly continued their victorious progress. In 1125 the Kitan empire was destroyed. It will be remembered that the Sung were at once attacked, although they had recently been allied with the Chin against the Kitan. In 1126 the Sung capital was taken. The Chin invasions were pushed farther south, and in 1130 the Yangtze was crossed. But the Chin did not hold the whole of these conquests. Their empire was not yet consolidated. Their partial withdrawal closed the first phase of the Chin empire.

But a few years after this maximum expansion, a withdrawal began which went on much more quickly than usual in such cases. The reasons were to be found both in external and in internal politics. The Juchên had gained great agrarian regions in a rapid march of conquest. Once more, great cities with a huge urban population and immense wealth had fallen to alien conquerors. Now the Juchên wanted to enjoy this wealth as the Kitan had done before them. All the Juchên people counted as citizens of the highest class; they were free from taxation and only liable to military service. They were entitled to take possession of as much cultivable land as they wanted; this they did, and they took not only the 'state domains' actually granted to them but also peasant properties, so that Chinese free peasants had to be contented with the remaining, poorer land, unless they became tenants on Juchên estates. A united front was therefore formed between all Chinese, both peasants and landowning gentry, against the Chin, such as it had not been possible to form against the Kitan. This made an important contribution later to the rapid collapse of the Chin empire.

The Chin who had thus come into possession of the cultivable land and at the same time of the wealth of the towns, began a sort of competition with each other for the best winnings, especially after the government had returned to the old Sung capital, Pien-liang (now K'aifeng, in eastern Honan). Serious crises developed in their own ranks. In 1149 the ruler was assassinated by his chancellor (a member of the imperial family), who in turn was murdered in 1161. The Chin thus failed to attain what had been secured by all earlier conquerors, a reconciliation of the various elements of the population and the collaboration of at least one group of the defeated Chinese.

2 Start of the Mongol empire

The cessation of fighting against the Sung brought no real advantage in external affairs, though the tribute payments appealed to the greed of the rulers and were therefore welcomed. There could be no question of further campaigns against the south, for the Hsia empire in the west had not been destroyed, though some of its territory had been annexed; and a new peril soon made its appearance in the rear of the Chin. When in the tenth century the Sha-t'o had had to withdraw from their dominating position in China, because of their great loss of numbers and consequently of strength, they went back into Mongolia and there united with the Ta-tan (Tatars), among whom a new small league of tribes had formed towards the end of the eleventh century, consisting mainly of Mongols and Turks. In 1139 one of the chieftains of the Juchên rebelled and entered into negotiations with the south Chinese. He was killed, but his sons and his whole tribe then rebelled and went into Mongolia, where they made common cause with the Mongols. The Chin pursued them, and fought against them and against the Mongols, but without success. Accordingly negotiations were begun, and a promise was given to deliver meat and grain every year and to cede twenty-seven military strongholds. A high title was conferred on the tribal leader of the Mongols, in the hope of gaining his favour. He declined it, however, and in 1147 assumed the title of emperor of the 'greater Mongol empire'. This was the beginning of the power of the Mongols, who remained thereafter a dangerous enemy of the Chin in the north, until in 1189 Genghiz Khan became their leader and made the Mongols the greatest power of Central Asia. In any case, the Chin had reason to fear the Mongols from 1147 onward, and therefore were the more inclined to leave the Sung in peace.

In 1210 the Mongols began the first assault against the Chin, the moment they had conquered the Hsia. In the years 1215–1217 the Mongols took the military key-positions from the Chin. After that there could be no serious defence of the Chin empire. There came a respite only because the Mongols had turned against the West. But in 1234 the empire finally fell to the Mongols.

Many of the Chin entered the service of the Mongols, and with their permission returned to Manchuria; there they fell back to the cultural level of a warlike nomad people. Not until the sixteenth century did these Tunguses recover, reorganize, and appear again in history this time under the name of Manchus.

The north Chinese under Chin rule did not regard the Mongols as enemies of their country, but were ready at once to collaborate with them. The Mongols were even more friendly to them than to the south Chinese, and treated them rather better.

14 Aborigines of South China, of the 'Black Miao'
tribe, at a festival. Water-colour drawing of the
eighteenth century.

(Collection of the Museum für Völkerkunde, Berlin,
No. ID 8756, 68.)

15 Pavilion on the 'Coal Hill' at Peking, in which
the last Ming emperor committed suicide.

(Photo Eberhard.)

CHAPTER TEN

The Period of Absolutism

(A) THE MONGOL EPOCH (1280–1368)

1 Beginning of new foreign rules

During more than half of the second period of 'Modern Times' which now began, China was under alien rule. Of the 631 years from 1280 to 1911, China was under national rulers for 276 years and under alien rule for 355. The alien rulers were first the Mongols, and later the Tungus Manchus. It is interesting to note that the alien rulers in the earlier period came mainly from the north-west, and only in modern times did peoples from the north-east rule over China. This was due in part to the fact that only peoples who had attained a certain level of civilization were capable of dominance. In antiquity and the Middle Ages, eastern Mongolia and Manchuria were at a relatively low level of civilization, from which they emerged only gradually through permanent contact with other nomad peoples, especially Turks. We are dealing here, of course, only with the Mongol epoch in China and not with the great Mongol empire, so that we need not enter further into these questions.

Yet another point is characteristic: the Mongols were the first alien people to rule the whole of China; the Manchus, who appeared in the seventeenth century, were the second and last. All alien peoples before these two ruled only parts of China. Why was it that the Mongols were able to be so much more successful than their predecessors? In the first place the Mongol political league was numerically stronger than those of the earlier alien peoples; second, the military organization and technical equipment of the Mongols were exceptionally advanced for their day. It must be borne in mind, for instance, that during their many years of war against the Sung dynasty in south China the Mongols already made use of small cannon in laying siege to towns. We have no exact knowledge of the number of Mongols who invaded and occupied China, but it is estimated that there were more than a million Mongols living in China. Not all of them, of course, were really Mongols! The name covered Turks, Tunguses, and others.

The name Meng-ku (Mongol) is found in sources much earlier than the thirteenth century; apparently, this was the name of a tribe, once belonging to the Shih-wei tribal federation. Early Western sources often call the Mongols 'Tatars', which is not quite correct, though the Tatar federation was, as far as we know, speaking a Mongol language, the Mongols as a political unit had broken off from the Tatars and formed their own federation. Among the auxiliaries of the Mongols were Uighurs, men from Central Asia and the Middle East, and even Europeans. When the Mongols attacked China they had the advantage of all the arts and crafts and all the new technical advances of Western and Central Asia. At their court, we even find some European technicians. They also had learned much from the Chinese, for instance the use of firearms. Thus, they were technically more advanced than earlier conquerors of China had been.

2 'Nationality legislation'

It was only after the Hsia empire in north China, and then the empire of the Juchên, had been destroyed by the Mongols, and only after long and remarkably modern tactical preparation, that the Mongols conquered south China, the empire of the Sung dynasty. They were now faced with the problem of ruling their great new empire, with a population of certainly more than sixty million (always omitting the western parts of the Mongol empire). The conqueror of that empire, Kublai, himself recognized that China could not be treated in quite the same way as the Mongol's previous conquests; he therefore separated the empire in China from the rest of the Mongol empire. Mongol China became an independent realm within the Mongol empire, a sort of dominion. The Mongol rulers were well aware that in spite of their numerical strength they were still only a minority in China, and this implied certain dangers. They therefore elaborated a 'nationality legislation', the first of its kind in the Far East. The purpose of this legislation was, of course, to be the protection of the Mongols. The population of conquered China was divided into four groups—(1) Mongols, themselves falling into four sub-groups (the oldest Mongol tribes, the White Tatars, the Black Tatars, the Wild Tatars); (2) Central Asian auxiliaries (Naimans, Uighurs, and various other Turkish people, Tanguts, and so on); (3) north Chinese; (4) south Chinese. The Mongols formed the privileged ruling class. They remained militarily organized, and were distributed in garrisons over all the big towns of China as soldiers, maintained by the state. All the higher government posts were reserved for them, so that they also formed the heads of the official staffs. The auxiliary peoples were also admitted into the government service; they, too, had privileges, but were not all soldiers but in many cases merchants, who used their privileged position to promote business. Not a few of these merchants were Uighurs and Mohammedans; many Uighurs were also employed as clerks, as the Mongols were very often unable to read and write Chinese, and the government offices were bilingual, working in Mongolian and Chinese. The clever Uighurs quickly learned enough of both languages for official purposes, and made themselves indispensable assistants to the Mongols. Persian, the main language of administration in the western parts of the Mongol empire besides Uighuric, also was a lingua franca among the new rulers of China.

In the Mongol legislation the south Chinese had the lowest status, and virtually no rights. Intermarriage with them was prohibited. The Chinese were not allowed to carry arms. For a time they were forbidden even to learn the Mongol or other foreign languages. In this way they were to be prevented from gaining official positions and playing any political part. Their ignorance of the languages of northern, central, and western Asia also prevented them from engaging in commerce like the foreign merchants, and every possible difficulty was put in the way of their travelling for commercial purposes. On the other hand, foreigners were, of course, able to learn Chinese, and so to gain a footing in Chinese internal trade.

Through legislation of this type the Mongols tried to build up and to safeguard their domination over China. Yet their success did not last a hundred years.

3 *Military position*

In foreign affairs the Mongol epoch was for China something of a breathing space, for the great wars of the Mongols took place at a remote distance from China and without any Chinese participation. Only a few concluding wars were fought under Kublai in the Far East. The first was his war against Japan (1281): it ended in complete failure, the fleet being destroyed by a storm. In this campaign the Chinese furnished ships and also soldiers. The subjection of Japan would have been in the interest of the Chinese, as it would have opened a market which had been almost closed against them in the Sung period. Mongol wars followed in the south. In 1282 began the war against Burma; in 1284 Annam and Cambodia were conquered; in 1292 a campaign was started against Java. It proved impossible to hold Java, but almost the whole of South-East Asia came under Mongol rule, to the satisfaction of the Chinese, for South-East Asia had already been one of the principal export markets in the Sung period. After that, however, there was virtually no more warfare, apart from small campaigns against rebellious tribes. The

Mongol soldiers now lived on their pay in their garrisons, with nothing to do. The old campaigners died and were followed by their sons, brought up also as soldiers; but these young Mongols were born in China, had seen nothing of war, and learned of the soldiers' trade either nothing or very little; so that after about 1320 serious things happened. An army nominally 1,000 strong was sent against a group of barely fifty bandits and failed to defeat them. Most of the 1,000 soldiers no longer knew how to use their weapons, and many did not even join the force. Such incidents occurred again and again.

4 *Social situation*

The results, however, of conditions within the country were of much more importance than events abroad. The Mongols made Peking their capital as was entirely natural, for Peking was near their homeland Mongolia. The emperor and his entourage could return to Mongolia in the summer, when China became too hot or too humid for them; and from Peking they were able to maintain contact with the rest of the Mongol empire. But as the city had become the capital of a vast empire, an enormous staff of officials had to be housed there, consisting of persons of many different nationalities. The emperor naturally wanted to have a magnificent capital, a city really worthy of so vast an empire. As the many wars had brought in vast booty, there was money for the building of great palaces, of a size and magnificence never before seen in China. They were built by Chinese forced labour, and to this end men had to be brought from all over the empire—poor peasants, whose fields went out of cultivation while they were held in bondage far away. If they ever returned home, they were destitute and had lost their land. The rich gentry, on the other hand, were able to buy immunity from forced labour. The great increase in the population of Peking (the huge court with its enormous expenditure, the mass of officials, the great merchant community, largely foreigners, and the many servile labourers), necessitated vast supplies of food. Now, as mentioned in earlier chapters, since the time of the Later T'ang the region round Nanking had become the main centre of production in China, and the Chinese population had gone over more and more to the consumption of rice instead of millet or wheat. As rice could not be grown economically in the north, practically the whole of the food supplies for the capital had to be brought from the south. The transport system taken over by the Mongols had not been created for long-distance traffic of this sort. The capital of the Sung had lain in the main centre of production. Consequently, a great fleet had suddenly to be built, canals and rivers had to be regulated, and some new canals excavated. This again called for a vast quantity of forced labour, often brought from afar to the points at which it was needed. The Chinese peasants had been exploited by the large landowners. The Mongols had not removed these landowners, as the Chinese gentry had gone over to their side. The Mongols had deprived them of their political power, but had left them their estates, the basis of their power. In past changes of dynasty the gentry had either maintained their position or been replaced by a new gentry: the total number of their class had remained virtually unchanged. Now, however, in addition to the original gentry there were about a million Mongols, for whose maintenance the peasants had also to provide, and their standard of maintenance was high. This was a great increase in the burdens of the peasantry.

Two other elements further pressed on the peasants in the Mongol epoch—organized religion and the traders. The upper classes among the Chinese had in general little interest in religion, but the Mongols, owing to their historical development, were very religious. Some of them and some of their allies were Buddhists, some were still shamanists. The Chinese Buddhists and the representatives of popular Taoism approached the Mongols and the foreign Buddhist monks trying to enlist the interest of the Mongols and their allies. The old shamanism was unable to compete with the higher religions, and the Mongols in China became Buddhist or interested themselves in popular Taoism. They showed their interest especially by the endowment of temples and monasteries. The temples were given great estates, and the peasants on those estates became temple servants. The land belonging to the temples was free from taxation.

We have as yet no exact statistics of the Mongol epoch, only approximations. These set the total area under cultivation at some six million ch'ing (a ch'ing is the ideal size of the farm worked by a peasant family, but it was rarely held in practice); the population amounted to fourteen or fifteen million families. Of this total tillage some 170,000 ch'ing were allotted to the temples; that is to say, the farms for some 400,000 peasant families were taken from the peasants and no longer paid taxes to the state. The peasants, however, had to make payments to the temples. Some 200,000 ch'ing with some 450,000 peasant families were turned into military settlements; that is to say, these peasants had to work for the needs of the army. Their taxes went not to the state but to the army. Moreover, in the event of war they had to render service to the army. In addition to this, all higher officials received official properties, the yield of which represented part payment of their salaries. Then, Mongol nobles and dignitaries received considerable grants of land, which was taken away from the free peasants; the peasants had then to work their farms as tenants and to pay dues to their landlords, no longer to the state. Finally, especially in north China, many peasants were entirely dispossessed, and their land was turned into pasturage for the Mongol's horses; the peasants themselves were put to forced labour. All this meant an enormous diminution in the number of free peasants and thus of taxpayers. As the state was involved in more expenditure than in the past owing to the large number of Mongols who were its virtual pensioners, the taxes had to be continually increased. Meanwhile the many peasants working as tenants of the great landlords, the temples, and the Mongol nobles were entirely at their mercy. In this period, a second migration of farmers into the southern provinces, mainly Fukien and Kwangtung, took place; it had its main source in the lower Yangtze valley. A few gentry families whose relatives had accompanied the Sung emperor on their flight to the south, also settled with their followers in the Canton basin.

The many merchants from abroad, especially those belonging to the peoples allied to the Mongols, also had in every respect a privileged position in China. They were free of taxation, free to travel all over the country, and received privileged treatment in the use of means of transport. They were thus able to accumulate great wealth, most of which went out of China to their own country. Chinese merchants fell more and more into dependence on the foreign merchants; the only field of action really remaining to them was the local trade within China and the trade with South-East Asia, where the Chinese had the advantage of knowing the language.

The impoverishment of China began with the flow abroad of her metallic currency. To make up for this loss, the government was compelled to issue great quantities of paper money, which very quickly depreciated, because after a few years the government would no longer accept the money at its face value, so that the population could place no faith in it. The depreciation further impoverished the people.

Thus we have in the Mongol epoch in China the imposing picture of a commerce made possible with every country from Europe to the Pacific; this, however, led to the impoverishment of China. We also see the raising of mighty temples and monumental buildings, but this again only contributed to the denudation of the country. The Mongol epoch was thus one of continual and rapid impoverishment in China, simultaneously with a great display of magnificence. The enthusiastic descriptions of the Mongol empire in China offered by travellers from the Near East or from Europe, such as Marco Polo, give an entirely false picture: as foreigners they had a privileged position, living in the cities and seeing nothing of the situation of the general population. It seems to be certain that Marco Polo, in spite

242

of his long stay in China, never learned to speak Chinese. His statement that he had a high administrative post in China may not be true, according to some scholars who even doubt that he saw as many parts of China as he claimed to have seen. If we read his reports, we are again and again amazed about what he did not write about, though he must have observed it: for instance, he does not seem to have appreciated Chinese painting and had no understanding of the complexities of Chinese religion.

5 Cultural developments

During the Mongol epoch a large number of the Chinese scholars withdrew from official life. They lived in retirement among their friends, and devoted themselves mainly to the pursuit of poetry, which had been elaborated in the Southern Sung epoch, without themselves arriving at any important innovations in form. Their poems were built up meticulously on the rules laid down by the various schools; they were routine productions rather than the outcome of any true poetic inspiration. In the realm of prose the best achievements were the 'miscellaneous notes' already mentioned, collections of learned essays. The foreigners who wrote in Chinese during this epoch are credited with no better achievements by the Chinese historians of literature. Chief of them were a statesman named Yeh-lü Ch'u-ts'ai, a Kitan in the service of the Mongols; and a Mongol named T'o-t'o (Tokto). The former accompanied Genghiz Khan in his great campaign against western Sinkiang, and left a very interesting account of his journeys, together with many poems about Samarkand and Sinkiang. His other works were mainly letters and poems addressed to friends. They differ in no way in style from the Chinese literary works of the time, and are neither better nor worse than those works. He shows strong traces of Taoist influence, as do other contemporary writers. We know that Genghiz Khan was more or less inclined to Taoism, and admitted a Taoist monk to his camp (1221–1224). This man's account of his travels has also been preserved, and with the numerous European accounts of Central Asia written at this time it forms an important source. The Mongol Tokto was the head of an historical commission that issued the annals of the Sung dynasty, the Kitan, and the Juchên dynasty. The annals of the Sung dynasty became the largest of all the historical works, but they were fiercely attacked from the first by Chinese critics on account of their style and their hasty composition, and, together with the annals of the Mongol dynasty, they are regarded as the worst of the annals preserved. Tokto himself is less to blame for this than the circumstance that he was compelled to work in great haste, and had not time to put into order the overwhelming mass of his material.

The greatest literary achievements, however, of the Mongol period belong beyond question to the theatre (or, rather, opera). The emperors were great theatre-goers, and the wealthy private families were also enthusiasts, so that gradually people of education devoted themselves to writing librettos for the operas, where in the past this work had been left to others. Most of the authors of these librettos remained unknown: they used pseudonyms, partly because play-writing was not an occuption that befitted a scholar, and partly because in these works they criticized the conditions of their day. These works are divided in regard to style into two groups, those of the 'southern' and the 'northern' drama; these are distinguished from each other in musical construction and in their intellectual attitude: in general the northern works are more heroic and the southern more sentimental, though there are exceptions. The most famous northern works of the Mongol epoch are 'P'i-p'a-chi' ('The Story of a Lute'), written about 1356, probably by Kao Ming, and 'Chao-shih ku-erh-chi' ('The Story of the Orphan of Chao'), a work that enthralled Voltaire, who made a paraphrase of it; its author was the otherwise unknown Chi Chün-hsiang. One of the most famous of the southern dramas is 'Hsi-hsiang-chi' ('The Romance of the Western Chamber'), by Wang Shih-fu and Kuan Han-ch'ing. Kuan lived under the Juchên dynasty as a physician, and then among the Mongols. He is said to have written fifty-eight dramas, many of which are still preserved. Kuan (c. 1220–1307) was highly praised during one period of the present regime and was called the Chinese Shakespeare. A newly composed opera depicted him as a populist, a friend of the common man. The Yüan drama introduced a new language into Chinese literature: a highly colloquial, northern dialect with a number of Mongolisms. A southern style of opera, which also began to emerge in this period, differs in language as well as in the music. Perhaps we should remark here that in Chinese operas the music is not newly composed for each opera, but each style of opera uses a number of standard melodies which the audience knows, just as they usually also know the content of the action. What is admired is mainly the art of acting and singing, and here, the actor in spite of being bound by tradition, can show his individuality.

In the fine arts, foreign influence made itself felt during the Mongol epoch much more than in literature. This was due in part to the Mongol rulers' predilection for the Lamaism that was widespread in their homeland. Lamaism is a special form of Buddhism which developed in Tibet, where remnants of the old national Tibetan cult (Bon) were fused with Buddhism into a distinctive religion. During the rise of the Mongols this religion, which closely resembled the shamanism of the ancient Mongols, spread in Mongolia, and through the Mongols it made great progress in China, where it had been insignificant until their time. Religious sculpture especially came entirely under Tibetan influence (particularly that of the sculptor Aniko, who came from Nepal, where he was born in 1244). This influence was noticeable in the Chinese sculptor Liu Yüan; after him it became stronger and stronger, lasting until the Manchu epoch.

In architecture, too, Indian and Tibetan influence was felt in this period. The Tibetan pagodas came into special prominence alongside the previously known form of pagoda, which has many storeys, growing smaller as they go upward; these towers originally contained relics of Buddha and his disciples. The Tibetan pagoda has not this division into storeys, and its lower part is much larger in circumference, and often round. To this day Peking is rich in pagodas in the Tibetan style.

The Mongols also developed in China the art of carpet-knotting, which to this day is found only in north China in the zone of northern influence. There were carpets before these, but they were mainly of felt. The knotted carpets were produced in imperial workshops—only, of course, for the Mongols, who were used to carpets. A further development probably also due to west Asian influence was that of cloisonné technique in China in this period.

Painting, on the other hand, remained free from alien influence, with the exception of the craft painting for the temples. The most famous painters of the Mongol epoch were Chao Mêng-fu (also called Chao Chung-mu, 1254–1322), a relative of the deposed imperial family of the Sung dynasty, and Ni Tsan (1301–1374).

In the fields of technology, we observe some further developments. We now find that the use of machines using water power became more widely spread. There were silk-reeling machines already in Sung time, but in 1313 we hear about a machine with 32 spindles, driven by water. But otherwise, the great developments now come to a standstill. China did not move into the industrial age. This surprising fact has been explained in different ways. Recently a cold period lasting from about A.D. 1200 to 1400 has been made responsible for the standstill, and it is said that between the end of the twelfth and the end of the fourteenth century the population of China decreased and only after 1400 began to go up regularly to the end of the sixteenth century. M. Elvin has proposed the theory of a 'high level equilibrium' which is tempting but needs further research. In briefest form, this theory explains that at around 1300 Chinese technology had developed to a point where industrialization comparable to the 'industrial revolution' in Europe in the eighteenth century was possible. It did not take place because the intensive agriculture of China could keep many more people alive than European agriculture, so that there was always an over-supply of human labour which made the use of machines uneconomical. Thus technology had no chance to develop to a level which made cheap mass production possible and competitive; everywhere, the earliest machines were somewhat quicker and more efficient than human labour, but required too much investment to be competitive. Others have made another observation which is not incompatible with Elvin's theory. The men who developed these machines were, for the most part, members of the gentry or 'leisure class' who took an interest in the crafts or the farmers. They worked together with craftsmen who built for them the machines they had invented. They even had these machines working on their properties, but they really did not need extra income; they had enough secure income. On the other hand, the craftsmen were not yet free and remained until the fifteenth century tied to the government, forced to do labour services. They were hardly in a position in which they could accumulate enough capital to set up their own workshops or machine factories.

There is no doubt that not only in the field of technology, but also in applied sciences, like medicine, the period of great progress was over with the Yüan, and new impulses came only in the late sixteenth and the seventeenth centuries. At this time, the best explanation seems to be to accept Elvin's explanation and the other explanation together with the impact of a foreign rule, i.e. to take internal as well as external reasons to explain the standstill.

6 Popular revolts

Possibly due to the cold period, possibly due to Mongol exploitation of farmers, or due to both factors, popular risings began early in the Mongol dynasty. The first popular rising came in 1325. Statistics of 1329 show that there were then some 7,600,000 persons in the empire who were starving; as this was only the figure of the officially admitted sufferers, the figure may have been higher. In any case, seven-and-a-half million were a substantial percentage of the total population. The risings that now came incessantly were led by men of the lower orders—a cloth-seller, a fisherman, a peasant, a salt smuggler, the son of a soldier serving a sentence, an office messenger, and so on. They never attacked the Mongols as aliens, but always the rich in general, whether Chinese or foreign. Wherever they came, they killed all the rich and distributed their money and possessions.

As already mentioned, the Mongol garrisons were unable to cope with these risings. But how was it that the Mongol rule did not collapse until some forty years later? The Mongols parried the risings by raising loans from the rich and using the money to recruit volunteers to fight the rebels. The state revenues would not have sufficed for these payments, and the item was not one that could be included in the military budget. What was of much more importance was that the gentry themselves recruited volunteers and fought the rebels on their own account, without the authority or the support of the government. Thus it was the Chinese gentry, in their fear of being killed by the insurgents, who fought them and so bolstered up the Mongol rule.

In 1351 the dykes along the Yellow river burst. The dykes had to be reconstructed and further measures of conservancy undertaken. To this end the government impressed 170,000 men. Following this action, great new revolts broke out. Everywhere in Honan, Kiangsu, and Shantung, the regions from which the labourers were summoned, revolutionary groups were formed, some of them amounting to 100,000 men. Some groups had a religious tinge; others declared their intention to restore the emperors of the Sung dynasty. Before long great parts of central China were wrested from the hands of the government. The government recognized the menace to its existence, but resorted to contradictory measures. In 1352 southern Chinese were permitted to take over certain official positions. In this way it was hoped to gain the full support of the gentry, who had a certain interest in combating the rebel movements. On the other hand, the government tightened up its nationality laws. All the old segregation laws were brought back into force, with the result that in a few years the aim of the rebels became no longer merely the expulsion of the rich but also the expulsion of the Mongols: a social movement thus became a national one. A second element contributed to the change in the character of the popular rising. The rebels captured many towns. Some of these towns refused to fight and negotiated terms of submission. In these cases the rebels did not murder the whole of the gentry, but took some of them into their service. The gentry did not agree to this out of sympathy with the rebels, but simply in order to save their own lives. Once they had taken the step, however, they could not go back; they had no alternative but to remain on the side of the rebels.

In 1352 Kuo Tzŭ-hsing rose in southern Honan. Kuo was the son of a wandering soothsayer and a blind beggar-woman. He had success; his group gained control of a considerable area around his home. There was no longer any serious resistance from the Mongols, for at this time the whole of eastern China was in full revolt. In 1353 Kuo was joined by a man named Chu Yüan-chang, the son of a small peasant, probably a tenant farmer. Chu's parents and all his relatives had died from a plague, leaving him destitute. He had first entered a monastery and become a monk. This was a favourite re-source—and has been almost to the present day—for poor sons of peasants who were threatened with starvation. As a monk he had gone about begging, until in 1353 he returned to his home and collected a group, mostly men from his own village, sons of peasants and young fellows who had already been peasant leaders. Monks were often peasant leaders. They were trusted because they promised divine aid, and because they were usually rather better educated than the rest of the peasants. Chu at first also had contacts with a secret society, a branch of the White Lotus Society which several times in the course of Chinese history has been the nucleus of rebellious movements. Chu took his small group, which identified itself by a red turban and a red banner, to Kuo, who received him gladly, entered into alliance with him, and in sign of friendship gave him his daughter in marriage. In 1355 Kuo died, and Chu took over his army, now many thousands strong. In his campaigns against towns in eastern China, Chu succeeded in winning over some capable members of the gentry. One was the chairman of a committee that yielded a town to Chu; another was a scholar whose family had always been opposed to the Mongols, and who had himself suffered injustice several times in his official career, so that he was glad to join Chu out of hatred of the Mongols.

These men gained great influence over Chu, and persuaded him to give up attacking rich individuals, and instead to establish an assured control over large parts of the country. He would then, they pointed out, be permanently enriched, while otherwise he would only be in funds at the moment of the plundering of a town. They set before him strategic plans with that aim. Through their counsel Chu changed from the leader of a popular rising into a fighter against the dynasty. Of all the peasant leaders he was now the only one pursuing a definite aim. He marched first against Nanking, the great city of central China, and captured it with ease. He then crossed the Yangtze, and conquered the rich provinces of the south-east. He was a rebel who no longer slaughtered the rich or plundered the towns, and the whole of the gentry with all their followers came over to him en masse. The armies of volunteers went over to Chu, and the whole edifice of the dynasty collapsed.

The years 1355–1368 were full of small battles. After his conquest of the whole of the south, Chu went north. In 1368 his generals captured Peking almost without a blow. The Mongol ruler fled on horseback with his immediate entourage into the north of China, and soon after into Mongolia. The Mongol dynasty had been brought down, almost without resistance. The Mongols in the isolated garrisons marched northward wherever they could. A few surrendered to the Chinese and were used in southern China as professional soldiers, though they were always regarded with suspicion.

The only serious resistance offered came from the regions in which other Chinese popular leaders had established themselves, especially the remote provinces in the west and south-west, which had a different social structure and had been relatively little affected by the Mongol regime.

Thus the collapse of the Mongols came for the following reasons: (1) They had not succeeded in maintaining their armed strength or that of their allies during the period of peace that followed Kublai's conquest. The Mongol soldiers had become effeminate through their life of idleness in the towns. (2) The attempt to rule the empire through Mongols or other aliens, and to exclude the Chinese gentry entirely from the administration, failed through insufficient knowledge of the sources of revenue and through the abuses due to the favoured treatment of aliens. The whole country, and especially the peasantry, was completely impoverished and so driven into revolt. (3) There was also a psychological reason. In the middle of the fourteenth century it was obvious to the Mongols that their hold over China was growing more and more precarious, and that there was little to be got out of the impoverished country: they seem in consequence to have lost interest in the troublesome task of maintaining their rule, preferring, in so far as they had not already entirely degenerated, to return to their old home in the north. It is important to bear in mind these reasons for the collapse of the Mongols, so that we may compare them later with the reasons for the collapse of the Manchus.

No mention need be made here of the names of the Mongol rulers in China after Kublai. After his death in 1294, grandsons and great-grandsons of his followed each other in rapid succession on the throne; not one of them was of any personal significance. Their life was spent in intriguing against one another. In part, these intrigues had to do with the conditions of the whole Mongol empire, especially with the homeland of the Mongols. Some cliques wanted to strengthen their hold over Mongolia, others tried to rely upon Chinese collaborators and make their rule over China more 'Chinese', accepting more and more typically Chinese techniques of governing.

(B) CHINESE ABSOLUTISM (1368–1644)

1 *Popular rebellion*

The many popular risings during the latter half of the period of Mongol rule in China were all of a purely economic and social character, and at first they were not directed at all against the Mongols as representatives of an alien people. Conditions in the fourteenth century were harsh. In addition to the factors already mentioned, the common man suffered from inflation because of the emission of more and more paper money which was not convertible. Overseas trade along the coast had more or less stopped, and even the grain transports from central to north China could not go by sea any more because of increasing danger from pirates. Canal transport was costly, slow and required a large labour force. Chu Yüan-chang's revolt is one of many that started, but only three times in Chinese history has a man of the peasantry become emperor and founder of a dynasty. The first of these three men founded the Han dynasty; the second founded the first of the so-called 'Five Dynasties' in the tenth century; Chu was the third.

We have a tendency to see in peasant revolts revolutionary movements, i.e. movements which attempt to change the social and governmental system. Perhaps the revolt of Wang Tsê (1047–1048), celebrated in a folk novel and mentioned in at least five theatre plays, was a true revolutionary rebellion; smaller rebellions before and after him sometimes had revolutionary elements, often in messianic guise. Chu, in the beginning does not seem to have had an ideology. When he came into power, however, some revolutionary ideas appeared, perhaps because of his collaboration with a secret society, characterized by red flags and red scarves. But soon after his movement was joined by the gentry what had been a revolutionary movement became a struggle for the substitution of one dynasty for another without interfering with the existing social system. However, the fights against the Mongols and the tightening of the Mongol nationality laws as a reaction, developed among the Chinese a feeling of nationalism. This feeling should not be confounded with the very old feeling of Chinese as a culturally superior group according to which, at least in theory though rarely in practice, every person who assimilated Chinese cultural values and traits was a 'Chinese'. The roots of nationalism seem to lie in the Southern Sung period, growing up in the course of contacts with the Juchên and Mongols; but the discriminatory laws of the Mongols greatly fostered this feeling. From now on, it was regarded a shame to serve a foreigner as official, even if he was a ruler of China.

2 Wars against Mongols and Japanese

It had been easy to drive the Mongols out of China, though apparently a considerable number of individual Mongols, disguising themselves as Chinese, seem to have remained in China. There is even a tradition that some small caste-like groups in central China are assimilated Mongols, depressed to the status of outcasts. As a political unit, however, the Mongols were never really beaten in their own country. On the contrary, they seem to have regained

strength after their withdrawal from China: they reorganized themselves and were soon capable of counterthrusts, while Chinese
offensives had as a rule very little success, and at all events no
decisive success. In the course of time, however, the Chinese gained
a certain influence over Sinkiang, but it was never absolute, always
challenged. After the Mongol empire had fallen to pieces, small states
came into existence in Sinkiang, for a long time with varying fortunes; the most important one during the Ming epoch was that of
Hami, until in 1473 it was occupied by the city-state of Turfan. At
this time China actively intervened in the policy of Sinkiang in a
number of combats with the Mongols. As the situation changed
from time to time, these city-states united more or less closely
with China or fell away from her altogether. In this period, however, Sinkiang was of no military or economic importance to
China.

In the time of the Ming there also began in the east and south
the plague of Japanese piracy. Japanese contacts with the coastal
provinces of China (Kiangsu, Chêkiang and Fukien) had a very
long history: pilgrims from Japan often went to these places in order
to study Buddhism in the famous monasteries of central China;
businessmen sold at high prices Japanese swords and other Japanese products here and bought Chinese products; they also tried to
get Chinese copper coins which had a higher value in Japan. Chinese
merchants co-operated with Japanese merchants and also with
pirates in the guise of merchants. Some Chinese, who were or felt
persecuted by the government, became pirates themselves. This
trade-piracy had started already at the end of the Sung dynasty,
when Japanese navigation had become superior to Korean shipping
which had in earlier times dominated the eastern seaboard. These
conditions may even have been one of the reasons why the Mongols
tried to subdue Japan. As early as 1387 the Chinese had to begin the
building of fortifications along the eastern and southern coasts of
the country. The Japanese attacks now often took the character of
organized raids: a small, fast-sailing flotilla would land in a bay, as
far as possible without attracting notice; the soldiers would march
against the nearest town, generally overcoming it, looting, and withdrawing. The defensive measures adopted from time to time during
the Ming epoch were of little avail, as it was impossible effectively
to garrison the whole coast. Some of the coastal settlements were
transferred inland, to prevent the Chinese from co-operating with
the Japanese, and to give the Japanese so long a march inland as to
allow time for defensive measures. The Japanese pirates prevented
the creation of a Chinese navy in this period by their continual
threats to the coastal cities in which the shipyards lay. Not until

much later, at a time of unrest in Japan in 1467, was there any peace from the Japanese pirates.

The Japanese attacks were especially embarrassing for the Chinese government for one other reason. Large armies had to be kept all along China's northern border, from Manchuria to Central Asia. Food supplies could not be collected in north China which did not have enough surpluses. Canal transportation from central China was not reliable, as the canals did not always have enough water and were often clogged by hundreds of ships. And even if canals were used, grain still had to be transported by land from the end of the canals to the frontier. The Ming government, therefore, had organized an overseas flotilla of grain ships which brought grain from central China directly to the front in Liao-tung and Manchuria. And these ships, vitally important, were so often attacked by the pirates that this plan later had to be given up again.

These activities along the coast led the Chinese to the belief that basically all foreigners who came by ships were 'barbarians'; when towards the end of the Ming epoch the Japanese were replaced by Europeans who did not behave much differently and were also pirate-merchants, the nations of Western Europe, too, were regarded as 'barbarians' and were looked upon with great suspicion. On the other side, continental powers, even if they were enemies, had long been regarded as 'states', sometimes even as equals. Therefore, when at a much later time the Chinese came into contact with Russians, their attitude towards them was similar to that which they had taken towards other Asian continental powers.

3 Social legislation within the existing order

At the time when Chu Yüan-chang conquered Peking, in 1368, becoming the recognized emperor of China (Ming dynasty), it seemed as though he would remain a revolutionary in spite of everything. His first laws were directed against the rich. Many of the rich were compelled to migrate to the capital, Nanking, thus losing their land and the power based on it. Land was redistributed among poor peasants; new land registers were also compiled, in order to prevent the rich from evading taxation. The number of monks living in idleness was cut down and precisely determined; the possessions of the temples were reduced, land exempted from taxation being thus made taxable—all this, incidentally, although Chu had himself been a monk! These laws might have paved the way to social harmony and removed the worst of the poverty of the Mongol epoch. But all this was frustrated in the very first years of Chu's reign. The laws were only half carried into effect or not at all, especially in the hinterland of the present Shanghai. That region had been conquered by Chu at the very beginning of the Ming epoch; in it lived the wealthy land-owners who had already been paying the bulk of the taxes under the Mongols. The emperor depended on this wealthy class for the financing of his great armies, and so could not be too hard on it.

Chu Yüan-chang and his entourage were also unable to free themselves from some of the ideas of the Mongol epoch. Neither Chu, nor anybody else before and long after him, discussed the possibility of a form of government other than that of a monarchy. The first ever to discuss this question, although very timidly, was Huang Tsung-hsi (1610–1695), at the end of the Ming dynasty. Chu's conception of an emperor was that of an absolute monarch, master over life and death of his subjects; it was formed by the Mongol emperors with their magnificence and the huge expenditure of their life in Peking; Chu was oblivious of the fact that Peking had been the capital of a vast empire embracing almost the whole of Asia, and expenses could well be higher than for a capital only of China. It did not occur to Chu and his supporters that they could have done without imperial state and splendour; on the contrary, they felt compelled to display it. The splendour of Peking, which we still admire today, is largely the result of the building activities in early Ming time, after the change of the capital from Nanking to Peking. Another sign of Chu's tendency to imitate the Mongol rulers were his grants: he conferred great land grants on all his relatives, friends, and supporters; he would give to a single person land sufficient for 20,000 peasant families; he ordered the payments of state pensions to members of the imperial family, just as the Mongols had done, and the total of these pension payments was often higher than the revenue of the region involved. For the capital alone over eight million *shih* of grain had to be provided in payment of pensions—that is to say, more than 160,000 tons! These pension payments were in themselves a heavy burden on the state; not only that, but they formed a difficult transport problem! We have no close figure of the total population at the beginning of the Ming epoch; about 1500 it is estimated to have been 53,280,000, and this population had to provide some 266,000,000 *shih* in taxes. At the beginning of the Ming epoch the population and revenue must, however, have been smaller.

The laws against the merchants and the restrictions under which the craftsmen worked remained under Chu essentially as they had been before, and changed only in the sixteenth century. But now the few remaining foreign merchants lost their privileged status and also fell under these laws, and their influence quickly diminished. All craftsmen, a total of some 300,000 men with families, were still registered and had to serve the government in the capital for three months once every three years; others had to serve ten days per month, if they lived close by. They were a hereditary caste as were the professional soldiers, and not allowed to change their occupation except by special imperial permission. When a craftsman or soldier died, another family member had to replace him; therefore, families of craftsmen were not allowed to separate into small nuclear families, in which there might not always be a suitable male. Yet, in an empire as large as that of the Ming, this system did not work too well: craftsmen lost too much time in travelling and often succeeded in running away while travelling. Therefore, from 1505 on, they had to pay a tax instead of working for the government, and from then on the craftsmen became relatively free.

4 *Colonization and agricultural developments*

As already mentioned, the Ming had to keep a large army along the northern frontiers. But they also had to keep armies in south China, especially in Yünnan. Here, the Mongol invasions of Burma and Thailand had brought unrest among the tribes, especially the Shan. The Ming did not hold Burma but kept it in a loose dependency as a 'tributary nation'. In order to supply armies so far away from all agricultural surplus centres, the Ming resorted to the old system of 'military colonies' which seems to have been invented in the second century B.C. and is still used even today (in Sinkiang). Soldiers were settled in camps called *ying*, and therefore there are so many place names ending with *ying* in the outlying areas of China. They worked as state farmers and accumulated surpluses which were used in case of war in which these same farmers turned soldiers again. Many criminals were sent to these state farms, too. This system, especially in south China, transformed territories formerly inhabited by native tribes or uninhabited, into solidly Chinese areas. In addition to these military colonies, a steady stream of settlers from central China and the coast continued to move into Kwangtung and Hunan provinces. They felt protected by the army against attacks by natives. Yet Ming texts are full of reports on major and minor clashes with the natives, from Kiangsi and Fukien to Kwangtung and Kwanghsi.

But the production of military colonies was still not enough to feed the armies, and the government in Chu's time resorted to a new design. It promised to give merchants who transported grain from central China to the borders, government salt certificates. Upon the receipt, the merchants could acquire a certain amount of salt and sell it with high profits. Soon, these merchants began to invest some of their capital in local land which was naturally cheap. They then attracted farmers from their home countries as tenants. The rent of the tenants, paid in form of grain, was then sold to the army, and the merchant's gains increased. Tenants could easily be found: the density of population in the Yangtze plains had further increased since the Sung time. This system of merchant colonization did not last long, because soon, in order to curb the profits of the merchants, money was given instead of salt certificates, and the merchants lost interest in grain transports. Thus, grain prices along the frontiers rose and the effectiveness of the armies was diminished.

Although the history of Chinese agriculture is as yet only partially known, a number of changes in this field, which began to show up from Sung time on, seem to have produced an 'agricultural revolution' in Ming time. We have already mentioned the Sung attempts to increase production near the big cities by deep-lying fields, cultivation on and in lakes. At the same time, there was an increase in cultivation of mountain slopes by terracing and by distributing water over the terraces in balanced systems. New irrigation machines, especially the so-called Persian wheel, were introduced in the Ming time. Perhaps the most important innovation, however, was the introduction of rice from Indo-China's kingdom Champa in 1012 into Fukien from where it soon spread. This rice had three advantages over ordinary Chinese rice: it was drought-resistant and could, therefore, be planted in areas with poor or even no irrigation. It had a great productivity, and it could be sown very early in the year. At first it had the disadvantage that it had a vegetation period of a hundred days. But soon, the Chinese developed a quick-growing Champa rice, and the speediest varieties took only sixty days from transplantation into the fields to the harvest. This made it possible to grow two rice harvests instead of only one, and more than doubled the production. Rice varieties which grew again after being cut and produced a second, but very much smaller harvest, disappeared from now on. Furthermore, fish were kept in the ricefields and produced not only food for the farmers but also fertilized the fields, so that continuous cultivation of ricefields without any decrease in fertility became possible. Incidentally, fish control the malaria mosquitoes; although the Chinese did not know this fact, large areas in south China which had formerly been avoided by Chinese because of malaria, gradually became inhabitable. Some enterpreneurs raised baby fish in hatcheries and sold them commercially.

The importance of alternating crops was also discovered and from now on, the old system of fallow cultivation was given up and continuous cultivation with, in some areas, even more than one harvest per field per year, was introduced even in wheat-growing areas. Considering that under the fallow system from one-half to one-third of all fields remained uncultivated each year, the increase in production under the new system must have been tremendous.

We believe that the population revolution which in China started about 1550, was the result of this earlier agrarian revolution. From the eighteenth century on we get reports of depletion of fields due to wrong application of the new system.

Another plant deeply affected Chinese agriculture: cotton. It is often forgotten that, from very early times, the Chinese in the south had used kapok and similar cotton-like fibres, and that all the time cocoons of different kinds of worms had been used for silk. Real cotton probably came from Bengal over South-East Asia first to the coastal provinces of China and spread quickly into Fukien and Kwangtung in Sung time.

On the other side, cotton reached China through Central Asia, and already in the thirteenth century we find it in Shensi in north-western China. Farmers in the north could in many places grow cotton in summer and wheat in winter, and cotton was a high-priced product. They ginned the cotton with iron rods; a mechanical cotton gin was not introduced until later. The raw cotton was sold to merchants who transported it into the industrial centre of the time, the Yangtze valley, and who re-exported cotton cloth to the north. Raw cotton, loosened by the string of the bow (a method which was known since Sung), could now in the north also be used for quilts and padded winter garments.

5 Commercial and industrial developments

Intensivation and modernization of agriculture led to strong population increases especially in the Yangtze valley from Sung time on. Thus, in this area commerce and industry also developed most quickly. Urbanization was greatest here. Nanking, the new Ming capital, grew tremendously because of the presence of the court and administration, and even when later the capital was moved, Nanking continued to remain the cultural capital of China. The urban population needed textiles and food. From Ming time on, fashions changed quickly as soon as government regulations which determined colour and material of the dress of each social class were relaxed or as soon as they could be circumvented by bribery or ingenious devices. Now, only factories could produce the amounts which the consumers wanted. We hear of many men who started out with one loom and later ended up with over forty looms, employing many weavers. Shanghai began to emerge as a centre of cotton cloth production. A system of middle-men developed who bought raw cotton and raw silk from the producers and sold it to factories.

Consumption in the Yangtze cities raised the value of the land around the cities. The small farmers who were squeezed out migrated to the south. Absentee landlords in cities relied partly on migratory, seasonal labour supplied by small farmers from Chêkiang who came to the Yangtze area after they had finished their own harvest. More and more, vegetables and mulberries or cotton were planted in the vicinity of the cities. As rice prices went up quickly a large organization of rice merchants grew up. They ran large ships up to Hankow where they bought rice which was brought down from Hunan in river boats by smaller merchants. The small merchants again made contracts with the local gentry who bought as much rice from the producers as they could and sold it to these grain merchants. Thus, local grain prices went up and we hear of cases where the local population attacked the grain boats in order to prevent the depletion of local markets.

While there always had been markets, from Sung time on, China became dotted with a network of markets of different types. There were markets in the cities, often comparable to the Near Eastern bazaars, and markets along the borders for trade with foreigners, both types strongly controlled by the government. But there were also farmers' markets, often called 'malaria markets' because they were held on alternate days (like the attacks by malaria tertiana). Such markets were often outside the villages ('mountain markets') and served as an exchange for the products of local villagers, but itinerant pedlars came to these places, too, and sold city-made textiles or iron implements. There were, separately, cattle and horse markets, held at times when it suited the farmers best. Finally, there were temple fairs, held on the birthday of the god of the temple. Here, more luxury articles were sold; scholars often found here valuable paintings or rare books, ordinary citizens bought toys and sweets for their children.

Grain, collected from farmers by agents or sent in by farmers, came to the cities and specialized big grain merchants. Their centre in central China soon became the district of Hui-chou, in particular Hsin-an, a city on the borders of Anhui and Chêkiang. When the grain transportation to the frontiers came to an end in early Ming time, the Hsin-an merchants specialized first in silver trade. Later in Ming time, they spread their activities all over China and often monopolized the salt, silver, rice, cotton, silk or tea businesses. In the sixteenth century they had well-established contacts with smugglers on the Fukien coast and brought foreign goods into the interior. Their home was also close to the main centres of porcelain production in Kiangsi which was exported overseas and to the urban centres. The demand for porcelain had increased so much that state factories could not fulfil it. The state factories seem often to have suffered from a lack of labour: indented artisans were imported from other provinces and later sent back on state expenses or were taken away from other state industries. Thus, private porcelain factories began to develop, and in connection with quickly changing fashions a great diversification of porcelain occurred.

One other industry should also be mentioned. With the development of printing, which will be discussed below, the paper industry was greatly stimulated. The state also needed special types of paper for the paper currency. Printing and book selling became a profitable business, and with the application of block print to textiles (probably first used in Sung time) another new field of commercial activity was opened.

As already mentioned, silver in form of bars had been increasingly used as currency in Sung time. The yearly government production of silver was about 10,000 kg. Mongol currency was actually based upon silver. The Ming, however, reverted to copper as basic unit, in addition to the use of paper money. This encouraged the use of silver for speculative purposes.

The development of business changed the face of cities. From Sung time on, the division of cities into wards with gates which were closed during the night, began to break down. Ming cities had no more wards. Business was no more restricted to official markets but grew up in all parts of the cities. The individual trades were no more necessarily all in one street. Shops did not have to close at sunset. The guilds developed and in some cases were able to exercise locally some influence upon the officials.

The increasing development of markets led to several other changes. We observe, for instance, a growing specialization and division of labour, so that, for instance, cloth was no more produced from the raw cotton to the finished product by one worker, but spinning, weaving and dyeing were done by different specialists, often in different cities.

In the countryside, too, the social organization became more and more complex. It seems, according to recent research, that the Hsin-an merchants have originated from landowner families who first went for diversification of cultivation, in order to protect themselves against catastrophies. They then invested in land in places outside; then they either had tenants working the land or bought up products of farmers and became merchants in the first place. Such merchant families had a stability, often over centuries, like the old gentry families and can be compared to the urban patricians in Europe.

From this period, we have enough contracts between landowners and tenants to see that, basically the relationship was contractual, so that, technically, we cannot call the producers 'serfs' any more.

Some tenants, though, could not leave the land and had servile obligations, such as to take care of the master's estate when he was away on business, or to take care of the master's family tombs. But at the same time, the master had to supply them with a house, had to give them gifts at the festivals, and often also gave them tools. Some landowners gave their tenants the housemaids as wives, thus saving the tenants from an expense which equalled a year's income. The tenant could pawn his land; he also could own land, and there were many farm labourers on one-year contracts, as well as free tenants who could move away or try to get a different piece of land from another landowner. There are cases in which a tenant, in order to get a wife, moved to the wife's family and served her family, in one case as long as twenty-two years—reminding us of the Old Testament and Jacob's service at Laban's house.

But there were also still slaves, apparently mainly criminals who were given to officials to work on their land. They were hereditary slaves and could not move. Thus, we observe a great complexity and diversity in Ming time.

6 Changing times

There appears in Ming times a different outlook on society and life. The old attitude is still found. For instance:

> Somebody gave to Lü Meng-cheng [Sung time] a mirror which could reflect 200 *li* afar. Lü said, his face was small, he needed no big mirror ('Ch'iu-yü-wan sui-pi', ch. 5).

Or:

> Formerly, women's work was with hemp, linen, and silk. They wove it and made yarn, and their product was solid and heavy, so that it did last a long time. In later times, women worked on stitching and embroidering; the product was light and easily spoiled. In the morning it was a splendid bed cover or dress; in the evening it was already thrown away. A waste of energy and of money, as it could not be worse ('Leng-lu tsa-chih', ch. 2).

This was a typical attitude against progress and change and in favour of frugality. At the base of it was what G. Foster called the concept of the 'limited good'. Now we find different opinions for the first time:

> Customs change from the simple to the vulgar, and this is irreversible, like the flowing of rivers downstream. From old times on, this was regretted. Our Sung-chiang [a city not far from Shanghai] was always known for its extravagant and artful, haughty customs. There was no more chance for a return

to simple life. But from the Chia-ching [1522–1566] and Lung-ch'ing [1567–1572] times on, the big houses, the honoured families indulged in extravagance, went towards sinfulness. . . . Every day unusual new things come up, every year there are hundreds of new things. Shepherd boys and village oldsters are competing to become 'rats' (i.e. oppressive officials), and rural women and country ladies change into seducing foxes ('Yün-chien chü-mu ch'ao', Ch. 2).

This author then gives a long list of changes. He regrets some of these changes. Thus he remarks that the rules for dress were made to 'clarify the fine distinctions between men and women, between high and low' and then says: 'When slaves compete for glorious (appearance), it will be difficult for them to become decent; if women copy the whores, it will be difficult for them to be decent.' He observes that formerly there were no shoe shops in town, but since 1573 male shoemakers began to make shoes. Shoes became lighter and finer. 'Slaves and masters use the same types now. This is the worst of all customs.' The forms and colours of hats changed rapidly, as did women's hair fashions. New brands of wine, new dishes were introduced. Since 1567 there were boatsmen at the gates of the city and excursions with parties on board became fashionable. 'Recently, wives and daughters of "small people" [i.e. rural land-owners], as soon as they can get out, immediately call themselves sales-women. They buy and sell gold and pearl head-dresses . . . and also indulge in prostitution.' Such a sales-woman rented herself out to a doctor who had no son and gave birth to a son for him. She became famous and the wealthy houses competed in inviting her. She later also sold sex drugs, and sex implements and became wealthy. Finally, the author complains about juvenile delinquency, another innovation, especially after 1580. These gangs divided the city up among the individual gangs, cheated country-people who wanted to sell merchandise in town, and blackmailed them. He even reports mob actions against officials. Thus, we may say that the changes in the sixteenth century were so quick and obvious that scholars observed them and got worried. It is only in the nineteenth century that some authors begin to regard the changes as a progress:

The use of *shih* [boys representing a dead ancestor] in funeral sacrifices; the use of human sacrifices for the dead; the use of cousins [of the wife] as concubines; the mutilating punishments by the courts; the divorce of women because of disabling diseases or barrenness: all these things occurred in the old time and have now disappeared. In such cases, the new is better than the old [custom] ('Leng-lu tsa-shih', Ch. 7).

And another author of the nineteenth century remarks that, apparently, even the gods change their customs: formerly, every man wore square boots, not pointed boots, now, deities appear in modern, pointed boots!

What I want to point out here is that great changes occurred during the lifetime of a person from Ming times on; that the thinkers wondered about them. Some regard them as bad, but unavoidable, others still long for the past. Only in the nineteenth century do some of them regard some changes as a progress towards a better society. Perhaps even more important is the growing social mobility, which, of course, the old gentry disliked.

7 Growth of the small gentry

There were still other factors which made for social mobility. With the spread of book printing, all kinds of books became easily accessible, including reprints of examination papers, Even businessmen and farmers increasingly learned to read and to write, and many people now could prepare themselves for the examinations. Attendance, however, at the examinations cost a good deal. The candidate had to travel to the local or provincial capital, and for the higher examinations to the capital of the country; he had to live there for several months and, as a rule, had to bribe the examiners or at least to gain the favour of influential people. There were many cases of candidates becoming destitute. Most of them were heavily in debt when at last they gained a position. They naturally set to work at once to pay their debts out of their salary, and to accumulate fresh capital to meet future emergencies. The salaries of officials were, however, so small that it was impossible to make ends meet; and at the same time every official was liable with his own capital for the receipt in full of the taxes for the collection of which he was responsible. Consequently every official began at once to collect more taxes than were really due, so as to be able to cover any deficits, and also to cover his own cost of living—including not only the repayment of his debts but the acquisition of capital or land so as to rise in the social scale. The old gentry had been rich landowners, and had had no need to exploit the peasants on such a scale.

The Chinese empire was greater than it had been before the Mongol epoch, and the population was also greater, so that more officials were needed. Thus in the Ming epoch there began a certain democratization, larger sections of the population having the opportunity of gaining government positions.

The new 'small gentry' did not consist of great families like the original gentry. When, therefore, people of that class wanted to play a political part in the central government, or to gain a position there, they had either to get into close touch with one of the families of the gentry, or to try to approach the emperor directly. In the immediate entourage of the emperor, however, were the eunuchs. Some members of the new class had themselves castrated after they had passed their state examination. Originally eunuchs were forbidden to acquire education. But soon the Ming emperors used the eunuchs as a tool to counteract the power of gentry cliques and thus to strengthen their personal power. When, later, eunuchs controlled appointments to government posts, long-established practices of bureaucratic administration were eliminated and the court, i.e. the emperor and his tools, the eunuchs, could create a rule by way of arbitrary decisions, a despotic rule. For such purposes, eunuchs had to have education, and these new educated eunuchs, when they had once secured a position, were able to gain great influence in the immediate entourage of the emperor; later such educated eunuchs were preferred, especially as many offices were created which were only filled by eunuchs and for which educated eunuchs were needed. Whole departments of eunuchs came into existence at court, and these were soon made use of for confidential business of the emperor's outside the palace.

These eunuchs worked, of course, in the interest of their families. On the other hand, they were very ready to accept large bribes from the gentry for placing the desires of people of the gentry before the emperor and gaining his consent. Thus the eunuchs generally accumulated great wealth, which they shared with their small gentry relatives. The rise of the small gentry class was therefore connected with the increased influence of the eunuchs at court.

8 Literature, art, crafts

The growth of the small gentry which had its stronghold in the provincial towns and cities, as well as the rise of the merchant class and the liberation of the artisans, are reflected in the new literature of Ming time. While the Mongols had developed the theatre, the novel may be regarded as the typical Ming creation. Its precursors were the stories of story-tellers centuries ago. The novels pretended to be stories of story-tellers: they were cut into chapters, not according to logical principles, but the cuts were made at the most interesting places, to induce the reader to read further on—just as the story-teller stopped at the interesting place, collected money, and then continued. Like the stories, the novels were interspersed with poems, some of which were summaries of the content of the chapter and served as a kind of memory-aid to the teller, other poems gave descriptions of nature or of human emotions, interrupting the more factual stories. But, most important, the novels were written in everyday language, not in the language of the gentry. To this day every

Chinese knows and reads with enthusiasm 'Shui-hu-chuan' ('The Story of the River Bank'), probably written about 1550 by Wang Tao-k'un, in which the ruling class was first described in its decay. Against it are held up as ideals representatives of the middle class in the guise of the gentleman brigand. Every Chinese also knows the great satirical novel 'Hsi-yu-chi' ('The Westward Journey'), by Feng Mêng-lung (1574–1645), in which ironical treatment is meted out to all religions and sects against a mythological background, with a freedom that would not have been possible earlier. The characters are not presented as individuals but as representatives of human types: the intellectual, the hedonist, the pious man, and the simpleton, are drawn with incomparable skill, with their merits and defects. A third famous novel is 'San-kuo yen-i' ('The Tale of the Three Kingdoms'), by Lo Kuan-chung. Just as the European middle class read with avidity the romances of chivalry, so the comfortable class in China was enthusiastic over romanticized pictures of the struggle of the gentry in the third century. 'The Tale of the Three Kingdoms' became the model for countless historical novels of its own and subsequent periods. Later, mainly in the sixteenth century, the sensational and erotic novel developed, most of all in Nanking. It has deeply influenced Japanese writers, but was mercilessly suppressed by the Chinese gentry which resented the frivolity of this wealthy and luxurious urban class of middle or small gentry families who associated with rich merchants, actors, artists and musicians. Censorship of printed books had started almost with the beginning of book printing as a private enterprise: to the famous historian, anti-Buddhist and conservative Ou-yang Hsiu (1007–1072), the enemy of Wang An-shih, belongs the sad glory of having developed the first censorship rules. Since Ming time, it became a permanent feature of Chinese governments.

The best known of the erotic novels is the 'Chin-p'ing-mei', which is still forbidden by the Communists as well as by the Nationalists, except in expurgated versions. Similarly, there is only one German translation which is not expurgated, but the objectionable sections are not in the commercial edition and have to be ordered separately; other translators used Latin at the same places. Much less 'erotic' and closer to the form of an historical novel is the 'Amorous adventures of Yang Ti, emperor of Sui' ('Sui Yang Ti yen-shih'), which does not yet exist in a translation but would deserve one. It might be pointed out that many novels were printed in Hui-chou, the commercial centre of the time.

The short story which formerly served the entertainment of the educated only and which was, therefore, written in classical Chinese, now also became a literary form appreciated by the middle classes.

The collection 'Chin-ku ch'i-kuan' ('Strange Stories of New Times and Old'), compiled by Feng Mêng-lung, is the best known of these collections in vernacular Chinese.

Little original work was done in the Ming epoch in the fields generally regarded as 'literature' by educated Chinese, those of poetry and the essay. There are some admirable essays, but these are only isolated examples out of thousands. So also with poetry: the poets of the gentry, united in 'clubs', chose the poets of the Sung epoch as their models to emulate.

The Chinese drama made further progress in the Ming epoch. Many of the finest Chinese dramas were written under the Ming; they are still produced again and again to this day. The most famous dramatists of the Ming epoch are Wang Shih-chen (1526–1590) and T'ang Hsien-tsu (1556–1617). T'ang wrote the well-known drama 'Mu-tan-t'ing' ('The Peony Pavilion'), one of the finest love-stories of Chinese literature, full of romance and remote from all reality. This is true also of the other dramas by T'ang, especially his 'Four Dreams', a series of four plays. In them a man lives in dream through many years of his future life, with the result that he realizes the worthlessness of life and decides to become a monk.

Together with the development of the drama (or, rather, the opera) in the Ming epoch went an important endeavour in the modernization of music, the attempt to create a 'well-tempered scale' made in 1584 by Chu Tsai-yü. This solved in China a problem which was not tackled till later in Europe. The first Chinese theorists of music who occupied themselves with this problem were Ching Fang (77–37 B.C.) and Ho Ch'êng-t'ien (A.D. 370–447).

In the Mongol epoch, most of the Chinese painters had lived in central China; this remained so in the Ming epoch. Of the many painters of the Ming epoch, all held in high esteem in China, mention must be made especially of Ch'iu Ying (c. 1525), T'ang Yin (1470–1523), and Tung Ch'i-ch'ang (1555–1636). Ch'iu Ying painted in the Academic Style, indicating every detail, however small, and showing preference for a turquoise-green ground. T'ang Yin was the painter of elegant women; Tung became famous especially as a calligraphist and a theoretician of the art of painting; a textbook of the art was written by him.

Just as puppet plays and shadow plays are the 'opera of the common man' and took a new development in Ming time, the wood-cut and block-printing developed largely as a cheap substitute of real paintings. The new urbanites wanted to have paintings of the masters and found in the wood-cut which soon became a multi-colour print a cheap mass medium. Block-printing in colours, developed in the Yangtze valley, was adopted by Japan and found its highest refinement there. But the Ming are also famous for their monumental architecture which largely followed Mongol patterns. Among the most famous examples is the famous Great Wall which had been in dilapidation and was rebuilt; the great city walls of Peking; and large parts of the palaces of Peking, begun in the Mongol epoch. It was at this time that the official style which we may observe to this day in north China was developed, the style employed everywhere. Nationalist China on the mainland and in Taiwan transformed this style into concrete.

In the Ming epoch the porcelain with blue decoration on a white ground became general; the first examples, from the famous kilns in Ching-te-chen, in the province of Kiangsi, were relatively coarse, but in the fifteenth century the production was much finer. In the sixteenth century the quality deteriorated, owing to the disuse of the cobalt from the Middle East (perhaps from Persia) in favour of Sumatra cobalt, which did not yield the same brilliant colour. In the Ming epoch there also appeared the first brilliant red colour, a product of iron, and a start was then made with three-colour porcelain (with lead glaze) or five-colour (enamel). The many porcelains exported to western Asia and Europe first influenced European ceramics (Delft), and then were imitated in Europe (Böttger); the early European porcelains long showed Chinese influence (the so-called onion pattern, blue on a white ground). In addition to the porcelain of the Ming epoch, of which the finest specimens are in the palace at Istanbul, especially famous are the lacquers (carved lacquer, lacquer painting, gold lacquer) of the Ming epoch and the cloisonné work of the same period. These are closely associated with the contemporary work in Japan.

Finally a few words about religious developments in Ming time. It seems that the present religious situation came to full development during Ming, after early beginnings, probably in Sung time. By this I mean that now each Chinese uses three systems for the main problems he has to deal with, paralleling the division of the world into three spheres: the upper world, our world, and the netherworld. These three worlds are symbolized by three kinds of buildings: temples for the deities of the upper world—they are 'clean'; houses in this world for humans—they are clean as well as polluted; tombs for the ghosts in the netherworld—they are polluted. Taoist priests can deal with the deities above; they have to be unpolluted and keep the temples clean. Buddhist priests can handle the ghosts and the dead, because being chaste and living outside the world of family and state in their monasteries they cannot be polluted. The cult in the house is often regarded as Confucianist. In the house, the ancestors above are honoured, because their *hun* soul is thought to be above;

at the tomb of an ancestor the dead are honoured as helpful spirits, and in the house the family lives and reproduces.

This is a predominantly 'cultic' approach, the approach that the common man has to religion. And thus, cultic Buddhism from Ming time on interests mainly the common man. There is a kind of revival of populist Buddhist sects in Ming, but philosophical Buddhism does not show much development. A great number of so-called *shan-shu* (books which should turn you to the Good) appears now in which the consequences of sinful actions are described and people are admonished to avoid falling into sin. This may be some reaction against the loosening of society as described above. It also shows that the common man was expected to act morally not because he is afraid of shame (external), but of sin (internalized feeling).

9 *Politics at court*

After the founding of the dynasty by Chu Yüan-chang, important questions had to be dealt with apart from the social legislation. What was to be done, for instance, with Chu's helpers? Chu, like many revolutionaries before and after him, recognized that these people had been serviceable in the years of struggle but could no longer remain useful. He got rid of them by the simple device of setting one against another so that they murdered one another. In the first decades of his rule the dangerous cliques of gentry had formed again, and were engaged in mutual struggles. The most formidable clique was led by Hu Wei-yung. Hu was a man of the gentry of Chu's old homeland, and one of his oldest supporters. Hu and his relations controlled the country after 1370, until in 1380 Chu succeeded in beheading Hu and exterminating his clique. New cliques formed before long and were exterminated in turn.

Chu had founded Nanking in the years of revolution, and he made it his capital. In so doing he met the wishes of the rich grain producers of the Yangtze delta. But the north was the most threatened part of his empire, so that troops had to be permanently stationed there in considerable strength. Thus Peking, where Chu placed one of his sons as 'king', was a post of exceptional importance.

In Chu Yüan-chang's last years (he was named T'ai Tsu as emperor) difficulties arose in regard to the dynasty. The heir to the throne died in 1391; and when the emperor himself died in 1398, the son of the late heir-apparent was installed as emperor (Hui Ti, 1399–1402). This choice had the support of some of the influential Confucian gentry families of the south. But a protest against his enthronement came from the other son of Chu Yüan-chang, who as king in Peking had hoped to become emperor. With his strong army this prince, Ch'eng Tsu, marched south and captured Nanking, where the palaces were burnt down. There was a great massacre of supporters of the young emperor, and the victor made himself emperor (better known under his reign name, Yung-lo). As he had established himself in Peking, he transferred the capital to Peking, where it remained throughout the Ming epoch. Nanking became a sort of subsidiary capital.

This transfer of the capital to the north, as the result of the victory of the military party and Buddhists allied to them, produced a new element of instability: the north was of military importance, but the Yangtze region remained the economic centre of the country. The interests of the gentry of the Yangtze region were injured by the transfer. The first Ming emperor had taken care to make his court resemble the court of the Mongol rulers, but on the whole had exercised relative economy. Yung-lo (1403–1424), however, lived in the actual palaces of the Mongol rulers, and all the luxury of the Mongol epoch was revived. This made the reign of Yung-lo the most magnificent period of the Ming epoch, but beneath the surface decay had begun. Typical of the unmitigated absolutism which developed now, was the word of one of the emperor's political and military advisers, significantly a Buddhist monk: 'I know the way of heaven. Why discuss the hearts of the people?'

10 *Navy. Southward expansion*

After the collapse of Mongol rule in Indo-China, partly through the simple withdrawal of the Mongols, and partly through attacks from various Chinese generals, there were independence movements in south-west China and Indo-China. In 1393 wars broke out in Annam. Yung-lo considered that the time had come to annex these regions to China and so to open a new field for Chinese trade, which was suffering continual disturbance from the Japanese. He sent armies to Yünnan and Indo-China; at the same time he had a fleet built by one of his eunuchs, Cheng Ho. The fleet was successfully protected from attack by the Japanese. Cheng Ho, who had promoted the plan and also carried it out, began in 1405 his famous mission to Indo-China, which had been envisaged as giving at least moral support to the land operations, but was also intended to renew trade connections with Indo-China, where they had been interrupted by the collapse of Mongol rule. This was the first of several expeditions by which Chinese ships ultimately reached the east coast of Africa and Arabia. Cheng Ho was a member of a Chinese Muslim family, so that he was an ideal person to contact the holy cities of Islam. This may give us one of the possible explanations for these very expensive expeditions: they could have been an attempt by the Chinese to counteract the occupation of large parts of the Near East by Timur (died in 1406). We know that Timur actually had planned to attack China and preparations came to a standstill with his death. If the Chinese could have interested the Muslims of the Near East in a collaboration with China, this would have made an attack against China very dangerous for Timur. The death of Timur and the breakdown of his empire eliminated this danger and reopened Central Asia for trade with China. Soon, trade missions from the kingdom of Shahruk in north Iran were able to come to China (the famous mission of 1409–1411).

Chinese and other scholars have often regarded these expeditions as either an outgrowth of the interest of the Yung-lo emperor in rare luxury goods, or merely as a 'friendship mission'. However, the fleet of Cheng Ho was loaded with soldiers and weapons, sufficient to overwhelm the small South-East Asian kingdoms into submission. In at least one case, Cheng Ho directly interfered in the politics of a south Asian kingdom and deported its ruler, setting up a puppet regime. It seems more likely that further expeditions were stopped after the death of Timur and the re-establishment of caravan trade. The cost of supplying the great fleet was certainly in no relation to the material advantages. A final reason for ending the expeditions may have been that the fleet would have had to be permanently guarded against the Japanese, as it had been stationed not in south China but in the Yangtze region. As early as 1411 the canals had been repaired, and from 1415 onward all the traffic of the country went by the canals, so evading the Japanese peril. This ended the short chapter of Chinese naval history.

These travels of Cheng Ho seem to have had two, more cultural, results: a large number of fairy-tales from the Middle East were brought to China, or at all events reached China at that time. The Chinese, being a realistically minded people, have produced relatively few fairy-tales of their own. The bulk of their finest fairy-tales was brought by Buddhist monks, in the course of the first millennium A.D., from India by way of Central Asia. The Buddhists made use of them to render their sermons more interesting and impressive. As time went on, these stories, spread all over China, modified in harmony with the spirit of the people and adapted to the Chinese environment. Only the fables failed to strike root in China: the matter-of-fact Chinese was not interested in animals that talked and behaved to each other like human beings. In addition, however, to these early fairly-tales, there was another group of stories that did not spread throughout China, but were found only in the south-eastern coastal provinces. These came from the Middle East, especially from Persia. The fairy-tales of Indian origin spread not only to Central Asia but at the same time to Persia, where they found a very

16 The imperial summer palace of the Manchu rulers, at Jehol.
(Photo H. Hammer-Morrisson.)

17 Tower on the city wall of Peking.
(Photo H. Hammer-Morrisson.)

congenial soil. The Persians made radical changes in the stories and gave them the form in which they came to Europe by various routes—through North Africa to Spain and France; through Constantinople, Venice, or Genoa to France; through Russian Central Asia to Russia, Finland, and Sweden; through Turkey and the Balkans to Hungary and Germany. Thus the stories found a European home. And this same Persian form was carried by sea in Cheng Ho's time to south China. Thus we have the strange experience of finding some of our own finest fairy-tales in almost the same form in south China. Another result of these travels was a great increase of the knowledge of the Western world. Chinese now had some general knowledge of the shape of Africa and heard details about countries of the Mediterranean. It has recently been asserted that the Koreans received information of the same quality through Central Asian contacts which, we may guess, the Chinese also could have received.

11 *Struggles between cliques*

Yung-lo's successor died early. Under the latter's son, the emperor Hsüan Tsung (1426–1435; reign name Hsüan-tê), fixed numbers of candidates were assigned for the state examinations. It had been found that almost the whole of the gentry in the Yangtze region sat at the examinations; and that at these examinations their representatives made sure, through their mutual relations, that only their members should pass, so that the candidates from the north were virtually excluded. The important military clique in the north protested against this, and a compromise was arrived at: at every examination one-third of the candidates must come from the north and two-thirds from the south. This system lasted for a long time, and led to many disputes.

At his death Hsüan Tsung left the empire to his eight-year-old son Ying Tsung (1436–1449 and 1456–1464), who was entirely in the hands of the Yang clique, which was associated with his grandmother. Soon, however, another clique, led by the eunuch Wang Chen, gained the upper hand at court. The Mongols were very active at this time, and made several raids on the province of Shansi; Wang Chen proposed a great campaign against them, and in this campaign he took with him the young emperor, who had reached his twenty-first birthday in 1449. The emperor had grown up in the palace and knew nothing of the world outside; he was therefore glad to go with Wang Chen; but that eunuch had also lived in the palace and also knew nothing of the world, and in particular of war. Consequently he failed in the organization of reinforcements for his army, some 100,000 strong; after a few brief engagements the Oirat-Mongol prince Esen had the imperial army surrounded and the emperor a prisoner. The eunuch Wang Chen came to his end, and his clique, of course, no longer counted. The Mongols had no intention of killing the emperor; they proposed to hold him to ransom, at a high price. The various cliques at court cared little, however, about their ruler. After the fall of the Wang clique there were two others, of which one, that of General Yü, became particularly powerful, as he had been able to repel a Mongol attack on Peking. Yü proclaimed a new emperor—not the captive emperor's son, a baby, but his brother, who became the emperor Ching Tsung. Yü Ch'ien (1398–1457) is celebrated in many operas as a patriot; there were temples devoted to his memory. Wang Chen, on the other hand, became the symbol of a traitor. The Yang clique insisted on the rights of the imperial baby. From all this the Mongols saw that the Chinese were not inclined to spend a lot of money on their imperial captive. Accordingly they made an enormous reduction in the ransom demanded, and more or less forced the Chinese to take back their former emperor. The Mongols hoped that this would at least produce political disturbances by which they might profit, once the old emperor was back in Peking. And this did soon happen. At first the ransomed emperor was pushed out of sight into a palace, and Ching Tsung continued to reign. But in 1456 Ching Tsung fell ill, and a successor to him had to be chosen. The Yü clique wanted to have the son of Ching Tsung; the Yang clique wanted the son of the deposed emperor Ying Tsung. No agreement was reached, so that in the end a third clique, led by the soldier Shih Heng, who had helped to defend Peking against the Mongols, found its opportunity, and by a coup d'état reinstated the deposed emperor Ying Tsung.

This was not done out of love for the emperor, but because Shih Heng hoped that under the rule of the completely incompetent Ying Tsung he could best carry out a plan of his own, to set up his own dynasty. It is not so easy, however, to carry a conspiracy to success when there are several rival parties, each of which is ready to betray any of the others. Shih Heng's plan became known before long, and he himself was beheaded (1460).

The next forty years were filled with struggles between cliques, which steadily grew in ferocity, particularly since a special office, a sort of secret police headquarters, was set up in the palace, with functions which it extended beyond the palace, with the result that many people were arrested and disappeared. This office was set up by the eunuchs and the clique at their back, and was the first dictatorial organ created in the course of a development towards despotism that made steady progress in these years.

In 1505 Wu Tsung came to the throne, an inexperienced youth of fifteen who was entirely controlled by the eunuchs who had brought him up. The leader of the eunuchs was Liu Chin, who had the support of a group of people of the gentry and the middle class. Liu Chin succeeded within a year in getting rid of the eunuchs at court who belonged to other cliques and were working against him. After that he proceeded to establish his power. He secured in entirely official form the emperor's permission for him to issue all commands himself; the emperor devoted himself only to his pleasures, and care was taken that they should keep him sufficiently occupied to have no chance to notice what was going on in the country. The first important decree issued by Liu Chin resulted in the removal from office or the punishment or murder of over three hundred prominent persons, the leaders of the cliques opposed to him. He filled their posts with his own supporters, until all the higher posts in every department were in the hands of members of his group. He collected large sums of money which he quite openly extracted from the provinces as a special tax for his own benefit. When later his house was searched there were found 240,000 bars and 57,800 pieces of gold (a bar was equivalent of ten pieces), 791,800 ounces and 5,000,000 bars of silver (a bar was five ounces), three bushels of precious stones, two gold cuirasses, 3,000 gold rings, and much else—of a total value exceeding the annual budget of the state! The treasure was to have been used to finance a revolt planned by Liu Chin and his supporters.

Among the people whom Liu Chin had punished were several members of the former clique of the Yang, and also the philosopher Wang Yang-ming (1473–1529), who later became so famous, a member of the Wang family which was allied to the Yang. In 1510 the Yang won over one of the eunuchs in the palace and so became acquainted with Liu Chin's plans. When a revolt broke out in western China, this eunuch (whose political allegiance was, of course, unknown to Liu Chin) secured appointment as army commander. With the army intended for the crushing of the revolt, Liu Chin's palace was attacked when he was asleep, and he and all his supporters were arrested. Thus the other group came into power in the palace, including the philosopher Wang Yang-ming. Liu Chin's rule had done great harm to the country, as enormous taxation had been expended for the private benefit of his clique. On top of this had been the young emperor's extravagance: his latest pleasures had been the building of palaces and the carrying out of military games; he constantly assumed new military titles and was burning to go to war.

12 Risings

The emperor might have had a good opportunity for fighting, for his misrule had resulted in a great popular rising which began in the west, in Szechwan, and then spread to the east. As always, the rising was joined by some ruined scholars, and the movement, which had at first been directed against the gentry as such, was turned into a movement against the government of the moment. No longer were all the wealthy and all officials murdered, but only those who did not join the movement. In 1512 the rebels were finally overcome, not so much by any military capacity of the government armies as through the loss of the rebels' fleet of boats in a typhoon.

In 1517 a new favourite of the emperor's induced him to make a great tour in the north, to which the favourite belonged. The tour and the hunting greatly pleased the emperor, so that he continued his journeying. This was the year in which the Portuguese Fernão Pires de Andrade landed in Canton—the first modern European to enter China.

In 1518 Wang Yang-ming, the philosopher general, crushed a rising in Kiangsi. The rising had been the outcome of years of unrest, which had had two causes: local risings of the sort we described above, and loss for the gentry due to the transfer of the capital. The province of Kiangsi was a part of the Yangtze region, and the great landowners there had lived on the profit from their supplies to Nanking. When the capital was moved to Peking, their takings fell. They placed themselves under a prince who lived in Nanking. This prince regarded Wang Yang-ming's move into Kiangsi as a threat to him, and so rose openly against the government and supported the Kiangsi gentry. Wang Yang-ming defeated him, and so came into the highest favour with the incompetent emperor. When peace had been restored in Nanking, the emperor dressed himself up as an army commander, marched south, and made a triumphal entry into Nanking.

One other aspect of Wang Yang-ming's expeditions has not yet been studied: he crushed also the so-called salt-merchant rebels in the southernmost part of Kiangsi and adjoining Kwangtung. These merchants-turned-rebels had dominated a small area, off and on since the eleventh century. At this moment, they seem to have had connections with the rich inland merchants of Hsin-an and perhaps also with foreigners. Information is still too scanty to give more details, but a local movement as persistent as this one deserves attention.

We know, however, that Wang fought against the minorities in south China and his war also has to be seen as a part of the great drive towards subjugation and 'assimilation' of minorities into the Chinese state.

Wang Yang-ming became acquainted as early as 1519 with the first European rifles, imported by the Portuguese who had landed in 1517. (The Chinese then called them Fu-lang-chi, meaning Franks. Wang was the first Chinese who spoke of the 'Franks'.) The Chinese had already had mortars which hurled stones, as early as the second

272

century A.D. In the seventh or eighth century their mortars had sent stones of a couple of hundredweights some four hundred yards. There is mention in the eleventh century of cannon which apparently shot with a charge of a sort of gunpowder. The Mongols were already using true cannon in their sieges. In the early years of the Ming, the Chinese armies also had bombs and muskets. This was at a time when the armies of Ming had more than three million soldiers. This number was, however, much reduced in the fourteenth century.

In 1519, the first Portuguese were presented to the Chinese emperor in Nanking, where they were entertained for about a year in a hostel, a certain Lin Hsün learned about their rifles and copied them for Wang Yang-ming. In general, however, the Chinese had no respect for the Europeans, whom they described as 'bandits' who had expelled the lawful king of Malacca and had now come to China as its representatives. Later they were regarded as a sort of Japanese, because they, too, practised piracy.

13 *Machiavellism*

All main schools of Chinese philosophy were still based on Confucius. Wang Yang-ming's philosophy also followed Confucius, but he liberated himself from the Neo-Confucian tendency as represented by Chu Hsi, which started in the Sung epoch and continued to rule in China in his time and after him; he introduced into Confucian philosophy the conception of 'intuition'. He regarded intuition as the decisive philosophic experience; only through intuition could man come to true knowledge. This idea shows an element of meditative Buddhism along lines which the philosopher Lu Hsiang-shan (1139–1192) had first developed, while classical Neo-Confucianism was more an integration of monastic Buddhism into Confucianism. Lu had felt himself close to Wang An-shih (1021–1086), and this whole school, representing the small gentry of the Yangtze area, was called the southern or the Lin-ch'uan school, Lin-ch'uan in Kiangsi being Wang An-shih's home. During the Mongol period, a Taoist group, the *Cheng-i-chiao* (Correct Unity Sect) had developed in Lin-ch'uan and had accepted some of the Lin-ch'uan school's ideas. Originally, this group was a continuation of Chang Ling's church Taoism. Through the *Cheng-i* adherents, the southern school had gained political influence on the despotic Mongol rulers. The despotic Yung-lo emperor had favoured the monk Tao-yen (c. 1338–1418) who had also Taoist training and proposed a philosophy which also stressed intuition. He was, incidentally, in charge of the compilation of the largest encyclopaedia ever written, the 'Yung-lo ta-tien', commissioned by the Yung-lo emperor.

Wang Yang-ming followed the Lin-ch'uan tradition. The introduction of the conception of intuition, a highly subjective conception, into the system of a practical state philosophy like Confucianism could not but lead in the practice of the statesman to machiavellism. The statesman who followed the teaching of Wang Yang-ming had the opportunity of justifying whatever he did by his intuition.

Wang Yang-ming failed to gain acceptance for his philosophy. His disciples also failed to establish his doctrine in China, because it served the interests of an individual despot against those of the gentry as a class, and the middle class, which might have formed a counterweight against them, was not yet politically ripe for the seizure of the opportunity here offered to it. In Japan, however, Wang's doctrine gained many followers, because it admirably served the dictatorial state system which had developed in that country. Incidentally, Chiang Kai-shek in those years in which he showed rightist tendencies, also became interested in Wang Yang-ming.

14 *Foreign relations in the sixteenth century*

The feeble emperor Wu Tsung died in 1521, after an ineffective reign, without leaving an heir. The clique then in power at court looked among the possible pretenders for the one who seemed least likely to do anything, and their choice fell on the fifteen-year-old Shih Tsung, who was made emperor. The forty-five years of his reign were filled in home affairs with intrigues between the cliques at court, with growing distress in the country, and with revolts on a larger and larger scale. Abroad there were wars with Annam, increasing raids by the Japanese, and, above all, long-continued fighting against the famous Mongol ruler Anda (1529–1567), from 1549 onward. At one time Anda reached Peking and laid siege to it. Anda's raids went as far south as Szechwan and Shansi. The emperor, who had no knowledge of affairs, and to whom Anda had been represented as a petty bandit, was utterly dismayed and ready to do whatever Anda asked; in the end he was dissuaded from this, and an agreement was arrived at with Anda for state-controlled markets to be set up along the frontier, where the Mongols could dispose of their goods against Chinese goods on very favourable terms. After further difficulties lasting many years, a compromise was arrived at: the Mongols were earning good profits from the markets, and in 1571 Anda accepted a Chinese title. On the Chinese side, this Mongol trade, which continued in rather different form in the Manchu epoch, led to the formation of a local merchant class in the frontier province of Shansi, with great experience in credit business; later the first Chinese bankers came almost entirely from this quarter.

After a brief interregnum there came once more to the throne a ten-year-old boy, the emperor Shen Tsung (reign name Wan-li; 1573–

1619). He, too, was entirely under the influence of various cliques, at first that of his tutor, the scholar Chang Chü-chan. Then, another man, Yen Sung, became the most influential, and at the same time harmful figure in politics. Recently, Yen Sung came into the limelight in connection with Hai Jui (1514–1587). Hai seems to have been an honest official and judge, praised in classical operas as much as his enemy Yen was cursed. At the beginning of the so-called 'Cultural Revolution' a newly written drama praised Hai as a model of a member of the upper class who was not, as the others, corrupt and did not harm his people. The author was attacked and, to some degree, the outbreak of the Cultural Revolution was caused by this drama.

At about the time of the death of Anda, we hear for the first time of a new people. In 1581 there had been unrest in southern Manchuria. The Mongolian tribal federation of the Tümet attacked China, and there resulted collisions not only with the Chinese but between the different tribes living there. In southern and central Manchuria were remnants of the Tungus Juchên. The Mongols had subjugated the Juchên, but the latter had virtually become independent after the collapse of Mongol rule over China. They had formed several tribal alliances, but in 1581–1583 these fought each other, so that one of the alliances to all intents was destroyed. The Chinese intervened as mediators in these struggles, and drew a demarcation line between the territories of the various Tungus tribes. All this is only worth mention because it was from these tribes that there developed the tribal league of the Manchus, who were then to rule China for some three hundred years.

In 1592 the Japanese invaded Korea. This was their first real effort to set foot on the continent, a purely imperialistic move. Korea, as a Chinese vassal, appealed for Chinese aid. At first the Chinese army had no success, but in 1598 the Japanese were forced to abandon Korea. They revenged themselves by intensifying their raids on the coast of central China; they often massacred whole towns, and burned down the looted houses. The fighting in Korea had its influence on the Tungus tribes: as they were not directly involved, it contributed to their further strengthening.

The East India Company was founded in 1600. At this time, while the English were trying to establish themselves in India, the Chinese tried to gain increased influence in the south by wars in Annam, Burma, and Thailand (1594–1604). These wars were for China colonial wars, similar to the colonial fighting by the British in India. But there began to be defined already at that time in the south of Asia, the outlines of the states as they exist at the present time.

In 1601 the first European, the Jesuit Matteo Ricci, succeeded in gaining access to the Chinese court, through the agency of a eunuch.

He made some presents, and the Chinese regarded his visit as a mission from Europe bringing tribute. Ricci was therefore permitted to remain in Peking. He was an astronomer and was able to demonstrate to his Chinese colleagues the latest achievements of European astronomy. In 1613, after Ricci's death, the Jesuits and some Chinese whom they had converted were commissioned to reform the Chinese calendar. In the time of the Mongols, Arabs had been at work in Peking as astronomers, and their influence had continued under the Ming until the Europeans came. By his astronomical labours Ricci won a place of honour in Chinese literature; he is the European most often mentioned. Only Western scholars regarded the Jesuit astronomers as 'harmful', because they did not spread the new Copernican concepts among the Chinese, supposedly because of the danger which these ideas harboured for Christian doctrine. It may be fair to say that they were not yet convinced that the new system was superior and better founded than theirs.

The missionary work was less effective. The missionaries penetrated by the old trade routes from Canton and Macao into the province of Kiangsi and then into Nanking. Kiangsi and Nanking were their chief centres. They soon realized that missionary activity that began in the lower strata would have no success; it was necessary to work from above, beginning with the emperor, and then, they hoped, the whole country could be converted to Christianity. When later the emperors of the Ming dynasty were expelled and fugitives in south China, one of the pretenders to the throne was actually converted—but it was politically too late. The missionaries had, moreover, mistaken ideas as to the nature of Chinese religion; we know today that a universal adoption of Christianity in China would have been impossible even if an emperor had personally adopted that foreign faith: there were emperors who had been interested in Buddhism or in Taoism, but that had been their private affair and had never prevented them, as heads of the state, from promoting the religious system which politically was the most expedient—that is to say, usually Confucianism. What we have said here in regard to the Christian mission at the Ming court is applicable also to the missionaries at the court of the first Manchu emperors, in the seventeenth century. Early in the eighteenth century missionary activity was prohibited—not for religious but for political reasons, and only under the pressure of the Capitulations in the nineteenth century were the missionaries enabled to resume their labours.

15 *External and internal perils*

Towards the end of the reign of Wan-li, about 1620, the danger that threatened the empire became more and more evident. The Manchus complained, no doubt with justice, of excesses on the part of Chinese officials; the friction constantly increased, and the Manchus began to attack the Chinese cities in Manchuria. in 1616, after his first considerable successes, their leader Nurhachu assumed the imperial title; the name of the dynasty was Tai Ch'ing (interpreted as 'The great clarity', but probably a transliteration of a Manchurian word meaning 'hero'). In 1618, the year in which the Thirty Years War started in Europe, the Manchus conquered the greater part of Manchuria, and in 1621 their capital was Liaoyang, then the largest town in Manchuria.

But the Manchu menace was far from being the only one. On the south-east coast Cheng Ch'eng-kung (in European sources usually Coxinga), the son of a Chinese merchant and a Japanese mother, made himself independent; later, with his family, he dominated Taiwan and fought many battles with the Dutch and Spaniards there. In western China there came a great popular rising, in which some of the natives joined, and which spread through a large part of the southern provinces. This rising was particularly sanguinary, and when it was ultimately crushed by the Manchus the province of Szechwan, formerly so populous, was almost depopulated, so that it had later to be resettled. And in the provinces of Shantung in the east there came another great rising, also very sanguinary, that of the secret society of the 'White Lotus'. We have already pointed out that these risings of secret societies were always a sign of intolerable conditions among the peasantry. This was now the case once more. All the elements of danger which we mentioned at the outset of this chapter began during this period, between 1610 and 1640, to develop to the full.

Then there were the conditions in the capital itself. The struggles between cliques came to a climax. On the death of Shen Tsung (or Wan-li; 1573–1619), he was succeeded by his son, who died scarcely a month later, and then by his sixteen-year-old grandson. The grandson had been from his earliest youth under the influence of a eunuch, Wei Chung-hsien, who had castrated himself. With the emperor's wet-nurse and other people, mostly of the middle class, this man formed a powerful group. The moment the new emperor ascended the throne, Wei was all-powerful. He began by murdering every eunuch who did not belong to his clique, and then murdered the rest of his opponents. Meanwhile the gentry had concluded among themselves a defensive alliance that was a sort of party; this party was called the Tung-lin Academy. It was confined to literati among the gentry, and included in particular the literati who had failed to make their way at court, and who lived on their estates in central China and were trying to gain power themselves. This group was opposed to

Wei Chung-hsien, who ruthlessly had every discoverable member murdered. The remainder went into hiding and organized themselves secretly under another name. As the new emperor had no son, the attempt was made to foist a son upon him; at his death in 1627, eight women of the harem were suddenly found to be pregnant! He was succeeded by his brother, who was one of the opponents of Wei Chung-hsien and, with the aid of the opposing clique, was able to bring him to his end. The new emperor tried to restore order at court and in the capital by means of political and economic decrees, but in spite of his good intentions and his unquestionable capacity he was unable to cope with the universal confusion. There was insurrection in every part of the country. The gentry, organized in their 'Academies', and secretly at work in the provinces, no longer supported the government; the central power no longer had adequate revenues, so that it was unable to pay the armies that should have marched against all the rebels and also against external enemies. It was clear that the dynasty was approaching its end, and the only uncertainty was as to its successor. The various insurgents negotiated or fought with each other; generals loyal to the government won occasional successes against the rebels; other generals went over to the rebels or to the Manchus. The two most successful leaders of bands were Li Tzŭ-ch'êng and Chang Hsien-chung. Li came from the province of Shensi; he had come to the fore during a disastrous famine in his country. The years around 1640 brought several widespread droughts in north China, a natural phenomenon that was repeated in the nineteenth century, when unrest again ensued. Chang Hsien-chung returned for a time to the support of the government, but later established himself in western China. It was typical, however, of all these insurgents that none of them had any great objective in view. They wanted to get enough to eat for themselves and their followers; they wanted to enrich themselves by conquest; but they were incapable of building up an ordered and new administration. Li ultimately made himself 'king' in the province of Shensi and called his dynasty 'Shun', but this made no difference: there was no distribution of land among the peasants serving in Li's army; no plan was set into operation for the collection of taxes; not one of the pressing problems was faced.

Meanwhile the Manchus were gaining support. Almost all the Mongol princes voluntarily joined them and took part in the raids into north China. In 1637 the united Manchus and Mongols conquered Korea. Their power steadily grew. What the insurgents in China failed to achieve, the Manchus achieved with the aid of their Chinese advisers: they created a new military organization, the 'Banner Organization'. The men fit for service were distributed among eight 'banners', and these banners became the basis of the

Manchu state administration. By this device the Manchus emerged from the stage of tribal union, just as before them Turks and other northern peoples had several times abandoned the traditional authority of a hierarchy of tribal leaders, a system of ruling families, in favour of the authority, based on efficiency, of military leaders. At the same time the Manchus set up a central government with special ministries on the Chinese model. In 1638 the Manchus appeared before Peking, but they retired once more. Manchu armies even reached the province of Shantung. They were hampered by the death at the critical moment of the Manchu ruler Abahai (1626–1643). His son Fu Lin was not entirely normal and was barely six years old; there was a regency of princes, the most prominent among them being Prince Dorgon.

Meanwhile Li Tzǔ-ch'êng broke through to Peking. The city had a strong garrison, but owing to the disorganization of the government the different commanders were working against each other; and the soldiers had no fighting spirit because they had had no pay for a long time. Thus the city fell, on 24 April 1644, and the last Ming emperor killed himself. A prince was proclaimed emperor; he fled through western and southern China, continually trying to make a stand, but it was too late; without the support of the gentry he had no resource, and ultimately, in 1659, he was compelled to flee into Burma.

Thus Li Tzǔ-ch'êng was now emperor. It should have been his task rapidly to build up a government, and to take up arms against the other rebels and against the Manchus. He had a good chance. His revolt was not a revolt of uneducated peasants. Peasants were his soldiers, but most of them were forced to join him. The core of his armies were professional bandits and disgruntled soldiers. But early in his rising, numerous gentry members had joined him or found themselves forced to join him. Among those who joined him of their own free will were officials who had been exiled, banished, or demoted by the government. We would think that such men would not again try to get into an official post and take the risk to suffer again a similar, often very cruel punishment after a few years. We would also think that the new government would not accept them, if they thought that these officials had deserved their punishment by the former dynasty. This has always been different in China and still is different today. Whenever we study the life history of an official, we see his career going upward for a time; but then comes a fall; the great majority of high officials at least once in their life had to suffer severe beatings, exile, or other punishments, and often solely because of the intrigues of an opposing faction, or because of an advice which did not please the ruler. Almost all of these men, as soon as they could, again served the ruler and their career began to turn upward. Very few of them felt so dishonoured and shamed that they never again served. Li Tzŭ-ch'êng got some of these proud men. When he was emperor, they were given important posts. Other officials changed their loyalty and were willing to go over to Li. Still others preferred to commit suicide instead of serving two masters. Thus, Li was in a position to build up a qualified staff. However, he, too, had no money. The treasury was empty. Requisitions and forced 'gifts' did not bring in enough cash. So his troops began to loot and to kill; Li got more and more suspicious of all those who had joined him only recently.

A rule of terror began. Li behaved in such a way that he was unable to gain any support from the existing officials in the capital; and as there was no one among his former supporters who had any positive, constructive ideas, just nothing was done.

This, however, improved the chances of all the other aspirants to the imperial throne. General Wu San-kui, who was defending the frontiers against the Manchus, thought that in the existing conditions he could easily occupy the capital and take revenge for the emperor who had been forced to commit suicide, as well as his own father who had been tortured to death. But when he moved south the Manchu threatened him from the north, so that he was forced to negotiate with the Manchu Prince Dorgon, to form an alliance with the Manchus. With them he entered Peking on 6 June 1644. Li Tzŭ-ch'êng quickly looted the city, burned down whatever he could, and fled into the west, continually pursued by Wu San-kui. In the end he was abandoned by all his supporters and killed by peasants. The Manchus, however, had no intention of leaving Wu San-kui in power: they established themselves in Peking, and Wu became their general.

(C) THE MANCHU DYNASTY (1644–1911)

1 *Installation of Manchus*

The Manchus had gained the mastery over China owing rather to China's internal situation than to their military superiority. How was it that the dynasty could endure for so long, although the Manchus were not numerous, although the first Manchu ruler (Fu Lin, known under the rule name Shun-chih; 1644–1662) was a psychopathic youth, although there were princes of the Ming dynasty ruling in south China, and although there were strong groups of rebels all over the country? The Manchus were aliens; at that time the national feeling of the Chinese had already been awakened; aliens were despised. In addition to this, the Manchus demanded that as a sign of their subjection the Chinese should wear pigtails and assume Manchurian clothing (law of 1645). Such laws could not but offend national pride. Moreover, marriages between Manchus and Chinese were prohibited, and a dual government was set up, with Manchus always alongside Chinese in every office, the Manchus being of course in the superior position. The Manchu soldiers were distributed in military garrisons among the great cities, and were paid state pensions, which had to be provided by taxation. They were the master race, and had no need to work. Manchus did not have to attend the difficult state examinations which the Chinese had to pass in order to gain an appointment. How was it that in spite of all this the Manchus were able to establish themselves?

The conquering Manchu generals first went south from eastern China, and in 1645 captured Nanking, where a Ming prince had ruled. The region round Nanking was the economic centre of China. Soon the Manchus were in the adjoining southern provinces, and thus they conquered the whole of the territory of the landowning gentry, who after the events of the beginning of the seventeenth century had no longer trusted the Ming rulers. The Ming prince in Nanking was just as incapable, and surrounded by just as evil a clique, as the Ming emperors of the past. The gentry were not inclined to defend him. A considerable section of the gentry were reduced to utter despair; they had no desire to support the Ming any longer; in their own interest they could not support the rebel leaders; and they regarded the Manchus as just a particular sort of 'rebels'. Interpreting the refusal of some Sung ministers to serve the foreign Mongols as an act of loyalty, it was now regarded as shameful to desert a dynasty when it came to an end and to serve the new ruler, even if the new regime promised to be better. Many thousands of officials, scholars, and great landowners committed suicide. Many books, often really moving and tragic, are filled with the story of their lives. Some of them tried to form insurgent bands with their peasants and went into the mountains, but they were unable to maintain themselves there. The great bulk of the élite soon brought themselves to collaborate with the conquerors when they were offered tolerable conditions. In the end the Manchus did not interfere in the ownership of land in central China.

At the time when in Europe Louis XIV was reigning, the Thirty Years War was coming to an end, and Cromwell was carrying out his reforms in England, the Manchus conquered the whole of China. Chang Hsien-chung and Li Tzŭ-ch'êng were the first to fall; Coxinga lasted a little longer and was even able to plunder Nanking in 1659, but in 1661 he had to retire to Formosa (Taiwan). Wu San-kui, who meanwhile had conquered western China, saw that the situation was becoming difficult for him. His task was to drive out the last Ming pretenders for the Manchus. As he had already been opposed to the Ming in 1644, and as the Ming no longer had any following among the gentry, he could not suddenly work with them against the Manchus. He therefore handed over to the Manchus the last Ming prince, whom the Burmese had delivered up to him in 1661. Wu San-kui's only possible allies against the Manchus were the gentry. But in the west, where he was in power, the gentry counted for nothing; they had in any case been weaker in the west, and they had been decimated by the insurrection of Chang Hsien-chung. Thus Wu San-kui was compelled to try to push eastward, in order to unite with the gentry of the Yangtze region against the Manchus. The Manchus guessed Wu San-kui's plan, and in 1673, after every effort at accommodation had failed, open war came. Wu San-kui made himself emperor, and the Manchus marched against him. Meanwhile, the Chinese gentry of the Yangtze region had come to terms with the Manchus, and they gave Wu San-kui no help. He vegetated in the south-west, a region too poor to maintain an army that could conquer all China, and too small to enable him to last indefinitely as an independent power. He was able to hold his own until his death, although, with the loss of the support of the gentry, he had had no prospect of final success. Not until 1681 was his successor, his grandson Wu Shih-fan, defeated. The end of the rule of Wu San-kui and his successor (1683) marked the end of the national governments of China; the whole country was now under alien domination, for the simple reason that all the opponents of the Manchus had failed. Only the Manchus were accredited with the ability to bring order out of the universal confusion, so that there was clearly no alternative but to put up with the many insults and humiliations they inflicted—with the result that the national feeling that had just been aroused died away, except, it seems, in some secret societies.

In the first phase of the Manchu conquest the gentry had refused to support either the Ming princes or Wu San-kui, or any of the rebels, or the Manchus themselves. A second phase began about twenty years after the capture of Peking, when the Manchus won over the gentry by desisting from any interference with the ownership of land, and by the use of Manchu troops to clear away the 'rebels' who were hostile to the gentry. A reputable government was then set up in Peking, free from eunuchs and from all the old cliques; in their place the government looked for Chinese scholars for its administrative posts. Literati and scholars streamed into Peking, especially members of the 'Academies' that still existed in secret, men who had been the chief sufferers from the conditions at the end of the Ming epoch. The young emperor Sheng Tsu (1663–1722; K'ang-hsi is the name by which his rule was known, not his name) was keenly interested in Chinese culture and gave privileged treatment to the scholars of the gentry who came forward. A rapid recovery quite clearly took place. The disturbances of the years that had passed had got rid of the worst enemies of the people, the formidable rival cliques and the individuals lusting for power; the gentry had become more cautious in their behaviour to the peasants; and bribery had been largely stamped out. Finally, the empire had been greatly expanded. All these things helped to stabilize the regime of the Manchus.

2 Decline in the eighteenth century

The improvement continued until the middle of the eighteenth century. About the time of the French Revolution there began a continuous decline, slow at first and then gathering speed. The European works on China offer various reasons for this: the many foreign wars (to which we shall refer later) of the emperor, known by the name of his ruling period, Ch'ien-lung, his craze for building, and the irruption of the Europeans into Chinese trade. In the eighteenth century the court surrounded itself with great splendour, and countless palaces and other luxurious buildings were erected, but it must be borne in mind that so great an empire as the China of that day possessed very considerable financial strength, and could support this luxury. The wars were certainly not inexpensive, as they took place along the Russian frontier and entailed expenditure on the transport of reinforcements and supplies; the wars against Sinkiang and Tibet were carried on with relatively small forces. This expenditure should not have been beyond the resources of an ordered budget. Interestingly enough, the period between 1640 and 1840 belongs to those periods for which scholarly interest has begun only recently. Western scholars have been too much interested in the impact of Western economy and culture or in the military events. Chinese scholars thus far have shown a prejudice against the Manchu dynasty and were mainly interested in the study of anti-Manchu movements and the downfall of the dynasty. On the other hand, the documentary material for this period is extremely extensive, and many years of work are necessary to reach any general conclusions even in one single field. The following remarks should, therefore, be taken as very tentative and preliminary, and they are, naturally, fragmentary.

The decline of the Manchu dynasty began at a time when the European trade was still insignificant, and not as late as after 1842, when China had had to submit to the foreign capitulations. These cannot have been the true cause of the decline. Above all, the decline was not so noticeable in the state of the Exchequer as in a general impoverishment of China. The number of really wealthy persons among the gentry diminished, but the middle class, that is to say the people who had education but little money and property, grew steadily in number.

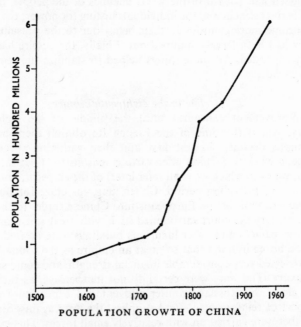

POPULATION GROWTH OF CHINA

One of the deeper reasons for the decline of the Manchu dynasty seems to lie in the enormous increase in the population. Here are a few Chinese statistics:

Year	Population			
1578 (before the Manchus)	10,621,463 families or	60,692,856	individuals	
1662	19,203,233 ,,	100,000,000	,,	*
1710	23,311,236 ,,	116,000,000	,,	*
1729	25,480,498 ,,	127,000,000	,,	*
1741		143,411,559	,,	
1754		184,504,493	,,	
1778		242,965,618	,,	
1796		275,662,414	,,	
1814		374,601,132	,,	
1850		414,493,899	,,	
(1953)		(601,938,035	,,)	*

*Approximately

284

It may be objected that these figures are incorrect and exaggerated. Undoubtedly they contain errors. But the first figure (for 1578) of some sixty millions is in close agreement with all other figures of early times; the figure for 1850 seems high, but cannot be far wrong, for even after the great T'ai P'ing Rebellion of 1851, which, together with its after-effects, cost the lives of countless millions, all statisticians of today estimate the population of China at more than four hundred millions. If we enter these data together with the census of 1953 into a chart (see p. 284), a fairly smooth curve emerges; the special features are that already before the end of the Ming the population was increasing and, second, that the high rate of increase in the population began with the long period of internal peace since about 1700. From that time onward, all China's wars were fought at so great a distance from China proper that the population was not directly affected. Moreover, in the seventeenth and eighteenth centuries the government saw to the maintenance of the river dykes so that the worst inundations were prevented. Thus there were not so many of the floods which had often cost the lives of many million people in China; and there were no internal wars, with their heavy cost in lives.

But while the population increased, the tillage failed to increase in the needed proportion. I have, unfortunately, no statistics for all periods; but the general tendency is shown by the following table:

Date	Cultivated area in *mou*	*mou* per person
1578	701,397,600	11·6
1662	531,135,800	
1719	663,113,200	
1729	878,176,000	6·1
(1953)	(1,627,930,000)	(2·7)

Six *mou* are about one acre. In 1578, there were 66 *mou* land per family of the total population. This was close to the figures regarded as ideal by Chinese early economists for the producing family (100 *mou*) considering the fact that about 80 per cent of all families at that time were producers. By 1729 it was only 35 *mou* per family, i.e. the land had to produce almost twice as much as before. We have shown that the agricultural developments in the Ming time greatly increased the productivity of the land. This then, obviously resulted in an increase of population. But by the middle of the eighteenth century, assuming that production doubled since the sixteenth century, population pressure was again as heavy as it had been then. And after

c. 1750, population pressure continued to build up to the present time.

Internal colonization continued during the Manchu time; there was a continuous but slow flow of people into Kwangsi, Kweichou, Yünnan, accompanied by periodic uprisings of the native, non-Chinese, population which lost their land to Chinese settlers. In spite of laws which prohibited emigration, Chinese also moved into South-East Asia. Chinese settlement in Manchuria was allowed only in the last years of the Manchus. But such internal colonization or emigration could alleviate the pressure only in some areas, while it continued to build up in others.

In Europe as well as in Japan, we find a strong population increase; in Europe at almost the same time as in China. But before population pressure became too serious in Europe or Japan, industry developed and absorbed the excess population. Thus, farms did not decrease too much in size. Too small farms are always and in many ways uneconomical. With the development of industries, the percentage of farm population decreased. In China, however, the farm population was still as high as 73·3 per cent of the total population in 1932 and the percentage rose to 81 per cent in 1950.

European farmers could produce more once the American plants, such as corn and potato, were introduced, plants with a higher yield per acre and at the same time plants which could utilize soils of lower quality. Corn came to China, too; and potato was not superior (in south China) to the indigenous sweet potatoes and yams. Thus, the new plants from the New World did not help China much.

In the first years of Manchu rule, we hear of serfs' rebellions in the areas of highest intensity of farming, Kiangsu, Kiangsi and Kwangtung. It seems that this is the beginning of a new trend. Many absentee landowners seem to find that it is difficult to get rent from serfs in villages, even with the help of managers. Investment in land is no longer the best investment, though still the safest. There seems to be a shift away from keeping bonded tenants, at least in the most developed areas, and towards pawnbroking, as a method of getting much more money out of the pocket of the farmer. Thus, bonded tenantship became changed into free tenantship. The relaxation of the landowners over their dependants and their move into towns seems also to have led to the emergence of organizations in villages, such as youth crop protection associations, dyke protection, canal cleaning and repair associations, i.e. many of the necessary activities were now taken over by farmers and tenants themselves. The farmers also had better access to the numerous markets, even markets in towns, and could sell there their farm products as well as the products of home industries. They were now better informed about price oscillations and could attempt, to some degree, to manipulate the market.

Thus, we cannot say that the level of living of the farmers went down in comparison to the level of living of city people. Rather, there was a slow, general downward trend, expressed, it seems, in a lowering of the life expectancy among all classes.

From the middle of the seventeenth century on, commercial activities, especially along the coast, continued to increase and we find gentry families who equip sons who were unwilling or not capable to study and to enter the ranks of the officials, but who were too unruly to sit in villages and collect the rent from the tenants of the family, with money to enter business. The newly settled areas of Kwangtung and Kwangsi were ideal places for them: here they could sell Chinese products to the native tribes or to the new settlers at high prices. Some of these men introduced new techniques from the old provinces of China into the 'colonial' areas and set up dye factories, textile factories, etc., in the new towns of the south. The new products replaced the hand-made textiles of the minorities and induced them to become more and more dependent upon the Chinese merchants who also brought good Chinese wine. We find a development among the minorities which has many parallels in other colonial areas: with the breakdown of the native culture and economy, the men become addicted to alcohol and lose first their money, then their land, finally their daughters to the colonial masters.

But the greatest stimulus for these commercial activities was foreign, European trade. American silver which had flooded Europe in the sixteenth century, began to flow into China from the beginning of the seventeenth century on. The influx was stopped not until between 1661 and 1684 when the government again prohibited coastal shipping and removed coastal settlements into the interior in order to stop piracy along the coasts of Fukien and independence movements on Formosa (Taiwan). But even during these twenty-three years, the price of silver was so low that home production was given up because it did not pay off. In the eighteenth century, silver again continued to enter China, while silk and tea were exported. This demand led to a strong rise in the prices of silk and tea, and benefited the merchants. When, from the late eighteenth century on, opium began to be imported, the silver left China again. The merchants profited this time from the opium trade, but farmers had to suffer: the price of silver went up, and taxes had to be paid in silver, while farm products were sold for copper. By 1835, the ounce of silver had a value of 2,000 copper coins instead of one thousand before 1800. High gains in commerce prevented investment in industries, because they would give lower and later profits than commerce.

At the latest in the eighteenth century, Chinese banks began to develop. Most famous were the bankers of Shansi, but Ningpo banks, too, were important. These banks are a good example of the commercial attitude that had developed: the bankers did not employ family members (which, according to the familistic attitude, they were supposed to do), but non-related men, to operate the branch offices. The families of these men lived as a kind of hostage in the head office, and the employee was personally responsible for any business losses he incurred. Similarly, the guards whom the bankers hired to transport cash from one place to another were not related to the boss. Thus, we have enough indications to say that capital was available for the development of industries. It is true that the government and the gentry tried to get into any larger business, either to control the business which then took the form of a joint private-government operation, or in order to draw income from co-operation with a businessman who, on the other side, got 'protection' against extortion from other officials. Such operations could not be fully successful, especially because the officials were not technical experts and often prevented the development of an enterprise by their political interference. Still, modern research is of the opinion that none of these factors was decisive, that there was an 'entrepreneurial spirit', but that perhaps the size of the industrial enterprises (except the state-operated ones) was too small to really lead to industrial development.

3 *Expansion in Central Asia; the first state treaty*

The rise of the Manchu dynasty actually began under the K'ang-hsi rule (1663–1722). The emperor had three tasks. The first was the removal of the last supporters of the Ming dynasty and of the generals, such as Wu San-kui, who had tried to make themselves independent. This necessitated a long series of campaigns, most of them in the south-west or south of China; these scarcely affected the population of China proper. In 1683 Formosa (Taiwan) was occupied and the last of the local rulers was defeated. It was shown above that the situation of all these leaders became hopeless as soon as the Manchus had occupied the rich Yangtze region and the intelligentsia and the gentry of that region had gone over to them.

A quite different type of insurgent commander was the Mongol prince Galdan. He, too, planned to make himself independent of Manchu overlordship. At first the Mongols had readily supported the Manchus, when the latter were making raids into China and there was plenty of booty. Now, however, the Manchus, under the influence of the Chinese gentry whom they brought, and could not but bring, to their court, were rapidly becoming Chinese in respect to culture. Even in the time of K'ang-hsi the Manchus began to forget Manchurian; they brought tutors to court to teach the young

Manchus Chinese. Later even the emperors did not understand Manchurian! As a result of this process, the Mongols became alienated from the Manchurians, and the situation began once more to be the same as at the time of the Ming rulers. Thus Galdan tried to found an independent Mongol realm, free from Chinese influence.

The Manchus could not permit this, as such a realm would have threatened the flank of their homeland, Manchuria, and would have attracted those Manchus who objected to sinification. Between 1690 and 1696 there were battles, in which the emperor actually took part in person. Galdan was defeated. In 1715, however, there were new disturbances, this time in western Mongolia. Tsewang Rabdan, whom the Chinese had made khan of the Ölöt, rose against the Chinese. The wars that followed, extending far into Sinkiang and also involving its Turkish population together with the Dzungars, ended with the Chinese conquest of the whole of Mongolia and of Sinkiang. As Tsewang Rabdan had tried to extend his power as far as Tibet, a campaign was undertaken also into Tibet, Lhasa was occupied, a new Dalai Lama was installed there as supreme ruler, and Tibet was made into a protectorate. Since then Tibet, Sinkiang and Inner Mongolia have remained to this day under Chinese colonial rule.

This penetration of the Chinese into Central Asia took place just at the time when the Russians were enormously expanding their empire in Asia, and this formed the third problem for the Manchus. In 1650 the Russians had established a fort by the river Amur. The Manchus regarded the Amur (which they called the 'River of the Black Dragon') as part of their own territory, and in 1685 they destroyed the Russian settlement. After this there were negotiations, which culminated in 1689 in the Treaty of Nerchinsk. This treaty was the first concluded by the Chinese state with a European power. Jesuit missionaries played a part in the negotiations as interpreters. Owing to the difficulties of translation the text of the treaty, in Chinese, Russian, and Manchurian, contained some obscurities, particularly in regard to the frontier line. Accordingly, in 1727 the Russians asked for a revision of the old treaty. The Chinese emperor, whose rule name was Yung-cheng, arranged for the negotiations to be carried on at the frontier, in the town of Kyakhta, in Mongolia, where after long discussions a new treaty was concluded. Under this treaty the Russians received permission to set up a legation and a commercial agency in Peking, and also to maintain a church. This was the beginning of the foreign capitulations. The present Chinese regime regards the treaties dealing with the Amur region and with the western parts of Sinkiang as unfair, and even before the revolution armed conflicts had begun; they still continue. The Chinese expected the Russians to cancel the treaties which they regard as 'unequal'.

On the other hand, the Chinese saw nothing extraordinary in granting the Russians quarters for their legation in Peking and other privileges, such as having their own churches. For some fifteen centuries all the 'barbarians' who had to bring tribute had been given houses in the capital, where their envoys could wait until the emperor would receive them—usually on New Year's Day. The custom had sprung up at the reception of the Huns. Moreover, permission had always been given for envoys to be accompanied by a few merchants, who during the envoy's stay did a certain amount of business. Furthermore the time had been when the Uighurs were permitted to set up a temple of their own. At the time of the permission given to the Russians to set up a 'legation', a similar office was set up (in 1729) for 'Uighur' peoples (meaning Mohammedans), again under the control of an office, called the Office for Regulation of Barbarians. The Mohammedan office was placed under two Mohammedan leaders who lived in Peking. The Europeans, however, had quite different ideas about a 'legation', and about the significance of permission to trade. They regarded this as the opening of diplomatic relations between states on terms of equality, and the carrying on of trade as a special privilege, a sort of capitulation. This reciprocal misunderstanding produced in the nineteenth century a number of serious political conflicts. The Europeans charged the Chinese with breach of treaties, failure to meet their obligations, and other such things, while the Chinese considered that they had acted with perfect correctness.

4 Culture

In this K'ang-hsi period culture began to flourish again. The emperor had attracted the gentry, and so the intelligentsia, to his court because his Manchus could not alone have administered the enormous empire; and he showed great interest in Chinese culture, and himself delved deeply into it. Following his example, many young Manchus also began to study Chinese and soon we find Manchu scholars and poets who were in no way inferior to Chinese. To increase his knowledge of China, the emperor had many works compiled, especially works of an encyclopaedic character. The encyclopaedias enabled information to be rapidly gained on all sorts of subjects, and thus were just what an interested ruler needed, especially when, as a foreigner, he was not in a position to gain really thorough instruction in things Chinese. The Chinese encyclopaedias of the seventeenth and especially of the eighteenth century were thus the outcome of the initiative of the Manchurian emperor, and were compiled for his information; they were, of course, inspired by the great Ming time encyclopaedia, the 'Yung-lo ta-tien', but this work was never printed and remained accessible only to the court, while the Manchu encyclopaedias were printed and copies were found in many parts of the country. However, they were not a part of a movement to spread knowledge among the people, like the French encyclopaedias of the eighteenth century. For this latter purpose the gigantic encyclopaedias of the Manchus, each of which fills several bookcases, were much too expensive and were printed in much too limited editions. The compilations began with the great geographical encyclopaedia of Ku Yen-wu (1613–1682), and attained their climax in the gigantic eighteenth-century encyclopaedia 'T'u-shu chi-ch'eng', scientifically impeccable in the accuracy of its references to sources. Here were already the beginnings of the 'Archaeological school', built up in the course of the eighteenth century. This school was usually called 'Han school' because the adherents went back to the commentaries of the classical texts written in Han time and discarded the orthodox explanations of Chu Hsi's school of Sung time. Later, its most prominent leader was Tai Chen (1723–1777). Tai was greatly interested in technology and science; he can be regarded as the first philosopher who exhibited an empirical, scientific way of thinking. Late nineteenth and early twentieth century Chinese scholarship is greatly obliged to him.

The most famous literary works of the Manchu epoch belong once more to the field which Chinese do not regard as that of true literature—the novel, the short story, and the drama. Poetry did exist, but it kept to the old paths and had few fresh ideas. All the various forms of the Sung period were made use of. The essayists, too, offered nothing new, though their number was legion. One of the best known is Yüan Mei (1716–1797), who was also the author of the collection of short stories 'Tse-pu-yü' ('The Master Did Not Tell'), which is regarded very highly by the Chinese. Yüan Mei, a kind of 'eccentric', deserves mention also because he tried to attract young daughters of the upper class to become his students, in spite of his somewhat doubtful reputation. The volume of short-stories entitled 'Liao-chai chih-i' ('Strange Stories from a Chinese Studio') by P'u Sung-ling (1640–1715?) is world-famous and has been translated into many languages. The collection is important for the folklorist because P'u was interested in folk beliefs. Both collections are distinguished by their simple but elegant style. The short story was popular among the greater gentry; it abandoned the popular style it had had in the Ming epoch, and adopted the polished language of scholars.

The Manchu epoch has left to us what is by general consent the finest novel in Chinese literature, 'Hung-lou-meng' ('The Dream of the Red Chamber'), by Ts'ao Hsüeh-ch'in, who died in 1763. It describes the downfall of a rich and powerful family from the highest rank of the gentry, and the decadent son's love of a young and emotional lady of the highest circles. The story is clothed in a mystical garb that does something to soften its tragic ending. Western readers appreciate this novel mainly because it is the only classical novel in which individual characters are clearly depicted, and in which emotions are openly expressed. This was and remained unusual, because to the present time, Chinese do not like to express their emotions openly. Down to the nineteenth century, the novel was from time to time forbidden, and parents were warned not to let their children read it. Even at the present time, surveys indicate that, though almost all young Chinese have read it, many regard it as a decadent book which is depressing and therefore has no moral value.

The interesting novel 'Ju-lin wai-shih' ('Private Reports from the Life of Scholars'), by Wu Ching-tzŭ (1701-1754), is a mordant criticism of Confucianism with its rigid formalism, of the social system, and of the examination system. Social criticism is the theme of many novels. The most modern in spirit of the works of this period is perhaps the treatment of feminism in the novel 'Ching-hua-yüan', by Li Yu-chên (d. 1830), which demanded equal rights for men and women, long before any Western influence could be felt. In particular, the novel is against the custom of foot-binding. Some of its economic and social proposals were later taken over by the T'ai P'ing, and at that time, too, the movement against foot-binding took roots and eventually led to its end.

In the nineteenth century, novels which describe the more intimate aspects of Chinese social life come forth. There are depictions of marital happiness, but also descriptions of the life of prostitutes in Shanghai (in the novel 'Hai-shang-hua lieh-chuan'), a novel from the end of the nineteenth century which—and this is another important novelty—was written in Shanghai dialect, not in the usual half-colloquial style of other novels. Somewhat later (published in 1907) is the most intimate story of a big Cantonese merchant, describing in detail the ways by which he made his fortunes, the corruption in the highest places, and the operation of a household with numerous concubines ('Erh-shih-tsai Fan-hua-meng').

The drama developed quickly in the Manchu epoch, particularly in quantity, especially since the emperors greatly appreciated the theatre. A catalogue of plays compiled in 1781 contains 1,013 titles! Some of these dramas were of unprecedented length. One of them was played in 26 parts containing 240 acts; a performance took two years to complete! Probably the finest dramas of the Manchu epoch are those of Li Yü (born 1611), who also became the first of the Chinese dramatic critics. What he had to say about the art of the theatre, and about aesthetics in general, is still worth reading.

About the middle of the nineteenth century the influence of Europe became more and more marked. Translation began with Yen Fu (1853–1921), who translated the first philosophical and scientific books and books on social questions and made his compatriots acquainted with Western thought. At the same time Lin Shu (1852–1924) translated the first Western short stories and novels. With these two began the new style, which was soon elaborated by Liang Ch'i-ch'ao, a collaborator of Sun Yat-sen's, and by others, and which ultimately produced the 'literary revolution' of 1917. Translation has continued to this day; almost every book of outstanding importance in world literature is translated within a few months of its appearance, and on the average these translations are of a fairly high level.

Particularly fine work was produced in the field of porcelain in the Manchu epoch. In 1680 the famous kilns in the province of Kiangsi were reopened, and porcelain that is among the most artistically perfect in the world was fired in them. Among the new colours were especially green shades (one group is known as 'famille verte'), and also black and yellow compositions. Monochrome porcelain also developed further, including very fine dark blue, brilliant red (called 'ox-blood'), and white. In the eighteenth century, however, there began an unmistakable decline, which has continued to this day, although there are still a few craftsmen and a few kilns that produce outstanding work (usually attempts to imitate old models), often in small factories.

In painting, European influence soon shows itself. The best-known example of this is Lang Shih-ning, an Italian missionary whose original name was Giuseppe Castiglione (1688–1766); he began to work in China in 1715. He learned the Chinese method of painting, but introduced a number of technical tricks of European painters, especially the Western way of depicting perspective. Many of these innovations were taken over by the official court painters: the painting of the scholars who lived in seclusion remained uninfluenced. Dutch flower-painting also had some influence in China as early as the eighteenth century.

The missionaries played an important part at court. The first Manchu emperors were as generous in this matter as the Mongols had been, and allowed the foreigners to work in peace. They showed special interest in the European science introduced by the missionaries; they had less sympathy for their religious message. The missionaries, for their part, sent to Europe enthusiastic accounts of the wonderful conditions in China, and so helped to popularize the idea that was being formed in Europe of an 'enlightened', a constitutional, monarchy. The leaders of the Enlightenment read these reports with enthusiasm, with the result that they had an influence on the French Revolution. Confucius was found particularly attractive, and was regarded as a forerunner of the Enlightenment. The philosopher Leibniz (1646–1716) was informed by the writings of the Jesuits of Chinese ideas, and it seems that the 'I-ching' ('Book of Changes') in which he detected a binary counting system, influenced his own development of a binary system—the system which is now basic for all computer work.

The missionaries gained a reputation at court as 'scientists', and in this they were of service both to China and to Europe. The behaviour of the European merchants who followed the missions, spreading gradually in growing numbers along the coasts of China, was not by any means so irreproachable. The Chinese were certainly justified when they declared that European ships often made landings on the coast and simply looted, just as the Japanese had done before them. Reports of this came to the court, and captured foreigners described themselves as 'Christians' and also seemed to have some connection with the missionaries living at court. When, additionally, quarrels between Jesuits and Franciscans broke out concerning the character of the Chinese ancestral cult (honouring the ancestors or venerating them?), the Yung-cheng emperor (1723–1736; his name as emperor was Shih Tsung) regarded the missionaries as a part of a secret organization and forbade their activities.

5 Relations with the outer world

During the Yung-cheng period, when Chinese population increases were very quick, long fights against the minorities in south-west China took place, but at the beginning of the Ch'ien-lung period (1736–1796), fighting started again in Sinkiang. Mongols, now called Kalmuks, defeated by the Chinese, had migrated to the Ili region, where after heavy fighting they gained supremacy over some of the Kazaks and other Turkish peoples living there and in western Sinkiang. Some Kazak tribes went over to the Russians, and in 1735 the Russian colonialists founded the town of Orenburg in the western Kazak region. The Kalmuks fought the Chinese without cessation until, in 1739, they entered into an agreement under which they ceded half their territory to Manchu China, retaining only the Ili region. The Kalmuks subsequently reunited with other sections of the Kazaks against the Chinese. In 1754 peace was again concluded with China, but it was followed by raids on both sides, so that the Manchus determined to enter on a great campaign against the Ili region. This ended with a decisive victory for the Chinese (1755). In the years that followed, however, the Chinese began to be afraid that the various Kazak tribes might unite in order to occupy the territory of the Kalmuks, which was almost unpopulated owing to the mass slaughter

of Kalmuks by the Chinese. Unrest began among the Mohammedans throughout the neighbouring western Sinkiang, and the same
Chinese generals who had fought the Kalmuks marched into Sinkiang
and captured the Mohammedan city states of Uch, Kashgar, and
Yarkand.

The reinforcements for these campaigns, and for the garrisons
which in the following decades were stationed in the Ili region and in
the west of Sinkiang, marched along the road from Peking that leads
northward through Mongolia to the far distant Uliassutai and
Kobdo. The cost of transport for one *shih* (about 66 lb.) amounted to
120 pieces of silver. In 1781 certain economies were introduced, but
between 1781 and 1791 over 30,000 tons, making some 8 tons a day,
were transported to that region. The cost of transport for supplies
alone amounted in the course of time to the not inconsiderable sum
of 120,000,000 pieces of silver. In addition to this there was the cost
of the transported goods and of the pay of soldiers and of the administration. These figures apply to the period of occupation, of relative
peace: during the actual wars of conquest the expenditure was
naturally far higher. Thus these campaigns, though I do not think
they brought actual economic ruin to China, were nevertheless a
costly enterprise, and one which produced little positive advantage.

In addition to this, these wars brought China into conflict with the
European colonial powers. In the years during which the Chinese
armies were fighting in the Ili region, the Russians were putting out
their feelers in that direction, and the Chinese annals show plainly
how the Russians intervened in the fighting with the Kalmuks and
Kazaks. The Ili region remained thereafter a bone of contention
between China and Russia, until it finally went to Russia, bit by bit,
between 1847 and 1881. The present Chinese government still regards
the Ili area as a part of China which should be returned to China.

The Kalmuks and Kazaks played a special part in Russo-Chinese
relations. The Chinese had sent a mission to the Kalmuks farthest
west, by the lower Volga, and had entered into relations with them,
as early as 1714. As Russian pressure on the Volga region continually
grew, these Kalmuks (mainly the Turgut tribe), who had lived there
since 1630, decided to return into Chinese territory (1771). During
this enormously difficult migration, almost entirely through hostile
territory, a large number of the Turgut perished; 85,000, however,
reached the Ili region, where they were settled by the Chinese on the
lands of the eastern Kalmuks, who had been largely exterminated.

In the south, too, the Chinese came into direct touch with the
European powers. In 1757 the English occupied Calcutta, and in
1766 the province of Bengal. In 1767 a Manchu general, Ming Jui,

who had been victorious in the fighting for Sinkiang, marched against Burma, which was made a dependency once more in 1769. And in 1790–1791 the Chinese conquered Nepal, south of Tibet, because Nepalese had made two attacks on Tibet. Thus English and Chinese political interests came here into contact.

For the Ch'ien-lung period's many wars of conquest there seem to have been two main reasons. The first was the need for security. The Mongols had to be overthrown because otherwise the homeland of the Manchus was menaced; in order to make sure of the suppression of the eastern Mongols, the western Mongols (Kalmuks) had to be overthrown; to make them harmless, Sinkiang and the Ili region had to be conquered; Tibet was needed for the security of Sinkiang and Mongolia—and so on. Vast territories, however, were conquered in this process which were of no economic value, and most of which actually cost a great deal of money and brought nothing in. They were conquered simply for security. That advantage had been gained: an aggressor would have to cross great areas of unproductive territory, with difficult conditions for reinforcements, before he could actually reach China. In the second place, the Chinese may actually have noticed the efforts that were being made by the European powers, especially Russia and England, to divide Asia among themselves, and accordingly they made sure of their own good share.

6   Decline; revolts

The period of Ch'ien-lung is that of the greatest expansion of the Chinese empire, also that of the greatest under the Manchu regime. But there began at the same time to be signs of internal decline. If we are to fix a particular year for this, perhaps it should be the year 1774, in which came the first great popular rising, in the province of Shantung. In 1775 there came another popular rising, in Honan—that of the 'Society of the White Lotus'. This society, which had long existed as a secret organization and had played a part in the Ming epoch, had been reorganized by a man named Liu Sung. Liu Sung was captured and was condemned to penal servitude. His followers, however, regrouped themselves, particularly in the province of Anhui. These risings seem to have been stimulated by local excesses of administrators or landlords, but began to become dangerous because of their connection with a sect which was widely spread over China and had an internal organization and leaders. Under such conditions, local uprisings of farmers can become dangerous. As the anger of the population was naturally directed also against the idle Manchus of the cities, who lived on their state pensions, did no work, and behaved as a ruling class, the government saw in these movements a nationalist spirit, and took drastic steps against them. The popular leaders now altered their programme, and acclaimed a supposed descendant from the Ming dynasty as the future emperor. Government troops caught the leader of the 'White Lotus' agitation, but he succeeded in escaping. In the regions through which the society had spread, there then began a sort of Inquisition, of exceptional ferocity. Six provinces were affected, and in and around the single city of Wuch'ang in four months more than 20,000 people were beheaded. The cost of the rising to the government ran into millions. In answer to this oppression, the popular leaders tightened their organization and marched north-west from the western provinces of which they had gained control. The rising was suppressed only by a very big military operation, and not until 1802. There had been very heavy fighting between 1793 and 1802—just when in Europe, in the French Revolution, another oppressed population won its freedom.

The Ch'ien-lung emperor abdicated on New Year's Day, 1795, after ruling for sixty years. He died in 1799. His successor was Jen Tsung (1796–1821; reign name: Chia-ch'ing). In the course of his reign the rising of the 'White Lotus' was suppressed, but in 1813 there began a new rising, this time in north China—again that of a secret organization, the 'Society of Heaven's Law'. One of its leaders bribed some eunuchs, and penetrated with a group of followers into the palace; he threw himself upon the emperor, who was only saved through the intervention of his son. At the same time the rising spread in the provinces. Once more the government succeeded in suppressing it and capturing the leaders. But the memory of these risings was kept alive among the Chinese people. For the government failed to realize that the actual cause of the risings was the general impoverishment, and saw in them a nationalist movement, thus actually arousing a national consciousness, stronger than in the Ming epoch, among the middle and lower classes of the people, together with hatred of the Manchus. They were held responsible for every evil suffered, regardless of the fact that similar evils had existed earlier.

7 European imperialism in the Far East

With the Tao-kuang period (1821–1850) began a new period in Chinese history which came to an end only in 1911.

In foreign affairs these ninety years were marked by the steadily growing influence of the Western powers, aimed at turning China into a colony. Culturally this period was that of the gradual infiltration of Western civilization into the Far East; it was recognized in China that it was necessary to learn from the West. In home affairs we see the collapse of the dynasty and the destruction of the unity of the empire; of four great civil wars, one almost brought the dynasty to its end. North and south China, the coastal area and the interior, developed in different ways.

Great Britain had made several attempts to improve her trade relations with China, but the mission of 1793 had no success, and that of 1816 also failed. English merchants, like all foreign merchants, were only permitted to settle in a small area adjoining Canton and at Macao, and were only permitted to trade with a particular group of monopolists, known as the 'Hong'. The Hong had to pay taxes to the state, but they had a wonderful opportunity of enriching themselves. The Europeans were entirely at their mercy, for they were not allowed to travel inland, and they were not allowed to try to negotiate with other merchants, to secure lower prices by competition.

The Europeans concentrated especially on the purchase of silk and tea; but what could they import into China? The higher the price of the goods and the smaller the cargo space involved, the better were the chances of profit for the merchants. It proved, however, that European woollens or luxury goods could not be sold; the Chinese would probably have been glad to buy food, but transport was too expensive to permit profitable business. Thus a new article was soon discovered—opium, carried from India to China: the price was high and the cargo space involved was very small. The Chinese were familiar with opium, under its Near-Eastern name, *afyûn* (*a-fu-yung*), probably since Sung times. In Ming time, the emperor received 200 pounds for himself and 100 for the empress from Thailand, but from the eighteenth century on, opium arrived in China from the coast. At the time of Ch'ien-lung, the court received between 200 and 1,000 crates from the Portuguese. In 1729, the government confiscated 34 pounds in the storeroom of a merchant in Chang-chou (Fukien). Thus, opium is not a drug, recently imported into China, but has a long history in China. The problem, which to my knowledge is not yet satisfactorily explained is, why opium smoking suddenly became a fashion in China and took proportions which threatened public health. Was it perhaps that only from the late eighteenth century on, opium was smoked and not taken internally only? In any case, from 1800 onward opium became more and more the chief article of trade, especially for the English, who were able to bring it conveniently from India. The opium trade resulted in certain groups of merchants being inordinately enriched; a great deal of Chinese money went abroad. The government became apprehensive and sent Lin Tsê-hsü as its commissioner to Canton. In 1839 he prohibited the opium trade and burned the chests of opium found in British possession. The British view was that to tolerate the Chinese action might mean the destruction of British trade in the Far East and that, on the other hand, it might be possible by active intervention to compel the Chinese to open other ports to European trade and to shake off the monopoly of the Canton merchants. In 1840 British ships-of-war appeared off the south-eastern coast of China and bombarded it. In 1841 the Chinese opened negotiations and dismissed Lin Tsê-hsü. As the Chinese concessions were regarded as inadequate, hostilities continued; the British entered the Yangtze estuary and threatened Nanking. In this first armed conflict with the West, China found herself defenceless owing to her lack of a navy, and it was also found that the European weapons were far superior to those of the Chinese. In 1842 China was compelled to capitulate: under the Treaty of Nanking Hong Kong was ceded to Great Britain, a war indemnity was paid, certain ports were thrown open to European trade, and the monopoly was brought to an end. A great deal of opium came, however, into China through smuggling—regrettably, for the state lost the customs revenue!

Opium cultivation in China became widely spread; in 1934, 7 per cent of the farmland in Yünnan was planted with opium, in spite of strict regulations against its cultivation and use. In the borderland between Yünnan and Burma, opium cultivation existed until the present time.

The treaty introduced the period of the capitulations. It contained the dangerous clause which added most to China's misfortunes—the Most Favoured Nation clause, providing that if China granted any privilege to any other state, that privilege should also automatically be granted to Great Britain. In connection with this treaty it was agreed that the Chinese customs should be supervised by European consuls; and a trade treaty was granted. Similar treaties followed in 1844 with France and the United States. The missionaries returned; until 1860, however, they were only permitted to work in the treaty ports. Shanghai was thrown open in 1843, and developed with extraordinary rapidity from a town to a city of a million and a centre of world-wide importance.

The terms of the Nanking Treaty were not observed by either side; both evaded them. In order to facilitate the smuggling, the British had permitted certain Chinese junks to fly the British flag. This also enabled these vessels to be protected by British ships-of-war from pirates, which at that time were very numerous off the southern coast owing to the economic depression. The Chinese, for their part, placed every possible obstacle in the way of the British. In 1856 the Chinese held up a ship sailing under the British flag, pulled down its flag, and arrested the crew on suspicion of smuggling. In connection with this and other events, Britain decided to go to war. Thus began the 'Lorcha War' of 1857, in which France joined for the sake of the booty to be expected. Britain had just ended the Crimean War, and was engaged in heavy fighting against the Moguls in India. Consequently only a small force of a few thousand men could be landed in China; Canton, however, was bombarded, and also the forts of Tientsin. There still seemed no prospect of gaining the desired objectives by negotiation, and in 1860 a new expedition was fitted out, this time some 20,000 strong. The troops landed at Tientsin and marched on Peking; the emperor fled to Jehol and did not return; he died in 1861. The new Treaty of Tientsin (1860) provided for (a) the opening of further ports to European traders; (b) the cession of Kowloon, the strip of land lying opposite Hong Kong; (c) the establishment of a British legation in Peking; (d) freedom of navigation along the Yangtze; (e) permission for British subjects to purchase land in China; (f) the British to be subject to their own consular courts and not to the Chinese courts; (g) missionary activity to be permitted throughout the country. In addition to this, the commercial treaty was revised, the opium trade was permitted once more, and a war indemnity was to be paid by China. In the eyes of Europe, Britain had now succeeded in turning China not actually into a colony, but at all events into a semi-colony; China must be expected soon to share the fate of India. China, however, with her very different conceptions of intercourse between states, did not realize the full import of these terms; some of them were regarded as concessions on unimportant points, which there was no harm in granting to the trading 'barbarians', as had been done in the past; some were regarded as simple injustices, which at a given moment could be swept away by administrative action.

But the result of this European penetration was that China's balance of trade was adverse, and became more and more so, as under the commercial treaties she could neither stop the importation of European goods nor set a duty on them; and on the other hand she could not compel foreigners to buy Chinese goods. The efflux of silver brought general impoverishment to China, widespread financial stringency to the state, and continuous financial crises and inflation. China had never had much liquid capital, and she was soon compelled to take up foreign loans in order to pay her debts. At that time internal loans were out of the question (the first internal loan was floated in 1894): the population did not even know what a state loan meant; consequently the loans had to be issued abroad. This, however, entailed the giving of securities, generally in the form of economic privileges. Under the Most Favoured Nation clause, however, these privileges had then to be granted to other states which had made no loans to China. Clearly a vicious spiral, which in the end could only bring disaster.

The only exception to the general impoverishment, in which not only the peasants but the old upper classes were involved, was a certain section of the trading community and the middle class, which had grown rich in its dealings with the Europeans. These people now accumulated capital, became Europeanized with their staffs, acquired land from the impoverished gentry, and sent their sons abroad to foreign universities, and learned European capitalist methods. This class was, of course, to be found mainly in the treaty ports in the south and in their environs. The south, as far north as Shanghai, became more modern and more advanced; the north made no advance. In the south, European ways of thought were learnt, and Chinese and European theories were compared. Criticism began. The first revolutionary societies were formed in this atmosphere in the south.

8 Risings in Sinkiang and within China:
the T'ai-p'ing Rebellion

But the emperor Hsüan Tsung (reign name Tao-kuang), a man in poor health though not without ability, had much graver anxieties than those caused by the Europeans. He did not yet fully realize the seriousness of the European peril.

In Sinkiang, where Turkish Mohammedans lived under Chinese rule, conditions were far from being as the Chinese desired. The Chinese, a fundamentally rationalistic people, regarded religion as a purely political matter, and accordingly required every citizen to take part in the official form of worship. Subject to that, he might privately belong to any other religion. To a Mohammedan, this was impossible and intolerable. The Mohammedans were only ready to practise their own religion, and absolutely refused to take part in any other. The Chinese also tried to apply to Sinkiang in other matters the same legislation that applied to all China, but this proved irreconcilable with the demands made by Islam on its followers. All this produced continual unrest.

Sinkiang had had a feudal system of government with a number of feudal lords (*beg*), who tried to maintain their influence and who had the support of the Mohammedan population. The Chinese had come to Sinkiang as soldiers and officials, to administer the country. They regarded themselves as lords of the land and occupied themselves with the extraction of taxes. Most of the officials were also associated with the Chinese merchants who travelled throughout Central Asia and as far as Siberia. The conflicts implicit in this situation produced great Mohammedan risings in the nineteenth century. The first came in 1825–1827; in 1845 a second rising flamed up, and thirty years later these revolts led to the temporary loss of the whole of Sinkiang.

In 1848, native unrest began in the province of Hunan, as a result

of the growing pressure of the Chinese settlers on the native population; in the same year there was unrest farther south, in the province
of Kwangsi, this time in connection with the influence of the Europeans. The leader was a quite simple man of Hakka blood, Hung
Hsiu-ch'üan (born 1814), who gathered impoverished Hakka peasants
round him as every peasant leader had done in the past. Very often
the nucleus of these peasant movements had been a secret society
with a particular religious tinge; this time the peasant revolutionaries
came forward as at the same time the preachers of a new religion of
their own. Hung had heard of Christianity from missionaries (1837),
and he mixed Christian ideas with those of ancient China and proclaimed to his followers a doctrine that promised the Kingdom of
God on earth. He called himself 'Christ's younger brother', and his
kingdom was to be called T'ai P'ing ('Supreme Peace'). He made his
first comrades, charcoal makers, local doctors, pedlars and farmers,
into kings, and made himself emperor. The movement, like many
before it, was religious as well as social, and it produced a great
response from the peasants. The programme of the T'ai P'ing, in
some points influenced by Christian ideas but more so by traditional
Chinese thought, was in many points revolutionary: (a) all property
was communal property; (b) land was classified into categories
according to its fertility and equally distributed among men and
women. Every producer kept of the produce as much as he and his
family needed and delivered the rest into the communal granary; (c)
administration and tax systems were revised; (d) women were given
equal rights: they fought together with men in the army and had
access to official position. They had to marry, but monogamy was
requested; (e) the use of opium, tobacco and alcohol was prohibited,
prostitution was illegal; (f) foreigners were regarded as equals,
capitulations that the Manchus had accepted were not recognized. A
large part of the officials, and particularly of the soldiers sent against
the revolutionaries, were Manchus, and consequently the movement
very soon became a nationalist movement, much as the popular movement at the end of the Mongol epoch had done. Hung made rapid
progress; in 1852 he captured Hankow, and in 1853 Nanking, the
important centre in the east. With clear political insight he made
Nanking his capital. In this he returned to the old traditions of the
beginning of the Ming epoch, no doubt expecting in this way to
attract support from the eastern Chinese gentry, who had no liking
for a capital far away in the north. He made a parade of adhesion to
the ancient Chinese tradition: his followers cut off their pigtails and
allowed their hair to grow as in the past.

He did not succeed, however, in carrying his reforms from the
stage of sporadic action to a systematic reorganization of the country,

and he also failed to enlist the elements needed for this as for all other administrative work, so that the good start soon degenerated into a terrorist regime.

Hung's followers pressed on from Nanking, and in 1853–1855 they advanced nearly to Tientsin; but they failed to capture Peking itself.

The new T'ai P'ing state faced the Europeans with big problems. Should they work with it or against it? The T'ai P'ing always insisted that they were Christians; the missionaries hoped now to have the opportunity of converting all China to Christianity. The T'ai P'ing treated the missionaries well but did not let them operate. After long hesitation and much vacillation, however, the Europeans placed themselves on the side of the Manchus. Not out of any belief that the T'ai P'ing movement was without justification, but because they had concluded treaties with the Manchu government and given loans to it, of which nothing would have remained if the Manchus had fallen; because they preferred the weak Manchu government to a strong T'ai P'ing government; and because they disliked the socialistic element in many of the measures adopted by the T'ai P'ing.

At first it seemed as if the Manchus would be able to cope unaided with the T'ai P'ing, but the same thing happened as at the end of the Mongol rule: the imperial armies, consisting of the 'banners' of the Manchus, the Mongols, and some Chinese had lost their military skill in the long years of peace; they had lost their old fighting spirit and were glad to be able to live in peace on their state pensions. Now three men came to the fore—a Mongol named Seng-ko-lin-ch'in, a man of great personal bravery, who defended the interests of the Manchu rulers; and two Chinese, Tsêng Kuo-fan (1811–1892) and Li Hung-chang (1823–1901), who were in the service of the Manchus but used their position simply to further the interests of the gentry. The Mongol saved Peking from capture by the T'ai P'ing. The two Chinese were living in central China, and there they recruited, Li at his own expense and Tsêng out of the resources at his disposal as a provincial governor, a sort of militia, consisting of peasants out to protect their homes from destruction by the peasants of the T'ai P'ing. Thus the peasants of central China, all suffering from impoverishment, were divided into two groups, one following the T'ai P'ing, the other following Tsêng Kuo-fan. Tsêng's army, too, might be described as a 'national' army, because Tsêng was not fighting for the interests of the Manchus. Thus the peasants could choose between two sides, between the T'ai P'ing and Tsêng Kuo-fan. Although Tsêng represented the gentry and was thus not the man of the simple common people, peasants fought in masses on his side, for he paid better, and especially more regularly. Tsêng, being a good strategist, won successes and gained adherents. Thus by 1856 the T'ai

P'ing were pressed back on Nanking and some of the towns round it; in 1864 Nanking was captured.

While in the central provinces the T'ai P'ing rebellion was raging, China was suffering grave setbacks owing to the Lorcha War of 1856; and there were also great and serious risings in other parts of the country. In 1855 the Yellow river had changed its course, entering the sea once more at Tientsin, to the great loss of the regions of Honan and Anhui. In these two central provinces the peasant rising of the so-called 'Nien Fei' had begun, but it only became formidable after 1855, owing to the increasing misery of the peasants. This purely peasant revolt was not suppressed by the Manchu government until 1868, after many collisions. Then, however, there began the so-called 'Mohammedan risings'. Here there are, in all, five movements to distinguish: (1) the Mohammedan rising in Kansu (1864–1865); (2) the Salar movement in Shensi; (3) the Mohammedan revolt in Yünnan (1855–1873); (4) the rising in Kansu (1895); (5) the rebellion of Yakub Beg in Sinkiang (from 1866 onward).

While we are fairly well informed about the other popular risings of this period, the Mohammedan revolts have not yet been well studied. We know from unofficial accounts that these risings were suppressed with great brutality. To this day there are many Mohammedans in, for instance. Yünnan, but the revolt there is said to have cost a million lives. The figures all rest on very rough estimates: in Kansu the population is said to have fallen from fifteen million to one million; the Sinkiang revolt is said to have cost ten million lives. There are no reliable statistics; but it is understandable that at that time the population of China must have fallen considerably, especially if we bear in mind the equally ferocious suppression of the risings of the T'ai P'ing and the Nien Fei within China, and smaller risings of which we have made no mention.

The Mohammedan risings were not elements of a general Mohammedan revolt, but separate events only incidentally connected with each other. The risings had different causes. An important factor was the general distress in China. In addition to this, owing to the national feeling which had been aroused in so unfortunate a way, the Chinese felt a revulsion against non-Chinese, such as the Salars, who were of Turkish race. Here there were always possibilities of friction, which might have been removed with a little consideration but which swelled to importance through the tactless behaviour of Chinese officials. Finally there came divisions among the Mohammedans of China which led to fighting between themselves.

All these risings were marked by two characteristics. They had no general political aim such as the founding of a great and universal Islamic state. Separate states were founded, but they were too small to endure; they would have needed the protection of great states. But they were not moved by any pan-Islamic idea. Second, they all took place on Chinese soil, and all the Mohammedans involved, except in the rising of the Salars, were Chinese. These Chinese who became Mohammedans are called Dungans. The Dungans are, of course, no longer pure Chinese, because Chinese who have gone over to Islam readily form mixed marriages with Islamic non-Chinese, that is to say with Turks and Mongols.

The revolt, however, of Yakub Beg in Sinkiang had a quite different character. Yakub Beg (his Chinese name was An Chi-yeh) had risen to the Chinese governorship when he made himself ruler of Kashgar. In 1866 he began to try to make himself independent of Chinese control. He conquered Ili, and then in a rapid campaign made himself master of all Sinkiang.

His state had a much better prospect of endurance than the other Mohammedan states. He had full control of it from 1874. Sinkiang was connected with China only by the few routes that led between the desert and the Tibetan mountains. The state was supported against China by Russia, which was continually pressing eastward, and in the south by Great Britain, which was pressing towards Tibet. Farther west was the great Ottoman empire; the attempt to gain direct contact with it was not hopeless in itself, and this was recognized at Istanbul. Missions went to and fro, and Turkish officers came to Yakub Beg and organized his army; Yakub Beg recognized the Turkish sultan as Khalif. He also concluded treaties with Russia and Great Britain. But in spite of all this he was unable to maintain his hold of Sinkiang. In 1877 the famous Chinese general Tso Tsung-t'ang (1812–1885), who had fought against the T'ai P'ing and also against the Mohammedans in Kansu, marched into Sinkiang and ended Yakub Beg's rule.

Yakub was defeated, however, not so much by Chinese superiority as by a combination of circumstances. In order to build up his kingdom he was compelled to impose heavy taxation, and this made him unpopular with his own followers: they had had to pay taxes under the Chinese, but the Chinese collection had been much less rigorous than that of Yakub Beg. It was technically impossible for the Ottoman empire to give him any aid, even had its internal situation permitted it. Britain and Russia would probably have been glad to see a weakening of the Chinese hold over Sinkiang, but they did not want a strong new state there, once they had found that neither of them could control the country while it was in Yakub Beg's hands. In 1881 Russia occupied the Ili region, Yakub's first conquest. In the end the two great powers considered it better for Sinkiang to return officially into the hands of the weakened China, hoping that in practice they would be able to bring Sinkiang more and more under their control. Consequently, when in 1880, three years after the removal of Yakub Beg, China sent a mission to Russia with the request for the return of the Ili region to her, Russia gave way, and the Treaty of Ili was concluded, ending for the time the Russian penetration of Sinkiang. In 1882 the Manchu government raised the conquered area to a 'new frontier' (Sinkiang) with a special administration.

This process of colonial penetration of Sinkiang continued. Until the end of the First World War there was no fundamental change in the situation in the country, owing to the rivalry between Great Britain and Russia. But after 1920 a period began in which Sinkiang became almost independent, under a number of rulers of parts of the country. Then, from 1928 onward, a more and more thorough penetration by Russia began, so that by 1940 Sinkiang could almost be called a Soviet Republic. The Second World War diverted Russian attention to the West, and at the same time compelled the Chinese to retreat into the interior from the Japanese, so that by 1943 the country was more firmly held by the Chinese government than it had been for seventy years. After the creation of the People's Democracy a directed immigration into Sinkiang began, in connection with the development of oil fields and of many new industries in the border area between Sinkiang and China proper. Roads and air communications opened Sinkiang. Yet, the differences between immigrant Chinese and local Muslim Turks continue to play a role.

9 Collision with Japan; further capitulations

The reign of Wen Tsung (reign name Hsien-feng 1851–1861) was marked throughout by the T'ai P'ing and other rebellions and by wars with the Europeans, and that of Mu Tsung (reign name T'ung-chih: 1862–1874) by the great Mohammedan disturbances. There began also a conflict with Japan which lasted until 1945. Mu Tsung came to the throne as a child of five, and never played a part of his own. It had been the general rule for princes to serve as regents for minors on the imperial throne, but this time the princes concerned won such notoriety through their intrigues that the Peking court circles decided to entrust the regency to two concubines of the late emperor. One of these, called Tzǔ Hsi (born 1835), of the Manchu tribe of the Yehe-Nara, quickly gained the upper hand. The empress Tzǔ Hsi was one of the strongest personalities of the later nineteenth century who played an active part in Chinese political life. She played a more active part than any emperor had played for many decades.

Meanwhile great changes had taken place in Japan. The restoration of the Meiji had ended the age of feudalism, at least on the surface. Japan rapidly became Westernized, and at the same time entered on an imperialist policy. Her aims from 1868 onward were clear, and remained unaltered until the end of the Second World War: she was to be surrounded by a wide girdle of territories under Japanese domination, in order to prevent the approach of any enemy to the Japanese homeland. This girdle was divided into several zones—(1) the inner zone with the Kurile Islands, Sakhalin, Korea, the Ryukyu archipelago, and Taiwan; (2) the outer zone with the Marianne, Philippine, and Caroline Islands, eastern China, Manchuria, and eastern Siberia; (3) the third zone, not clearly defined, including especially the Netherlands Indies, Indo-China, and the whole of China, a zone of undefined extent. The outward form of this sub-jugated region was to be that of the Greater Japanese Empire, described as the Imperium of the Yellow Race (the main ideas were contained in the Tanaka Memorandum 1927 and in the Tada Inter-view of 1936). Round Japan, moreover, a girdle was to be created of producers of raw materials and purchasers of manufactures, to provide Japanese industry with a market. Japan had sent a delegation of amity to China as early as 1869, and a first Sino-Japanese treaty was signed in 1871; from then on, Japan began to carry out her imperialistic plans. In 1874 she attacked the Ryukyu islands and Formosa (Taiwan) on the pretext that some Japanese had been murdered there. Under the treaty of 1874 Japan withdrew once more, only demanding a substantial indemnity; but in 1876, in violation of the treaty and without a declaration of war, she annexed the Ryukyu Islands. These islands (one of which is in Japanese called Okinawa) were since centuries in a loose dependency with China, while, on the other hand, they paid tribute to some lords in Kyushu. The popula-tion of the islands has a culture and social structure of its own, and their language differs from standard Japanese. They felt discriminated against by the Japanese and gained after the Second World War some kind of independence while under American occupation; finally, however, Japan reassumed its control over the islands. In 1876 began the Japanese penetration into Korea; by 1885 she had reached the stage of a declaration that Korea was a joint sphere of interest of China and Japan; until then China's protectorate over Korea had been unchallenged. At the same time (1876) Great Britain had secured further capitulations in the Chefoo Convention; in 1862 France had acquired Cochin China, in 1864 Cambodia, in 1874 Tongking, and in 1883 Annam. This led in 1884 to war between France and China, in which the French did not by any means gain an indubitable victory; but the Treaty of Tientsin left them with their acquisi-tions.

Meanwhile, at the beginning of 1875, the young Chinese emperor died of smallpox, without issue. Under the influence of the two empresses, who still remained regents, a cousin of the dead emperor, the three-year-old prince Tsai T'ien was chosen as emperor Tê Tsung (reign name Kuang-hsü: 1875–1909). He came of age in 1889 and took over the government of the country. The empress Tzŭ Hsi retired, but did not really relinquish the reins.

In 1894 the Sino-Japanese War broke out over Korea, as an outcome of the undefined position that had existed since 1885 owing to the imperialistic policy of the Japanese. China had created a North China squadron, but this was all that can be regarded as Chinese preparation for the long-expected war. The governor-general of Chihli (now Hopei—the province in which Peking is situated), Li Hung-chang, was a general who had done good service, but he lost the war, and at Shimonoseki (1895) he had to sign a treaty on very harsh terms, in which China relinquished her protectorate over Korea and lost Taiwan. The intervention of France, Germany, and Russia compelled Japan to content herself with these acquisitions, abandoning her demand for South Manchuria. Korea and Formosa (Taiwan) became colonies, Taiwan first, Korea later, and remained so until the end of the Second World War.

10 Russia in Manchuria

After the Crimean War, Russia had turned her attention once more to the East. There had been hostilities with China over eastern Siberia, which were brought to an end in 1858 by the Treaty of Aigun, under which China ceded certain territories in northern Manchuria. This made possible the founding of Vladivostok in 1860. Russia received Sakhalin from Japan in 1875 in exchange for the Kurile Islands. She received from China the important Port Arthur as a leased territory, and then tried to secure the whole of south Manchuria. This brought Japan's policy of expansion into conflict with Russia's plans in the Far East. Russia wanted Manchuria in order to be able to pursue a policy in the Pacific; but Japan herself planned to march into Manchuria from Korea, of which she already had possession. This imperialist rivalry made war inevitable: Russia lost the war; under the Treaty of Portsmouth in 1905 Russia gave Japan the main railway through Manchuria, with adjoining territory. Thus Manchuria became Japan's sphere of influence and was lost to the Manchus without their being consulted in any way. The Japanese penetration of Manchuria then proceeded stage by stage, not without occasional setbacks, until she had occupied the whole of Manchuria from 1932 to 1945. After the end of the Second World War, Manchuria was returned to China, with certain reservations in favour of the Soviet Union, which were later revoked. Japan also got half of the island of Sakhalin (Japanese: Karafuto), which it had to return back to the Soviet Union after the defeat of 1945.

11   *Reform and reaction: the Boxer Rising*

China had lost the war with Japan because she was entirely without modern armament. While Japan went to work at once with all her energy to emulate Western industrialization, the ruling class in China had shown a marked repugnance to any modernization; and the centre of this conservatism was the dowager empress Tzŭ Hsi. She was a woman of strong personality, but too uneducated—in the modern sense—to be able to realize that modernization was an absolute necessity for China if it was to remain an independent state. The empress failed to realize that the Europeans were fundamentally different from the neighbouring tribes or the pirates of the past; she had not the capacity to acquire a general grasp of the realities of world politics. She felt instinctively that Europeanization would wreck the foundations of the power of the Manchus and the gentry, and would bring another class, the middle class and the merchants, into power. She has often been blamed for not thinking of the possibility that China might become a colony of one or several Western countries; with hindsight, we have today to admit that such a development could not have been successful.

There were reasonable men, however, who had seen the necessity of reform—especially Li Hung-chang, who has already been mentioned. In 1896 he went on a mission to Moscow, and then toured Europe. The reformers were, however, divided into two groups. One group advocated the acquisition of a certain amount of technical knowledge from abroad and its introduction by slow reforms, without altering the social structure of the state or the composition of the government. The others held that the state needed fundamental changes, and that superficial loans from Europe were not enough. According to the dominant sociological theory until about 1960, the introduction only of Western technology and technical knowledge could not have succeeded. Today, we are much more cautious in our judgement. We now know of numerous examples where social changes came long after successful technical changes. The failure in the war with Japan made the general desire for reform more and more insistent not only in the country but in Peking. Until now Japan had been despised as a barbarian state; now Japan had won! The Europeans had been despised; now they were all cutting bits out of China for themselves, extracting from the government one privilege after another, and quite openly dividing China into 'spheres of interest', obviously as the prelude to annexation of the whole country.

309

In Europe at that time the question was being discussed over and over again, why Japan had so quickly succeeded in making herself a modern power, and why China was not succeeding in doing so; the Japanese were praised for their capacity and the Chinese blamed for their lassitude. Both in Europe and in Chinese circles it was overlooked that there were fundamental differences between both societies. When Japan modernized under the Meiji regime, the old upper class co-operated fully with the government out of fear that otherwise Japan would be unable to preserve its integrity. Thus, the upper class remained intact and led the modernization, willing even to give up numerous of its privileges. In China, nobody seriously feared the loss of independence of the country. Further, there was a cleft between the ruling dynasty, the Manchu conquerors, and the Chinese élite, and the tension between the two absorbed the energy that should have gone into modernization. The leaders of China remained, except for small attempts, inactive and when modernization later began, it was not carried through by the élite. Additionally, Japan had a developed middle class, the merchants, who entered into a symbiosis with the feudal lords. Thus, changes initiated by Japan's élite, were taken up and sponsored by the middle class. China's middle class of merchants was weak. It was not a willing partner of the disunited élite. It had still to gain the strength to liberate itself before it could become the support for a capitalistic state. And the gentry were still strong enough to maintain their dominance and so to prevent a radical reconstruction; all they would agree to were a few reforms during the so-called 'T'ung-chih reforms' or 'Self-strengthening Movement' (1861–1895).

In 1895 and in 1898 a scholar, K'ang Yo-wei (1858–1927), who was admitted into the presence of the emperor, submitted to him memoranda in which he called for radical reform. K'ang was a scholar who belonged to the empiricist school of philosophy of the early Manchu period, the so-called Han school. He was a man of strong and persuasive personality, and had such an influence on the emperor that in 1898 the emperor issued several edicts ordering the fundamental reorganization of education, law, trade, communications and the army. These laws were not at all bad in themselves; they would have paved the way for a liberalization of Chinese society. But they aroused the utmost hatred in the conservative gentry and also in the moderate reformers among the gentry. K'ang Yo-wei and his followers, to whom a number of well-known modern scholars belonged, had strong support in south China. We have already mentioned that owing to the increased penetration of European goods and ideas, south China had become more progressive than the north; this had added to the tension already existing for other reasons between north and south. In foreign policy the north was more favourable to Russia and radically opposed to Japan and Great Britain; the south was in favour of co-operation with Britain and Japan, in order to learn from those two states how reform could be carried through. In the north the men of the south were suspected of being anti-Manchu and revolutionary in feeling. This was to some extent true, though K'ang Yo-wei and his friends, among them the publicist Liang Ch'i-ch'ao (1873–1929), were as yet largely unconscious of it.

When the empress Tzŭ Hsi saw that the emperor was actually thinking about reforms, she went to work with lightning speed. Very soon the reformers had to flee; those who failed to make good their escape were arrested and executed. The emperor was made a prisoner in a palace near Peking, and remained a captive until his death; the empress resumed her regency on his behalf. The period of reforms lasted only for a few months of 1898. A leading part in the extermination of the reformers was played by troops from Kansu under the command of a Mohammedan, Tung Fu-hsiang. General Yüan Shih-k'ai, who was then stationed at Tientsin in command of 7,000 troops with modern equipment, the only ones in China, could have removed the empress and protected the reformers; but he was already pursuing a personal policy, and thought it safer to give the reformers no help.

There now began, from 1898, a reactionary rule of the dowager empress. But China's general situation permitted no breathing-space. In 1900 came the so-called Boxer Rising, a new popular movement against the gentry and the Manchus similar to the many that had preceded it. The Peking government succeeded, however, in negotiations that brought the movement into the service of the government and directed it against the foreigners. This removed the danger to the government and at the same time helped it against the hated foreigners. But incidents resulted which the Peking government had not anticipated. An international army was sent to China, and marched from Tientsin against Peking, to liberate the besieged European legations and to punish the government. The Europeans captured Peking (1900); the dowager empress and her prisoner, the emperor, had to flee; some of the palaces were looted. The peace treaty that followed exacted further concessions from China to the Europeans and enormous war indemnities, the payment of which continued into the 1940s, though most of the states placed the money at China's disposal for educational purposes. When in 1902 the dowager empress returned to Peking and put the emperor back into his palace-prison, she was forced by what had happened to realize that at all events a certain measure of reform was necessary. The reforms, however, which she decreed, mainly in 1904, were very modest and were never fully carried out. They were only intended to make an impression on the outer world and to appease the continually growing body of supporters of the reform party, especially numerous in south China. The south remained, nevertheless, a focus of hostility to the Manchus. After his failure in 1898, K'ang Yo-wei went to Europe, and no longer played any important political part. His place was soon taken by a young Chinese physician who had been living abroad. Sun Yat-sen (1866–1925), who turned the reform party into a middle-class revolutionary party.

12 End of the dynasty

Meanwhile the dowager empress held her own. General Yüan Shih-k'ai, who had played so dubious a part in 1898, was not impeccably loyal to her, and remained unreliable. He was beyond challenge the strongest man in the country, for he possessed the only modern army; but he was still biding his time.

In 1908 the dowager empress fell ill; she was seventy-four years old. When she felt that her end was near, she seems to have had the captive emperor Tê Tsung assassinated (at 5 p.m. on 14 November); she herself died next day (15 November, 2 p.m.): she was evidently determined that this man, whom she had ill-treated and oppressed all his life, should not regain independence. As Tê Tsung had no children, she nominated on the day of her death the two-year-old prince P'u Yi as emperor (reign name Hsüan-t'ung, 1909–1911).

The empress Tzŭ Hsi is still regarded as responsible for the sufferings that China had to suffer for about half a century, and popular stories about her abound in description of her misdeeds. Together with the Empress Lü in the early Han time, and the Empress Wu in T'ang time, she became the symbol of evil: what would become of a country under the rule of a woman. This may well be one of the reasons why still so few women are in high positions and recognized as capable in the People's China.

The fact that another child was to reign and a new regency to act for him, together with all the failures in home and foreign policy, brought further strength to the revolutionary party. The government believed that it could only maintain itself if it allowed Yüan Shih-k'ai, the commander of the modern troops, to come to power. The chief regent, however, worked against Yüan Shih-k'ai and dismissed him at the beginning of 1909; Yüan's supporters remained at their posts. Yüan himself now entered into relations with the revolutionaries, whose centre was Canton, and whose undisputed leader was now Sun Yat-sen. At this time Sun and his supporters had already made attempts at revolution, but without success, as his following was as yet too small. It consisted mainly of young intellectuals who had been educated in Europe and America; the great mass of the

Chinese people remained unconvinced: the common people could not understand the new ideals, and the middle class did not entirely trust the young intellectuals.

The state of China in 1911 was as lamentable as could be: the European states, Russia, America, and Japan regarded China as a field for their own plans, and in their calculations paid scarcely any attention to the Chinese government. Foreign capital was penetrating everywhere in the form of loans or railway and other enterprises. If it had not been the mutual rivalries of the powers, China would long ago have been annexed by one of them. The government needed a great deal of money for the payment of the war indemnities, and for carrying out the few reforms at last decided on. In order to get money from the provinces, it had to permit the viceroys even more freedom than they already possessed. The result was a spectacle altogether resembling that of the end of the T'ang dynasty, about A.D. 900: the various governors were trying to make themselves independent. In addition to this there was the revolutionary movement in the south.

The government made some concession to the progressives, by providing the first beginnings of parliamentary rule. In 1910 a national assembly was convoked. It had a Lower House with representatives of the provinces (provincial diets were also set up), and an Upper House, in which sat representatives of the imperial house, the nobility, the gentry, and also the protectorates. The members of the Upper House were all nominated by the regent. It very soon proved that the members of the Lower House, mainly representatives of the provincial gentry, had a much more practical outlook than the routineers of Peking. Thus the Lower House grew in importance, a fact which, of course, brought grist to the mills of the revolutionary movement.

In 1910 the first risings directed actually against the regency took place, in the province of Hunan. In 1911 the 'railway disturbances' broke out in western China as a reply of the railway shareholders in the province of Szechwan to the government decree of nationalization of all the railways. The modernist students, most of whom were sons of merchants who owned railway shares, supported the movement, and the government was unable to control them. At the same time a great anti-Manchu revolution began in Wuch'ang, one of the cities of which Wuhan, on the Yangtze, now consists. The revolution was the result of government action against a group of terrorists. Its leader was an officer named Li Yüan-hung. The Manchus soon had some success in this quarter, but the other provincial governors now rose in rapid succession, repudiated the Manchus, and declared themselves independent. Most of the Manchu garrisons in the provinces were murdered. The governors remained at the head of their troops in their provinces, and for the moment made common cause with the revolutionaries, from whom they meant to break free at the first opportunity. The Manchus themselves failed at first to realize the gravity of the revolutionary movement; they then fell into panic-stricken desperation. As a last resource, Yüan Shih-k'ai was recalled (10 November 1911) and made prime minister.

Yüan's excellent troops were loyal to his person, and he could have made use of them in fighting on behalf of the dynasty. But a victory would have brought no personal gain to him; for his personal plans he considered that the anti-Manchu side provided the springboard he needed. The revolutionaries, for their part, had no choice but to win over Yüan Shih-k'ai for the sake of his troops, since they were not themselves strong enough to get rid of the Manchus, or even to wrest concessions from them, so long as the Manchus were defended by Yüan's army. Thus Yüan and the revolutionaries were forced into each other's arms. He then began negotiations with them, explaining to the imperial house that the dynasty could only be saved by concessions. The revolutionaries—apart from their desire to neutralize the prime minister and general, if not to bring him over to their side—were also readier than ever to negotiate, because they were short of money and unable to obtain loans from abroad, and because they could not themselves gain control of the individual governors. The negotiations, which had been carried on at Shanghai, were broken off on 18 December 1911, because the revolutionaries demanded a republic, but the imperial house was only ready to grant a constitutional monarchy.

Meanwhile the revolutionaries set up a provisional government at Nanking (29 December 1911), with Sun Yat-sen as president and Li Yüan-hung as vice-president. Yüan Shih-k'ai now declared to the imperial house that the monarchy could no longer be defended, as his troops were too unreliable, and he induced the Manchu government to issue an edict on 12 February 1912, in which they renounced the throne of China and declared the Republic to be the constitutional form of state. The young emperor of the Hsüan-t'ung period, after the Japanese conquest of Manchuria in 1931, was installed there. He was, however, entirely without power during the melancholy years of his nominal rule, which lasted until 1945.

In 1912 the Manchu dynasty came in reality to its end. On the news of the abdication of the imperial house, Sun Yat-sen resigned in Nanking, and recommended Yüan Shih-k'ai as president.

314

CHAPTER ELEVEN

The Republic (1912–1948)

1 Social and intellectual position

In order to understand the period that now followed, let us first
consider the social and intellectual position in China in the period
between 1911 and 1927. The Manchu dynasty was no longer there,
nor were there any remaining real supporters of the old dynasty. The
gentry, however, still existed. Alongside it was a still numerically
small middle class, with little political education or enlightenment.

The political interests of these two groups were obviously in
conflict. But after 1912 there had been big changes. The gentry were
largely in a process of decomposition. They still possessed the basis
of their existence, their land, but the land was falling in value, as
there were now other opportunities of capital investment, such as
export-import, shareholding in foreign enterprises, or industrial
undertakings. It is important to note, however, that there was not
much fluid capital at their disposal. In addition to this, cheaper rice
and other foodstuffs were streaming from abroad into China, bringing the prices for Chinese foodstuffs down to the world market prices,
another painful business blow to the gentry. Silk had to meet the
competition of Japanese silk and especially of rayon; the Chinese silk
was of very unequal quality and sold with difficulty. On the other
hand, through the influence of the Western capitalistic system, which
was penetrating more and more into China, land itself became
'capital', an object of speculation for people with capital; its value
no longer depended entirely on the rents it could yield but, under
certain circumstances, on quite other things—the construction of
railways or public buildings, and so on. These changes impoverished
and demoralized the gentry, who in the course of the past century
had grown fewer in number. The gentry were not in a position to
take part fully in the capitalist manipulations, because they had
never possessed much capital; their wealth had lain entirely in their
land, and the income from their rents was consumed quite un-
productively in luxurious living.

Moreover, the class solidarity of the gentry was dissolving. In the
past, politics had been carried on by cliques of gentry families, with

315

the emperor at their head as an unchangeable institution. This edifice had now lost its summit; the struggles between cliques still went on, but entirely without the control which the emperor's power had after all exercised, as a sort of regulative element in the play of forces among the gentry. The arena for this competition had been the court. After the destruction of the arena, the field of play lost its boundaries: the struggles between cliques no longer had a definite objective; the only objective left was the maintenance or securing of any and every hold on power. Under the new conditions cliques or individuals among the gentry could only ally themselves with the possessors of military power, the generals or governors. In this last stage the struggle between rival groups turned into a rivalry between individuals. Family ties began to weaken and other ties, such as between school mates, or origin from the same village or town, became more important than they had been before. For the securing of the aim in view any means were considered justifiable. Never was there such bribery and corruption among the officials as in the years after 1912. This period, until 1927, may therefore be described as a period of dissolution and destruction of the social system of the gentry.

Over against this dying class of the gentry stood, broadly speaking, a tripartite opposition. To begin with, there was the new middle class, divided and without clear political ideas; anti-dynastic of course, but undecided especially as to the attitude it should adopt towards the peasants who, to this day, form over 80 per cent of the Chinese population. The middle class consisted mainly of traders and bankers, whose aim was the introduction of Western capitalism in association with foreign powers. There were also young students who were often the sons of old gentry families and had been sent abroad for study with grants given them by their friends and relatives in the government; or sons of businessmen sent away by their fathers. These students not always accepted the ideas of their fathers; they were influenced by the ideologies of the West, Marxist or non-Marxist, and often created clubs or groups in the University cities of Europe, the United States, and Japan. In 1906 there were about 30,000 students in Japan alone. Such groups of people who had studied together or passed examinations together, had already begun to play a role in politics in the nineteenth century. Now, the influence of such organizations of usually informal character increased. Against the returned students who often had difficulties in adjustment, stood the students at Chinese universities, especially the National University in Peking (Peita). They represented people of the same origin, but of the lower strata of the gentry or of business; they were more nationalistic and politically active and often less influenced by Western ideologies.

In the second place, there was a relatively very small genuine proletariat, the product of the first activities of big capitalists in China, found mainly in Shanghai. Third and finally, there was a gigantic peasantry, uninterested in politics and mostly uneducated, but ready to give unthinking allegiance to anyone who promised to make an end of the conditions in the matter of rents and taxes, conditions that were growing steadily worse with the decay of the gentry. These peasants were thinking of popular risings on the pattern of all the risings in the history of China—attacks on the towns and the killing of the hated landowners, officials, and money-lenders, that is to say, of the gentry.

Such was the picture of the middle class and those who were ready to support it, a group with widely divergent interests, held together only by its opposition to the gentry system and the monarchy. It could not but be extremely difficult, if not impossible, to achieve political success with such a group. Sun Yat-sen (1866–1925), the 'Father of the Republic', accordingly laid down three stages of progress in his many works, of which the best-known are 'San-min chu-i' ('The Three Principles of the People'), and 'Chien-kuo fang-lüeh' ('Plans for the Building up of the Realm'). The three phases of development through which republican China was to pass were: the phase of struggle against the old system, the phase of educative rule, and the phase of truly democratic government. The phase of educative rule was to be a sort of authoritarian system with a democratic content, under which the people should be familiarized with democracy and enabled to grow politically ripe for true democracy.

Difficult as was the internal situation from the social point of view, it was no less difficult in economic respects. China had recognized that she must at least adopt Western technical and industrial progress in order to continue to exist as an independent state. But the building up of industry demanded large sums of money. The existing Chinese banks were quite incapable of providing the capital needed; but the acceptance of capital from abroad led at once, every time, to further political capitulations. The gentry, who had no cash worth the mention, were violently opposed to the capitalization of their properties, and were in favour of continuing as far as possible to work the soil in the old style. Quite apart from all this, all over the country there were generals, the so-called 'warlords', who had come from the ranks of the gentry, and who collected the whole of the financial resources of their region for the support of their private armies. Investors had little confidence in the republican government so long as they could not tell whether the government would decide in favour of its right or of its left wing.

No less complicated was the intellectual situation at this time. Confucianism, and the whole of the old culture and morality bound up with it, was unacceptable to the middle-class element. In the first place, Confucianism rejected the principle, required at least in theory by the middle class, of the equality of all people; second, the Confucian great-family system was irreconcilable with middle-class individualism, quite apart from the fact that the Confucian form of state could only be a monarchy. Every attempt to bolster up Confucianism in practice or theory was bound to fail and did fail. Even the gentry could scarcely offer any real defence of the Confucian system any longer. With Confucianism went the moral standards especially of the upper classes of society. Philosophical Taoism was out of the question as a substitute, because of its anarchistic and egocentric character. Consequently, in these years, part of the gentry turned to Buddhism and part to Christianity. Some of the middle class who had come under European influence also turned to Christianity, regarding it as a part of the European civilization they had to adopt. Others adhered to modern philosophic systems such as pragmatism and positivism. Marxist doctrines spread rapidly.

Education was secularized. Great efforts were made to develop modern schools, though the work of development was continually hindered by the incessant political unrest. Only at the universities, which became foci of republican and progressive opinion, was any positive achievement possible. Many students and professors were active in politics, organizing demonstrations and strikes. They pursued a strong national policy, often also socialistic. At the same time real scientific work was done; many young scholars of outstanding ability were trained at the Chinese universities, often better than the students who went abroad. There is a permanent disagreement between these two groups of young men with a modern education: the students who return from abroad claim to be better educated, but in reality they often have only a very superficial knowledge of things modern and none at all of China, her history, and her special circumstances. The students of the Chinese universities have been much better instructed in all the things that concern China, and most of them are in no way behind the returned students in the modern sciences. They are therefore a much more serviceable element.

The intellectual modernization of China goes under the name of the 'Movement of May Fourth', because on 4 May 1919, students of the National University in Peking demonstrated against the government and their pro-Japanese adherents. When the police attacked the students and jailed some, more demonstrations and student strikes and finally a general boycott of Japanese imports were the consequence. In these protest actions, professors such as Ts'ai Yüan-p'ei (1876–1940), later president of the Academia Sinica, took an active part. The forces which had now been mobilized, rallied around the journal 'New Youth' ('Hsin Ch'ing-nien'), created in 1915 by Ch'en Tu-hsiu (1879–1942). The journal was progressive, against the monarchy, Confucius, and the old traditions. Ch'en Tu-hsiu who put himself strongly behind the students, was more radical than other contributors but at first favoured Western democracy and Western science; he was influenced mainly by John Dewey who was guest professor in Peking in 1919–1920. Similarly tending towards liberalism in politics and Dewey's ideas in the field of philosophy were others, mainly Hu Shih. Finally, some reformers criticized conservatism purely on the basis of Chinese thought. Hu Shih (1892–1962) gained greatest acclaim by his proposal for a 'literary revolution', published in the 'New Youth' in 1917. This revolution was the logically necessary application of the political revolution to the field of education. The new 'vernacular' replaced the old 'classical' literary language. The language of the classical works is so remote from the language of daily life that no uneducated person can understand it. A command of it requires a full knowledge of all the ancient literature, entailing decades of study. The gentry had elaborated this style of speech for themselves and their dependants; it was their monopoly; nobody who did not belong to the gentry and had not attended its schools could take part in literary or in administrative life. The literary revolution introduced the language of daily life, the language of the people, into literature: newspapers, novels, scientific treatises, translations, appeared in the vernacular, and could thus be understood by anyone who could read and write, even if he had no Confucianist education.

It may be said that the literary revolution has achieved its main objects. As a consequence of it, a great quantity of new literature has been published. Not only is every important new book that appears in the West published in translation within a few months, but modern novels and short stories and poems have been written, some of them of high literary value.

At the same time as this revolution there took place another fundamental change in the language. It was necessary to take over a vast number of new scientific and technical terms. As Chinese, owing to the character of its script, is unable to write foreign words accurately and can do no more than provide a rather rough paraphrase, the practice was started of expressing new ideas by newly formed native words. Thus modern Chinese has very few foreign words, and yet it has all the new ideas. For example, a telegram is a 'lightning-letter'; a wireless telegram is a 'not-have-wire-lightning-communication'; a fountain-pen is a 'self-flow-ink-water-brush'; a typewriter is a 'strike-letter-machine'. Most of these neologisms are identical in the modern languages of China and Japan.

There had been several proposals in recent decades to do away with the Chinese characters and to introduce an alphabet in their place. They have all proved to be unsatisfactory so far, because the character of the Chinese language, as it is at this moment, is unsuited to an alphabetical script. They would also destroy China's cultural unity: there are many dialects in China that differ so greatly from each other that, for instance, a man from Canton cannot understand a man from Shanghai. If Chinese were written with letters, the result would be a Canton literature and another literature confined to Shanghai, and China would break up into a number of areas with different languages. The old Chinese writing is independent of pronunciation. A Cantonese and a Pekingese can read each other's newspapers without difficulty. They pronounce the words quite differently, but the meaning is unaltered. Even a Japanese can understand a Chinese newspaper without special study of Chinese, and a Chinese with a little preparation can read a Japanese newspaper without understanding a single word of Japanese.

The aim of modern education in China is to work towards the establishment of 'High Chinese', the former official (Mandarin) language, throughout the country, and to set limits to the use of the various dialects. Once this has been done, it will be possible to proceed to a radical reform of the script without running the risk of political separatist movements, which are always liable to spring up, and also without leading, through the adoption of various dialects as the basis of separate literatures, to the break-up of China's cultural unity. In the last years, the unification of the spoken language has made great progress. Yet, alphabetic script is used only in cases in which illiterate adults have to be enabled in a short time to read very simple information. More attention is given to a simplification of the script as it is; Japanese had started this some forty years earlier. Unfortunately, the new Chinese abbreviated forms of characters are not always identical with long-established Japanese forms, and are not developed in such a systematic form as would make learning of Chinese characters easier.

2   First period of the Republic: The warlords

The situation of the Republic after its foundation was far from hopeful. Republican feeling existed only among the very small groups of students who had modern education, and a few traders, in other words, among the 'middle class'. And even in the revolutionary party to which these groups belonged there were the most various conceptions of the form of republican state to be aimed at. The left wing of the party, mainly intellectuals and manual workers, had in view more or less vague socialistic institutions; the liberals, for instance the traders, thought of a liberal democracy, more or less on the American pattern; and the nationalists merely wanted the removal of the alien Manchu rule. The three groups had come together for the practical reason that only so could they get rid of the dynasty. They gave allegiance to Sun Yat-sen as their leader. He succeeded in mobilizing the enthusiasm of continually widening circles for action, not only by the integrity of his aims but also because he was able to present the new socialistic ideology in an alluring form. The anti-republican gentry, however, whose power was not yet entirely broken, took a stand against the party. The generals who had gone over to the republicans had not the slightest intention of founding a republic, but only wanted to get rid of the rule of the Manchus and to step into their place. This was true also of Yüan Shih-k'ai, who in his heart was entirely on the side of the gentry, although the European press especially had always energetically defended him. In character and capacity he stood far above the other generals, but he was no republican.

Thus the first period of the Republic, until 1927, was marked by incessant attempts by individual generals to make themselves independent. The Government could not depend on its soldiers, and so was impotent. The first risings of military units began at the outset of 1912. The governors and generals who wanted to make themselves independent sabotaged every decree of the central government; especially they sent it no money from the provinces and also refused to give their assent to foreign loans. The province of Canton, the actual birthplace of the republican movement and the focus of radicalism, declared itself in 1912 an independent republic.

Within the Peking government matters soon came to a climax. Yüan Shih-k'ai and his supporters represented the conservative view, with the unexpressed but obvious aim of setting up a new imperial house and continuing the old gentry system. Most of the members of the parliament came, however, from the middle class and were opposed to any reaction of this sort. One of their leaders was murdered, and the blame was thrown upon Yüan Shih-k'ai; there then came, in the middle of 1912, a new revolution, in which the radicals made themselves independent and tried to gain control of south China. But Yüan Shih-k'ai commanded better troops and won the day. At the end of October 1912 he was elected, against the opposition, as president of China, and the new state was recognized by foreign countries.

China's internal difficulties reacted on the border states, in which the European powers were keenly interested. The powers considered that the time had come to begin the definitive partition of China. Thus there were long negotiations and also hostilities between China

321

and Tibet, which was supported by Great Britain. The British demanded the complete separation of Tibet from China, but the Chinese rejected this (1912); the rejection was supported by a boycott of British goods. In the end the Tibet question was left undecided. Tibet remained until recent years a Chinese dependency with a good deal of internal freedom. The Second World War and the Chinese retreat into the interior brought many Chinese settlers into Eastern Tibet which was then separated from Tibet proper and made a Chinese province (Hsi-k'ang) in which the native Khamba will soon be a minority. The communist regime soon after its establishment conquered Tibet (1950) and has tried to change the character of its society and its system of government which led to the unsuccessful attempt of the Tibetans to throw off Chinese rule (1959) and the flight of the Dalai Lama to India. The construction of highways, air and missile bases and military occupation have thus tied Tibet closer to China than ever since early Manchu times.

In Outer Mongolia Russian interests predominated. In 1911 there were diplomatic incidents in connection with the Mongolian question. At the end of 1911 the Hutuktu of Urga declared himself independent, and the Chinese were expelled from the country. A secret treaty was concluded in 1912 with Russia, under which Russia recognized the independence of Outer Mongolia, but was accorded an important part as adviser and helper in the development of the country. In 1913 a Russo-Chinese treaty was concluded, under which the autonomy of Outer Mongolia was recognized, but Mongolia became a part of the Chinese realm. After the Russian revolution had begun, revolution was carried also into Mongolia. The country suffered all the horrors of the struggles between White Russians (General Ungern-Sternberg) and the Reds; there were also Chinese attempts at intervention, though without success, until in the end Mongolia became a Soviet Republic. Hemmed in on all sides by China and the Soviet Union, with no access to the sea, the small country had to manoeuvre between its two big neighbours. Since the establishment of the People's Republic and especially since the crisis between China and the Soviet Union, Outer Mongolia has moved closer to the Soviet Union as the—at the moment—less dangerous side. China did not quickly recognize Mongolia's independence, and in his work 'China's Destiny' (1944) Chiang Kai-shek insisted that China's aim remained the recovery of the frontiers of 1840, which means among other things the recovery of Outer Mongolia. In spite of this, after the Second World War Chiang Kai-shek had to renounce de jure all rights in Outer Mongolia. Inner Mongolia was always united to China much more closely; only for a time during the war with Japan did the Japanese maintain there a puppet government. The disappearance of this government went almost unnoticed.

At the time when Russian penetration into Mongolia began, Japan had entered upon a similar course in Manchuria, which she regarded as her 'sphere of influence'. On the outbreak of the First World War Japan occupied the former German-leased territory of Tsingtao, at the extremity of the province of Shantung, and from that point she occupied the railways of the province. Her plan was to make the whole province a protectorate; Shantung is rich in coal and especially in metals. Japan's plans were revealed in the notorious 'Twenty-one Demands' (1915). Against the furious opposition especially of the students of Peking, Yüan Shih-k'ai's government accepted the greater part of these demands. In negotiations with Great Britain, in which Japan took advantage of the British commitments in Europe, Japan had to be conceded the predominant position in the Far East.

Meanwhile Yüan Shih-k'ai had made all preparations for turning the Republic once more into an empire, in which he would be emperor; the empire was to be based once more on the gentry group. In 1914 he secured an amendment of the constitution under which the governing power was to be entirely in the hands of the president; at the end of 1914 he secured his appointment as president for life, and on 12 December 1915 he induced the parliament to resolve that he should become emperor.

This naturally aroused the resentment of the republicans, but it also annoyed the generals belonging to the gentry, who had had the same ambition. Thus there were disturbances, especially in the south, where Sun Yat-sen with his followers agitated for a democratic republic. The foreign powers recognized that a divided China would be much easier to penetrate and annex than a united China, and accordingly opposed Yüan Shih-k'ai. Before he could ascend the throne, he died suddenly (June 1916)—and this terminated the first attempt to re-establish monarchy.

Yüan was succeeded as president by Li Yüan-hung. Meanwhile five provinces had declared themselves independent. Foreign pressure on China steadily grew. She was forced to declare war on Germany, and though this made no practical difference to the war, it enabled the European powers to penetrate further into China. Difficulties grew to such an extent in 1917 that a dictatorship was set up and soon after an interlude, the recall of the Manchus and the reinstatement of the deposed emperor (1st–8th July 1917).

This led to various risings of generals, each aiming simply at the satisfaction of his thirst for personal power. Ultimately the victorious group of generals, headed by Tuan Ch'i-jui, secured the election of Fêng Kuo-chang in place of the retiring president. Fêng was succeeded at the end of 1918 by Hsü Shih-ch'ang, who held office until 1922. Hsü, as a former ward of the emperor, was a typical representative of the gentry, and was opposed to all republican reforms.

The south held aloof from these northern governments. In Canton an opposition government was set up, formed mainly of followers of Sun Yat-sen; the Peking government was unable to remove the Canton government. But the Peking government and its president scarcely counted any longer even in the north. All that counted were the generals, the most prominent of whom were: (1) Chang Tso-lin, who had control of Manchuria and had made certain terms with Japan, but who was ultimately murdered by the Japanese (1928); (2) Wu P'ei-fu, who held north China; (3) the so-called 'Christian general', Fêng Yü-hsiang, and (4) Ts'ao K'un, who became president in 1923.

At the end of the First World War Japan had a hold over China amounting almost to military control of the country. China did not sign the Treaty of Versailles, because she considered that she had been duped by Japan, since Japan had driven the Germans out of China but had not returned the liberated territory to the Chinese. In 1921 peace was concluded with Germany, the German privileges being abolished. The same applied to Austria. Russia, immediately after the setting up of the Soviet government, had renounced all her rights under the capitulations. The present regime is of the opinion that the Soviet Union also should have returned to China the land which they had forced the Manchu to give up. The Russian view is that these outlying territories had been conquered by China's foreign rulers, not by the Chinese. But still, this was the first step in the gradual rescinding of the capitulations; the last of them went only in 1943, as a consequence of the difficult situation of the Europeans and Americans in the Pacific produced by the Second World War.

At the end of the First World War the foreign powers revised their attitude towards China. The idea of territorial partitioning of the country was replaced by an attempt at financial exploitation; military friction between the Western powers and Japan was in this way to be minimized. Financial control was to be exercised by an international banking consortium (1920). It was necessary for political reasons that this committee should be joined by Japan. After her Twenty-one Demands, however, Japan was hated throughout China. During the World War she had given loans to the various governments and rebels, and in this way had secured one privilege after another. Consequently China declined the banking consortium. She tried to secure capital from her own resources; but in the existing political situation and the acute economic depression internal loans had no success.

In an agreement between the United States and Japan in 1917, the United States, in consequence of the war, had had to give their assent to special rights for Japan in China. After the war the international conference at Washington (November 1921–February 1922) tried to set narrower limits to Japan's influence over China, and also to redetermine the relative strength in the Pacific of the four great powers (America, Britain, France, Japan). After the failure of the banking plan this was the last means of preventing military conflicts between the powers in the Far East. This brought some relief to China, as Japan had to yield for the time to the pressure of the Western powers.

The years that followed until 1927 were those of the complete collapse of the political power of the Peking government—years of entire dissolution. In the south Sun Yat-sen had been elected generalissimo in 1921. In 1924 he was re-elected with a mandate for a campaign against the north. In January 1924 there also met in Canton the first general congress of the Kuomintang ('People's Party') with 165 delegates. The party, which had, in 1929, 653,000 members, or roughly 0·15 per cent of the population, is the continuation of the Komingtang ('Revolutionary Party') founded by Sun Yat-sen, which as a middle-class party had worked for the removal of the dynasty. The new Kuomintang was more socialistic, as is shown by its admission of Communists and the stress laid upon land reform.

The Communist party had been created under Soviet stimulation in July 1921. Twelve men came together in a school in the protected French concession of Shanghai. The party had two wings. The Peking wing was created by Li Ta-chao. Li was a librarian at the Peking University who in 1918 created a society which in 1919 openly became a 'Marxist Research Society'. He was soon joined by a student, Ch'ü Chiu-pai, and a young library assistant, Mao Tsê-tung. Ch'en Tu-hsiu founded in 1920 in Shanghai the Marxist Study Society. Ch'en held on to the Western Communist programme which said that a revolution would have to be led by the urban proletariat—though, at that time, only Shanghai had some 'proletariat'. Li, who was executed in 1927, found that without the peasants, the majority of all Chinese, no revolution could succeed, an idea which his pupil Mao later accepted. At the time of the constitution of the KMT, Sun Yat-sen was advised by two Russian Communists, Borodin, adviser for party organization, and Galen, adviser for military affairs. Both men together with some forty other Russians, reorganized the southern armies which now came under the leadership of Chiang Kai-shek (1866–1975). Due to the presence of the Russian advisers, the KMT accepted co-operation with Communists, a co-operation which was resented by both sides and did not last long.

At the end of 1924 Sun Yat-sen with some of his followers went to Peking, to discuss the possibility of a reunion between north and south on the basis of the programme of the People's Party. There, however, he died on 12 March 1925 before any definite results had been attained; there was no prospect of achieving anything by the negotiations, and the south broke them off. But the death of Sun Yat-sen had been followed after a time by tension within the party between its right and left wings. Sun's successor, Hu Han-min (died 1936), represented the more rightist wing, but Chiang soon emerged as the true leader, based upon his new, modernized army which he trained in the military academy at Whampoa, near Canton.

The People's Party of the south and its governments, at that time fairly radical in politics, were disliked by the foreign powers; only Japan supported them for a time, owing to the anti-British feeling of the south Chinese and in order to further her purpose of maintaining disunion in China. The first serious collision with the outer world came on 30 May 1925, when British soldiers shot at a crowd demonstrating in Shanghai. This produced a widespread boycott of British goods in Canton and in British Hong Kong, inflicting a great loss on British trade with China and bringing considerable advantages in consequence to Japanese trade and shipping: from the time of this boycott began the Japanese grip on Chinese coastwise shipping.

The second party congress was held in Canton in 1926. Chiang Kai-shek already played a prominent part. The People's Party, under Chiang Kai-shek and with the support of the Communists, began the great campaign against the north (27 July 1926). At first it had good success: the various provincial governors and generals and the Peking government were played off against each other, and in a short time one leader after another was defeated. The Yangtze was reached, and in 1926 the southern government moved to Hankow. All over the southern provinces there now came a genuine rising of the masses of the people, mainly the result of Communist propaganda and of the government's promise to give land to the peasants, to set limits to the big estates, and to bring order into the taxation. In spite of its Communist element, at the beginning of 1927 the southern government was essentially one of the middle class and the peasantry, with a socialistic tendency.

3 Second period of the Republic: Nationalist China

With the continued success of the northern campaign, and with Chiang Kai-shek's southern army at the gates of Shanghai (21 March 1927), a decision had to be taken. Should the left wing be allowed to gain the upper hand, and the great capitalists of Shanghai be expropriated as it was proposed to expropriate the gentry? Or should the right wing prevail, an alliance be concluded with the capitalists, and limits be set to the expropriation of landed estates? Chiang Kai-shek, through his marriage with Sun Yat-sen's wife's sister, had become allied with one of the greatest banking families. In the days of the siege of Shanghai, Chiang, together with his closest colleagues (with the exception of Hu Han-min and Wang Ching-wei, a leftist leader who will be mentioned later), decided on the second alternative. Shanghai came into his hands without a struggle, and the capital of the Shanghai financiers, and soon foreign capital as well, was placed at his disposal, so that he was able to pay his troops and finance his administration. At the same time the Russian advisers were dismissed or executed. The Communists in Shanghai, on Russian advice, did not rise against Chiang, when he approached the city, which made his victory much easier. On the other hand, Chiang's army did not trust the Communists, so that the dismissal of the advisers and actions against Communists within the army was also possible.

The decision arrived at by Chiang Kai-shek and his friends did not remain unopposed, and he parted from the 'left group' (1927) which formed a rival government in Hankow, while Chiang Kai-shek made Nanking the seat of his government (April 1927). The choice of Nanking as the new capital pleased both the industrialists and the agrarians: the great bulk of China's young industries lay in the Yangtze region, and that region was still the principal one for agricultural produce; the landowners of the region were also in a better position with the great market of the capital in their neighbourhood. In this situation, Chiang could not alienate the landowners by a radical land reform. He needed the industrialists and the capital which was safely in Shanghai. Now, the Nanking government succeeded in carrying its dealings with the northern generals to a point at which they were largely out-manoeuvred and became ready for some sort of collaboration (1928). There were now five supreme commanders—Chiang Kai-shek, Fêng Yü-hsiang (the 'Christian general'), Yen Hsi-shan, the governor of Shansi, Chang Tso-lin (killed 4 June 1928, and replaced by his son Chang Hsüeh-liang), and the Muslim Li Chung-yen. Naturally this was not a permanent solution; not only did Chiang Kai-shek's four rivals try to free themselves from his ever-growing influence and to gain full power themselves, but various groups under military leadership rose again and again, even in the home of the Republic, Canton itself. These struggles, which were carried on more by means of diplomacy and bribery than at arms, lasted until 1936. Chiang Kai-shek, as by far the most skilful player in this game, and at the same time the man who had the support of the foreign governments and of the financiers of Shanghai, gained the victory. However, there still was no peace. Since 1934, the

Communists emerged a real danger in central China, and from 1928 on, Japan's attitude towards a unified China became more and more threatening. We will discuss the developments in central China later and first focus on the foreign interventions.

In April 1928, Japan landed troops in Shanghai, apparently in order to weaken Chiang's power, and to strengthen Chang Tso-lin who tended towards Japan. When, however, after fighting in Shantung (3 May 1928), Chang seemed to dissociate himself from Japan, he was killed in a railway accident which was, according to rumours, arranged by Japanese. During the next three years, the Japanese who had, as we have heard, control over the South Manchurian Railway and adjacent territory, tried to strengthen their position in Manchuria, and finally, in 1931, took it over. At that time, Nanking was helpless, since Manchuria was only loosely associated with Nanking, and its governor, Chang Hsüeh-liang, had tried to remain independent of it. Thus Manchuria was lost almost without a blow. On the other hand, the fighting with Japan that broke out soon afterwards in Shanghai brought credit to the young Nanking army, though owing to its numerical inferiority it was unsuccessful. China protested to the League of Nations against its loss of Manchuria. The League sent a commission (the Lytton Commission), which condemned Japan's action, but nothing further happened, and China indignantly broke away from her association with the Western powers (1932–1933). In view of the tense European situation (the beginning of the Hitler era in Germany, and the Italian plans of expansion), the Western powers did not want to fight Japan on China's behalf, and without that nothing more could be done. They pursued, indeed, a policy of playing off Japan against China, in order to keep those two powers occupied with each other, and so to divert Japan from Indo-China and the Pacific.

China had thus to be prepared for being involved one day in a great war with Japan. Chiang Kai-shek wanted to postpone war as long as possible. He wanted time to establish his power more thoroughly within the country, and to strengthen his army. In regard to external relations, the great powers would have to decide their attitude sooner or later. America could not be expected to take up a clear attitude: she was for peace and commerce, and she made greater profits out of her relations with Japan than with China; she sent supplies to both (until 1941). On the other hand, Britain and France were more and more turning away from Japan, and Russo-Japanese relations were at all times tense. Japan tried to emerge from her isolation by joining the 'axis powers', Germany and Italy (1936); but it was still doubtful whether the Western powers would proceed with Russia, and therefore against Japan, or with the Axis, and therefore in alliance with Japan.

Japan for her part considered that if she was to raise the standard of living of her large population and to remain a world power, she must bring into being her 'Greater East Asia', so as to have the needed raw material resources and export markets in the event of a collision with the Western powers; in addition to this, she needed a security girdle as extensive as possible in case of a conflict with Russia. In any case, 'Greater East Asia' must be secured before the European conflict should break out.

4 *The Sino-Japanese war (1937–1945)*

Accordingly, from 1933 onward Japan followed up her conquest of Manchuria. A military, rather unsuccessful intervention by the Japanese army in January 1932 was followed on 9 March by the declaration of Manchukuo, as an independent state under Japanese control. The Japanese made the last Manchu emperor, P'uYi, 'emperor' of this puppet state in March 1934, probably hoping that the glory of an emperor could attract Chinese to desert Chiang. Already in 1933, Japanese armies had moved close to Peking, and the result of this was that the whole area north of Peking became a demilitarized zone, under a semi-dependent government. Japan also began to exercise pressure on inner Mongolia and succeeded, by means of an immense system of smuggling, currency manipulation, and propaganda, in bringing a number of Mongol princes over to her side.

The signal for the outbreak of war was an 'incident' by the Marco Polo Bridge, south of Peking (7 July 1937). The Japanese government profited by a quite unimportant incident, undoubtedly provoked by the Japanese, in order to extend its dominion a little further. China still hesitated; there were negotiations. Japan brought up reinforcements and put forward demands which China could not be expected to be ready to fulfil. Japan then occupied Peking and Tientsin and wide regions between them and south of them. The Chinese soldiers stationed there withdrew almost without striking a blow, but formed up again and began to offer resistance. In order to facilitate the planned occupation of north China, including the province of Shantung, Japan decided on a diversionary campaign against Shanghai. The Nanking government sent its best troops to the new front, and held it for nearly three months against superior forces; but meanwhile the Japanese steadily advanced in north China. On 9 November Nanking fell into their hands, followed by a mass massacre. By the beginning of January 1938, the province of Shantung had also been conquered.

Chiang Kai-shek and his government fled to Ch'ung-ch'ing (Chung-king), the most important commercial and financial centre of the interior after Hankow, which was soon threatened by the Japanese fleet. By means of a number of landings the Japanese soon conquered the whole coast of China, so cutting off all supplies to the country; against hard fighting in some places they pushed inland along the railways and conquered the whole eastern half of China, the richest and most highly developed part of the country. Chiang Kai-shek had the support only of the agriculturally rich province of Szechwan, and of the scarcely developed provinces surrounding it. Here there was as yet no industry. Everything in the way of machinery and supplies that could be transported from the hastily dismantled factories was carried westward. Students and professors went west with all the contents of their universities, and worked on in small villages under very difficult conditions—one of the most memorable achievements of this war for China. But all this was by no means enough for waging a defensive war against Japan. Even the famous Burma Road could not save China.

By 1940–1941 Japan had attained her war aim: China was no longer a dangerous adversary. She was still able to engage in small-scale fighting, but could no longer secure any decisive result. Puppet governments were set up in Peking, Canton, and Nanking, and the Japanese waited for these governments gradually to induce supporters of Chiang Kai-shek to come over to their side. Most was expected of Wang Ching-wei, who headed the new Nanking government. He was one of the oldest followers of Sun Yat-sen, and was regarded as a democrat with leftist tendencies. In 1925, after Sun Yat-sen's death, he had been for a time the head of the Nanking government, and for a short time in 1930 he had led a government in Peking that was opposed to Chiang Kai-shek. Beyond any question Wang still had many followers, including some in the highest circles at Chungking, men of eastern China who considered that collaboration with Japan, especially in the economic field, offered good prospects. Japan paid lip service to this policy: there was talk of sister peoples, which could help each other and supply each other's needs. There was propaganda for a new 'Greater East Asian' philosophy, *Wang-tao*, in accordance with which all the peoples of the East could live together in peace under a thinly disguised dictatorship. What actually happened was that everywhere Japanese capitalists established themselves in the former Chinese industrial plants, bought up land and securities, and exploited the country for the conduct of their war.

After the great initial successes of Hitlerite Germany in 1939–1941, Japan became convinced that the time had come for a decisive blow against the positions of the Western European powers and the United States in the Far East. Lightning blows were struck at Hong Kong and Singapore, at French Indo-China, and at the Netherlands

East Indies. The American navy seemed to have been eliminated by the attack on Pearl Harbor (December 1941), and one group of islands after another fell into the hands of the Japanese. Japan was at the gates of India and Australia. Russia was carrying on a desperate defensive struggle against the Axis, and there was no reason to expect any intervention from her in the Far East. Greater East Asia seemed assured against every danger.

The situation of Chiang Kai-shek's Chungking government seemed hopeless. Even the Burma Road was cut, and supplies could only be sent by air; there was shortage of everything. With immense energy small industries were begun all over western China, often organized as co-operatives; roads and railways were built—but with such resources would it ever be possible to throw the Japanese into the sea? Everything depended on holding out until a new page was turned in Europe. Infinitely slow seemed the progress of the first gleams of hope—the steady front in Burma, the reconquest of the first groups of islands; the first bomb attacks on Japan itself. Even in May 1945, with the war ended in Europe, there seemed no sign of its ending in the Far East. Then came the atom bomb, bringing the collapse of Japan; the Japanese armies receded from China, and suddenly China was free, mistress once more in her own country as she had not been for decades.

Before we have to come back to events of the War, it might be useful to throw a look at the non-political developments of this period between 1927 and 1945.

Until the time of the 'Manchurian incident' (1931), the Nanking government steadily grew in strength. It gained the confidence of the Western powers, who proposed to make use of it in opposition to Japan's policy of expansion in the Pacific sphere. On the strength of this favourable situation in its foreign relations, the Nanking government succeeded in getting rid of one after another of the capitulations. Above all, the administration of the 'Maritime Customs', that is to say of the collection of duties on imports and exports, was brought under the control of the Chinese government (1927): until then it had been under foreign control. Now that China could act with more freedom in the matter of tariffs, the government had greater financial resources, and through this and other measures it became financially more independent of the provinces. It succeeded in building up a small but modern army, loyal to the government and superior to the still existing provincial armies. This army gained its military experience in skirmishes with the Communists and the remaining generals and later fought gallantly the Japanese invaders. The financial situation, however, deteriorated quickly during the War, because large parts of China were not under the control of the Nationalists, and the cost of the War climbed higher and higher.

On the literary front, many writers began to publish in the 1920s and 1930s who now are recognized as representatives of China's modern literature. Some of these writers were leftists, after a start along liberal lines, such as Lu Hsün (1881–1936) whose 'Diary of a Madman' and 'True Story of Ah O' have gained general acclaim. Mao Tun's (1898–   ) 'Twilight', a novel about life in Shanghai, is equally well known. On the other side of the liberal writers, we should mention Lao Shê (1898–   ), whose 'Ricksha Boy' found many readers even in the West, Pa Chin (1904–   ), a more romantic writer, and Lin Yü-t'ang. Lin is probably best known in the West for those of his works in which he wanted to show the West what China was and is, and how we should look at China. But Lin has also ventured into other fields, such as the project of a large, modern Chinese–English dictionary, which was recently published, or his translations of Chinese classics and literary masterpieces into English.

CHAPTER TWELVE

Present-day China

(A) THE GROWTH OF COMMUNISM

In order to understand today's China, we have to go back in time to report events which were cut short or left out of our earlier discussion in order to present them in the context of this chapter.

Although Socialism and Communism had been known in China long ago, this line of development of Western philosophy had interested Chinese intellectuals much less than liberalistic, democratic Western ideas. It was widely believed that Communism had no real prospects for China, as a dictatorship of the proletariat seemed to be relevant only in a highly industrialized and not in an agrarian society. Thus, in its beginning the 'Movement of May Fourth' of 1919 had Western ideological traits but was not communistic. This changed with the success of Communism in Russia and with the theoretical writings of Lenin. Here it was shown that Communist theories could be applied to a country similar to China in its level of development.

Thus, we may regard the 'Movement of May Fourth' as the critical point at which the division began which finally ended with the establishment of the People's Democratic Republic. We mentioned already that the Communist Party (CCP) was founded in Shanghai in 1921. As in all Communist movements, the leaders were members of the middle class and well-educated men who deserted their own class, made themselves fighters for the proletariat, and worked for the destruction of the other classes. The leaders who emerged in the first years after the founding of the CCP came in part from the Peking group, and from the Shanghai group, but also from Chinese who had been students in Europe: Chou En-lai and Li Li-san learned about Communism when they were students in Paris; Chu Tê in Germany.

When Chiang Kai-shek entered Shanghai and tried to exterminate the Communists, some leaders could escape to the interior. Mao Tsê-tung moved close to his home and took a position which is described well in the classic novel 'Shui-hu-chuan' which he knows so well and quotes often: he settled on the Chin-kang shan, a mountain area between the provinces of Hunan and Kiangsi, i.e. an area in which the powers of either province were weak and where by clever moves any danger from one province could be avoided by moving into the adjacent one. Like the heroes of the novel. Mao collected men around him and made his first, unsuccessful rising in September 1927. Chu Tê and Ch'en Yi attempted a coup in Kiangsi, which also failed. The rest of the party assembled in Hankow, replaced Ch'en Tu-hsiu by the pro-Soviet Li Li-san (until 1930).

The years following the débâcle of 1927 are years of political 'soul-searching' in China as well as in the Soviet Union. The main question was: why was the attempt to establish a socialist regime in China a failure? The tactic which Chinese Communists, operating together with Chiang's armies, and supported by the Russian advisers, adopted had been developed on the basis of classical Marxist-Leninist doctrine, which assumed that a socialist revolution has to be carried by the urban proletariat. This was the tactic which had brought Communism in the Soviet Union to success, it was said. The other side, the ideological leader of which was K. A. Wittfogel, was of the opinion that the failure had been caused by the application of a strategy which was based upon European economy and society; however, China's society was an 'Oriental society', based not on rain agriculture, but on irrigation agriculture. In such a society, revolutionary tactics and strategy have to be different, and the fight has to be carried out by a group other than the urban proletariat, at least in the beginnings. Within the Chinese CCP, Ch'en Tu-hsiu was the representative of the 'classical' theory; it would be wrong to call Li Ta-chao the representative of the theory of 'Oriental Society', because these ideas became known in China more widely only after 1927, but Li was of the opinion that for a revolution the collaboration of the peasantry was essential.

In the Hankow talks, the Soviet side got the victory and Mao's opinions were rejected. Yet Mao gained some successes in Kiangsi and P'eng Te-huei emerged as one of his best military leaders. Thus, a small Communist republic was proclaimed on 7 November 1931 in Kiangsi.

Chiang tried to consolidate China, as we have seen, and naturally, the elimination of Communism was one of his aims. Between 1930 and 1934, he launched five campaigns against Kiangsi. At first, he was not successful, partly because the 19th Route Army which had fought the Japanese in Shanghai (1932) upon its return to Fukien turned itself into a 'People's Revolutionary Army' and took up contacts with the Kiangsi regime. From 1934 on, however, the new strategy which Chiang, with his German advisers developed, forced the Communists to give up Kiangsi. On 15 October 1934, they decided to move. It is said that over 100,000 men started out their 'legendary' Long March through all of west China, often through areas inhabited by minorities, always on the flight before Chiang's and other armies, troubled by dissensions within the Party. It is during these years that Chou En-lai emerged as the military and political leader. In December 1936 the marchers settled in Yen-an (Yenan) in Shensi province; only some 30,000 made it. It is here, in an area which was remote, poor, and not yet under the control of Chiang's forces, Mao Tsê-tung came up as the leader of the CCP. The Party took up some contacts with Chang Hsüeh-liang, the son of Chang Tso-lin, who had control over Manchuria (Chinese term: 'Eastern Three Provinces', later and today 'North East'), who was afraid of Chiang's strength. On 12 December 1936 his men succeeded in kidnapping Chiang and in extorting some concessions from him. This was the time when a Japanese attack was in the air, and a proposal for a 'United Front' was made.

When the Japanese began their war with the Marco Polo Bridge 'incident' (7 July 1937), Chiang's forces were fully engaged, while Mao's CCP began to organize guerrilla units behind the Japanese forces and to strengthen his own territory which was not yet threatened by the Japanese. In the summer of 1938. Mao again committed himself to collaborate with the KMT, however, the situation remained the same: neither party trusted the other. Thus, many troops which could well have been used to fight the Japanese had to be kept in waiting.

As everywhere, the attack by Hitler upon the Soviet Union produced great changes in Communist parties. Suddenly, the Soviet Union, which now had to assume that Japan would attack Russia once it had sufficiently subdued China, shifted from an interest in the Communist Yenan group to the Chiang government and supplied it with material assistance, as the United States did. The United States, deeply involved in the fight against the Japanese and against Hitler, had an interest in persuading the KMT to co-operate with the CCP and made, through General Stillwell, attempts to form a United Front. Like so many democratic countries, they did not understand that for Communists a 'United Front' of any kind is a strategic movement at the time of relative weakness, to lull the enemy in security, to get its men inside the other side and to move into important or key positions so that later they can take the organization over; reading of Lenin would have given insight into this strategy.

When the War in Europe was over and the defeat of Japan expected, the Soviet Union entered the war against Japan (8 August 1945) by occupying Manchuria, Jehol and Chahar. They looted Manchuria, the most industrialized part of China, and were also able to supply the CCP with the weapons they took from the Japanese. This enabled the CCP to move into Manchuria and parts of north China, by accepting Japanese surrender, until Chiang by agreement with the Japanese succeeded in having the Japanese surrender to his armies.

The Soviet Union offered Chiang (14 August 1945) a treaty of friendship, but under the condition that they were given special privileges in Manchuria, similar to those imperial Russia had had until 1904. However, they promised to evacuate Manchuria as quickly as possible.

In the face of the Yenan government's moves, Chiang had to ask the United States to assist him in airlifting troops from west China to the east. Thus, his troops could occupy the great cities of the east when the Japanese surrendered. On 2 August 1945, Chiang made an attempt to reach an agreement with Mao in Chungking, but any agreement was now impossible. When the Soviets retreated from Manchuria, they let the CCP move in and prevented as much as they could the move of Chiang's troops into Manchuria. Again, General Marshall's mission in late 1945 attempted to induce the KMT and the CCP to form an integrated National Army, to convoke a political conference and a cease-fire. Fighting began soon, as negotiations were, as predictable, unsuccessful. In the first phase Chiang's troops were successful; in March 1947, they even entered Yenan. Finally, Chiang could move large numbers of his troops into Manchuria, where he was opposed by Lin Piao. Lin, well equipped with Japanese arms, defeated him, so that Chiang lost his best troops. With this defeat, general demoralization began. September 1948, Ch'en Yi occupied Shantung. Then came in late 1948 the decisive battle near Hsü-chou, which ended with defections from Chiang and therefore, a defeat. On 23 January 1949 Peking fell; on 24 April Nanking; and by 1 October 1949, all of China's mainland was in the hand of the Communist regime.

The end of Chiang on the mainland was not simply a military defeat. When the Nationalist government took over the administration, it lacked popular support in the areas liberated from the Japanese. Farmers who had been given land by the Communists, or who had been promised it, were afraid that their former landlords, whether they had remained to collaborate with the Japanese or had fled to west China, would regain control of the land. Workers hoped for new social legislation and rights. Businessmen and industrialists were faced with destroyed factories, worn-out or antiquated equipment, and an unchecked inflation which induced them to shift their accounts into foreign banks or to favour short-term gains rather than long-term investments. As in all countries which have suffered from a long war and an occupation, the youth believed that the old regime had been to blame, and saw promise and hope on the political left. And, finally, the Nationalist soldiers, most of whom had been separated for years from their homes and families, were not willing to fight other Chinese in the civil war now well under way; they wanted to go home and start a new life. The Communists, however, were now well organized militarily and were constantly strengthened by deserters from the KMT.

(B) NATIONALIST CHINA IN TAIWAN

The Nationalist government retreated to Taiwan (Formosa) with those soldiers who remained loyal. This island was returned to China after the defeat of Japan, though final disposition of its status had not yet been determined.

Taiwan's original population had been made up of more than a dozen tribes who are probably distant relatives of tribes in the Philippines. These are Taiwan's 'aborigines', altogether about 200,000 people in 1948.

At about the time of the Sung dynasty, Chinese began to establish outposts on the island; these developed into regular agricultural settlements towards the end of the Ming dynasty. Immigration increased in the eighteenth and especially the nineteenth centuries. These Chinese immigrants and their descendants are the 'Taiwanese', Taiwan's main population of about 8 million people as of 1948.

Taiwan was at first a part of the province of Fukien, whence most of its Chinese settlers came; there was also a minority of Hakka, Chinese from Kuangtung province. When Taiwan was ceded to Japan, it was still a colonial area with much lawlessness and disorder, but with a number of flourishing towns and a growing population. The Japanese, who sent administrators but no settlers, established law and order, protected the aborigines from land-hungry Chinese settlers, and attempted to abolish headhunting by the aborigines and to raise the cultural level in general. They built a road and railway system and strongly stressed the production of sugar cane and rice. During the Second World War, the island suffered from air attacks and from the inability of the Japanese to protect its industries.

After Chiang Kai-shek and the remainder of his army and of his government officials arrived in Taiwan, they were followed by others fleeing from the Communist regime, mainly from Chekiang, Kiangsu, and the northern provinces of the mainland. Eventually, there were on Taiwan about two million of these 'mainlanders', as they have sometimes been called.

When the Chinese Nationalists took over from the Japanese, they assumed all the leading positions in the government. The Taiwanese nationals who had opposed the Japanese were disappointed; for their part, the Nationalists felt threatened because of their minority position. The next years, up to 1952, were characterized by bloody confrontations. Tensions persisted for many years, but have lessened since about 1960.

The new government of Taiwan resembled China's pre-war government under Chiang Kai-shek. First, to maintain his claim to the legitimate rule of all of China, Chiang retained—and controlled through his party, the KMT—his former government organization, complete with cabinet ministers, administrators, and elected parliament, under the name 'Central Government of China'. Second, the actual government of Taiwan, which he considered one of China's provinces, was organized as the 'Provincial Government of Taiwan', whose leading positions were at first in the hands of KMT mainlanders. There have since been regular elections for the provincial assembly, for local government councils and boards, and for various provincial and local positions. Third, the military forces were organized under the leadership and command of mainlanders. And finally, the education system was set up in accordance with former mainland practices by mainland specialists. However, evolutionary changes soon occurred.

The government's aim was to make Mandarin Chinese the language of all Chinese in Taiwan, as it had been in mainland China long before the War, and to weaken the Taiwanese dialects. Soon almost every child had a minimum of six years of education (increased in 1968 to nine years), with Mandarin Chinese as the medium of instruction. In the beginning few Taiwanese qualified as teachers because, under Japanese rule, Japanese had been the medium of instruction. As the children of Taiwanese and mainland families went to school together, the Taiwanese children quickly learned Mandarin, while most mainland children became familiar with the Taiwan dialect. For the generation in school today, the difference between mainlander and Taiwanese has lost its importance. At the same time, more teachers of Taiwanese origin, but with modern training, have begun to fill first the ranks of elementary, later of high-school, and now even of university, instructors, so that the end of mainland predominance in the educational system is foreseeable.

The country is still ruled by the KMT, but although at first hardly any Taiwanese belonged to the Party, many of the elective jobs and almost all positions in the provincial government are at present in the hands of Taiwanese independents, or KMT members, more of whom are continuously entering the central government as well. Because military service is compulsory, the majority of common soldiers are Taiwanese: as career officers grow older and their sons show little interest in an army career, more Taiwan-Chinese are occupying higher army positions. Foreign policy and major political decisions still lie in the hands of mainland Chinese, but economic power, once monopolized by them, is now held by Taiwan-Chinese.

This shift gained impetus with the end of American economic aid. which had tied local businessmen to American industry and thus worked to the advantage of mainland Chinese, for these had contacts in the United States, whereas the Taiwan-Chinese had contacts only in Japan. After the termination of American economic aid, Taiwanese trade with Japan, the Philippines, and Korea grew in importance and with it the economic strength of Taiwan-Chinese businessmen. After 1964, Taiwan became a strong competitor of Hong Kong and Japan in some export industries, such as electronics and textiles. We can regard Taiwan from 1964 on as occupying the 'take-off' stage, to use Rostow's terminology—a stage of rapid development of new, principally light and consumer, industries. There has been a rapid rise of industrial towns around the major cities, and there are already many factories in the countryside, even in some villages. Electrification is essentially completed, and heavy industries, such as fertilizer and assembly plants and oil refineries, now exist.

This rapid industrialization was accompanied by an unusually fast development of agriculture. A land-reform programme limited land ownership, reduced rents, and redistributed formerly Japanese-owned land. This was the programme that the Nationalist government had attempted unsuccessfully to enforce in liberated China after the Pacific War. It is well known that the abolition of landlordism and the distribution of land to small farmers do not in themselves improve or enlarge production. The Joint Council on Rural Reconstruction, on which American advisers worked with Chinese specialists to devise a system comparable to American agricultural extension services but possessing elements of community development, introduced better seeds, more and better fertilizers, and numerous other innovations which the farmers quickly adopted, with the result that the island became self-supporting, in spite of a steadily growing population (16 million in 1974).

At the same time, the government succeeded in stabilizing the currency and in eliminating corruption, thus re-establishing public confidence and security. Good incomes from farming as well as from industries were invested on the island instead of flowing into foreign banks. In addition, the population had enough surplus money to buy the products of the new domestic industries as these appeared. Thus, the industrialization of Taiwan may be called 'industrialization without tears', without the suffering, that is, of proletarian masses who produce objects which they cannot afford for themselves. Today, even lower middle-class families have television consoles which cost the equivalent of US $300; they own electric fans and radios; they are buying Taiwan-produced refrigerators and air conditioners; and more and more think of buying Taiwan-assembled cars. They encourage their children to finish high school and to attend college if at all possible; competition for admission is very strong in spite of the continuous building of new schools and universities. Education to the level of the B.A. is of good quality, but for some graduate study students are still sent abroad. Taiwan complains about the 'brain drain', as about 93 per cent of its students who go overseas do not return, but it has more than sufficient trained manpower to continue its development, and in any case there would not be enough jobs available if all the students returned.

When Chiang Kai-shek died (5 April 1975), Taiwan had changed from an underdeveloped colony into the country with the second-highest standard of living in Asia. His son Chiang Ching-kuo became leader of the KMT and remained premier, the office he had held in the last years of his father's life. With Chiang died the last of the four great men of the Second World War, and at the same time ended a period of world history. For the first time, a group of small countries which produce an essential raw material, oil, could cause a serious depression among the industrialized countries (1973); for the first time, America lost a war (Vietnam) which it could not win after the decision was made not to invade North Vietnam; public pressure forced a withdrawal (1973). America gave up its role in South-East Asia which caused the breakdown of Vietnam, Cambodia and Laos (1975), and the creation of three new Communist states. This will change the total power relation in the Far East and South-East Asia and initiate a new period. Of all countries which might be affected by these changes, Taiwan is the one which is most united, but also one of the smallest.

(C) PEOPLE'S REPUBLIC OF CHINA (1949–   )

1   *General remarks*

Perhaps a historian should not write about anything that is still ongoing or less than a hundred years old, and leave the field to a political scientist. Writing about a controlled society is even more dangerous. We cannot freely travel and freely speak to the common man. If we can speak to a political leader we know that he says what he wants us to believe; and if a common man talks to us, he, too, would say what he is supposed to say or what he wants us to believe. We can read those books, pamphlets, and papers which the regime lets out, i.e. certainly not all existing publications; we can listen to some radio and television emissions, but they are sent out for specific purposes. History in a controlled socialist society is not a field of scholarship, but a piece of political education, subjected to constant rewriting when political conditions change. Many specialists try to decipher the messages contained in these materials, but the results are never reliable. From this results the fact that those who study a totalitarian regime often are the victims of propaganda. Or, they see and know the truth but do not dare to write it, because it would make it impossible for them to get an entry visa next time. This is aggravated by the credulity and ignorance of many Americans: they hear words like 'democracy' and think of American democracy; they think Chinese react in the same way as we do and interpret what they see as we would interpret information in our countries. Many of the visitors of today's China have seen China during the War, in its worst time, and, compared to that, they are greatly impressed with the changes; but had they travelled in China before 1937, they would have a different impression. Others talk about mainland China without having seen Taiwan: this would give them some possibility of evaluation. Thus, I do not think it is possible for any of us to write an accurate and objective history of the last thirty years of China; all we can do is to try.

Let us first discuss a few general points. The quick development of the People's Republic is not astonishing. Both Taiwan and mainland China have developed extremely quickly. The reasons do not seem to lie solely in the form of government, for the preconditions for a 'take-off' existed in China as early as the 1920s, if not earlier. That is, the quick development of China could have started forty years ago but was prevented, primarily for political reasons. One of the main preconditions for quick development is that a large part of the population is inured to hard and repetitive work. The Chinese farmer was accustomed to such work; he put more time and energy into his land than any other farmer. He and his fellows were the industrial workers of the future: reliable, hard-working, tractable, intelligent. To train them was easy, and absenteesim was never a serious problem, as it is in other developing nations. Another pre-condition is the existence of sufficient trained people to manage industry. Forty years ago China had enough such men to start modernization; foreign assistance would have been necessary in some fields, but only briefly.

Another requirement (at least in the period before radio and television) is general literacy. Meaningful statistical data on literacy in China before 1937 are lacking. Some authors remark that before 1800 probably all upper-class sons and most daughters were educated, and that men in the middle and even in the lower classes often had some degree of literacy. In this context 'educated' means that these persons could read classical poetry and essays written in literary Chinese, which was not the language of daily conversation. 'Literacy', however, might mean only that a person could read and write some 600 characters, enough to conduct a business and to read simple stories. Although newspapers today have a stock of about 6,000 characters, only some 600 characters are commonly used, and a farmer or worker can manage well with a knowledge of about 100 characters. Statements to the effect that in 1935 some 70 per cent of all men and 95 per cent of all women were illiterate cannot include all those millions who could read what they had to read in their professions; probably not even those who could read some 600 characters. There are sufficient data to establish that the literacy programme of the KMT had penetrated the countryside and had reached even outlying villages before 1940.

The transportation system in China before the war was not highly developed, but numerous railroads connecting the main industrial centres did exist, and bus and truck services connected small towns with the larger centres. What were missing in the pre-war years were laws to protect the investor, efficient credit facilities, an insurance system supported by law, and a modern tax structure. In addition, the monetary system was inflation-prone. Although sufficient capital probably could have been mobilized within the country, the available resources went into military construction and preparation.

The failure to capitalize on existing means of development before the War resulted from the chronic unrest caused by warlordism, revolutionaries and foreign invaders, which occupied the energies of the Nationalist government from its establishment to its fall. Once a stable government free from internal troubles arose, national development, whether private or socialist, could proceed at a rapid pace.

Thus, the development of Communist China is not a miracle, possible only because of its form of government. What is unusual about Communist China is the fact that it is the only nation possessing a highly developed culture of its own to have jettisoned it in favour of a foreign one. What missionaries had dreamed of for centuries and knew they would never accomplish, Mao Tsê-tung achieved; he imposed an ideology created by Europeans and understandable only in the context of central Europe in the nineteenth century. We speak of 'Maoism' today, and admittedly, in a few points, Maoism differs from Russian Communism as developed by Lenin and Stalin. But the steps which were taken in China to develop the new society are much too similar to those taken in the Soviet Union to enable us to regard Maoism as a completely different system. Confrontations between China and the Soviet Union show again and again that China believes that its form of Communism is the correct one and that China should be the leader of the Communist world, not Russia, which has 'deviated'.

This may change over time. One school of analysts believes that the friction between Soviet Russia and Communist China indicates that China's Communism has become Chinese. These men point out that Communist Chinese practices are often direct continuations of earlier Chinese practices, customs, and attitudes. And they predict that this trend will continue, resulting in a form of socialism or communism distinctly different from that found in any other country. Another school, however, believes that Communism precedes 'Sinism', and that the regime will slowly eliminate traits which once were typical of China and replace them with institutions developed out of Marxist thinking. In any case, for the present, we believe that in present-day China many traits are preserved which were developed in the old time but can be easily integrated in so far as they contribute to the stability of the system. Later we will discuss some of these traits.

2 *Political development*

After the foundation of the 'People's Democratic Republic' on 1 October 1948, a government was created which was modelled after the Soviet system. It did, in the beginning, recognize the existence of other, small, parties which never had any say in politics, and recognized four classes of people: workers, farmers, small and big capitalists, all under the 'democratic dictatorship under the leadership of the CCP', as Russia had in the early years. Executive, legislative, and judicial powers were in the hands of the Central People's Government Council, which had 71 members and Mao Tsê-tung as chairman. The actual work was done by a State Administrative Council, somewhat comparable to a cabinet, responsible to the Government Council or to Mao. The country remained subdivided into provinces and districts. A new constitution was proclaimed in 1954 which created an All China People's Congress which laid down the general line of politics. Below this was a Party Congress, inside which there was the Central Committee, appointed for a five-year period. The actual political decisions were made here. The constitution established two classes of citizens: men and women over 18 were full citizens; people regarded as landlords and as counter-revolutionaries were excluded. The CCP, which in 1949 already had, it is said, 4·5 million members, was the élite of the citizens. It should be mentioned that to this day even the descendants of the outcasts are outcasts and do not have the same rights as other citizens.

In order to solidify the regime, the great land reform was begun in

June 1950, following in its steps very closely the Russian model. The first step was the elimination of those people who were declared to be landlords. If we think of landlords as men who own hundreds of acres and had these worked by tenants, we are mistaken. In comparison to Western farms, even 'big' landlords had little land. The CCP had already, during their Kiangsi period, difficulties in establishing whom they wanted to define as landlord and as 'rich peasant'. The land situation was so complicated that in one case almost half of those persons who first had been regarded as landlords or rich peasants had to be reclassified as ordinary farmers, because some farmers owned some land and rented more land; some used hired labour only in some seasons and not permanently, some had become relatively rich recently through their own labour, and so on. In general, according to estimates, four-fifths of the land was operated by owners in north China, three-fifths in central China, and one-half in south China. Landlordism was not as extensive as had been asserted. The cost of this land reform and the elimination of other enemies in human lives is not known. However, the most conservative estimates mention two million.

As in Soviet Russia, this land reform, which gave land to those who work on the land, was followed by taking the land away from them in the drive towards collectivization, at first the establishment of co-operative farms (1953–1957). The last step then began in 1958 with the establishment of communes and collectivization. Some 26,000 communes were created, each one made up of thirty former co-operatives; each commune with a population of about 25,000 people. The communes were units which included farmers as well as rural industries. It may well be that the original aim of this was to enable each such unit to continue to offer resistance in case of a war and a breakdown of central organization. The famous creation of the 'backyard furnaces', which produced high-cost iron of low quality, seems to have had a similar purpose: to teach citizens how to produce iron for armaments in case of war and enemy occupation, when only guerrilla resistance would be possible. In the same year, aggressive actions against offshore, Nationalist-held islands increased. China may have believed that war with the United States was imminent. To this day, no analysis of the communes is possible. Several scholars assert that the lowest units within the communes are the old, village- and kinship-based groupings, now centrally directed and obliged to follow the plans laid out by the government. Even so, the 'Great Leap Forward' of 1958 brought on a serious crisis, as the Russian advisers had predicted. The years 1961–1964 provided a needed respite from the failures of the Great Leap. Farmers regained limited rights to income from private efforts, and improved farm techniques such as better seed and the use of fertilizer began to produce results. China can now feed her population in normal years.

It should be mentioned that at the same time that rural communes were established, urban communes, too, began to appear. These, however, seem to be not much more than a further attempt at control of what formerly were block and city quarter organizations.

Soon after the establishment of the Peking regime, a pact of friendship and alliance with the Soviet Union was concluded (February 1950), and Soviet specialists and civil and military products poured into China to speed its development. China had to pay for this assistance as well as for the loans it received from Russia, but the application of Russian experience, often involving the duplication of whole factories, was successful. In a few years, China developed its heavy industry, just as Russia had done. It should not be forgotten that Manchuria, as well as other parts of China, had had modern heavy industries long before 1949. The Manchurian factories ceased production because, when the Russians invaded Manchuria at the end of the war, they removed the machinery to Russia.

Similar to Soviet Russia, China developed its five-year plans; the first one only actually began in 1955 and stressed, after the initial work of reconstruction of the damages of revolution, the building of heavy industries. This work was connected with a change of higher instruction. The government stressed training in the technical fields, in order to have sufficient competent technicians; similar to the practice in the Soviet Union, the young men and women were given a relatively brief and specialized training which meant that the manpower needs could quickly be eliminated. There has been great progress since 1955 and China astonished the world when it exploded its first atomic bomb (1966), built with the help of American-trained scientists. We know now that the building of atomic bombs is relatively easy. However, it requires a great investment in means and trained manpower, and the question has been raised whether the propaganda value of the bomb was so great. Other projects had to be postponed which probably were more urgent. Was it done to impress the world with the war potential of a young socialist country? Or was it in response to Soviet threats?

Today, problems in industry still continue. China has discovered oil, mainly in the innermost provinces of Sinkiang, Shensi and Kansu; only the oil from Hei-lung-kiang in northern Manchuria is relatively close to big industrial centres. Offshore oil drilling is planned and the outlook is good, but China has already begun to export oil, to get needed foreign exchange as well as to impress the oil-hungry nations of Asia; yet in spite of stepped-up production, China's production is not yet sufficient (estimated 70 million tons for 1974) to supply its petro-chemical industries, especially fertilizer factories, its agriculture (machines), and its transportation problems (cars, trucks). There are still problems with iron and steel, after the dismal failure of the 'backyard furnaces' which produced at a high cost in fuel and labour very low-quality iron. By 1974, it is estimated, China produced about 400 million tons of coal, an increase of 6 per cent over 1973, but the needs are growing much quicker than the supply.

As in the Soviet Union, the stress upon heavy and military industry together with the farm policy produced strains which found their expression in the so-called 'Hundred Flowers' movement (1956). This event has been explained in different ways. One explanation is that Mao Tsê-tung envisaged that China would rapidly industrialize, and that for this aim China would need all of China's human resources, and that he, therefore, wanted to liberalize the restrictions posed upon non-Party members, so that different opinions could be brought forth and that, at the same time a bureaucratization of the Party could be prevented by the influx of new blood. The other explanation which, to me, seems to be more likely, is that by permitting discussions, the Party could find out who was not in agreement with the Party line and could eliminate such persons. In any case, the outpour of opposition seems to have frightened the leaders and the 'Hundred Flowers' were stopped. The years of 1956–1957 are also the years in which in the Soviet Union the de-Stalinization began and unrest in Eastern Europe developed. Mao and his group remained closer to the Stalin line and the personality cult which was criticized so strongly in the Soviet Union became even stronger in China in the form of a cult of Mao. On the other side, the first measures against bureaucratization of the Party which are to be seen in these years and which grew strongly in the 1960s indicate a position much closer to Trotsky than to Stalin. Perhaps the most important element behind all these 'ideological' speculations is what has always been behind political changes in China: the fight for ultimate power between two cliques.

Certainly, not only the pro-Stalin attitude of Mao, but also the 'deviation' of China in creating communes at a state which, according to the Soviets was premature, and the attempt of China to build up military and atomic strength, was a strain upon the Soviet–Chinese relations. The Russian advisers left and Russian assistance stopped around 1960. From then on, tensions between the two Communist countries began to increase. The Chinese believed that the Soviet Union might try to destroy China's developing atomic industry. There were also numerous clashes of a military character along the northernmost frontier: the Chinese claimed some islands in the frontier river which the Soviets regarded as theirs. And finally, there was a considerable flight of the Turkish (Uighur) inhabitants of Sinkiang into the adjacent areas of the Soviet Union where they had tribal relatives and where the standard of living was a good deal higher, combined with an influx of cadres trained in the Soviet Union which were supposed to incite Sinkiang to rebellion. All these developments which became more and more large-scale in the 1960s forced both countries to keep large armies, fully war-equipped, along the almost endless frontiers (most important in 1969).

This, combined with bad harvests which the government attributed to inclement climate but which seem to have mainly been caused by the commune policy, made the years between 1957 and 1962 years of crisis. The first big outward sign of crisis was the Lu-shan Conference in August 1959 of the Central Committee. Defence Minister P'eng Tê-huai, just returned from Moscow, spoke up against Mao's policies. Mao and his faction were strong enough to swing the situation by dismissing P'eng and replacing him by Lin Piao as new Minister of Defence. The more radical party of Mao decided in favour of 'red' against 'expert' in the discussion whether a Communist should in the first place be a good Communist and only in the second place a good specialist, or whether at this stage of development the most important problem was to mobilize and utilize as many experts as were available and look at ideology only in the second place. Only in the field of agriculture, the Conference made some concessions in the form of temporary relaxations, so that farm production would increase again. The other result of the Conference was that Liu Shao-ch'i emerged as Chairman of the Republic. He had been Vice-Chairman since 1949. Mao did not lose prestige, on the contrary, the cult of Mao was stepped up, but he did lose direct political control. It seems that the developments of 1965 and 1966 are an attempt of Mao to regain full political control.

Major political changes are often in totalitarian societies initiated by outwardly unimportant events. Wu Han, deputy major of Peking, had written in 1961 a play about an official in the Ming time who, supposedly, fought for the right of the common man and opposed the emperor, Hai Jui (1514–1587). This was nothing extraordinary, as Hai Jui was the hero of at least eight classical plays. In late 1965 he published 'Hai Jui dismissed from Office', and this work was strongly attacked by Yao Wen-yüan in Shanghai at the same time that Mao was staying in Shanghai. The 'theoretical question' with Hai Jui was whether a member of the former upper class, the élite, could under any circumstances be regarded as a 'good' man, or, in application to the present, whether an outcast member of Communist society could under any circumstances turn out to be a friend of the people. The criticism was regarded as an attack of the Mao clique against Liu Shao-ch'i to whose clique Wu Han belonged. This event became the forerunner of the so-called 'Great Socialist Cultural Revolution' which officially began on 18 April 1966. The term 'cultural' should not be taken in the common meaning. The first action was that all universities and most schools were closed and remained closed for more than a year, at a time when China needed trained manpower most urgently and quickly. During the course of the 'Cultural Revolution' numerous cultural treasures of China were destroyed. The term seems to mean that a different group of people would come into power and change China's political culture. In fact, Mao mobilized China's youngsters against Liu Shao-ch'i and his clique. The so-called 'Red Guards' rose up everywhere in the country, a sign that the movement was well prepared, and masses stormed offices of Party officials as well as houses of officials and other persons disliked by the regime; they attacked professors and dishonoured Party leaders. Masses of them streamed through the country up to Peking. Much more so than during the 'Hundred Flowers' movement, the young radicals went overboard, alienated even the friends of Mao and threatened to become a danger to all the over-aged party leaders, so that, finally, the army had to interfere and to restore some order again. The worst was over in the autumn of 1967, when a few schools began to open again, but fights, especially in provincial centres, continued until late 1968. By that time, Mao was in full control and had gained a decisive victory over Liu Shao-ch'i who from then on disappeared from the political horizon. With him went Chu Tê, the man who had created the Red Army (People's Liberation Army). Lin Piao became the First Vice-Chairman of the Central Committee, that is, he became the second most powerful man in the regime and the designated successor of Mao. With him rose Ch'en Po-ta and Chiang Ch'ing, Mao's third wife. Chiang had been an actress and film heroine before the Revolution and after a life full of changes had felt forced to leave Shanghai and the film world and joined the Communist camp in Yenan, where she became the lover and later the wife of Mao. The Party Congress of April 1969 made these changes official; it was the first congress since 1958.

In 1971, Lin Piao (born 1908) died in a plane crash in Outer Mongolia. The background of this event is still not quite clear. It is said that Lin tried to assume the highest power and control with the help of parts of the military in the areas of Central China; that his plans, however, were betrayed by his own daughter, so that the revolt could not start, Lin had to escape, and was either shot down or crashed on his flight to Soviet Russia. As Lin had been designated to become Mao's successor, major reshuffling was necessary. This was finalized in the People's Congress of 13–17 January 1974, in Peking. The result was a kind of compromise. Chou En-lai (age 76), of weak health, was elected as Premier. Chou is certainly the most able living politician of China and regarded as a moderate man, though close to Mao. His friend Yeh Chien-ying, Party Vice-Chairman, became Minister of Defence.

But the new government included Teng Hsiao-p'ing (age 70), who became the most senior of the Vice-Premiers. Teng was one of the most prominent victims of the 'Cultural Revolution'. Chu Tê (age 88) was also rehabilitated and became Chairman of the National People's Congress. On the other, radical, side, only Chang Chun-chiao of the Shanghai group, became a Vice-Premier, and Mrs Chiang Ch'ing is now only a member of the Central Politburo. Mao received new powers and, most important, the control of the army. Many regard this cabinet as a 'patchwork' to prepare for the moment when Mao as well as Chou En-lai will disappear (Chou died 1975). It is impossible to predict what then will come. Certainly, the tension between the radical (Mao) and the 'revisionist' (former Liu Shao-ch'i) cliques is still as strong as before.

3 Foreign relations

In contrast to the opinion of many western scholars who, like Western politicians, have swallowed the Confucian myth of the peaceful Chinese, China has a long military tradition. The most popular folk novels and theatre plays glorify war and military heroes. The backbone of the People's Republic is the army which consists of a central military élite and five other élite groups which emerged as the 'People's Liberation Army' during the revolutionary wars. Within these army groups exist tensions and rivalries. More important, however, are the tensions which are created by the existence of two power groups within each army: the unit commanders and the political commissars—a copy of the Soviet system of the early revolutionary period. The third partner in these rivalries are the civil party administrators whose role is similar to the civil administrators in imperial China. These tensions played a decisive role in the liquidation of the 'Red Guards' during the 'Cultural Revolution' and in the 1975 Party Congress.

However, thus far, the army has been successful not only in the preservation of the regime in the country, but also in conflicts on and beyond its frontiers.

China's military strength was first demonstrated in the Korean War when Chinese armies entered Korea (October 1950). Their successes contributed to the prestige of the Peking regime at home and abroad, but while South Korea retained its independence, North Korea came under Soviet and not under Chinese influence.

In the same year, China invaded and conquered Tibet. Tibet, under Manchu rule until 1911, had achieved a certain degree of independence thereafter: no republican Chinese regime ever ruled Lhasa. The military conquest of Tibet is regarded by many as an act of Chinese imperialism, or colonialism, as the Tibetans certainly did not want to belong to China or be forced to change their traditional form of government. Having regarded themselves as subjects of the Manchu but not of the Chinese, they rose against the Communist rulers in March 1959, but without success.

Chinese control of Tibet, involving the construction of numerous roads, airstrips, and military installations, as well as differences concerning the international border, led in 1959 to conflicts with India. It seems today that the military conflicts, in which India was the loser, were started by India rather than by China. It is true that the borders between China and India were uncertain and looked different depending on whether one used Manchu or Indian maps. But looking at the recent consolidation of India's grip over Kashmir, its domination of Sikkim, its action in Bengal, we see a clear pattern into which the conflict with China fits well.

China's other border problem was with Burma. Early in 1960 the two countries concluded a border agreement which ended disputes dating from British colonial times. But as Burma's policy oscillates between different forms of Socialism, at the moment apparently China seems to be more interested in influencing the outcome of these internal tensions.

Very early in its existence Communist China assumed control of Sinkiang, Chinese Central Asia, a large area originally inhabited by Turkish and Mongolian tribes and states, later conquered by the Manchu, and then integrated into China in the early nineteenth century. The Communist action was to be expected, although after the Revolution of 1911 Chinese rule over this area had been erratic, and during the Pacific War some Soviet-inspired hope had existed that Sinkiang might gain independence, following the example of Outer Mongolia, another country which had been attached to the Manchu until 1911 and which, with Russian assistance, had gained its independence from China. Sinkiang is of great importance to Communist China as the site of large sources of oil and of atomic industries and testing grounds. The government has stimulated and often forced Chinese immigration into Sinkiang, so that the erstwhile Turkish and Mongolian majorities have become minorities, envious of their ethnic brothers in Soviet Central Asia who now enjoy a much higher standard of living and more freedom.

Inner Mongolia had a brief dream of independence under Japanese protection during the War. But the majority of the population was

Chinese, and already before the Pacific War, the country had been divided into three Chinese provinces, of which the Chinese Communists gained control without delay.

In general, when the Chinese Communists discuss territorial claims, they appear to seek the restoration of borders that China claimed in the eighteenth century. Thus, they make occasional remarks about the Ili area and parts of Eastern Siberia, which the Manchu either lost to the Russians or claimed as their territory. North Vietnam is probably aware that Imperial China exercised political rights over Tongking and Annam (the present-day North and part of South Vietnam). China does not seem to have participated in the Vietnam War with its army, but has supplied the North Vietnamese with military equipment and advisers, as did the Soviet Union. The whole Asian situation should be seen in world perspective. Clearly, the Korean War was the beginning of the decline of American power; in fact, it was a war which the United States lost. The war in Vietnam, Cambodia and Laos was also lost: the United States succeeded in their 'Peace with honour' only in being allowed to bring their troops out of the area, while the war continued uninterrupted. Thus, while the United States faded out of Asia like Great Britain had during and right after the Second World War, the real question is now whether China or the Soviet Union should take over. The countries of South-East Asia are in a difficult situation: China is a close neighbour, and it is always the best policy to be allied with the power which is in the rear of the neighbour, which in this case would be the Soviet Union. But will they be able to sustain their factual independence with the assistance of distant Russia? Or will they end up with a nominal independence?

China's South Asia policy was, to this date, not fully successful. One result of the war with India was that China came closer to Pakistan, but on the other side, India turned towards the Soviet Union, which supported it in the interference in East Pakistan and the creation of Bangladesh. China's attempts to gain influence in the Near East, too, were not successful, and the African situation is still too unclear: both countries try to gain influence but none has yet shown much success.

These tensions between the two powers show up clearly in the international party meetings. Here, the split with the Russian Communist Party deepened strongly during the meetings of 1966 and 1969. The Russian party could neither reintegrate the Chinese party into the old framework, nor prevent China's influence over Communist parties in countries thus far aligned with the Soviet Union who became interested in China. The Chinese Party regards itself as the true successor of the Communist Party after the decease of

Stalin, and brands the Soviet Party as being revisionist. China has also indicated that it is the true representative of the Third World, or in other words, of the non-white world, and pointed to the fact that the Soviet Union and its Eastern European colonies are, after all, heirs of white supremacy.

President Nixon's first China visit (1972) was an attempt to exploit the tensions and achieve a solution of some kind in South-East Asia, and, finally, to open trade with Communist China. For China, this visit was one of its easiest and greatest successes. Nixon's visit was seen as a 'tributary mission' of the old time: a foreign power sends its ruler to show its submission to China, by bringing rare animals and other 'products of the country' to China and asking for favours. No other measure could have strengthened the prestige of China inside the country more than this one. The visit could have taken place at a neutral location, or the conference in Warsaw which had been held for many years could have been stepped up or been transferred to a neutral place if the main aim had been to increase contacts and trade. Thus far, the trade relations are unimportant and depend fully on the political aims of China which can step them up or stop them at will. The United States also had to indicate its readiness to sell out Taiwan, a process which is now under way, in order to get trade promises. China finally could use the 'friendship' with the United States to exercise some pressure upon the Soviet Union. There cannot be any doubt, however, that China still regards the United States as a main enemy, and that the United States will not at all succeed in playing the Soviets against China and vice versa: in the ultimate case, both countries would go together against the common enemy.

A further result of the Nixon visit was the acceptance of China into the United Nations and the rejection of, what would seem natural, the recognition of Taiwan as a member of the United Nations, though with a status different from its former one. China has always openly declared that it does not agree with the principles of the United Nations, but can now use this platform to propagate its ideas and aims.

Another line of Chinese foreign policy is similar to policies of Fascist Italy and Nazi Germany: the attempt to make use of ethnic minorities as a political tool. The events in Indonesia which ended with a complete failure and the death of a great number of Indonesian Chinese, and the attempts to influence Chinese-Americans, which have thus far not been successful either, are examples. Many overseas Chinese who have been invited to visit China have not returned with enthusiasm for the new China, but have kept quiet in order not to endanger their relatives inside China and so as not to make a second visit to their families impossible. Like other countries under a dictatorial regime, China does not allow its citizens to leave the country; exceptions are made only in special cases, mainly with old people who are unable to work productively. As the only way by which ethnic Chinese can secretly leave the country is Hong Kong, and as Hong Kong, already overcrowded, is not happy to receive more people, while China tries to prevent illegal emigration, the number of emigrants is a kind of thermometer of the internal situation. The high point of illegal emigration was in 1962 (165,000 persons). After 1962, the numbers decreased, to increase again steadily from 1967 on. The estimated number in 1974 was 70,000. We have no data on the number of inhabitants of Sinkiang leaving for the Soviet Union.

4 *Social developments*

Chinese leaders realize that an improved level of living is difficult to attain while the birth rate remains high. They have hesitated to adopt a family-planning policy, which would fly in the face of Marxist doctrine, although for a short period family planning was openly recommended. Their most efficient method of limiting the birth rate has been to recommend postponement of marriage. Birth control pills are available, and to women who have already two children, sterilization is mentioned in case of a third child. We have, however, no statistical data on average age at marriage, extent of use of family-planning devices and number of actual sterilizations. It is said that the average life expectancy, supposedly 53 years in 1949, has gone up to over 70 years. In Taiwan during the War and under Japanese rule, life expectancy for men was 41, for women 45·7 years (1950); it is now 65·5 for men and 71 for women (end of 1974); the Taiwanese data seem quite reliable. The total population of China has been variously estimated between 600 and 800 million. The 1953 census was, as research could show, based on some sample census results and an extrapolation of earlier, also unreliable census data from the pre-revolutionary time.

China has also claimed to have eradicated infectious diseases; thus, no cases of syphilis were reported in 1974. Not knowing to what degree all these data may be true, it seems that the Chinese government has made attempts on the one hand to limit great population increases and on the other hand to increase general health by mainly preventive methods. In the field of medicine there were indeed only few 'Western' doctors available, i.e. doctors with a training in Western medicine. There were, however, many 'Chinese' doctors in the country, i.e. persons with a more or less formal training in the classical Chinese medical techniques. Before the Revolution, there was a considerable tension between the two groups. The new regime employed both types on an equal level, requiring the Western doctors to learn the basics of Chinese medicine, and vice versa. This had the result that there were more doctors at hand; that the competition among both kinds disappeared, and that in the time period in which a Chinese chemical industry was not yet able to supply sufficient Western drugs, Chinese herb medicines could be used. In order to educate a greater number of doctors, the general medical training was reduced to three years. In addition large numbers of so-called 'barefoot doctors' were trained in very short training periods. These men and women correspond roughly to our nurse's helpers; they can treat the most common and not too serious illnesses and are supposed to transfer the patients to the fully trained doctors in complex cases. This is probably the most realistic policy if the aim of the government is to create very quickly a medical organization which can combat efficiently infectious diseases and thus create socialized medical care. Acupuncture, which existed in China for more than two thousand years but was more or less given up when Western medical knowledge came to China, has been taken up again and some amazing successes have been reported, though the cases which were in the press could not be regarded as scientifically supervised so as to exclude suggestion or even the use of additional medicines. Yet much research has been stimulated all over the world.

China had a developed educational system before the Revolution, as indicated above. The level of universities was remarkably high. The War interrupted this development. The new regime tried to build up higher education with, as far as possible, students only from the lower classes, excluding descendants of the old upper class from higher education. Great stress was laid upon the ideological indoctrination of students. With the Cultural Revolution all universities were closed. The new system which is now accepted has shortened college training to three years only. Only such men and women are allowed to study who have been working in factories or rural communes and are recommended by the local party leaders as politically reliable. This, naturally, brings a special type of student to the colleges, often persons who have little ability and no great interest in acquiring scientific and scholarly training. We read about a movement to eliminate all examinations and to stress only political worth. In general, the universities have taken the function they have in the Soviet Union: they are training schools for teachers and the professors have to give the students standardized information. There are no research scholars as in Western universities. What we would regard as graduate work goes on in academies in which a few selected students work under the direct guidance of recognized scholars and political educators as in the Soviet Union. There is no knowledge yet of whether this system can produce the great number of highly specialized scientists which a developing country needs. Moreover, the students who have finished college are normally sent back to the rural and often outlying parts of China, supposedly to bring their knowledge to the farmers and workers and, in co-operation with them, to develop the countryside. We have numerous reports that the students resent this very much, and there is no doubt that they will have hardly any opportunity to increase their knowledge and keep abreast of new progress in their fields.

One field of social change which has been praised very much by the People's Republic is the 'liberation' of women. In fact, the marriage law of April 1950 was one of the few new laws which were introduced. As in the Soviet Union, much of the legal procedure is still based on hearings before groups of reliable citizens, of arbitration or mediation in the absence of law codes. Now, Nationalist China earlier created a modern and liberal marriage law; moreover, women were never the slaves that they have sometimes been painted. In many parts of China, long before the Pacific War, women worked in the fields with their husbands. Elsewhere they worked in secondary agricultural industries (weaving, preparation of food conserves, home industries, and even textile factories) and provided supplementary income for their families. All that 'liberation' in 1950 really meant was that women had to work a full day as their husbands did, and had, in addition, to do housework and care for their children much as before. The new marriage law did, indeed, make both partners equal; it also made it easier for men to divorce their wives, political incompatibility becoming a ground for divorce.

The ideological justification for a new marriage law was the desirability of destroying the traditional Chinese family and its economic basis because a close family, and all the more an extended family or a clan, could obviously serve as a centre of resistance. Land collectivization and the nationalization of business destroyed the economic basis of families. The 'liberation' of women brought them out of the house and made it possible for the government to exploit dissension between husband and wife, thereby increasing its control over the family. Finally, the new education system, which indoctrinated all children from nursery to the end of college, separated children from parents, thus undermining parental control and enabling the state to intimidate parents by encouraging their children to denounce their 'deviations'. Sporadic efforts to dissolve the family completely by separating women from men in communes—recalling an attempt made almost a century earlier by the T'ai P'ing—were unsuccessful.

The central problem facing China or any nation that modernizes and industrializes in the twentieth century can be simply stated.

Nineteenth-century industry needed large masses of workers which only the rural areas could supply; and, with the development of farming methods, the countryside could afford to send its youth to the cities. Twentieth-century industry, on the other hand, needs technicians and highly qualified personnel, often with college degrees, but few unskilled workers. China has traditionally employed human labour and did not make use of inventions which could have freed human labour, as we saw above. Now, it needs modern industries very urgently and quickly, especially in order to preserve its military preparedness and to produce the fertilizers that are necessary to raise the production of food per acre, so that it can safely feed its population. As the new industries need relatively few people and as cities already are crowded, the government attempts to prevent a further influx into the cities and to keep people in the countryside. Not only students, but many others have been removed from cities and forced to settle in villages. As every citizen is registered and needs food coupons (grain, cloth and cooking oil are still rationed), it is difficult to circumvent such orders. But if more and more people have to be kept in farming occupations, it will be very difficult to raise the general standard of living, especially as the farmers know that life in the cities is more interesting and offers a higher standard of living. The Soviet Union is faced with a similar problem, but at least it has much land which is practically empty and at least parts of it still can be taken under cultivation. This is not the case in China; within its present territory, there is very little empty land, and even little under-used land. The foreign press has often given the fantastically low prices of goods such as bicycles, motorcycles or watches, but compared to the average urban worker's income, to buy a bicycle means the expense of three months' salary; a motorcycle costs eight months' salary, and a watch, two months'.

Another related problem is that China can hardly afford to build a network of highways that eat up much productive land, and to tear down large parts of the cities to make room for broad streets. This means that China will have to develop a system of transportation different from that of Western countries, even if it can produce enough oil.

Finally, a word about the minorities in China. The government has recognized 54 ethnic groups as minorities and has given them a status very similar to that given to minorities in the Soviet Union. Some of the minorities are millions strong, such as the Tibetans; others are small tribal units. There has been some effort to bring the small units —with all their own dialects or languages—together into more or less artificial larger units, but the general line of policy is the same as in the Soviet Union. Children in elementary schools receive lectures in their own languages, but the textbooks are in Chinese, and higher education is fully in Chinese. Large numbers of settlers as well as 'instructors' have been sent into the minority areas, and when we hear that these areas have a large increase in population, larger than the purely Chinese areas, it means that the Chinese population is quickly increasing so that soon in most of these minority areas, the native population will numerically be a minority, while at the time of the creation of the 'autonomous' areas, they were still the majority in these areas. Under the guidance of Party workers, the old élite in these areas has been eliminated, as among the Chinese, and in the Minority Institute in Peking new, reliable Party cadres are trained. The Institute, in addition, prepares some dictionaries of the native languages, collects some local legends, local music and dances in order to keep up the appearance in conformity with Lenin's slogan 'Nationalist in form, socialist in content'.

5   Cultural developments

According to Marxian doctrine, culture and art are 'superstructures' and have to be shaped in accordance to the economic structure. This created a number of problems which we cannot expect to see solved within a decade or two. After the establishment of the People's Republic of China and during the period of strong Russian influence, experiments with 'socialist realism' in literature and art were made. This trend was given up when the friendship broke up, but the new literature is stylistically not basically different from the old socialist realism. The new literature wants to show the 'typical', not the exceptional or individual. The hero has to be the Communist hero of the time of the Long March, the Japanese War, the War against the KMT, or the Korean War. He and his followers are always heroic, fight happily to death, do acts of unheard-of heroism, protect equally heroic women and always come from the 'people'. Love and sex do not play a role in their lives. Their enemies are always ugly, mean, and even if they are courageous, they are in the end always defeated. If the hero fights until his own death, he dies for the glory of the Party, not for his own glory. In some cases, he ends his life with his own hands, when no other way is seen, but he never surrenders. He willingly sacrifices his wife and even his son for the Party and its victory. He is often shown in a heroic landscape, mountain cliffs are all over, and they have to be climbed: the hero struggles against and defeats nature. In some novels, minorities play a role; they always co-operate with the Chinese Communist Party against their own traditional leaders who co-operate with the bad old Chinese leaders.

Thus, novels do not, with few exceptions, depict heroes of history.

The past is always dark and black, while the future looms bright. All this means that the new literature is repetitive and limited, yet we have to keep in mind that with the exception of the early years of this century, literature was always regarded as a tool of education. Thus, the new literature wants to show models which the population should admire and imitate. An interesting point here is the stress upon the fight against nature at a time when the world turns more and more towards an ecological view. Pre-modern China was very ecology-conscious, expressed in the stress laid upon geomancy: man should try to fit himself into nature, should adjust to and not destroy nature. China here adheres more to Western Marxism which praised the power of man to make nature his servant. Similarly to the expression of this attitude in literature, we observe in photographs and paintings the proud chimneys of factories, pouring their pollution into nature, in contrast to classical Chinese art which showed only the vapours of virginal nature in which man is a small, insignificant element.

Art and poetry were, in pre-modern China, two upper-class activities. We can hardly name one painting which shows ordinary men or women doing ordinary work. When farmers, fishermen, or woodcutters are depicted, they seem to be leisurely working, while often a scholar looks benignly at their activities. The new regime, in agreement with Marxist doctrine, stimulated the ordinary man to paint, and wanted to have paintings which show people hard at work, producing something that is of social or simply practical use. Thus, we find the new paintings are more like posters, realistic, didactic; and if these paintings show some traces of old Chinese painting traditions, they seem to be almost as outlandish as if they were painted by a Western poster-designer who tries to paint in the 'Chinese style'. In contrast to the traditional paintings, they want to be clear, easy to understand, in harmony with socialist thought; I must confess that I never found a satisfactory way to explain the paintings of Sung, Ming and Ch'ing as expressions of a gentry ideology, though certainly, the more one studied their every single detail, the more one was impressed by the hidden meanings and allusions. For the educated viewer this was still the case with most of the works of China's most famous modern and modernistic painter, Ch'i Pai-shih, and the honours given him by the new regime seem to be given mainly because he was one of the few modern painters who was known and loved by foreign art lovers.

It is equally difficult to detect an ideology in Chinese poems: they, too, are technical masterpieces, following numerous complex rules of construction, and are full of allusions and quotations, rather than vehicles for the expression of very personal emotions. Recently, Tu

Fu, the T'ang poet, received praise because he describes in many poems the sufferings of the common man in the time of unrest and revolt in which the poet lived and under which he, personally, also suffered. Yet, no person without a full classical education can understand his poems and their hidden meanings. The new regime took two approaches towards the poem. First, they stimulated the common man to make poems; many thousands of such 'worker-poems' have been published and praised. This was done in order to give the ordinary man the belief that the making of poems is something he, too, can do, and not only the members of the old upper class. The other approach was to collect and to publish folk songs and folk poems, especially those in which the exploitation of the farmer by the landlord is described. These songs and poems were presented as models of real poetry. Folklorists have difficulties in deciding whether such 'poems of protest' were real folk poems or how many of them were; because many of the poems made by living workers and farmers were also published as 'folk poems', because these persons were 'folk'.

The strong interest in folklore—which also has its parallels in the Soviet Union—decreased from about 1960 on; after all, most existing and loved folk songs were simply love songs, romantic and not heroic, and, therefore, not educational and not in harmony with the new spirit. The same is true with folk tales and more so with fairy tales. And in most of the great number of jokes and jests, the scoundrel and the butt of the joke is not the landlord or the monk, but the stupid daughter-in-law or her equally stupid husband. We pointed out already that China's classical opera is also an art form which resists transformation into a revolutionary art. Attempts to collect and then to perform folk operas, which existed in all parts of China, were not satisfactory. Thus, we now see ballets or musicals in which some American traits, but many Russian traditions are obvious. Gone are the elegant sword dances of the warriors and the fleeting, flowing steps of the heroines, replaced by Russian interpretations of old Viennese traditions. The few operas which the new regime recognizes, like 'The East is Red', which was also made into a film, emulate the same virtues that the new novels show; some are made on the basis of novels. Pure dance performances of 'Chinese folk dances' bring dances of minorities, a fact which is not always clearly stated.

Thus, in the field of art there are problems which derive from an attempt to translate abstract Marxian art theory into practical life. Soviet Russia had made similar attempts, and after more than fifty years an 'underground art' begins to emerge which tries to liberate itself from stifling control. It can be expected that in the long run the same development will appear in China.

Finally, the field of religion has to be mentioned. Naturally, a socialist regime has to regard religion as superstition and as a super-structure resulting from an earlier economic system. Thus, most Taoist and Buddhist temples as well as Christian churches have been closed or destroyed; monks and nuns have been returned to 'productive life'. Foreign visitors are shown some temples and some monks or nuns; to judge from pictures and films, the temples were reorganized and filled with figures which normally do not belong together in one temple or on one altar. Monks and nuns are usually old and unable to work; some of them who have been interviewed inside or outside China were clearly rather uneducated in their field.

Instead of religious processions, temple fairs, and other religious events, political processions, demonstrations, and celebrations have been performed, in a conscious attempt to change the mind of the citizen.

When saying all this, we should not forget that religion as well as theatre, play, and literature were always in imperial China controlled and censored by the emperor's officials: they were stimulated only when the regime believed that some educational or political aim could be achieved by permitting them. Thus, the ideology has changed, and techniques of control have been improved, but the general attitude is very similar.

6 Concluding observations

We have in the preceding sections always attempted to show to what degree modern Communist China is following the line of old Chinese tradition, i.e. to what degree it still is 'China'; but we also tried to indicate to what degree it is 'Western' in the sense that the official doctrine, Maoism, is a child of German and Russian parents. Our observations can best be summarized by a look at the present 'Anti-Confucius, anti-Lin Piao' campaign (1974–1975). Confucius is the symbol of Chinese social and cultural values of the old time. With his name the basic values of Chinese society are connected. All these values are class-based values; only one of them can easily be accepted by the present regime. For Confucius, the family was the unit of society; and the family was hierarchically ordered. Some family members had more power and more rights than others. The present government attempts to replace the family by the Party. Though nominally egalitarian, the Party, too, is hierarchically organized. But the main difference between family and Party is that the family is tied together by bonds of blood and emotion, bonds which, ideally can never be untied. The Party is tied together by political activity, and the bonds do not remain the same under all conditions. Many members have been thrown out of the Party or lost their status in the Party.

The second Confucian value is loyalty to the 'son of heaven'—to the emperor who, in theory at least, represented heaven and the order of Nature. This value has been transferred to loyalty to the Party and its leader, because to transfer it to the nation could possibly give impetus to the rise of nationalism; nationalism is undesirable for an organization which claims to represent all the oppressed in the world.

The only Confucian value which could easily be accepted and used is the belief in education and the role of the leader as educator.

Confucius is also a symbol of 'civil culture', a man who never did make war or advocated war. More symptomatic than the fight against Confucius is the praise for Shih Huang-ti, the all-time symbol of war against the independent states of the late Chou time, and the dictator who burned the books of morality and killed their makers, the educated. It sounds incongruous that Lin Piao, the military man, is put together with Confucius; but if we see Shih Huang-ti on the other side, it may mean that Lin is identified with a 'revisionist' soft line, and that Mao wants to promote the strong line of permanent revolution.

The future development of the People's Republic still cannot be guessed. We see developments, see a certain raising of the standard of living, but cannot foresee how the internal situation will look even in a few years from today. Similarly, we cannot predict the future of the Republic of China on Taiwan. Its economic development is amazing, but its fate does not lie in the hands of these 16 million people.

Notes and References

The following notes and references are intended to help the interested reader. They draw his attention to some more specialized literature in English, and occasionally in French and German. They also indicate for the more advanced reader the sources for some of the interpretations of historical events. As such sources are most often written in Chinese or Japanese and, therefore, inaccessible to most readers, only brief hints and not full bibliographical data are given. The specialists know the names and can easily find details in the standard bibliographies. The general reader will profit most from the bibliography on Chinese history published each year in the 'Journal of Asian Studies'. These Notes do not mention the original Chinese sources which are the factual basis of this book.

Chapter 1
Section 2

The best analysis of the results of archaeology in China is Chang Kwang-chih, 'The Archaeology of Ancient China', revised edition, New Haven, 1968.

Section 3

This discussion is mainly based upon my 'Kultur und Siedlung der Rand-völker Chinas', Leiden, 1942; 'Die Lokalkulturen des Nordens und Westens', Leiden, 1942; 'The Local Cultures of South and East China', Leiden, 1968. See also H. J. Wiens, 'China's March toward the Tropics', Hamden, 1954.

Sections 4, 5 and 6

I have made use of Chang Kwang-chih's book, the main excavation reports, and my own ethno-historical studies (see section 3).

Chapter 2
Section 1

The first and for a long time best study of the Shang period was H. G. Creel's 'The Birth of China', London, 1936. For the archaeological remains, Chang Kwang-chih is now the best analyst. For the dating and the social structure of the Shang I have made use of unpublished studies by

David N. Keightley (his Ph.D. dissertation 'Public Work in Ancient China: a Study of Forced Labour in the Shang and Western Chou', Columbia University, 1969, and several public lectures and personal discussions). Once these studies are completed and published, many of our old concepts will have to be changed.

Section 2

New insights can be expected from the forthcoming studies by D. N. Keightley. I have made use of my own studies ('Local Cultures', see above) and Chang Kwang-chih's book (see above).

Section 3

Again, Keightley's studies will probably necessitate revisions in this section. A general discussion of theories dealing with Chinese feudalism is given by D. Bodde, Feudalism in China in R. Coulborn, 'Feudalism in History', Princeton, 1956. For the origins of the Chinese city and its development, Paul Wheatley, 'The Pivot of the Four Corners', Edinburgh, 1970 is most stimulating because Wheatley has tried to develop a general theory of the ancient city.

Chapter 3
Sections 1 and 2

A different view of the basic character of Chou culture and development, especially concerning the use of horses in warfare and possible Western connections, is presented by Magdalene von Dewall, 'Pferd und Wagen als Kulturgut im frühen China', Hamburg, 1964. My own theory of feudalism is in 'Conquerors and Rulers', second edition, Leiden, 1965.

Section 3

The best discussion on 'shifting cultivation' is found in K. J. Pelzer, 'Population and Land Utilization', New York, 1941.

Sections 4 and 5

Important is H. G. Creel, 'The Origins of Statecraft in China', vol. 1: 'The Western Chou Empire', Chicago, 1970.

Sections 6 and 7

Here, I have made use of my own studies in 'Moral and Social Values of the Chinese', Taipei, 1971. These should be compared with studies like those of D. J. Munro, 'The Concept of Man in Early China', Stanford, 1969; Noah E. Fehl, 'Rites and Propriety in Literature and Life', Hong Kong, 1971; W. Eichhorn, 'Chinese Civilization', New York, 1969, and others. Discussion of the basic values of the Chinese, from ancient to modern times has given rise to numerous, often stimulating studies. I may refer here to Lily Abegg, 'Mind of Asia', New York, 1952 as one fairly extreme study, and to Li Yih-yüan (ed.), 'Symposium on the Character of the Chinese', Taipei, 1972, which takes a different approach. The stimulating book by Wolfgang Bauer, 'China und die Hoffnung auf Glück', Munich, 1971, studies diachronically the Chinese ideas about the good life. There is as yet, in my opinion, no satisfactory study on Lao Tzǔ and Chuang Tzǔ.

Chapter 4
Sections 1 *and* 2

The book by J. Prusek, 'Chinese Statelets and the Northern Barbarians in the Period 1400–300 B.C.', New York, 1971, is very helpful, though I do not agree with Prusek in many questions. For many special questions of settlement and clans G. Haloun's Contributions to the History of Clan Settlement in Ancient China in 'Asia Major', vol. 1, Leipzig, 1924, is still the best study. Perhaps even more important is his short article Die Rekonstruktion der chinesischen Urgeschichte durch die Chinesen in 'Japanisch-deutsche Zeitschrift für Wissenschaft und Technik', no. 3, of 7 July 1925. For all discussions about the development of Chinese science and technology, J. Needham's 'Science and Civilization in China', Cambridge, 1954–? (not yet completed), is indispensable, though a certain caution should be preserved in questions of interpretation. The separate study 'Clerks and Craftsmen in China and the West', Cambridge, 1970, is more important for the later periods of Chinese technology, but contains the same bias as the main work.

In several places in this book, I have referred to the possible influence of climatic changes upon the development of culture. I have relied upon G. Jenkins, A Note on Climatic Cycles and the Rise of Chinggis Khan, 'Central Asiatic Journal', vol. 18, 1974, pp. 217–26. Jenkins is familiar with other recent studies on this subject.

Section 3

There is no satisfactory, modern study of Chinese philosophy of this time. We often still use Fung Yu-lan's, 'History of Chinese Philosophy' (trans. by D. Bodde), Princeton, 1952. Charles A. Moore (ed.), 'The Chinese Mind, Essentials of Chinese Philosophy and Culture', Honolulu, 1967, is not satisfactory. Stimulating is H. G. Creel, 'What is Taoism?', Chicago, 1970.

Chapter 5
Sections 1, 2 *and* 3

The immediately earlier period is critically studied by J. I. Crump, 'Chan-Kuo Ts'e', Oxford, 1970; his interpretation gives new insight, and his translation of the text is the first one yet. For the Ch'in history, we still have to refer to D. Bodde's 'China's First Unifier', Leiden, 1938, and his 'Statesman, Patriot, and General in Ancient China', New Haven, 1940. From this period on, the impressive 'Geschichte des chinesischen Reiches', Berlin, 1930 (5 vols) by Otto Franke is still usable and for the medieval period still the best one; the earlier sections are now too antiquated. For the study of social changes in the time down to the Ch'in dynasty look into Hsu Cho-yün, 'Ancient China in Transition', Stanford, 1956.

Chapter 6
Section 1

The definition of 'gentry' is based on research which is discussed in my 'Social Mobility in Traditional China', Leiden, 1962. Other scholars use the term in a different sense as those men who have passed the imperial examinations and therefore achieved special status. In my definition, the gentry is a class in the Marxist sense and not in the contemporary American sense; moreover, the basic unit of the gentry is not the individual but his family.

Sections 2 and 4

There is still no modern, satisfactory study of the Hsiung-nu and their relations to the Chinese. W. M. MacGovern, 'The Early Empires of Central Asia', Chapel Hill, 1939, is very much out of date. A general survey of Central Asian societies is given by Lawrence Krader, 'Peoples of Central Asia', The Hague, 1963. Discussions on nomadism and on settlement of nomads can be found in W. Irons and N. Dyson-Hudson (eds), 'Perspectives on Nomadism', International Studies in Sociology and Social Anthropology, vol. 13, 1972, and Rolf Herzog, 'Sesshaftwerden von Nomaden', Köln, 1963. The process of interaction between Central Asian nomadic states and Chinese is studied in my 'Conquerors and Rulers', Leiden, 1965.

Sections 3 and 5

The basic historical texts are translated by H. H. Dubs, 'The History of the Former Han Dynasty', Baltimore, 1938. An extensive study of Han history and society in perhaps as much as 18 volumes is planned; thus far only the first volume is published: Ch'ü T'ung-tsu, 'Han Social Structure', Seattle, 1971. The best study of life in Han time is M. Loewe, 'Everyday Life in Early Imperial China', London, 1968. On Chinese bureaucracy see F. Balazs, 'Chinese Civilization and Bureaucracy', New Haven, 1964. For a theoretical discussion of pre-modern empires see S. N. Eisenstadt, 'The Political Systems of Empires: The Rise and Fall of the Historical Bureaucratic Societies', Glencoe, 1963. The concepts of K. A. Wittfogel, 'Oriental Despotism', New Haven, 1957, differ strongly from my own and those of Eisenstadt.

Sections 6, 7 and 8

H. Bielenstein, 'The Restoration of the Han Dynasty', Stockholm, 1953, is still the most detailed and careful study. An important study of Han China's foreign relations is Ying-shih Yü, 'Trade and Expansion in Han China', Berkeley, 1967.

Section 9

The religious book used by the Yellow Turbans and influential in later times has been studied by W. Eichhorn, in 'Mitteilungen des Instituts für Orientforschung', Berlin, 1954, vol. 2, no. 2, pp. 326 ff.

Section 10

The book of Wang Ch'ung has been translated by Alfred Forke, 'Lun Hêng, Philosophical Essays of Wang Ch'ung', Shanghai and London, 1907, continued in 'Mitteilungen des Seminars für orientalische Sprachen', Supplements 10 and 14 (1906–11). For alchemy see J. R. Ware (trans.),

'Alchemy, Medicine, and Religion in the China of A.D. 320', Cambridge, 1966. For the history of Buddhism in China, E. Zürcher, 'The Buddhist Conquest of China', is the best study. A. F. Wright, 'Buddhism in Chinese History', Stanford, 1959 discusses the general importance of Buddhism for China's culture.

Chapter 7

The political history of this whole period is best described in O. Franke's 'Geschichte des chinesischen Reiches', vol. 2, Berlin, 1936. For the Toba period see my 'Das Toba-Reich Nordchinas', Leiden, 1949. For Chinese–Central Asian relations see O. Lattimore, 'Inner Asian Frontiers of China', New York, 1951. A. C. Soper discusses the secular arts of this period in his 'Textual Evidence for the Secular Arts of China in the Period from Liu Sung through Sui', Ascona, 1967.

Chapter 8
Part A

For the creation of the Sui see A. F. Wright, The Formation of Sui Ideology in J. K. Fairbank (ed.), 'Chinese Thought and Institutions', Chicago, 1957, pp. 71–104. For the foundation of the T'ang see W. Bingham, 'The Founding of the T'ang Dynasty', Baltimore, 1941. On genealogies in general see my 'Social Mobility in Traditional China', Leiden, 1962; Chow Yung-teh, 'Social Mobility in China', New York, 1966, presents a strongly different view. On the principles of name-giving in China see the interesting study by Wolfgang Bauer, 'Der chinesische Personenname', Wiesbaden, 1959.

Part B

For an understanding of T'ang administration the book by D. C. Twitchett, 'Financial Administration under the T'ang Dynasty', New York, 1963, is indispensable. Among the many important works by Lien-sheng Yang, his 'Les Aspects économiques des travaux publics dans la Chine imperiale', Paris, 1964, is of special interest. R. Hartwell's A Cycle of Economic Change in Imperial China: Coal and Iron in North-east China, 750–1350, in 'Journal of the Economic and Social History of the Orient', vol. 10, 1967, pp. 102–59 is the first study marking a new approach to Chinese economic history. For the analysis of the Chinese upper class in this and the preceding period, David G. Johnson has made highly important studies. I have used his Ph.D. dissertation 'The Medieval Chinese Oligarchy', Department of History, University of California, Berkeley, 1970. The publication of a revised form of this thesis can be expected soon. Johnson has revised and refined some of my own studies and those of my Japanese colleagues. While Chinese official historiography has always treated the Empress Wu as a bad ruler, the novel 'Flowers in a Mirror' ('Ching-hua yüan') gives a completely different picture of her, representing the new interpretation of a novelist of the early nineteenth century. Some material for this chapter is found in my 'Moral and Social Values of the Chinese', Taipei, 1971, and in the 'Settlement and Social Change in Asia', Hong Kong, 1967.

Part C

This chapter is mainly based upon my own studies, which will soon (1976) be reprinted in a volume 'China und seine westlichen Nachbarn', Darmstadt.

Chapter 9
Parts A and B

Our evaluation of the Sung period will probably change in the next years, due to a multitude of work under way. Some indication of what is done can be found in the 'Sung Studies Newsletter'. For the Sung and the following periods important is the new theory developed by Mark Elvin, 'The Pattern of the Chinese Past', Stanford, 1974 (see also R. Myers's review in the 'Journal of Asian Studies', vol. 33, February 1974). Elvin has translated also Shiba Yoshinobu's 'Commerce and Society in Sung China', Ann Arbor, 1970, a book which summarizes much of the research done by Japanese specialists. See also Laurence J. C. Ma, 'Commerical Development and Urban Change in Sung China', Ann Arbor, 1971. Ma uses more Chinese publications. For aspects of the political history, a Marxist interpretation by G. Lewin, 'Die ersten 50 Jahre der Song Dynastie', Berlin, 1973, is interesting; for diplomatic history the article by Herbert Franke, Treaties between Sung and Chin in 'Sung Studies', series 1, History, 1970, pp. 55–84, is important.

For the development of science in this period see U. Libbrecht, 'Chinese Mathematics in the 13th Century', MIT East Asian Studies, 1973; further see J. Needham's above-cited great book and Shigeru Nakayama and N. Sivin, 'Chinese Science, Explorations of an Ancient Tradition', MIT Press, Cambridge, 1973.

For administration see Johanna Menzel (ed.), 'The Chinese Civil Service. Career Open to Talent?', Boston, 1963, and B. E. McKnight, 'Village and Bureaucracy in Southern Sung China', Chicago, 1971. For folk poetry, I have used P. Pelliot, 'Airs de Touen-huoang' (Mission P. Pelliot, II), Paris, 1972. Social life is excellently described by J. Gernet, 'Daily Life in China on the Eve of Mongol Invasion', Stanford, 1970. A detailed geographical study of the city of Hangchou by I. d'Argencé is, unfortunately, not yet published.

We should mention here some studies on the intimate life of the time, such as G. Schlegel, 'La Prostitution en Chine', Rouen, 1886, still not yet replaceable by a more modern study; R. Des Rotours, 'Courtisanes Chinoises à la fin des T'ang', Paris, 1968, Howard S. Levy, 'Chinese Footbinding. The History of a Curious Custom', New York, 1966, Cheng Wouchan, 'Érotologie de la Chine', Paris, 1963, and the classic in this field, R. H. van Gulik, 'Sexual Life in Ancient China', Leiden, 1961.

For the development of Chinese pharmacology and medicine the studies by P. U. Unschuld should be consulted, mainly his 'Pen-ts'ao, 2000 Jahre traditionelle pharmazeutische Literatur Chinas', Munich, 1973.

Chapter 10
Part A

For aspects of the economy during the Mongol period see Herbert Franke, 'Geld und Wirtschaft in China unter der Mongolen-Herrschaft', Leipzig,

1949 and Franz Schurman, 'Economic Structure of the Yüan Dynasty', Cambridge, 1956. The study on the Mongol postal system by Peter Olbricht, 'Das Postwesen in China unter der Mongolenherrschaft', Göttingen, 1954, is still important. P. Pelliot's 'Notes on Marco Polo', Paris, 1963, 2 vols, is a treasury of information concerning the cultural history of the period, and L. Olschki's 'Marco Polo's Asia', Berkeley, 1960, brings Marco Polo into the focus of European and Asian relations. The complex development among the Mongol rulers is shown by John W. Dardess, 'Conquerors and Confucians. Aspects of Political Change in Late Yüan China', New York, 1973.

Part B

For the developments in the field of philosophy in Ming time see W. Th. DeBary, 'Self and Society in Ming Thought', New York, 1970. On law and treatment of law cases in the last centuries of traditional China see D. Bodde and C. Morris, 'Law in Imperial China', Cambridge, 1967. A brief summary of the government structure is given by C. Hucker, 'The Traditional Chinese State in Ming Time,' New York, 1969. On schools and education see T. Grimm, 'Erziehung und Politik im konfuzianischen China der Ming-Zeit', Hamburg, 1960.

For China at the time of the early Christian missionaries see C. J. Gallagher, 'China in the 16th century', New York, 1953. For the last years of the Ming Dynasty I have made use of an unpublished manuscript by Fred Wakeman on the 'Shun Dynasty', and James B. Parsons, 'Peasant Rebellions of the Late Ming Dynasty', Tucson, 1970. A study on the merchants of the Hsin-an area by Harriet Zurndorfer will soon be completed; some of my remarks are influenced by discussions with her. Two books by Ho Ping-ti are of great value for questions of social mobility and of demography: 'The Ladder of Success in Imperial China', New York, 1962, and 'Studies on the Population of China, 1368–1953', Cambridge, 1959.

China's expansion during this time and the maritime policy are discussed by C. P. Fitzgerald, 'The Southern Expansion of the Chinese People', London, 1972, and Bodo Wiethoff, 'Die chinesische Seeverbotspolitik und der private Überseehandel von 1368 bis 1567', Hamburg, 1963.

The most recent study on eunuchs is by Taisuke Mitamura, 'Chinese Eunuchs, the Structure of Intimate Politics', Rutland, 1970. Although strongly biased, the following studies on sexual life and aberrations contain much material for this and later periods: Herbert D. Lamson, 'Social Pathology in China', Shanghai, 1935, and J. J. Matignon, 'La Chine hermétique', Paris, 1936. Michel Beurdeley, 'Chinese Erotic Art', Tokyo, 1969, is a serious study. On folk literature see now W. C. Idema, 'Chinese Vernacular Fiction', Leiden, 1974, and Cornelia Töpelmann's 'Shan-ko von Feng Meng-lung', Wiesbaden, 1973, brings translations of some Ming time folk poems. The study by Andrew Boyd, 'Chinese Architecture and Town Planning, 1500 B.C. to A.D. 1911', London, 1962, is disappointing, as is W. Speiser, 'Baukunst des Ostens. Von der Zeitenwende bis zum 19. Jahrhundert', Essen, 1963.

Part C

On General Chinese world concepts of the time see J. K. Fairbank (ed.), 'The Chinese World Order. Traditional China's Foreign Relations', Cambridge, 1968, and J. R. Levenson, 'Confucian China and its Modern Fate', Berkeley, 1968. A general history of the last century is found in Immanuel C. Y. Hsu, 'The Rise of Modern China', New York, 1970. A new light on the relations between England and China as well as India is given by Dilip K. Basu, 'A Comparative Study of Calcutta and Canton, 1800–1840', unpublished Ph.D. thesis, Berkeley, 1975.

The mechanisms of government are studied by Silas H. L. Wu, 'Communications and Imperial Control in China', Cambridge, 1970, and Th. A. Metzger, 'The Internal Organization of Ch'ing Bureaucracy: Legal, Normative, and Communication Aspects', Cambridge, 1973. On rural organization see K. Ch. Hsiao, 'Rural China: Imperial Control in the 19th Century', Seattle, 1960. On the economic situation of the government officials see Chung-li Chang, 'The Income of the Chinese Gentry', Seattle, 1962. The most important recent studies on the economy which have greatly modified our concepts are W. E. Wilmott (ed.), 'Economic Organization in Chinese Society', Stanford, 1972; Ramon H. Myers, 'The Chinese Peasant Economy: Agricultural Development in Hopei and Shantung 1890–1949', Cambridge, 1970; Evelyn S. Rawski, 'Agricultural Change and the Peasant Economy of South China', Cambridge, 1972; A. Feuerwerker, 'The Chinese Economy, ca. 1870–1911', Ann Arbor, 1969. W. Skinner's Marketing and Social Structure in Rural China, 'Journal of Asian Studies', vol. 24, 1964–5, is an application of theories developed in connection with Europe and will have to be modified, but is still the best available study. On the Chinese city see W. Skinner and M. Elvin, 'The Chinese Cities between the Two Worlds', Stanford, 1974. Still the only study on the settlement forms of villages is the Ph.D. thesis by H. D. Scholz, 'Die Formen der ländlichen Siedlung in China', Bonn, 1949 (unpublished). Two older studies should be mentioned: Heinrich Schmidthenner, 'Chinesische Landschaften und Städte', Stuttgart, 1925 and F. Gutkind, 'Revolution of Environment', London, 1946. Schmidthenner, but especially Gutkind, brings (on pp. 190–333) the ecological viewpoint which now has become so popular.

For the T'ai P'ing Rebellion, the best recent book is by Jen Yu-wen, 'The Taiping Revolutionary Movement', New Haven, 1973. On recent attitudes towards non-Chinese minorities see Henry G. Schwarz, 'Chinese Policies Towards Minorities', Western Washington State College, 1971.

For the position of women in pre-modern China see F. Ayscough, 'Chinese Women, Yesterday and Today', Boston, 1937; this should be compared with the two modern studies by Margery Wolf, 'Women and the Family in Rural Taiwan', Stanford, 1972, and Marilyn B. Young (ed.), 'Women in China', Ann Arbor, 1973. Ms Young's book treats mainly the situation in the People's Republic.

On Chinese religion, the book by C. K. Yang, 'Religion in Chinese Society', Berkeley, 1962, is too much of an adaptation of Max Weber's ideas to China; the new study by P. C. Baity, 'Religion in a Chinese Town',

Taipei, 1975 gives a very new approach, which to some degree is also apparent in Arthur P. Wolf (ed.), 'Religion and Ritual in Chinese Society', Stanford, 1974. For Buddhism see especially Holmes Welch, 'The Practice of Chinese Buddhism, 1900–1950', Cambridge, 1967. Concerning the practice and teachings of modern Taoists see Michael Saso, 'Taoism and the Rite of Cosmic Renewal', Washington State Univ. Press, 1972, and another forthcoming book by Saso.

Among the many socially interesting novels of the nineteenth century, 'Flowers in the Mirror', trans. by Lin Tai-yi, Berkeley, 1965; 'The Scholars' ('Ju-lin wai-shih') by Wu Ching-tzu, Peking, 1957, and the 'Chapters from a Floating Life' by Shen Fu, trans. by Lin Yutang, Boston, 1937, should be mentioned: 'Flowers' because of its modern attitude towards women and its criticism of existing society; 'Scholars' as a biting criticism of corruption, and 'Floating Life' as the best, most intimate and tender description of marital life. Many books on the Chinese opera are now available. For practical use, L. C. Arlington and H. Acton, 'Famous Chinese Plays', Peking, 1937, reprint 1963, is the best. See also A. C. Scott, 'The Classical Theatre of China', London, 1957.

The first study of Chinese psychiatry should perhaps be mentioned here. It is by G. Schaltenbrand, Psychiatrie in Peking, 'Zeitschr. f. d. gesamte Neurologie und Psychiatrie', vol. 137, 1931, no. 1, pp. 169–232; modern research dealing with this field has tended to forget this contribution.

Chapter 11

Out of the enormous mass of publications about China since 1911, only a few studies should be mentioned here, such as F. Wakeman, 'History and Will. Philosophical Perspectives of Mao Tse-tung's Thought', New Haven, 1974, because of his different approach; James P. Harrison, 'The Communists and Chinese Peasant Rebellions. A Study in the Rewriting of Chinese History', New York, 1969. Because of the new opinion concerning the character of peasant rebellions, Chiang Ch'ing (Mrs Mao), 'On the Revolution of the Peking Opera', Peking, 1968, because of the Party line concerning the classical opera and its substitute. G. V. H. Moseley, 'The Consolidation of the South China Frontier', Berkeley, 1973, because of the description of minority policy. M. J. Meijer, 'Marriage Law and Policy in the Chinese People's Republic', Hong Kong, 1971, as the first study of the new 'liberation' of women, and Wu Yüan-li, 'An Economic Survey of Communist China', New York, 1956, as one of many studies on the state of economy.

INDEX